Releas
Samford University Library

P9-CRX-385

CONSTITUTION MAKERS ON CONSTITUTION MAKING

CONSTITUTION MAKERS ON CONSTITUTION MAKING

THE EXPERIENCE OF EIGHT NATIONS

EDITED BY

ROBERT A. GOLDWIN & ART KAUFMAN

American Enterprise Institute for Public Policy Research

Washington, D.C.

Samford University Library

Distributed by arrangement with
UPA, Inc.

4720 Boston Way   3 Henrietta Street
Lanham, Md. 20706   London WC2E 8LU England

Library of Congress Cataloging-in-Publication Data
Constitution makers on constitution making: the experience of eight na-
tions / Robert A. Goldwin and Art Kaufman, editors.
  p. cm.—(AEI studies; 479)
  Contents: The drafting of the French constitution of 1958 / Jean
Foyer—Making the constitution of Greece / Constantine D. Tsatsos
—The writing of the constitution of the United States / Walter
Berns—The creation of the 1974 constitution of the Socialist
Federal Republic of Yugoslavia / Jovan Djordjevic—The writing of
the constitution of Spain / Francisco Rubio Llorente—The writing
of the 1971 Egyptian constitution / Ibrahim Saleh—The making of
the Venezuelan constitution / Gustavo Planchart Manrique—The
making of the Nigerian constitution / F. R. A. Williams.

ISBN 0-8447-3667-8 (alk. paper).
ISNB 0-8447-3666-X (pbk. : alk. paper)

  1. Constitutional history—Congresses.   I. Goldwin, Robert A.,
1922-   .   II. Kaufman, Art.   III. Series.

K3161.A3 1983b
342'.029—dc 19
[342.229]   88-15533
                                                                          CIP

1 3 5 7 9 10 8 6 4 2

AEI Studies 479

© 1988 by the American Enterprise Institute for Public Policy Research,
Washington, D.C. All rights reserved. No part of this publication may be
used or reproduced in any manner whatsoever without permission in
writing from the American Enterprise Institute except in the case of brief
quotations embodied in news articles, critical articles, or reviews. The
views expressed in the publications of the American Enterprise Institute
are those of the authors and do not necessarily reflect the views of the
staff, advisory panels, officers, or trustees of AEI.

"American Enterprise Institute" and (ᴂ)   are registered service
marks of the American Enterprise Institute for Public Policy Research.

Printed in the United States of America

Contents

K
3161
.A3
1983b

Preface

Americans are accustomed to thinking of constitution writing as something done hundreds of years ago by bewigged gentlemen wearing frock coats, knee breeches, and white stockings. But for the rest of the world, constitution writing is very much an activity of the present day. The Constitution of the United States is now more than 200 years old, but most of the other constitutions in the world are less than fifteen years old. That is, of the 160 or so national written constitutions in the world, more than half have been written since 1974.

This means that constitution writing is a common political activity of our time. On average, in the last few decades, more than five new national constitutions have come into effect somewhere or other every year. Some of these constitutions are, of course, for new nations, but the surprising fact is that most were written for very old nations, such as Spain, Portugal, Turkey, and Greece.

The frequency of constitution writing tells us at least two things: first, constitutions are considered very important, and great investments of time and effort are devoted to writing them; second, it is very difficult and rare to write a constitution that lasts—that is why there are so many new ones every year.

As a consequence of all this constitution writing, the world is full of living constitution writers, more than ever before in history. In every part of the world, in every sort of political regime, there are men (but very few, if any, women), still active in public life, who have played a significant role in the writing of the constitution of their own country.

It occurred to us and our colleagues at the American Enterprise Institute, as part of our decade-long program of study of the Constitution, that this extraordinary supply of constitution-making experience ought to be brought together and put to good use. The plan was quite simple. We would ask constitution writers from a wide variety of countries to tell the story of how their constitution came to be written. We would seek out two authors from each country who, either because of the different roles they played in the writing of their nation's constitution or because of their political differences, would present the story from a somewhat differing perspective.

In addition to the pairs of authors from eight countries from different parts of the world, with very different kinds of constitutions and regimes, we would also invite constitutional experts (many of them also constitution writers) from a dozen more countries to discuss the papers and help us interpret their lessons about constitution writing. These foreign authors and participants included a former national president, cabinet members, legislators, political party leaders, and judges, almost all of whom were also noted constitutional scholars. This international group formed a fraternity of constitution makers who knew each other's names and works but who had never met before coming together for this conference.

And finally, to complete the group of forty, we invited twelve American men and women knowledgeable about constitutions—judges, lawyers, historians, political scientists—with a wide variety of backgrounds and viewpoints. The final element of the plan for the conference was that there would be nine discussion sessions, one discussion devoted to each country's pair of papers and a final session to assess what we had learned and to suggest topics for future study.

In September 1983, we gathered in the West Conference Room of the Supreme Court of the United States, with Chief Justice of the United States Warren E. Burger, serving as honorary chairman, keynote speaker, and gracious host. The conference proceeded almost exactly as planned, and this book is the result. (A complete list of the authors and participants appears in this volume.) In addition to the eight pairs of papers, giving two authoritative accounts of the writing of eight national constitutions, this volume presents the edited discussions among the participants. Because the papers had been distributed to the participants well in advance of the conference, it was unnecessary to devote time for authors to read their papers aloud to the participants. Instead, each session began with a question from the chairman of the conference, Robert A. Goldwin, AEI's director of constitutional studies, followed at once by response and discussion among the five members of a panel that included the two authors and three selected participants (the panel changed for each session, so that every one of the forty participants served on the panel for one of the eight sessions). After an hour or so of discussion among the panelists, discussion was opened to all members of the conference.

A transcript was made of the recorded remarks of the English speakers and the English translation of remarks made in French or Spanish. (Because of a mechanical malfunction, a portion of the discussion of the Egyptian papers was lost.) In the following years that transcript was edited, sent to the speakers all over the world for their corrections, and prepared for this publication.

The result is, to the best of our knowledge, the first and only book on constitution making by constitution makers. It has been many years in the making and has involved the cooperative efforts of many people, in addition to the authors and participants, whose assistance we here acknowledge, with gratitude: Richard Ware and the Earhart Foundation; Philip Merrill; Michael Schneider, Mark Blitz, and their colleagues at the U.S. Information Agency; Marilyn Zak and her colleagues at the Agency for International Development; Mark Cannon, Bradford Wilson, and their colleagues in the Office of the Chief Justice of the United States; Robert M. Warner and his colleagues at the National Archives; Charles H. Percy, chairman, and his fellow members of the Senate Foreign Relations Committee; William Bennett and his colleagues at the National Endowment for the Humanities; Kay Sterling, Larry Foust, and Katy Breen of AEI; Cecil Moore and his AEI staff; Ingeborg Wichmann and her team of simultaneous interpreters; and William J. Baroody, Jr., then president of AEI, and a staunch advocate of the project that led to completion of this book.

ROBERT GOLDWIN
ART KAUFMAN

Contributors

ROBERT A. GOLDWIN (United States) is resident scholar and director of constitutional studies at the American Enterprise Institute. He has served in the White House as special consultant to the president of the United States and, concurrently, as adviser to the secretary of defense. He has taught political science at the University of Chicago and Kenyon College, and was dean of St. John's College in Annapolis, Maryland. Among many other publications, he is the editor or co-editor of more than a score of books, including *How Democratic Is the Constitution?*, *How Capitalistic Is the Constitution?*, *How Does the Constitution Secure Rights?*, *How Federal Is the Constitution?*, and the author of, most recently, "Why Blacks, Women and Jews Are Not Mentioned in the Constitution," in *Commentary*, May 1987.

ART KAUFMAN (United States) is research assistant in the Department of Government, Georgetown University. He has served as acting director of educational programs, Commission on the Bicentennial of the U.S. Constitution; assistant director of constitutional studies, American Enterprise Institute; program officer, Institute for Educational Affairs; and assistant editor, *The Public Interest* magazine. He is the coeditor (with Robert A. Goldwin) of several volumes on constitutional subjects, including: *Separation of Powers: Does It Still Work?*, *How Does the Constitution Protect Religious Freedom?*, and *Slavery and Its Consequences: The Constitution, Race, and Equality*.

T. AKINOLA AGUDA (Nigeria) is director of the Nigerian Institute of Advanced Legal Studies, University of Lagos. He is the former chief justice of Ondo State and former dean of the faculty of law, University of Ife. His many articles include "Discriminatory Statutory Provisions and Fundamental Rights Provisions of the Constitutions of Botswana, Lesotho, and Swaziland," in *The South African Journal*; "Judicial Attitude to Some Fundamental Rights under the Constitution," in *Nigerian Bar Journal*; "Some Fundamental Rights in Nigeria and in the Sudan under Military Rule," in *African Law Journal*; and "The Role of the Judge with Special Reference to Civil Liberties," *East African Law*

Journal. His book, *The Judiciary in the Government of Nigeria*, has just been published.

AFONSO ARINOS DE MELO FRANCO (Brazil) is senator of the state of Rio de Janeiro and president of the committee preparing various proposals for the new Constitution of Brazil. He is director of the Institute of Public Law and Political Science, Getulio Vargas Foundation, Rio de Janeiro, and director of the *Magazine of Political Science*, published by the Institute. He has served as Brazil's ambassador to the United Nations, as minister of foreign relations, as president of the Justice and Foreign Relations Commission of the Federal Senate, and as Brazilian delegation chief to Vatican Council II. He has published more than fifty books on Brazilian history, literary criticism, plastic arts, constitutional law, political science, theater, and poetry.

WALTER BERNS (United States) is the John M. Olin University Professor at Georgetown University and an adjunct scholar at the American Enterprise Institute. He is the author of many books and articles on constitutional issues, including *The First Amendment and the Future of American Democracy, For Capital Punishment, In Defense of Liberal Democracy*, and, most recently, *Taking the Constitution Seriously*. He is a member of the National Council on the Humanities and has served on the American delegation to the United Nations Commission on Human Rights.

ALBERT P. BLAUSTEIN (United States) is professor of law at Rutgers University. He has served as a constitutional consultant and legal adviser to governments and liberation movements in Liberia, Cambodia, Bangladesh, Peru, Zimbabwe, and others. Dr. Blaustein is the author or coauthor of more than twenty books, including *Constitutions of the Countries of the World* (18 volumes, 1971–), *Independence Documents of the World* (2 volumes, 1977), and *Human Rights Source Book*. He is chairman and president of Human Rights Advocates International and is chairman of the Committee on the Influence of the U.S. Constitution Abroad for the League of Human Rights, World Peace through Law Center.

ALLAN R. BREWER-CARIAS (Venezuela) is a professor of the law faculty and director of the Institute of Public Law at the Central University of Venezuela. His other academic activities include professor of the Strasbourg International Law Faculty for the Teaching of Comparative Law; visiting professor at the International Institute of Public Administration in Paris; visiting fellow at Clare Hall (1972–1974), Simon

Bolivar Professor, University of Cambridge (1985–1986), fellow of Trinity College (1985–1986), and teaching member of the law faculty at Cambridge University. He has served as legal adviser to the Ministry of Justice, Comptroller's Office, Ministry of Finance, Attorney General's Office, and the Supreme Electoral Council. He served as president of the Public Administration Commission; as substitute justice in the Supreme Court; and as substitute senator for the Federal District. He has written extensively on legal, social, administrative, and constitutional issues.

DAVID CAMERON (Canada) is deputy minister of the Ministry of Intergovernmental Affairs. He was previously vice-president of institutional relations at the University of Toronto and a professor of political science. From 1982 to 1985, he was assistant under secretary of state for education support, Department of the Secretary of State. From 1980 to 1982, he was assistant secretary to the Cabinet for Strategic and Constitutional Planning, Federal-Provincial Relations Office, and was involved in planning for constitutional change. He was dean of arts and science at Trent University from 1975 to 1977, and chairman of its Department of Political Studies from 1970 to 1975.

MARK W. CANNON (United States) has been staff director of the Commission on the Bicentennial of the U.S. Constitution since 1985. He has served as administrative assistant to the chief justice of the United States, 1972–1985; director of international programs, Institute for Public Administration, 1965–1968; director of Venezuelan Urban Development Project, 1964–1965; and chairman of the Political Science Department of Brigham Young University, 1961–1964. He is the coauthor of *Views from the Bench: The Judiciary and Constitutional Politics; Urban Government for Valencia;* and *The Makers of Public Policy: American Power Groups and Their Ideologies.*

JORGE CARPIZO (Mexico) is director and tenured research fellow at the Institute of Legal Research, a professor of constitutional law at the faculty of law, and general executive secretary of the Ibero-American Institute of Constitutional Law. He recently received the 1982 Social Sciences Research Award of the Mexican Academy of Scientific Research, and the Henri Capitant Medal of France. He is the author of *La Constitucion Mexicana de 1917; Lineamientos Constitucionales de la Commonwealth; Federalismo en Latinoamerica; El presidencialismo mexicano;* and *Estudios Constitucionales;* and numerous scholarly articles.

WILLIAM T. COLEMAN, JR. (United States) is chairman of the board of the Legal Defense and Educational Fund of the National Association for the Advancement of Colored People, and served as a counsel in several key civil rights cases of the 1950s and 1960s, including *Brown v. Board of Education*. He was appointed *amicus curiae* by the Supreme Court of the United States in *Bob Jones University v. United States* and *Goldsboro Christian Schools, Ind. v. United States*, cases argued before the Supreme Court in October 1982. He served as secretary of transportation from 1975 to 1977, and is currently senior partner at O'Melveny and Myers in Washington, D.C. Mr. Coleman served as a U.S. Supreme Court law clerk to the late Justice Felix Frankfurter.

JOSEPH A. L. COORAY (Sri Lanka) was senior constitutional adviser to the parliamentary select committee on the drafting of the present (1978) Republican Constitution of Sri Lanka. He was also a member of the drafting committee as well as an adviser to the Constituent Assembly in the drafting of the 1972 Constitution of the First Republic. Dr. Cooray is the chairman of the Human Rights Commission of Sri Lanka and also vice-chairman of the United Nations Human Rights Committee. He has served as judge of the Constitutional Court of Sri Lanka and has taught constitutional law, international law and human rights at the Sri Lanka Law College. He was chairman, UN International Seminar on Human Rights, Peace and Development; and has been a member of the Sri Lanka Delegation to the UN General Assembly Sessions. His publications include *The Revision of the Constitution, Constitutional Government and Human Rights in a Developing Society*, and *Constitutional and Administrative Law of Sri Lanka*.

MICHAEL DECLERIS (Greece) is senior justice (councilor of state) at the Council of State, the Supreme Administrative Court in Greece. A pioneer of systems methodology in law and political science, he founded the Greek Systems Society. His publications include "Certain System Concepts in Law and Politics," "The Last Chance: Constitution-Making in Cyprus, 1972–1974," and "Lasswell's Empirical Theory of Law and Politics."

JOVAN DJORDJEVIC (Yugoslavia) was deputy president of the 1963 Constitutional Commission of Yugoslavia, a member of the 1974 Constitutional Commission, and president of the International Association for Constitutional Law. He has served as president of the Constitutional Sub-Commission for Human Rights and Freedom; vice-president of the International Association for Political Science; and a member of the Serbian Academy of Sciences.

CONTRIBUTORS

DANIEL ELAZAR (United States) is professor of political science and director of the Center for the Study of Federalism at Temple University. He has written and edited numerous books on American federalism, including *The American Partnership: Federal-State Relations in the Nineteenth Century* (1962), and *American Federalism: A View From the States* (3rd ed., 1984). Dr. Elazar is editor of *Publius: The Journal of Federalism* and is Senator N. M. Paterson Professor of Political Studies, and head of the Institute of Local Government at Bar-Ilan University in Israel. He is also president of the Jerusalem Center of Public Affairs.

BRUCE E. FEIN (United States) is visiting fellow for constitutional studies at the Heritage Foundation. Previously, Mr. Fein was general counsel for the Federal Communications Commission. He has written extensively on the Supreme Court and constitutional issues, with special attention to theories of separation of powers in the formulation of the Constitution of the United States. He is the author of several annual volumes *Significant Decisions of the Supreme Court*, published by the American Enterprise Institute.

JEAN FOYER (France) is a deputy to the National Assembly, and professor of private law at the University of Paris II. He was a member of the working group that prepared the text of the Constitution of 1958. He has been secretary of state, minister of cooperation, minister of justice, minister of public health, and president of the National Assembly committee on constitutional laws of legislation and administration.

DIOGO FREITAS DO AMARAL (Portugal) is professor of public law and political science at Lisbon University and the Portuguese Catholic University. He has served as vice prime minister and minister for foreign affairs, and minister for national defense. He was a member of the Portuguese Parliament from 1975 to 1982 and of the Council of State 1974–1975 and 1982. Founder and party leader of the Center Democratic Party (Christian Democrats) from 1974 to 1982, and again since January 1988, he was president of the European Union of Christian Democrats, 1981–1983. He is the author of numerous works on legal, administrative, and constitutional issues.

CARLOS JOSE GUTIERREZ (Costa Rica) is ambassador permanent representative of Costa Rica to the United Nations. He has been dean of the school of law of the University of Costa Rica (1966–1972), ambassador to the Federal Republic of Germany (1975–1976), minister of justice (1982–1983), and minister of foreign affairs and culture of the Republic of Costa Rica (1983–1986). He is the author of many books on constitutional law, including *The Central American Court of Justice* (1975), *Lessons on the Philosophy of Law* (4th ed., 1985), *Costa Rican Political Thought: Social Democracy* (1986), *Neutrality and Militant Democracy* (1987), and coauthor of *Costa Rican Constitutional Law* (1983).

A. E. DICK HOWARD (United States) is White Burkett Miller Professor of Law and Public Affairs at the University of Virginia School of Law. He directed the revision of Virginia's constitution from 1968 to 1970. He has been a frequent lecturer in other countries, speaking under the auspices of universities and learned societies in England, Australia, Spain, Sweden, Brazil, Hong Kong, the Philippines, and elsewhere.

BERNARD LEWIS (United States) is the Cleveland E. Dodge Professor of Near Eastern Studies, Emeritus, at Princeton University, and the director of the Annenberg Research Institute in Philadelphia.

FRANCOIS LUCHAIRE (France) is professor of constitutional law, University of Paris (Pantheon-Sorbonne), and director of the Center for Research of Constitutional Law. He was also interministerial deputy to the prime minister for liberal professions. In 1958 he was a member of the editorial committee of the new French Constitution and government commissioner to the Constitutional Consultative Committee and State Council. He was also a member of the Constitutional Council of the French Republic, president of the National Support Committee for François Mitterrand's candidacy for president, and is vice-president of the Movement of the Radical Left.

HARVEY C. MANSFIELD, JR. (United States) has been professor of government at Harvard University since 1969. He is the author of many books on political thought, including *Statesmanship and Party Government, A Study of Burke and Bolingbrook* (1965), *The Spirit of Liberalism* (1978), and *Selected Letters of Edmund Burke* (1984). He has provided a new translation of and introduction to Machiavelli's *The Prince* (1985). He is also the author of "The Forms and Formalities of Liberty," *The Public Interest* (1983), "Constitutionalism and the Rule of Law," *Harvard Journal of Law and Public Policy* (1985), "Constitutional Government: The Soul of Modern Democracy" (1987), "The Religious Issue and the Origin of Modern Constitutionalism" (1987), and "The Forms of Liberty" (1986).

TERENCE MARSHALL (United States) is professor of judicial and political sciences at the University of Paris X-Nanterre. Previously he taught political science at the University of Pennsylvania, North Carolina State University, the University of Paris I-Sorbonne-Pantheon, and L'École Normale Supérieure. His publications include "Leo Strauss, la Philosophie et la Science Politique," in *The Revue Française de Science Politique*, "John Locke et la Philosophie Constitutionnelle," in *Synthese*, *Vie et Institutions Politiques des États-Unis*, and "Rousseau Translations: A Review Essay," in *Political Theory*, among others. He is currently preparing a two-volume study in French on American constitutional theory and practice.

NANI A. PALKHIVALA (India) is senior advocate of the Supreme Court of India, New Delhi; former ambassador of India to the United States; and former professor of law at Bombay University and Tagore Professor of Law at Calcutta University. He has been counsel for India before the International Tribunal at Geneva (1964–1966) and before the International Civil Aviation Organization and the World Court. His many publications include *Our Constitution Defaced and Defiled; India's Priceless Heritage; Taxation in India;* and *We, The People.*

NAJDAN PASIC (Yugoslavia), former president of the Constitutional Court of Serbia and a member of the Central Committee of the League of Communists of Yugoslavia, was professor, faculty of political science, University of Belgrade, from 1960 until his retirement in 1986. He was editor-in-chief of the magazines *Our Reality* and *Socialism* and has been for many years a member of the Commissions for Constitutional Questions of both the federal and Serbian assemblies. He is active in current constitutional reform. His many publications include: *Public Corporation in Great Britain, The Contemporary State, Comparative Political Systems, The National Question in the Contemporary Epoch, Political Organization of Self-managing Society, Interests and the Political Process,* and *Essays and Treaties on Political Systems.*

JOSÉ PEDRO PÉREZ-LLORCA (Spain), now in private law practice, was Spain's foreign minister, 1980–1982. He was the Central Democratic Union (UDC) party's principal drafter of the 1978 Constitution. He was president of the parliamentary group of the Congress during the parliamentary constitutional period and later was a member of the combined Congressional-Senate Commission. He founded the Popular party and served as its secretary general until the party joined with other parties to form the UDC. Prior to becoming foreign minister, he served as minister for the presidency for relations with the Cortes (Parliament), and minister for Territorial Administration.

GUSTAVO PLANCHART MANRIQUE (Venezuela) is currently in private law practice. In addition to several other academic posts, he was a professor of constitutional law at the Central University of Venezuela and at the Catholic University Andres Bello, and was dean of the faculty of law of the Central University. He is a member of the Council of the University for Peace of the United Nations sitting in San Jose, Costa Rica, and of the Rectoral Council of the Simon Rodriguez University in Caracas, Venezuela; he was vice-president of the Advisory Commission for Foreign Relations of the Republic of Venezuela.

JACK N. RAKOVE (United States) is professor of history and director of the American Studies Program at Stanford University. He is the author of *The Beginning of National Politics: An Interpretive History of the Continental Congress*. He has written numerous articles on constitutional history and politics that have appeared in journals such as *William and Mary Quarterly*, *Perspectives in American History*, and *The Atlantic*.

FRANCISCO RUBIO LLORENTE (Spain) is tenured professor of constitutional law at the University of Madrid. As secretary general of the Spanish Parliament (Cortes) he participated in the drafting of the 1978 Spanish Constitution. Since 1980 he has been one of the twelve justices of the Spanish constitutional court. His most recent publications are "Problemas de la interpretacion constitucional en la jurisprudencia del Tribunal español," in *Festschrift fur Wolfgang Zeidler* (Berlin, New York, 1987) and "Constitutional Jurisdiction as Law Making," in *Law in the Making. A comparative study* (Heidelberg, Wien, New York, 1988).

IBRAHIM SALEH (Egypt) is deputy president of the Court of Cassation and counsellor to the speaker of the People's Assembly. He has been teaching at the faculty of law, the Faculty of Shariah and Law and Higher Institutes since 1968. He has represented Egypt in various international conventions around the world.

AMOS SAWYER (Liberia) is chairman of the Liberian Constitution Commission and dean of the University of Liberia Liberal Arts College.

MOHAMAD TAHA AL-SHAEIR (Egypt) is vice-president of the Ain Shams University in Cairo, Egypt, where he is also professor of public law, constitutional law, and administrative law. He has been a member of the Egyptian Senate and a member of the Egyptian delegation,

International Institute of Administrative Sciences. He is a former member of the State Council (1960–1961). His publications include "Theory of Constitutional Law," "The Egyptian Constitution," "Administrative Law," and "Constitutional Law in Kuwait."

VOJISLAV D. STANOVCIC (Yugoslavia) has been professor of political theory, faculty of political science, at the University of Belgrade since 1968. He has served previously as managing editor of *Our Reality*, a monthly review of social science, and editor of *Socialism*. He has written and edited three editions of *Political Encyclopedia* and is preparing a fourth edition. He also has edited the 1,159-page *Theory and Practice of Self-Management*. Among his other publications are: *Industrial Democracy, Utopian Theories of Society*, "Territorial and Functional Federalism," "Social Role, Ethical, and Political Teachings of the Founders of Great World Religions," "On the Character and Political Ideas of *The Federalist* Papers," as well as many other articles on federalism, human rights, political parties, and other subjects. Dr. Stanovcic has translated *The Federalist* into Serbo-Croation.

GERALD STOURZH (Austria) is a professor of modern history at the Institute for History, University of Vienna and a full member of the Austrian Academy of Sciences. He was a member of the Institute for Advanced Study, Princeton and an overseas fellow, Churchill College, Cambridge University. His publications include *Benjamin Franklin and American Foreign Policy, Alexander Hamilton and the Idea of Republican Government*, and the *History of the Austrian State Treaty Negotiations, 1945–1955*. He has written numerous papers on constitutional history, the history of political thought, and the history of international relations.

ARTURO M. TOLENTINO (Philippines) was minister of state for foreign affairs beginning in 1978 and has served in many diplomatic posts, including Philippine delegate to the Law of the Sea Conference. He served two terms in the Filipino House of Representatives (1949–1957), three terms as senator (1957–1973) and two terms in the National Assembly (1978–1986). He was head of the Philippine observer mission to the nonaligned summit and was elected vice-president in 1986. He is the author of various law books, among them *Commentaries on the Civil Code* (5 volumes), *Commentaries on Commercial Law* (2 volumes), and *Government of the Philippines*.

CONSTANTINE TSATSOS (Greece) was president of Greece from 1975 to 1980 and president of the constitutional committee that drafted the

Greek Constitution of 1975. At various times he served as minister of education, minister of justice, and minister of cultural affairs. He was a professor of philosophy of law, University of Athens, and a member of the European Academy of Arts, Sciences, and Humanities. He was the author of many books on the theory of law, philosophy, and literary criticism and was translator with commentary of classical Greek writings. He wrote poetry as well as political texts, including *At the Roots of American Democracy*. He died in 1987.

VAKUR VERSAN (Turkey) is dean of the political science faculty at Istanbul University. He was three times a visiting professor of Middle East Government at Columbia University, New York City. His publications include *Public Administration* (in Turkish, 9th ed., 1986), *Turkish Administrative Legislation* (in Turkish, coauthor), and *Turkish Contribution to Islamic Public Law and Statecraft* (1976).

J. CLIFFORD WALLACE (United States) is a judge on the U.S. Court of Appeals for the Ninth Circuit. He previously served as a judge on the U.S. District Court for the Southern District of California. He has been a visiting or adjunct professor at three law schools and is the author of many articles on constitutional interpretation and administrative problems of the judiciary. He is also the author of *Judicial Administration in a System of Independence: A Tribe with Only Chiefs*.

FREDERICK ROTIMI ALADE WILLIAMS (Nigeria) is currently in the private practice of law. He was chairman of the Nigerian Constitution Drafting Committee, and former attorney general and minister of justice in the old Western Region of Nigeria. He was chairman of the Council of the University of Ife, the National Universities Commission, and Council of the University of Nigeria. He has published a number of articles and papers.

LESLIE WOLF-PHILLIPS (United Kingdom) is senior lecturer in political science, department of government, London School of Economics and Political Science. He is also a consultant to the Third World Foundation for Economic and Social Studies, London. He was constitutional consultant to the Namibian National Convention (1974–1975), the National Constitutional Commission of Liberia (1982), and constitutional advisor to the prime minister of Pakistan (1975–1976). Among his published works are *Constitutions of Modern States; Comparative Constitutions;* and *Constitutional Legitimacy: The Doctrine of Necessity*.

Board of Trustees

Willard C. Butcher, *Chairman*
Chm. and CEO
Chase Manhattan Bank

Paul F. Oreffice, *Vice-Chm.*
Chairman
Dow Chemical Co.

Robert Anderson
Chm. and CEO
Rockwell International Corp.

Warren L. Batts
Chm. and CEO
Premark International

Winton M. Blount
Chm. and CEO
Blount, Inc.

Edwin L. Cox
Chairman
Cox Oil & Gas, Inc.

John J. Creedon
Pres. and CEO
Metropolitan Life Insurance Co.

Christopher C. DeMuth
President
American Enterprise Institute

Charles T. Fisher III
Chm. and Pres.
National Bank of Detroit

D. Gale Johnson
Chairman
AEI Council of Academic
    Advisers

Richard B. Madden
Chm. and CEO
Potlatch Corp.

Robert H. Malott
Chm. and CEO
FMC Corp.

Paul W. McCracken
Edmund Ezra Day University
    Professor Emeritus
University of Michigan

Randall Meyer
Former President
Exxon Co., U.S.A.

The American Enterprise Institute
for Public Policy Research

Founded in 1943, AEI is a nonpartisan, nonprofit, research and educational organization based in Washington, D.C. The Institute sponsors research, conducts seminars and conferences, and publishes books and periodicals.

AEI's research is carried out under three major programs: Economic Policy Studies; Foreign Policy and National Security Studies; and Social and Political Studies. The resident scholars and fellows listed in these pages are part of a network that also includes ninety adjunct scholars at leading universities throughout the United States and in several foreign countries.

The views expressed in AEI publications are those of the authors and do not necessarily reflect the views of the staff, advisory panels, officers, or trustees. AEI itself takes no positions on public policy issues.

Paul A. Miller
Chm. and CEO
Pacific Lighting Corp.

Richard M. Morrow
Chm. and CEO
Amoco Corp.

David Packard
Chairman
Hewlett-Packard Co.

Edmund T. Pratt, Jr.
Chm. and CEO
Pfizer, Inc.

Mark Shepherd, Jr.
Chairman
Texas Instruments, Inc.

Roger B. Smith
Chm. and CEO
General Motors Corp.

Richard D. Wood
Chairman of the Board
Eli Lilly and Co.

Walter B. Wriston
Former Chairman
Citicorp

Officers

Christopher C. DeMuth
President

David B. Gerson
Executive Vice President

James F. Hicks
Vice President, Finance and
    Administration; Treasurer; and
    Secretary

Patrick Ford
Vice President, Public Affairs

Council of Academic Advisers

D. Gale Johnson, *Chairman*
Eliakim Hastings Moore
    Distinguished Service Professor
    of Economics
University of Chicago

Paul M. Bator
John P. Wilson Professor of Law
University of Chicago

Gary S. Becker
University Professor of Economics
    and Sociology
University of Chicago

Donald C. Hellmann
Professor of Political Science and
    International Studies
University of Washington

Gertrude Himmelfarb
Distinguished Professor of
    History
City University of New York

Nelson W. Polsby
Professor of Political Science
University of California at
    Berkeley

Herbert Stein
A. Willis Robertson
    Professor of Economics
    Emeritus
University of Virginia

Murray L. Weidenbaum
Mallinckrodt Distinguished
    University Professor
Washington University

James Q. Wilson
James Collins Professor of
    Management
University of California at
    Los Angeles

Research Staff

Claude E. Barfield
Resident Fellow; Director,
    Science and Technology

Walter Berns
Adjunct Scholar

Douglas J. Besharov
Resident Scholar; Director,
    Social Responsibility Project

Robert H. Bork
John M. Olin Scholar in Legal
    Studies

Nicholas N. Eberstadt
Visiting Scholar

Mark Falcoff
Resident Scholar

Gerald R. Ford
Distinguished Fellow

Murray F. Foss
Visiting Scholar

Suzanne Garment
Resident Scholar

Allan Gerson
Resident Scholar

Robert A. Goldwin
Resident Scholar; Codirector,
    Constitution Project

Gottfried Haberler
Resident Scholar

William S. Haraf
J. Edward Lundy Visiting Scholar;
    Director, Financial Markets
    Regulation Project

Karlyn H. Keene
Resident Fellow; Managing
    Editor, *Public Opinion*

Alan L. Keyes
Resident Scholar

Jeane J. Kirkpatrick
Senior Fellow
Counselor to the President for
    Foreign Policy Studies

Marvin H. Kosters
Resident Scholar; Director,
    Economic Policy Studies

Irving Kristol
Senior Fellow

Robert Licht
Visiting Scholar;
Associate Director,
    Constitution Project

S. Robert Lichter
DeWitt Wallace Fellow

Chong-Pin Lin
Associate Director,
    China Studies Program

John H. Makin
Resident Scholar; Director,
    Fiscal Policy Studies

Brian F. Mannix
Resident Fellow; Managing
    Editor, *Regulation*

Constantine C. Menges
Resident Scholar

Joshua Muravchik
Resident Scholar

Michael Novak
George F. Jewett Scholar;
Director, Social and Political
    Studies

Norman J. Ornstein
Resident Scholar

Richard N. Perle
Resident Fellow

Thomas Robinson
Director, China
    Studies Program

William Schneider
Resident Fellow

Peter Skerry
Research Fellow

Herbert Stein
Senior Fellow;
    Editor, *AEI Economist*

Edward Styles
Director, Publications

Sir Alan Walters
Senior Fellow

Kazuhito Wantanabe
Visiting Fellow

Ben J. Wattenberg
Senior Fellow;
    Coeditor, *Public Opinion*

Carolyn L. Weaver
Resident Scholar; Editor,
    Regulation

*John C. Weicher
    F.K. Weyerhaeuser Scholar

Makoto Yokoyama
Visiting Fellow

*On leave for government service.

CONSTITUTION MAKERS ON CONSTITUTION MAKING

1

Introduction

Making a constitution, a special and rare political activity, is possible only at certain extraordinary moments in a nation's history, and its success or failure can have profound and lasting consequences for the nation and its people. In significant ways it is unlike other political action, though the differences are neither sufficiently studied nor well understood. This volume is intended, therefore, to encourage thoughtful consideration of the process of constituting a nation, study which we think has been neglected and which serious students of constitutions and constitutionalism ought to emphasize.

The small number of persons in the world down through history who have had constituting experience—an even smaller number have done it successfully—are not generally appreciated and have been grievously neglected as a source of information and understanding of the nature of constitutions and the importance of constitutionalism in the worldwide struggle for political freedom and the security of rights.

The explicit topic of these papers, and of the volume as a whole, is the making of constitutions, as one of the highest, if not the highest, form of political activity. But the essays and the discussions range far beyond the act of constitution making, offering a sustained exploration of the nature of constitutions as the foundation of all political activity and as a key to understanding the varieties of nations and how they are constituted.

The eight countries selected for inclusion in this volume—France, Greece, the United States, Yugoslavia, Spain, Egypt, Venezuela, and Nigeria—represent a variety of regimes, geographic regions, age of nationhood, and reasons for the decision to write a constitution. Of great importance, of course, is that each country selected has—or, as in the unhappy case of Nigeria, had—an "honest" constitution, that is, one that is not simply a facade but that has a direct and formative relationship to the daily political life of the nation. The United States was included in the selection—in part because it could not be left out but also because it has the *first* written national constitution—even though, obviously, in that case one criterion for choosing authors had, unavoidably, to be broken.

There are great differences among the essays because each author has a different story to tell. There are also fundamental similarities, however, in the process of making the constitution in all nations, however much they may differ, and special efforts were made to discover these similarities.

The device the editors used was, first, to compile a checklist of questions that any constitution maker would have to try to answer in the process of constitution making and, second, to adapt that checklist to the task the authors faced, of telling the story of how, in each different country, the constitution makers went about answering those questions. By providing the same list of questions to each author, we sought to make the essays readily comparable, so that the reader would be able to see the similarities in the tasks of the constitution makers, wherever they were and whatever kind of regime they were establishing, and at the same time see the differences in approach and results from country to country. Here is what we wrote to each author in advance of the writing of the essays:

> To facilitate fruitful comparisons, we propose a kind of checklist of thematic questions any constitution writer must deal with. We offer this in place of an outline, which we think would be too restrictive. We want our guidance to be helpful, not something imposed on you that makes it more difficult to tell the authoritative story of how your constitution got written and adopted. Some of the checklist questions will be more important in one account than in another, depending on the circumstances in which the new constitution was written, the history of the nation, the character of the people and the composition of the population, the number and range of political parties, the personalities of the political leadership, and many other factors. To give but one example: the constitutional task to make "one people"—to strengthen a sense of national unity by constitutional provisions—will be a greater concern in a multiethnic nation than in one whose population is more nearly homogeneous. And yet the task of promoting a sense of national unity is unlikely to be ignored by any competent constitutional convention.
>
> We ask, therefore, that you discuss all of the questions included in the checklist even if it is only to report that the matter was deemed of little importance or that it never came up. For example, the choice of a federal or a unitary system will in one account require several pages and in another be disposed of in a sentence or two.

The checklist of questions for constitution making follows:

I. The decision to make a new constitution

A. Why was a new constitution thought necessary or desirable? What events and circumstances led to the decision to try to write one? Was there some critical national problem that could be resolved only by means of a new constitution? Or was there some overriding national purpose or aim that could not be achieved under the old constitution? Was the task originally thought of as improving the existing constitution or designing a new one?

B. What were the great issues at the start—national unity, political and economic stability, reform of the party or election system, resolution of regional or ethnic conflict, increased democratization, protection of individual or group rights, a different principle of representation, greater or lesser power for the executive, some combination of the above, or something else entirely?

C. What were the chief controversies, the fundamental difficulties that had to be resolved? Were they such that the prospects of success were threatened or deliberations halted until resolved? How did they get resolved?

D. Was there an effort to state—in a preamble or elsewhere—the fundamental purposes or principles to be served by the constitution? Was there controversy over basic principles, and how was it resolved? Once there was agreement, how did it influence the form and substance of subsequent provisions of the constitution?

II. *The making of the constitution* (forming the committee or convention, drafting the constitution, adoption or ratification)

A. How were delegates to the constitutional committee or constituent assembly chosen? Was there controversy about the method of selection, and how was it resolved?

B. Were there controversies over procedure once the commission or assembly was chosen, and how were they resolved?

C. What place in the deliberations did the questions listed below have?

• What powers are assigned to the different branches of government, and what is their relationship (for example, presidential or parliamentary system, or some variation)?
• What are the limits of the powers of the government as a whole and of the various branches and officers, and by what means are the limits sustained?
• Elections: by what method are the various offices to be filled? direct popular election by universal suffrage, or some indirect method? winner take all, or some form of proportional representation? Which offices, if any (for example, judicial), are not elective, and what is the method of ap-

pointment? Are there different methods of election or selection for different offices?

• The executive: is there a single chief executive or a cabinet or some form of executive council? What are the executive powers, and how are they limited? What is the role of the head of state (if separate from the head of government)? If a monarchy, what is the role of the crown? How is the chief executive chosen, and what is the term of office?

• To whom are the powers assigned for the conduct of foreign policy (to what extent are they shared, and on what principle)?

• The legislature: is it unicameral or bicameral? What is the principle of representation? What is the length of term for members? How are salaries of members determined? Does the legislature have the power of the purse? taxing power? oversight powers? a role in appointments? impeachment power? budget-making powers? power over the monetary system? power to regulate domestic and foreign trade? a role in war making and treaty making?

• The judiciary: what is the system of justice and law enforcement? Are police powers national, or is there some form of local authority? What is the judicial system, and how independent are judges from executive and legislative control? How are judges appointed or elected and for what terms? What provisions protect judicial salaries? Is there a separate constitutional court? Are there powers of judicial review of the constitutionality of legislative and executive actions?

• Are there powers to suspend the constitution in emergencies? If so, by whom and under what conditions? Are there protections against abuse of emergency powers?

• Is the national government unitary or federal, and if the latter, what form of federalism? Whether unitary or federal, is it centralized or decentralized, or some combination?

• What is the constitutional status of the military? Who is the commander in chief of the armed forces? How much and what form of civilian control is there?

• What is the role of religion? Is there an established church? an official religion or several official religions? Or is there separation of church and state? Is freedom of religion protected, and by what means?

• To what extent are the executive, legislative, and judicial powers separated, and by what provisions are the separations maintained?

• What protections are there for the rights of individuals: speech, press, religion, peaceable assembly, habeus corpus, public trial, and so on? Is there a bill of rights? Are the rights primarily political and legal, or are social and economic rights included? Are the rights provisions stated negatively or affirmatively? What is the status under the constitution of international declarations of rights?

• What protections are there for the group rights of minorities (religious, ethnic, racial, regional, or other)?

• What is the constitutional status of political parties? Is it a one-party system, two-party system, multiparty system, or is that left undetermined?

• What are the powers for managing the economy? What is the status of private property? What are the regulatory and licensing powers? Are there government monopolies and, if so, of what kind? What are the copyright and patent provisions?

• What is the educational system, and how is it controlled or supervised? Is the school system centralized, regional, local, or some combination? Are there provisions for ethnic, religious, or language schools? Are private schools allowed?

• What are the provisions for the mass media? Are there government-owned, political party-owned, or privately owned newspapers and television and radio stations? Are the media regulated or licensed? What protections are there for freedom of the press, and how are abuses prevented?

• Are there different levels or kinds of citizenship; that is, are there qualifications or restrictions of voting rights, property rights, representation, access to education, or eligibility for public office based on race, sex, religion, language, or national origin? What are the naturalization provisions?

• What is the status of international law and international organizations in relation to national laws and institutions?

• What is the constitutional amending process? Is it designed to make amendment relatively easy or difficult? Does the amending process include the people as a whole, or is it limited to the legislature and other officials?

• What is the process for ratification of the constitution?

We think the influence of the checklist has given the essays a coherence they might otherwise not have had. Viewed in one way, the essays are simply a series of accounts of constitution writing in eight different countries. Looked at in another way, they present a progression of themes displaying the variety of constitutions, the variety of regimes, and the different kinds of occasions necessitating the adoption of a new constitution. France presents the opportunity to consider the role of "the towering figure" in the design of a constitution and the effect of national crisis on the constitution-making process. France and the United States present a contrast in unitary and federal design, and the United States and Yugoslavia present two quite different understandings of the meaning of federalism. Yugoslavia and Nigeria, unusually diverse multiethnic nations, present differing approaches to nation building or people building, the task of holding a nation together. Egypt and Greece present differing examples of the establishment of religion and the constitutional role of the church, and both are in contrast to the United States and several others. And the role of the military comes sharply to the fore in considering the Venezuelan and Nigerian Constitutions.

These themes are developed in steady progression from session to session with a rewarding continuity, so that in the end it became clear to the conference participants that they had been talking about much more than the technical or mechanical process of how to write a constitution.

We believe that this volume—bringing together constitution writers from around the world to present their knowledge and experience of constitution making—is the first effort of its kind. We hope it is also a step in drawing attention to the contribution that sound constitutional thought can make in the effort to foster, encourage, and strengthen governments devoted to political liberty and committed to the protection of fundamental rights. Learning more about the task of constitution writing is essential to the effort of building such nations on the basis of "reflection and choice" rather than by "accident and force," as Alexander Hamilton stated so long ago.

In that spirit and to that purpose, we offer this volume as our contribution to the bicentennial of the Constitution of the United States of America.

ROBERT A. GOLDWIN
ART KAUFMAN

2
The Drafting of the French Constitution of 1958

Jean Foyer

The Constitution promulgated on October 4, 1958, had been adopted by the French people in a referendum on September 28 of that year. In 1985 it celebrates its twenty-seventh anniversary, making it the most durable of all French constitutions with the exception of the constitution of 1875, which governed the Third Republic.

This essay, a study of political history and law, is also a testimony to the constitutional writing process. Divided into three parts, the essay attempts to answer the following questions:

1. Under what circumstances, according to what principles, and following what procedures was the drafting of the Constitution of 1958 undertaken?

2. What were the stages of, and the methods governing, the writing of the draft?

3. What were the important problems faced in the preparation of the constitutional text?

The Quest for Institutions Adapted to Modern Times, 1934–1958

The constitutional reform initiated in the autumn of 1958 was the conclusion of a long and sometimes dramatic history begun between World War I and World War II.

For half of a century, France had lived under the regime of the Third Republic. The authors of the laws of 1875 had wanted to found a constitutional monarchy based on the Orleanist model. The regime turned rather quickly into a government by assembly. The French accepted the regime. A phrase of Anatole France sums up rather well the general feeling of the time: "I forgive the Republic for governing poorly, because she governs little."

With the 1930s, everything changed. The regime showed signs of tiring, which was a natural consequence of the efforts sustained and the human losses incurred between 1914 and 1918 in resisting the shock of the enemy and at last grasping victory.

After 1930 the governments of the declining Third Republic were incapable of efficiently treating the economic crisis—they exhibited contradictory policy. They were also unable to react to the first encroachments of totalitarian states, and they did not prepare France for a new conflict that had become inevitable. The national consensus began to break apart.

The reform of the state and the revision of the Constitution became the themes of studies inciting governmental and parliamentary initiatives that led to nothing. After February 6, 1934, Gaston Doumergue, the former president of the Republic, was urgently recalled and appointed prime minister. He waited a few months too long to propose a timid and modest constitutional revision. His proposal aroused a strong opposition and forced his retirement. In reality, a large majority of the members of Parliament did not want a reform that would limit their sovereign power. The theme of revision is classified among the themes of the right, yet even those who supported the revision suspected that the powerlessness of the regime would lead to the establishment of a Fascist system.

Such a system was established in France as a consequence of the defeat by the Nazis in June 1940. Every kind of error was ascribed to the laws of 1875. On July 10, 1940, Marshal Henri Pétain obtained the authorization to promulgate a new constitution, which was to be ratified by the nation and applied by the assemblies it would create. This constitution would actually never be promulgated. Pétain invested himself with the powers of the head of state and issued a series of constitutional acts that concentrated all powers in the hands of the chief of state. Then, after the total occupation of France, all powers were concentrated in the hands of Prime Minister Pierre Laval, who returned to power in April 1942. Having taken power because of France's defeat, the Vichy regime disappeared in 1944 with the arrival of the allied armies.

During the years of the Nazi occupation, reflections on and propositions for constitutional reform were not lacking. The resistance inside France, animated by a spirit of reform and by a will to change, ardently desired to correct the political errors of the past. Numerous resistance movements elaborated drafts for a constitution.

General Charles de Gaulle, too, was moved by the concern to prevent the recurrence of the events he had witnessed in June 1940 and desired to reestablish a democratic regime in France.

In the summer of 1945, the provisional government presided over by de Gaulle, acting on the suggestion of René Capitant, professor of constitutional law and minister of national education, decided to consult the French people. In the referendum of October 21, 1945, the French people were consulted. At the same time, they were asked to elect a National Assembly. Two questions were posed in the referendum: Will the newly elected assembly be a Constituent Assembly? An affirmative response would abrogate the laws of 1875. The second question pertained to the period of the elaboration of the Constitution: Did the people want the public authorities to be provisionally organized according to the terms of a law elaborated by the government?

This law gave the Constituent Assembly six months to achieve its task. It also required that the text of the constitution adopted by the assembly be submitted to a referendum, which would also determine the mode of nominating the president of the provisional government and clarify the responsibility of the government before the National Assembly.

The voting public responded to the two questions in the affirmative. The text of the law organizing, in a provisional manner, the public powers was promulgated on November 2, 1945. The elected assembly then was a constituent assembly.

For the election of the assembly, the provisional government chose, as a mode of voting, a system of proportional representation based on the department. This decision had serious consequences: the development of the rule of parties. The assembly was divided into three large parties that dynamically would lead to a short-term regime giving primary power to the assembly. This development would have serious consequences for the future as realized by the constitution that would be prepared and adopted. The Socialists and Communists between them occupied a majority of the seats in the assembly.

After several skirmishes revealing the disposition of the assembly, de Gaulle, who had been elected president of the provisional government by unanimous vote, resigned.

The proposed constitution, adopted by the Constituent Assembly on April 16, 1945, established the sovereignty of the National Assembly. The assembly would be flanked by two councils without power. The president of the Republic, elected by the National Assembly, would be only a figurehead. The prime minister held his investiture from the National Assembly and was responsible to it. The government was given no serious counterweight to reestablish the equilibrium of the system.

Only the Socialist and Communist representatives would vote for the law establishing the new constitution. The influence of the Communists is obvious. The authors of the legislative proposal were fearful that de Gaulle would return to a leadership role, and because of this view they worked to weaken the executive.

An absolute unicameralism worried the public. In the referendum of May 2, 1946, the majority of the electorate rejected the legislative proposal.

Having been silent for six months, de Gaulle spoke on June 16, 1946, during a commemorative ceremony at Bayeux. For the first time he developed his constitutional ideas in a detailed and complete manner. His original ideas were not to be modified, and it is not surprising to find them in the Constitution of 1958 and again in the proposal contained in a referendum in April 1969.

De Gaulle thought he would be heard by most of the members of the second constitutional assembly, especially by the representatives of the Popular Republican Movement. He would be disappointed. Concerned to be done with the provisional government, the assembly made a few concessions to the positions that had won public support in the recent election, but it did not fundamentally modify the organization of power as proposed in April.

Returning to the political battle in a speech given at Epinal in September 1946, de Gaulle condemned the proposed constitution and asked the electorate to reject it. But the public was tired of the constitutional debates. In the referendum, the proposal was approved by a little more than a third of the registered voters. Abstentions were about as numerous. The Constitution of the Fourth Republic was promulgated on October 27, 1946.

In the spring of 1947, de Gaulle, clearly abandoning his aloof position, founded the Reassemblement du Peuple Français. Institutional reform would be one of its principal objectives.

Despite these campaigns directed at reform, the regime of the Fourth Republic efficaciously resisted by manipulating, when necessary, the electoral legislation.

In 1953 de Gaulle once again withdrew from political activity. The following year the parties agreed to introduce minor constitutional revisions (December 17, 1954). De Gaulle's undertaking to support institutional reform, supported by the Reassemblement, had failed.

The regime of the parties was powerless to resolve two major problems: decolonization and inflation. The solution to these problems could not be imposed by governments limited to five-month life spans and composed of representatives of parties often holding opposing opinions on these problems. The Fourth Republic would die of this congenital incapacity.

In 1954, after the disaster of Dien Bien Phu, the Geneva Accords ended the war in Indochina without any serious repercussions in France.

Algeria would be quite different: a million Europeans had been settled there for several generations and believed that Algeria was their home. A part of the officer corps, bruised by the end of the war in Indochina, tried to rally the Algerian Moslems to their integralist thesis. The Europeans of Algeria and the professional soldiers constituted a pressure group sufficiently strong to stop the formulation of any solution to the question of Algeria that disagreed with their own views.

During the two years following the legislative election of January 2, 1956, ministerial crises were unexceptional in frequency. The resolutions of these crises, however, were interminable.

Looking for ways to deal more with the effects than with the causes of instability, the last governments of the Fourth Republic tried to have the assembly vote a constitutional revision. These efforts would activate the ideas of a rationalized parliamentarianism.

At the last moment, Pierre Pflimlin's government obtained a vote of the National Assembly on its proposal, but it was too late. The situation in Algeria and the behavior of the army had made inevitable an appeal to "the most illustrious Frenchman" to constitute a government. In the context of an impending civil war de Gaulle was called by René Coty, the president of the Republic, to form a government. For three weeks, Algeria had not obeyed the legal government, and emissaries from Algiers arrived in Corsica to make it shift its allegiance to the side of Algeria. The army replaced the civil administration and pushed for control of the Committees on Public Safety, created by the leaders of the movement that had trained the European population of Algeria and had turned some Moslems against the policy of abandonment attributed to the last governments. The threat of a landing in Algeria had been heard; at least some feared such an eventuality.

After weeks of hesitation, an assembly was elected in 1956 to make peace in Algeria. The assembly actually intensified the war, however; the majority of the assembly was on the left, and it eventually resigned control. De Gaulle appeared to be the only man capable of preserving civil peace, of getting the army to respect a republican discipline, and of restoring the authority of the state. He placed the reform of the institutions as a primary objective of his government.

The Major Problems to Resolve

The return of de Gaulle to public life was greeted with satisfaction or, at least, with relief by the great majority of the public, although, in Algeria as well as in continental France, not everyone saw the same significance in his return to power. The seriousness of the problems, however, necessitated an urgent restoration of the power of the state and, in this regard, most of the French were in agreement, even if for different reasons.

The most immediate and urgent problems were tied to decolonization, dramatically in Algeria and, to a lesser degree, in black Africa.

After May 13, 1956, a revolutionary situation existed in Algeria. The army controlled the country by substituting itself for the civil authorities.

Opinions in most of the other political parties were divided between realism and sentiment. The first group considered indefinitely imposing the sovereignty of a European power on 10 million Moslems as impossible as granting the indigenous population of Algeria, whose birth rate was high, a political weight in French institutions in proportion to their numerical importance. The second group was sensitive to the existence of the colonial population with European roots and did not think abandoning or repatriating them was legitimate.

The inhabitants of French Algeria were persuaded that de Gaulle would defend this latter policy, although he was far from believing that it was possible or realistic.

In black Africa the situation was different and, fortunately, peaceful. In 1954, the Guy Mollet government had taken the initiative on voting a general law for the overseas territories. This law decentralized the administration of these territories, creating for territorial affairs governmental councils elected by the territorial assemblies, which themselves were derived from election by a unicameral college. The general law was clearly only a stage in this evolution, however, and this stage was brief. By the spring of 1958, it was already outdated. But unanimity did not reign with regard to the following stage. In continental France, public opinion was generally disposed to accept a significant change. A campaign was already active in part of the continental press. The campaign, called Cartierism, was named after the principal protagonist, Raymond Cartier.

The situation was less simple on the African side. Unanimity did not exist among the African people either on the question of new relations with France or on the question of relations among the overseas territories themselves.

In the French territories on the African continent, the most important and the best organized political formation was the Reassemblement Democratique Africain (RDA), the leader of which was Félix Houphouët-Boigny, a member of Parliament from the Ivory Coast. He had been a minister in the Mollet, Bourges-Maunoury, Pflimlin, and Gaillard governments. He would also be in the cabinet of de Gaulle. President Houphouët-Boigny envisaged the formation of a federal state that would include France and the African countries. His major preoccupation was developing the African countries, and he thought that a precondition for this development was close solidarity between France and the African countries. The solidarity also had, as a precondition, the federal character of the relationship, a guarantee that the Africans would participate in political decision making. Joined to these political and economic views were considerations of sentiment.

Within the RDA and, even more, among the other political formations of black Africa, this concept of federation was challenged. While most leaders wanted to conserve close ties with France, others desired immediate independence be given to their countries. Only then did they wish to establish, between sovereign states, a confederation or a "French Commonwealth." Ever since the English-speaking countries had become independent, numerous political leaders in Africa, even among those desiring close ties with France, thought that delaying the independence of their countries was no longer possible and that such a delay would have no other result than to encourage, especially among the young, those movements that were hostile to France and supported by certain foreign powers.

Concerning the relations of the territories among themselves, the African leaders and political parties fought on opposite fronts. The federalists in Franco-African affairs fought for the autonomy of each of the overseas territories. They succeeded in having their view reflected in the general law. This law created councils of government in each territory, but it did not permit them in the territories of French West Africa (AOF) and of French Equatorial Africa (AEF).

The law refused to allow for a federal executive at these levels. On the contrary, the confederalists desired the maintenance and enforcement in inter-African relations of those kinds of federations that constituted the groups of territories. The representatives of Senegal naturally were found in this camp. These leaders, fearing that Dakar would experience the destiny of Vienna—that of a capital of an empire out of proportion to the size of a small country—protested that the general law "Balkanized" Africa. The Ivory Coast, however, was reluctant to contribute a large share of the budget of the AOF from which it expected little in return.

The new government would have to decide between the federalist and confederalist theses to make its decision known in the constitution.

In the economic area, the task awaiting the new authorities was not simple. Having been the initiator of the European Economic Community, and having ratified the two treaties of Rome of March 25, 1957, France was in an economic situation that hardly permitted playing the game of the Common Market. The country could not cure, once and for all, the disequilibrium of its finances; and it was unable to find enough energy to modernize its industrial plants or the distribution system. The leaders of the Fourth Republic recognized the nature and the cause of the disease; they had the intelligence to accept the diagnosis and even to recommend the remedy; but they were powerless to apply the cure.

The powerlessness that paralyzed the initiation of a lucid policy was obviously attributable to the weakness of the state, engendered by the absence of a true majority in the assemblies. This absence of a majority was, without a doubt, a given of the collective psychology of the French; under the Fourth Republic, it was aggravated by an electoral regime based on the proportional system of representation. On several occasions, the return to a majority vote had been demanded as an electoral reform; but such a reform would have been a gamble.

Returning to power at a dramatic time, de Gaulle was determined to use his government to cure the country of its institutional weakness.

Despite the introduction of the constitutional referendum in 1945, which was never again called into question, the Fourth Republic had put into place bad institutions and had been incapable of reforming them. Without a doubt, the reason that the institutions could not be reformed was that the process for revision had been organized as an exclusively parliamentary procedure. This observation, the conditions for calling on de Gaulle, and the discredit into which the National Assembly had fallen explain the decision to confer on a new government the responsibility for initiating reform.

Named prime minister under provisions of the Constitution of 1946 and resolved to undertake all revisions according to these provisions, de Gaulle wanted to constitute a government with an ensured majority in the National Assembly when the vote on investiture was taken. He desired to involve all the political forces in the country in this process, excepting only the Communists and the extreme right. De Gaulle worked to obtain the largest consensus for the new institutions and obtained it without great difficulty.

The composition of the government influenced the drafting of the Constitution. The government on June 1, 1958, was not neatly divided in composition. Numerous ministers came from the civil service. The preparatory work on the Constitution was given to Michel Debré. To this end, he was named minister of justice. In addition, the eminent representatives of the large political factions came into the government as ministers of state. A former prime minister, Antoine Pinay, was named minister of finance. Both the political parties and the ministers of state participated directly in the drafting of the Constitution.

Félix Houphouët-Boigny devoted himself to the part concerning Franco-African relations. The former prime ministers focused on the rules concerning the relations between the government and Parliament. Having experienced the difficulties of the system of the Fourth Republic, Guy Mollet and Pierre Pflimlin wanted to correct them. As a consequence, many articles of Title V—the relations between the government and Parliament—which are derived from a rationalized parliamentarianism, are a result of their efforts. Mollet, however, remained faithful to constitutional concepts—the responsibility of the government before Parliament and the powers of the second parliamentary chamber—the dismissal of which would have created difficulties for the Socialist electorate at the moment of the referendum. On the second point, the Socialist view would assert itself during the drafting of the text. On the first point, it would be felt during the preparation of the law establishing the procedure for revision.

The Basis of Constitutional Reform

In the declaration presented to the National Assembly on June 1, 1958, in support of his request for investiture, de Gaulle stated that his government, if it received the assembly's vote of confidence, would immediately bring before the legislature a proposal for the reform of article 90 of the Constitution. The reform would ask the National Assembly to give the government a mandate for preparing indispensable changes that would then be proposed to the country in a referendum.

The National Assembly gave the government a vote of confidence by 329 votes to 224. Among those voting against was François Mitterrand, who is now president of the republic.

Independent of those representatives whose opposition was fore-seen, if not natural, other opponents manifested their disagreement with the conditions under which de Gaulle returned to power, rather than with his policy.

On the same day, the government placed before the National Assembly a proposal: constitutional law 58–7233. The text explaining the reasons for this proposal concluded that it was necessary to pro-ceed urgently to a reform of the Constitution "in order to place the Republic in a position to assure order in the state and the welfare of the Nation."

The proposed law sought to modify the procedure for revision. It allowed and authorized temporary derogations from the provisions of article 90. These deviations consisted in modification of both the initiative for revision and the power to decide on it. The initiative would belong to the government, deliberating in the Council of Min-isters, after having heard the opinion of the Council of State. The text announced the principles that the proposal would implement to en-sure the efficiency of the state and the protection of civil liberties. The power of decision would be exercised by the French people con-sulted through a referendum. The declaration of principles was fol-lowed by a brief text:

> The Government of the Republic, acting in the Council of Ministers after having heard the opinion of the Council of State, establishes a proposal for a constitutional law which is subject to referendum.
> The constitutional law bearing on the revision of the Constitution will be promulgated by the President of the Republic eight days after its adoption.

The Commission on Universal Suffrage was responsible for re-porting the declaration to the National Assembly. After a meeting between the ministers of state and the members of this commission, the government introduced a modification of the text. This latter mod-ification ensured the participation of the representatives in the prep-aration of the new Constitution by imposing on the government the obligation to consult a committee, two-thirds of whose members would be designated by the appropriate commissions of the National As-sembly and by the Council of the Republic.

The Commission on Universal Suffrage of the National Assembly, however, judged that this concession was insufficient. Following the proposition of its reporter, the commission replaced the draft version with a significantly different text. The proposal was then to be brought before the two assemblies, which would have three months to examine it and would adopt the text only if an absolute majority of their members voted in favor. Failing to adopt the text within three months, or failing to obtain an absolute majority, the government then would have the authority to present, in the form of a referendum, either the original proposal or the disposition adopted by Parliament without an absolute majority.

This was Parliament's last act of resistance.

The government could not accept the commission's draft, de Gaulle made clear. De Gaulle was equally clear in his refusal of an amendment offered by the Communist representative Robert Ballanger, which would have obliged the government to consult the National Assembly on the proposal to be presented in the referendum. The National Assembly, de Gaulle observed, could not be reduced to a consultative assembly.

Asked to vote on an amendment that complemented the government's proposal and that integrated the principles proclaimed in the text explaining the reasons for the changes, the National Assembly adopted the amendment in place of the text proposed by the commission. The Council of the Republic did the same thing. Immediately promulgated, the law bears the date of June 3, 1958.

This article of the law of June 3, 1958, contains two additions to the initial proposal, the first of which is a consequence of the government's letter of rectification:

- The consultation with a Consultative Committee composed of two-thirds of the members of Parliament will be obligatory.
- The proposal for the Constitution should carry out the principles enumerated in the text.

The following principles were set down by de Gaulle at the time of his investiture in 1958:

- Universal suffrage alone is the source of power. Legislative and executive power derive from universal suffrage or from the bodies elected by it.
- Executive and legislative power should be effectively separated so that the government and Parliament each assume responsibility for the exercise of their full attributions.
- The government is responsible before Parliament.
- The judicial power must remain independent of the other powers to be able to ensure respect for fundamental liberties, such as those defined by the Preamble to the Constitution of 1946 and by the Declaration of the Rights of Man to which it referred.
- The Constitution must allow for institutionalization of the rela-

tionship of the Republic with the peoples who are associated with it.

The Central Themes of the Constitutional Debate

The method established by the law of June 3, 1958, for drafting and preparing the proposal for revision did not allow for debate in the way that a procedure of revision pursued before an assembly would have.

Pressured by the deadline that it had imposed and desiring to preserve the spirit of republican continuity, the government did not break with the preceding constitution on a number of points. When it innovated even on significant points, it did so by following the example of the former regime. The Preamble followed the Constitution of 1946 in enumerating individual rights. The concept of community evolved from the 1956 general law for the overseas territories. A genuine debate, however, opened on the question of the Community and on the means needed to improve French parliamentarianism.

The Institutions of the Republic.

The choice of political regime. There never was a true debate about the presidential and parliamentary systems. A fundamental principle of the law of June 3, 1958, was, in effect, that the government should be responsible before Parliament. The government, whose work would be directed by the prime minister, would have the task of determining and carrying out the policy of the nation.

Similarly, the conviction was widely shared that the French parliamentary system, the cause of instability and government weakness, called for profound changes. According to the apt phrase of the minister of justice, the question was one of purifying the parliamentary system. By what means, however, should it be purified?

From the first efforts to revise the Constitution, two strikingly different orientations emerged. Simplifying, one might say that the first orientation was defended by the president of council; the second represented the views of the ministers of state. In the end, the ministers of justice synthesized the two views.

For de Gaulle, the correction or the healing of parliamentarianism had to be found in a modification of the role of the chief of state. The restoration of governmental authority depended on the presidential function, which alone was capable of acting as a counterweight to parliamentary excesses.

To reestablish presidential authority, the chief of state would no longer be elected only by the members of Parliament and by the senators. Furthermore, in accord with de Gaulle's 1946 speech at Bayeux, the chief of state would be indirectly elected. Because the electoral college of the president of the Republic closely resembled the body that elected the senators, the debate in 1958 focused on the place of the representatives of the town and of the rural communes.

The government had to be derived from the president: the president would give the government its legitimacy. He would name the prime minister and the other members of the government on the recommendation of the prime minister. It was not clear if the government would be obliged to ask the National Assembly for a vote of confidence. De Gaulle, on the contrary, solemnly declared before the Consultative Committee that the president should not be able to dismiss the prime minister; although he was appointed by the president, he was not responsible to the president.

Among the prerogatives of the president of the Republic two were to be mixed or, rather, composed of superimposed layers. The dividing line would be marked by the obligation of a countersignature. Under the obligation of a ministerial countersignature, the president of the Fifth Republic would conserve a group of executive functions that the preceding constitutions had given to the head of state (among them the nomination to certain public jobs, the negotiation and ratification of treaties, and the promulgation of laws) and would preside over the council of ministers. Traditionally these powers were exercised more by the government whose members countersigned the acts, than by the president of the Republic who signed them. In 1958 some might have thought, but nobody said, that different choices were possible under the new Constitution. Aside from these attributions of power, which would continue the president as the theoretical head of the executive function, the Constitution had to recognize in the president of the Republic the function of arbitrator and final appeal.

By the prerogatives that derived from this notion, the president of the Republic would have the means to guarantee the stability of the government he had appointed. Essentially these means ranged from a recourse to universal suffrage to direct democracy. The president of the Republic, without a countersignature, would be able to dissolve the National Assembly. In this regard there would be only one restriction on his power: having dissolved the assembly, he would have to wait for a year before dissolving another. In this way Parliament would be exposed to the threat of confronting the electorate if it created a crisis by provoking the resignation of the government. Similarly the president of the Republic would be able to end stalemates

19

by submitting to a referendum a project that the assemblies would be capable of adopting or rejecting.

The president of the Republic then would be a person of recourse in exceptional circumstances. If the regular functioning of public authority were threatened, he would be invested with all the powers necessary to give the constitutional authorities the means of fulfilling their functions without delay.

One final idea appeared essential to de Gaulle for healing parliamentarianism of its illness: governmental functions had to be made independent of a parliamentary mandate.

The constitutional proposal did not follow all of the principles set forth by de Gaulle. In the Interministerial Committee and in the government, the old tradition of distrust of the chief of state reappeared. It was also to appear in the debates of the Consultative Committee and force de Gaulle to make rather important concessions.

Ministers and members of Parliament placed their hopes in the techniques of rationalized parliamentarianism. In truth, the two conceptions were not exclusive, and the proposed text would reconcile them. The prerogatives of the head of state had, above all, a certain curative value, the procedures of rationalized parliamentarianism had a preventative function.

The first section of the proposal was inspired by the Fourth Republic and had been written by men who had lived under its rule. Knowing from experience the conflict that constantly threatened the existence of their governments, they worked carefully to eliminate the causes. The first section gives to the domain of the law the power to determine the priority on the agenda of the government's proposals. The assemblies would deliberate only on the government's text. If the law forbids propositions and amendments aimed at reducing resources or increasing spending, the National Assembly is saved from the necessity of voting down such propositions and bringing on itself or on the Senate the responsibility for this refusal. Failure to observe the deadlines imposed on the assemblies for voting on legislative proposals on finances would authorize the government to take recourse in an executive order to provide the funds for the approved services. The reduction in the number of permanent commissions, and their decline in relation to special commissions, would cause the disappearance of institutional representatives of pressure groups. One or several parliamentary precedents correspond to each of these rules.

One of the most important parts of the text concerned ministerial responsibility. The proposal eliminated the demand for a blocked vote, an occasion to invoke ministerial responsibility. The government could, in effect, use the blocked vote without having to be called to account by Parliament. Above all, the process for a motion of censure, whether spontaneous or provoked by the government engaging in its responsibility, came from a proposal that the Fourth Republic had been unable to adopt. Now only those voting in favor of the motion of censure would be counted. And when the government took responsibility for a text, the text would be adopted if a motion of censure were not voted within the time provided for in the Constitution.

These innovations disturbed normal patterns and traditions. The president of the Consultative Committee, Paul Reynaud, vehemently criticized the idea of the tacit approval of the law in the absence of a vote of censure. The councilors of state also had scruples about delimiting the domain of the law.

Every measure taken to correct, cleanse, and rationalize the parliamentary system had been conceived in terms of a system in which the cabinet had to govern with the support of small and unstable majorities. The utility of these measures would appear less certain the day the electorate would send to the National Assembly a massive majority elected on the president's program. The president himself would be elected, in virtue of the revision of 1962, by universal suffrage. But in 1958 who could have known?

The separation of powers. The second principle that the law of June 3, 1958, set forth was that the executive and legislative powers had to be separated in such a way as to permit the government and Parliament to exercise their full powers. The Declaration of 1789 made respect for this principle the criterion for the very existence of the constitution. Numerous modifications, however, were possible in the application of the principle.

De Gaulle revealed his understanding of the separation of powers to the Interministerial Committee on June 14, 1958. Legislative and executive powers were to be separate only in two senses: that they have different sources and that they have different compositions.

On the first point, de Gaulle's conception could be easily satisfied. The text of the Constitution empowered the president of the Republic to nominate the prime minister and exempted that nomination from the rule requiring a countersignature.

The second point could be admitted only with great difficulty. The original text proposed to the Interministerial Council went further than de Gaulle's declaration of June 13; it also derived from a slightly different idea. The minister of justice suggested establishing a rule whereby ministers' functions would be separated; ministers could not be members of Parliament or serve as presidents of a general council or as mayors. This text was set aside. De Gaulle differed. He wanted

21

to make the member of Parliament nominated to the government ineligible for a parliamentary mandate until the end of the legislature. Within the government, the principle of incompatibility was to be admitted only between governmental functions and the legislative mandate.

Defined in this way, the rule had a fundamental theory and a practical purpose. The fundamental theory held that separation of powers forbids simultaneous membership in the government and in the legislative body. The practical purpose concerns governmental stability. The deputy or senator who accepts a government portfolio takes little risks since he maintains his own mandate independent from Parliament. Therefore, members of Parliament would be moved to provoke a ministerial crisis only when necessary.

The Consultative Committee did not show the same resignation as the ministers of state. Most of the members of the committee stated that the proposed rule ran counter to tradition and to the nature of parliamentary government, which normally would require that the ministers be chosen by the two chambers.

De Gaulle tried to convince the committee that Parliament would remain the school of public life and the source of ministers; but his effort was in vain. The text amended by the committee began with the affirmation that the ministers could be chosen in Parliament. It then took up an idea that the Interministerial Committee had abandoned, namely, that the ministers could not support any policy that ran counter to the government's position nor could they be members of a political party. During the performance of their ministerial functions, they had to absent themselves from the respective assemblies.

These proposals were hardly realistic and were even contradictory. In the event of a narrow majority, choosing ministers from Parliament would be practically impossible.

Naturally, the government pushed aside the proposition of the Consultative Committee. The text addressed to the Council of State established the rule that the nomination of a member of Parliament to a governmental function would allow his replacement by a substitute elected at the same time for just this purpose. The concept of incompatibility was extended to every position having a professional representative function at the national level, which included public employment or professional activity.

Bicameralism. The principle of bicameralism was not called into question during the preparatory sessions of the Constitution. The Constitution of 1958 would call the second assembly the senate. In this way, it reintroduced the name of the powerful upper house of the Third Republic.

In 1958 the constitutional debate focused on a twofold question: What will be the composition and what will be the powers of the second assembly or Senate?

In his speech at Bayeux, de Gaulle had outlined the proposal for a second assembly that would represent the territorial collectivities of the Republic; the economic, social, and cultural forces; and the overseas territories.

During the first meeting of the Interministerial Council, de Gaulle had developed this idea, but he immediately abandoned it in the face of objections by the ministers of state, who were hostile to the association of political representatives and professional representatives. The proposal of July 29 made of the Senate a federal assembly even though it remained the grand council of the communes of France. As a consequence of this idea, the president of the Senate is charged with carrying out the functions of the president of the Republic during an interim period.

The legislative powers of the new Senate, and the accountability of the government before it, were discussed, and the texts were significantly modified over the course of successive examinations. The question concerning the respective powers of the two chambers was resolved by article 45.

In the draft, the dispositions in question were placed under article 40. The relation between the two chambers that the Council of the Cabinet had retained at this stage affirmed that any proposition should be examined by both assemblies to arrive at the adoption of an identical text. This disposition signified the character of complete bicameralism; however, a qualification significantly reduced its importance. In the event of disagreement, the draft conferred on the prime minister the ability to call for the formation of a mixed commission responsible for proposing a text on the points of disagreement. If the commission failed in its task of conciliation, or if its propositions were not accepted, the government could ask the National Assembly to make a definite pronouncement.

This system had a governmental, rather than a parliamentary, inspiration; and it was the realization of a remarkably incomplete form of bicameralism. The government was placed in the position of arbitrator.

Within the Constitutional Consultative Committee, in its second session (August 13, 1958), this question was the object of one of the most developed debates. Several opinions contended for attention.

The senatorial point of view was presented by the radicals, moderates, and even by a Gaullist senator who tried to acquire rights for the Senate equal to those of the National Assembly. The Socialists opposed this approach. In the end the government's text provided the basis for a compromise, proposed in the amendments of Jean Gilbert-Jules and of François Valentin. The essential modification consisted of making more difficult the adoption of amendments to the text being considered and proposed by the mixed commission. In the event that a compromise was beyond reach, the compromise required a new reading of the law before each assembly. Then the National Assembly could take final action.

In the text put before the Council of State, the government would reject the first part of the amendment. It would, however, retain the second half, which would become the text of article 45. On this point, the Constitution remains marked by the conditions of its preparation. The authors began from the hypothesis of an assembly consisting of an unstable and incoherent majority. The disposition of article 45 would have permitted the government to rely on the Senate to stop the adoption of an inopportune text accepted by a solid majority of the National Assembly.

The adopted draft was characterized by remarkable hypocrisy. To take into account the terms of the law of June 3, 1958, article 20 precisely states that the government is accountable before Parliament. To meet the demands of Guy Mollet and of the Socialists who opposed the Senate, however, the text added that the government was accountable under the conditions and according to the procedures stated in article 49 and 50. In this context, articles 45 and 50 authorized neither the government to accept responsibility for the text before the Senate nor the senators to place before the Senate a vote of no confidence.

Finally, to avoid any criticism associated with a possible violation of the law of June 3, 1958, the government would write at the end of article 49 that the government had the power to ask the Senate to approve a declaration of general policy.

Foreign policy: Treaties and international agreements. Section VI of the Constitution had a few of the most debated dispositions of the draft as well as dispositions imposed by the necessities of international relations.

According to constitutional tradition, two series of provisions were included in the Constitution: the first and most traditional regulated the attribution of treaty-making power. The other series asserted that treaties, regularly ratified and published, had a force superior to those of internal laws. The latter dispositions were introduced in 1946.

The draft contained two innovations: the first took into account the importance given to agreements related to contemporary practice; the second followed from recent political history.

1. Tradition recognized only solemnly honored treaties. It conferred on the head of state, sovereign or president, the power to negotiate these treaties, meaning the power to sign and to ratify agreements. Certain categories of treaties, however, could not be ratified without an act of law authorizing the president to ratify them. The list of these treaties has varied with the evolution of international relations.

In essence the Constitution of October 4, 1958, maintained this system; however, it complemented the system with an important provision. It no longer affected simply the power to conclude treaties; it now touched on the approbation of agreements.

The use of simple agreements had been conceived as a convenient response to the current practice of international relations. According to the terms of article 52, section 2, the president of the Republic "is informed of all negotiations leading to the conclusion of an international agreement exempted from ratification." These agreements, then, are not concluded without the knowledge of the head of state. Simple agreements do not require ratification.

2. Michel Debré, the minister of justice, was responsible for the innovative provisions concerning internal constitutional law and international law.

The Constitution of October 27, 1946, the result of the work of professors of public law, solemnly proclaimed the adherence of the French Republic to one of the proposed doctrines for solving the problem concerning the relations between internal law and international law. These doctrinal conceptions were to be tested during the 1950s. They would feed the controversies raised around the notion of supranationality made fashionable by the protagonists of the European communities.

Responsible for preparation of the texts submitted to the Interministerial Council, Debré introduced the provision that is now in article 54. The text went through several modifications. The final draft is primarily the result of an amendment that Coste-Floret placed before the Constitutional Council. It states that if the Constitutional Council, convoked by the president of the Republic, the prime minister, or the president of either of the assemblies, declares that an international agreement contains a clause contrary to the Constitution, then before that agreement can be ratified or approved the Constitution must be amended.

Without a doubt, the new provision is consistent with the doctrine of unified government. Article 55 reaffirms this position.

The controversy was much more heated concerning the provision introduced into article 55. This article takes up the substance of article 27 of the Constitution of 1946 (that is, the adherence to monism), but it adds something quite specific. The text states that regularly ratified and approved treaties and agreements can have force and authority over internal law only when, in a specific case, each party to the treaty agreement recognizes this to be the case.

During the examination of the draft by the Constitutional Council, opposition to the reciprocity clause was based on its perceived uselessness. The adversaries of this clause maintained that it was derived from common international law.

Actually, the debate turned more on political concerns than on juridical questions. Those opposed to the inclusion of the provision in the Constitution feared that it would constrain the force of supranationality. They argued that, while reciprocity was conceivable in the execution of a bilateral agreement, reciprocity was more difficult in the case of a multilateral engagement. The critics saw in this provision the means of escaping from the imperialism of the institutions of the European Community.

The Consultative Committee proposed rejection of the provision of reciprocity.

Refusing to hear the protests of certain jurists and of the European party, the government did not give in, and it reestablished the provision in the proposal submitted for the referendum.

Laws, Regulations, and Regulatory Power

The Constitution of 1958 was a genuine revolution in legal theory. Jurists, however, refused to accept its implications, and the revolution was finally ruined by its practical application and by jurisprudence. The revolution was useless.

As traditionally understood in France, separation of powers never reserved to the legislator the power to issue rules broad in scope. Such power traditionally belonged to numerous national and local administrative authorities. This power now is exercised through acts that are generally known as regulations. According to the law in force before the Constitution of 1958, however, laws and regulations were not on the same level in the hierarchy of norms. Under the Constitution, the legislature—that is Parliament—had not only an exclusive power in certain matters but also the liberty to bring every concern into the legislative domain. Regulatory power being subordinated to the law, regulations could not contradict the provisions of the law. In fact, a process of appealing regulations existed; there was an administrative jurisdiction that had the power to strike down regulations that violated the law. Between the two wars, Professor Carre de Malberg devised the basis for the theory of this condition of the law in his book *The Law: Expression of the General Will.*

Since World War I, juridical construction has suffered from several disorders. The activity of the assemblies continued to enlarge the range of affairs subject to legislation. Moreover, the constant development of state intervention profoundly changed the character of the law. Previously the law was conceived as an attempt to reflect justice; now it was quickly becoming a tool, much like the budget, for executing policy. To carry out its program, a government is obligated to obtain the passage of laws that have a legislative character. Bothersome for a government supported by a homogeneous and stable majority, this requirement often placed the governments of the Third and Fourth Republics in unenviable situations and would bring about their premature falls.

Although saying that to govern is to legislate may be an exaggeration, in many cases it is necessary to legislate in order to govern.

In the final years of the Third Republic, the issuance of decrees had become more common if not normal. The government would obtain by a law an enabling power to modify by decree existing laws. The enabling power was given in due time. It defined either the extent or the purpose to which the decree was restricted. The decrees would come under the jurisdictional control of the Council of State, but they had to be submitted to the bureaus of the assemblies for ratification. In practice, ratification was never forthcoming.

This procedure reached its culmination in the act founding the Vichy regime. This development, perhaps, explains the hostility to the decree-laws in the two constituent assemblies. These assemblies intended to prohibit the use of decree-laws. This unrealistic position was held for only two years.

Two juridical techniques were used during the Fourth Republic: the delegalization of certain domains and the delegation of powers. The delegalization was invalid and without constitutional support, however. The delegation of powers was also probably illegal.

How would the new Constitution resolve the problem? During the first preparatory stages, Minister of Justice Debré proposed a system of alternation based on legislative sessions. Between sessions, the government could modify legislative provisions by a regulatory

27

act. Parliament and the government would have equal legislative power depending on the period. Such a proposition was too bold to be accepted.

The Interministerial Committee resolved to put into effect two techniques used by the regime of 1946, and it gave these techniques constitutional validity.

The Institution of Delegalization. The texts concerning delegalization of French law were presented to the Interministerial Committee. The Constitution would define a natural legislative domain. Everything that was not included in this domain would belong to the domain of regulation.

This kind of reversal of perspectives generated concern and opposition. These reactions were greater among jurists than among politicians. In their thinking, the system of law, the expression of the general will, and the sovereignty of Parliament all would collapse.

In the Consultative Committee and in the Council of State, the provisions of articles 34 and 37 gave rise to the longest and most technical debates. The list of legislative matters was lengthened, and a distinction was introduced. In its final form, the text distinguished between those matters that are totally subject to legislation (in which the law fixes the rules) and those for which the law determines only the fundamental principles. It was a subtle distinction, and the criterion for differentiation was not indicated.

The General Assembly of the Council of State, however, tried to save the old principle of parliamentary sovereignty in the legislative domain. It added a final section, which described the limits of the areas of legislative concern; that is, it included "all matters recognized to be of a legislative nature by the organic law." The government would not retain this formula, which ruined its system, but it retained the idea under a less viable and less restraining formula: "The provisions of the present article can be made precise and can be complemented by an organic law."

According to the Constitution, the government has not only an ordinary regulatory power that permits it to regulate all matters not enumerated in article 34, it has also the means to oppose any discussion in the assemblies of proposed laws and amendments the objects of which do not fall into the legislative domain. If Parliament tries to move into the regulatory domain, the government has the power to modify Parliament's action by decree. The government can do this only if the Constitutional Council declares that Parliament's measure touches on regulatory matters. The Constitution, however, imposes no obligation on the government to use these means and does not even forbid the government to bring before Parliament proposals that do not properly address legislative matters.

Making the Delegation of Power Constitutional. Although it is limited, the legislative domain still includes the most important matters such as fiscal law. Delegation still has its utility. The law giving the government enabling power permits it to issue ordinances prepared in the Council of Ministers modifying provisions of a legislative nature. The ordinances have the same juridical application as the old decrees.

With a large measure of support, the constituents of 1958 agreed that the government could oppose the discussion of or the vote on any parliamentary initiative on a delegated subject. This agreement held during the period of the delegation as the law on the enabling power determined.

The Protection of Individual Rights

The constitutional history of France offers three models for the protection of individual rights. The constitutions of the revolutionary and imperial eras had been prefaced by a declaration of rights. Without using that expression, the constitutional charter had contained provisions of the same order under the title "Public Law of the French." Be that as it may, the guarantee of the rights proclaimed had not been well ensured. The constitutional laws of 1875 simply posed the rules of organization and procedure. In 1946 the first draft of the constitution, deliberated by the Socialist-Communist majority, contained a declaration of rights inspired by socialist tendencies. The text deliberated by the second constituent assembly, concerned about efficiency, had more modest ambitions. In place of declaration, the constitutional text was preceded by a preamble composed of two parts. First, the preamble referred to the Declaration of the Rights of Man and of the Citizen and to the general principles recognized by the laws of the Republic (this latter notion corresponded precisely to academic liberty). Second, the preamble stated several economic and social principles considered particularly necessary to our time. These two elements of the preamble were not coherent. The Declaration of 1789 was the expression of economic and political liberalism. The constitutional draft of 1946 expressed economic and social principles inspired by a distinctly socialist ideology.

The question of what should be put into the draft of the constitution confronted the drafters in 1958. It was rapidly resolved. Even though the Declaration of 1789 had been drafted in a short time, that experience could not be repeated. In 1958 there was great difficulty in obtaining sufficient support. The drafters of the constitution also thought (and, without a doubt, they were right) that the preparation of a declaration of rights was more suited to an assembly than to a government charged with the exceptional task of revising the constitution.

The government, however, could not purely and simply return to the laws of 1875. The absence of any reference to individual rights would have been taken as a step backward, an abandonment of the philosophy that had supported the constitution of the Fourth Republic.

A solution to the problem was found in the preamble. This brief text reaffirmed the dedication of the French people to the rights of man and to the principles of national sovereignty such as they were defined in the Declaration of 1789, confirmed and complemented by the preamble of the constitution of 1946.

A second section of the preamble offered the peoples of the overseas population new institutions, that is, the Community. This offer had to be accepted within a fixed deadline.

In the Consultative Committee, the preamble had not been the subject of a long debate. The committee refused to adopt an amendment that would have tried to define precisely the principles of the economic system in France.

The positive effect of the principles stated in the preamble would be seen only after the Constitution became effective. During the discussion in the Consultative Committee, the government's chief representative successfully opposed an amendment that tried to make the Constitutional Council the judge of the conformity of the law with the principles of the preamble. In its decision of July 16, 1971, the Constitutional Council recognized that it had the power to censure the law for failing to conform to the principles of the preamble of 1946. Since the revision of 1974, which conferred on sixty senators or on sixty members of Parliament the power to convoke the Constitutional Council, recourse to the council on matters related to the supposed violations of the principles of the preamble has become frequent.

In the final text of article 2, a second phrase was added to the first section. After having announced that France is an indivisible, secular, democratic and social republic, the article continues: "It ensures equality before the law of all citizens regardless of origin, race, or religion. It respects all beliefs." The first part of the phrase reproduces the text of 1946. If we are to believe an author who did not take part in the preparation of the text but is a specialist in ecclesiastical affairs, the second section was added at the extremely discreet request of the Catholic episcopate. I am unable, however, to confirm or refute this statement.

The Sources for the System of Public Liberties. The principles of liberty formulated in a preamble or in an article are much too general to provide the foundation of a complete law of public liberties. In the absence of a specific text, jurisprudence very naturally assumes this obligation of definition. The first of the objects to be included in the legislative domain by article 34 is constituted by "the rules concerning civil rights and the fundamental guarantees accorded to citizens for the exercise of public liberties." The text adds that the need for national defense can impose restrictions on citizens and their property.

The delegalization of the fine, however, is a result of an initiative of the Council of State. It has been suggested that the principle of legality be reserved for only the most serious infractions and that, within the regulatory powers, the power for determining fines and penalties should be recognized by the authors. The proposition was accepted by the government. The result is *a contrario* to the letter of article 34.

The Constitutional Guarantees of Liberty. The fundamental guarantees for the exercise of citizens' public liberties, as mentioned above, are in the domain of law. The constitution presents only one rule concerning power in this matter. The importance of individual liberty makes it the exception to the rule. Article 66 states that nobody can be "arbitrarily detained. The judiciary authority, guardian of individual liberty, ensures the respect of this principle under the conditions set down by the law." Concerning this text, one can speak of a French *habeas corpus*.

Problems of Jurisdictional Organization

Three sections of the Constitution deal with questions of jurisdictional organization: title VII, "On the Constitutional Council"; title VIII, "On Judicial Authority"; and title IX, "On the High Court of Justice." With the exception of the first, these three sections are brief. All of them refer to the organic law, and the second refers also to ordinary law.

This part of the Constitution has received less attention than the other parts. As the Consultative Committee had among its members a number of men of the law, the section later given the name "On Judicial Authority" was discussed in more detail. The minister of justice took part in this discussion. The most significant element in this judicial ensemble concerned the Constitutional Council. The importance of the Constitutional Council would later become manifest.

The Appearance of Constitutional Jurisdiction. In 1958 constitutional jurisdiction was not in the French republican tradition. The features instituted by the Constitution of October 27, 1946, appeared only in general form. The Constitutional Committee could be convoked only by the president of the Republic; insofar as its control was severely restricted by questions of procedure, it was rather the avenger of the rights of this assembly than the protector of the liberties of citizens. The committee had the power to sanction violations of the articles of the constitution; it had no power to sanction violations of the principles proclaimed in the preamble. It was convoked once.

Several factors militated in favor of innovation. The memory of all too recent experience pointed up institutional weaknesses and failings. The will to cleanse French parliamentarianism, by structuring the conduct of affairs in the assemblies, implied the institution of procedures and a controlling mechanism. As always, there was the concern for respecting the distinction between the legislative and regulatory domains. The early 1950s were poisoned by controversies over the treaty instituting a European Defense Community. Its adversaries maintained that according to French law the treaty was unconstitutional.

Constitutional jurisdiction was made necessary by these various concerns. As a result, framers of the 1958 Constitution could not fail to institute a general cover over the constitutionality of the laws. They also had to make such a control more effective than the provisions established in 1946. In addition to the verification of constitutional conformity of the organic laws and of parliamentary regulations before their promulgation, a recourse against ordinary laws was instituted in the Constitution.

No one proposed to institute this recourse by exceptional measures. Such a power would have posed the danger of creating a kind of juridical instability that French tradition condemned. The only recourse permitted was, during a very brief period, that given to the president of the Republic to promulgate the law. The verification of constitutional conformity can block all or part of the provisions of a new law; it cannot invalidate a law already in force. This supervision of constitutionality, however, still remains limited.

In the minds of the constituents, the verification of conformity was limited to the provisions contained in the constitutional features of the law itself, that is, to the rules of power and to the rules of form. In 1958 one thought to give the council the power to verify the conformity of the content of the law with the principles reaffirmed in the preamble. Later, the jurisprudence of the council achieved this extension by preterition.

Judiciary Authority. The classical doctrine of separation of powers put the judiciary authority after the legislative and executive. For some time, the expression of this doctrine did not appear in French constitutions. Since 1852, all French texts have been laconic concerning justice. No allusion is made to administrative justice. Concerning justice affecting private dispute and the function of repression, all the texts have been restricted to three issues: the power to nominate magistrates, the power to pardon, and the power in matters of amnesty.

In 1946 a profound modification was introduced by creation of the Conseil Supérieur de la Magistrature (Superior Magistrates Council). The results of this new organization were disappointing. The institute was unable to find a responsible path between politics and corporatism.

The draft version of the Constitution could not treat the problems of justice by preterition. One of the bases established by the law of June 3, 1958, which founded the government's power of initiative in constitutional matters, was precisely the independence of the judicial authority. This independence was thought necessary to ensure respect for liberties.

As soon as the new minister of justice, Michel Debré, assumed the responsibility of his office, he commissioned a study of the statute of the magistrature.

These facts explain the laconic nature of the provisions adopted by the government and present in the draft submitted to the Constitutional Consultative Committee under the title of "Justice." The first article affirms that the independence of the magistrates is ensured by law. This statement expressed the basic idea of the reform prepared simultaneously by the minister of justice. A second article, however, reaffirmed the traditional principle of the irremovability of the magistrates from office. The Superior Council was retained, but its powers were reduced and its composition changed. It was to see that discipline and the status of the magistrates were respected. Named by the president of the Republic, two-thirds of the members of the council must be magistrates or former magistrates. The mandate would be for six years and would not be renewable.

Deliberating on these texts during its seventh session, the Consultative Committee witnessed an exchange between the supporters and adversaries of the Superior Council as the Constitution of 1946 had organized it. Several modifications were introduced into the text with agreement by the minister of justice. The law fixing the status of magistrate would be considered an organic law. The Superior Council would retain the power proposing the advisers to the Cour de Cassation and the first presidents of the Courts of Appeals. Half the members of the Superior Council would be ex officio, and the other half would be named by the president of the Republic.

The final text would not retain all the propositions of the Constitutional Consultative Committee. The version submitted to the Council of State added to the faculties of the Superior Council the power of consultation in matters of pardon. This power was optional for the president of the Republic. But this version gave up any attempt of defining the composition of the Superior Council, which was referred to the organic law.

Nor would the section on the Council of the Cabinet retain the heading "On the Independence of the Magistrature," which the Constitutional Consultative Committee had adopted. Instead it was renamed "On Justice." Neither heading was chosen by the Council of State, which had proposed the retention of the term "judiciary authority," which appeared in the law of June 3, 1958.

After this examination, the final version was markedly different from the preceding versions. The purpose of ensuring the independence of the magistrature, attributed to the ordinary and organic law, was replaced by the purpose of guaranteeing the independence of the judicial authority as confided in the president of the Republic, who was assisted in this responsibility by the Superior Magistrates Council. The composition of the council was defined: nine members designated by the president under conditions fixed by organic law. In the exercise of its disciplinary function, the council was presided over by the first president of the Cour de Cassation.

The High Court of Justice. This institution is a traditional part of French constitutions, in spite of its often being the object of criticism formulated in respect to political justice. French constitutional history offers several models of high courts differing by organization and powers. In large measure, the type of high court is directly related to the organization of Parliament; when Parliament is bicameral, the high court is defined in terms of the powers of the Upper House. One can distinguish between the high courts that are constituted by the Upper House and the high courts that have special jurisdictions. In the composition of the latter, there are numerous variations; in most of these high courts, either Parliament or one of the houses of Parliament intervenes.

In 1958 the question of establishing high courts was posed in new terms. The Upper House was given the old name of Senate; and even if it did not regain all its powers, those shaping the Constitution decidedly attempted to restore its prestige. It is possible to imagine a return to the model of the Third Republic by reestablishing the division of tasks: accusation in the Lower House, judgment in the Upper House.

This model, however, was not used. The exact reason for its rejection is not clear. As a result, the model of special jurisdiction was used. The restoration of a more authentic form of bicameralism, however, required the recognition of identical prerogatives in each of the two houses in terms of the composition of the High Court and with regard to accusation.

Title IX had not been the object of extended discussions and underwent modification only after the publication of the draft on July 29, 1958.

In the Consultative Committee, the criticism focused on the presidency of the High Court, which opposed certain members of Parliament. The latter defended the prerogatives of the National Assembly to the majority of the members of the committee, who thought it was suitable to fill the presidency of the High Court with the president of the Senate. The opposition was easily eliminated by a change permitting the High Court itself to elect its president.

A second debate focused on the powers of the High Court. According to the draft, the High Court had power to judge the president of the Republic in case of high treason. High treason is the only case in which the president of the Republic is responsible for acts carried out in the name of his office. No text defined high treason. The High Court had the responsibility of determining the existence of high treason and of qualifying it without taking into account the principle of legality of the offenses or of the crimes.

The principle of legality did apply when the High Court was convoked on matters related to the members of the government for crimes or offenses committed in the exercise of their functions. The power of the High Court vis à vis the ministers was extended with regard to accomplices when the head of a plot was charged with violations against the security of the state.

A discussion ensued before the Consultative Committee on the question of whether it was wise to increase the power of the High Court concerning violations of the security of the state. Such was the tradition of the Third Republic, and the committee proposed to restore this rule. On this point, however, the modification proposed by the committee was not retained.

Centralization or Decentralization?

The tradition of French public law is hostile to federalism. This is expressed in the primary sense of the term "indivisibility of the Republic." Tradition, however, has accommodated itself to a certain decentralization. For instance, the Constitution of 1946 was the first constitutional text to include provisions establishing fundamental rules of law for the territorial collectives.

The 1946 Constitution distinguished the departments and the territories among the overseas territorial collectives. For the first, the rule was that of assimilation of the continental departments save for those excepted by the law. For the second group, particular statutes were set forth in the constitution.

Title XI of the Constitution of 1958, "On the Territorial Collectives," essentially updated the texts of 1946. Other titles opened the way for the formation of the Community, that is, a federal, rather than a simply decentralized, structure. These latter titles have obviously assumed a greater importance than the former.

The New Provision. After recognizing that the overseas territories were free to retain their status, article 76 opened the way for two other alternatives: the territories could become either departments within the Republic or they could have the status of a member state of the Community. They could accept the latter status grouped together or separately. By this last provision, the Constitution allowed the Africans the choice between two possibilities. Senegal defended one possibility; Ivory Coast defended the other. Whatever the choice, the decision on this aspect had to be taken within four months. At the beginning of the work on the draft, the option among the three kinds of status was open only to the overseas territories.

Article 16 and the Emergency Powers

Article 16 of the Constitution invests the president of the Republic with emergency powers when the institutions of the Republic, the defense of its territory, or the execution of its international agreements are threatened in a serious and immediate manner and when the smooth functioning of public authority accorded by the Constitution is interrupted. It is difficult to speak in this instance of a suspension of the Constitution. In effect, the hypothesis envisaged by the text is that of circumstances that have interrupted the regular functioning of the constitutionally empowered authorities. Article 16 authorizes the president of the Republic to take measures without a ministerial countersignature, to give to the constituted public authorities the means of carrying out their responsibilities as quickly as possible. Certain authors have compared the situation of the president of the Republic exercising the powers incorporated in article 16 to that of a dictator placed at the head of the Roman Republic in an emergency.

What are the origins of this provision already well known in 1958? De Gaulle, marked by the memory of June 1940, concluded that the head of state lacked the power to impose a policy he judged necessary for the salvation of the country at a moment when unforeseeable events threatened its honor and destiny.

In the first draft submitted by the minister of justice appeared the following: (1) a definition of the conditions for emergency powers—the threat against national unity or national independence; (2) the obligation to consult with the prime minister and the presidents of the assemblies; (3) the requirement of a message to the nation delivered before the Council of State; and (4) a proposition, which in the end was not retained, that Parliament be given a summary of the measures taken as well as a presentation of these measures for a judgement of conformity. To a certain degree, these requirements borrowed elements from the ordinances.

In the course of successive examinations, the text was enriched. Threats against the independence and security of the country were extended to mean threats against the institutions of the Republic. The requirements of a summary submitted to Parliament and the ratification of conformity of the measures no longer appeared, but their purpose was defined. The measures should be motivated by the will to give the constitutionally empowered public authorities the means of fulfilling their mission as quickly as possible. The stipulation was not to change. Finally, at the end of July 1958, a measure requiring consultation with the Constitutional Council and the convening of Parliament as soon as circumstances warranted was introduced. Indeed, the text would not say that the Constitutional Council in consultation decides on the conditions necessitating the application of article 16, but it would be difficult for a president of the Republic to employ the powers permitted under article 16 against an opposing opinion of the Constitutional Council. Public opinion would cry out against dictatorship. Concerning the calling of Parliament into session, the article would allow the two houses to impeach the president of the Republic if they thought that he had no right to employ the powers authorized by article 16 or that he had used those powers improperly. Such in substance was the text in the draft submitted to the Consultative Committee.

The Consultative Committee and other persons worked to reinforce the guarantees. The press stressed the importance of the issues involved.

Before the Constitutional Committee had formulated its opinion, the former prime minister, Paul Ramadier, presented de Gaulle with a modified draft of the article reintroducing the countersignature of the prime minister.

In place of the political control suggested by Ramadier, the Consultative Committee preferred the control by the Constitutional Council. The Consultative Committee, which had discussed the text of the article with the participation of de Gaulle, had clearly introduced two modifications. The first made the Constitutional Council the judge of the existence of the conditions necessary for the application of emergency powers. According to the draft of the Consultative Committee, even the initiative of the procedure for providing the existence of the conditions apparently would belong to the Constitutional Council. The second modification aimed at imposing consultation with the Constitutional Council before the measures of article 16 could be taken.

The government decided not to keep the draft of Ramadier and accepted only a modified draft of the proposition of the Consultative Committee. It would be necessary to consult the Constitutional Council.

After the debate ended, the Council of State was consulted. Its members severely criticized the draft of the article, and the council adopted a few editorial modifications that did not change the significance of the article. The government adopted these changes to the final draft.

Except for the systematic opposition, which consisted of the Communist party and the friends of Mitterrand, the political leaders did not challenge the principle of the article.

The Political Parties

In 1946, the first constituent assembly thought legislating on the subject of political parties was impossible. Throughout the Fourth Republic, interesting doctrinal studies were presented on the subject, and comparative law offered models, notably the Italian Constitution and the fundamental law of the German Federal Republic.

In the texts presented by Mr. Debré to the Interministerial Committee at the end of June 1958 is a section, "On Parties and Political Formations," containing four provisions: the obligation to follow democratic principles in party organization; the responsibility to declare and present their statutes to the Constitutional Council; the power conferred on the Constitutional Council to note any violations of Constitution provisions; and the power of the High Court to censure any failure of the party to dissolve if the government so demands. These requirements harmonized poorly with the liberal character of French legislation in the matter of associations. The government did not include the article in the draft version submitted to the Consultative Committee.

The discussion was opened again at the sixth session of the committee. Three of the committee's members, two members of Parliament belonging to the right and a university professor, presented an amendment stating that "the liberty of opinion and expression is recognized for all. Even so, the associations and political groups should be motivated by democratic principles and should obey no foreign interest." The authors of the amendment did not hide their intention: the amendment was aimed at the Communist party. It raised questions and reservations, not the least among which was that the amendment was motivated by an authoritarian spirit. As a result, it had little chance of acceptance. During this first review, the committee voted only to take the amendment into consideration and then sent it to a work group.

The new review was taken up in the plenary session two days later, on August 6, 1958. The work groups reported out a draft written in anticipated terms. The new article imposed on the political parties only a respect for democratic principles contained in the Constitution.

The amendment was adopted by the Consultative Committee. The government at first appeared to abandon the idea of an article on political parties and only at the last minute added a provision in the text sent to the Council of State. This new text was short. It began by borrowing from the fundamental law of the German Federal Republic and defined the political parties by their activity: "the parties and political groups competing for votes," that is, pursuing a democratic activity par excellence. The text continued by taking up the first idea of the amendment of the Consultative Committee. The parties had to respect the principles of national sovereignty and of democracy. The obligation of respecting the principle of national sovereignty meant the same as the negative obligation of not being obedient to any foreign interest.

The Council of State expressed serious reservations concerning the preparation of the draft on the general status of political parties. It adopted the article proposed by the government, after inserting a second phrase according to which parties and political groups would be formed freely and would exercise their activity freely.

Starting from an inquisitorial and suspicious attitude toward the political parties, the Constitution of 1958 expressly recognized their existence, guaranteed for them a sphere of action and their suffrage, and insured for them a system of liberty all under the single condition of respecting the rules of public order about which no one seemed to have serious concern. Although in the summer of 1958 political parties were not a matter of concern, the public did not intend to permit the policing of parties, including (perhaps) the Communist party. The cold war, however, had not ended.

Amending the Constitution

Under the title of "Revision"—a single procedure is stipulated. In conformity with the idea of constitutional rigidity, this procedure is more solemn and more cumbersome than the ordinary legislative procedure. Three specific elements characterize it.

First, the initiative of amendment belongs to the president of the Republic on a proposition from the prime minister. The initiative does not belong to the prime minister.

Second, the adoption of the draft or of the proposition of amendment is achieved only by a vote, on identical terms, of the two assemblies. This is a guarantee conferred on the Senate against any initiative that might suppress it or restrict its prerogatives.

Third, the referendum introduced in 1947 by de Gaulle on this constitutional matter was naturally maintained. The president of the Republic, however, could decide to have a draft amendment—not a proposal—ratified by Parliament convoked as a congress. A three-fifths majority must vote in favor for passage.

The only debate over the article focused on the possibility of whether an amendment, rejected by Parliament, could be resubmitted. This question was answered affirmatively in law but negatively from the political point of view.

In 1962 de Gaulle directly submitted to referendum, conforming to article 2, a legislative proposal that would modify the Constitution. Did this procedure accord with established norms? Debate on this question has not ended.

A Sketch for a Federal Structure

The Community. One of the principles established by the law on constitutional amendments of June 3, 1958, was that the text had to allow for the organization of ties between the Republic and the peoples associated with it. The draft for the Constitution remained silent concerning the solution of the Algerian question. An elementary prudence required this silence. According to the Europeans of Algeria and a part of the army, any allusion to a solution other than that of "integration" would have been a serious danger. Yet this silence made starting the negotiations desired by de Gaulle impossible. The Constitution treated only the relations of the Republic with the overseas territories and, more precisely, with the countries of black Africa and with Madagascar. The solution could be peaceful, but it would not be attained without difficulty and would not prevent secession.

If the Africans thought that the general law of June 23, 1956, was already out of date, the African parties and their leaders did not agree among themselves on the organization that was desirable. Their opposition would dominate the constitutional debate, and some thought that the agreement would be based on only a temporary solution and would eventually lead to a more radical solution.

The confrontation of theses. The Rassemblement Democratique Africain (RDA) was the largest party in Black Africa following the legislative elections of 1956, the municipal elections, and the territorial elections. Its president, Félix Houphouët-Boigny, who, since 1956, belonged to all the governments, was minister of state in de Gaulle's cabinet. The RDA favored the establishment of a federal state between France and the African countries. This new entity was often referred to as the Franco-African Community. The RDA freely admitted that the Community could become totally egalitarian only by stages. In principle, the RDA rejected the idea of independence.

According to the head of the RDA, this rejection was imposed by sentiment and by economic realism. The Parti du Regroupement Africain (PRA) supported a position exactly contrary to that of the RDA. The PRA would accept relations with France only as independent states in the framework of a confederation. It favored in Africa a federation of territories within the framework of the older groups. These latter would become independent states.

Madagascar, which had enjoyed independence and insularity, avoided these discussions. The leaders that came to power when the general law was instituted gave their country a special status and manifested an indifference to the doctrinal conflicts separating the Africans.

If the RDA was the only political formation to have one of its leaders in the government, the defenders of the other doctrines would find a tribune in the Consultative Committee. Beside Gabriel Lisette, the vice-president of the Government Council of Chad who belonged to the RDA, the committee included persons who would join the PRA and who were distinguished members of Parliament, such as President Léopold Senghor and the Major of Dakar, Amadou Lamine Gueye. The president of the Government Council of Madagascar, Philibert Tasiranana, was also a member.

The provisions concerning the relations of the Republic and the African peoples and Madagascar are those on which the committee's action could be the most efficacious.

The text did not satisfy the defenders of either doctrine.

The transformation of the draft. The text presented to the Consultative Committee carried two sections concerning the relations with the overseas territories. The first was entitled "On the Federation"; the other, "On the Association of Free Peoples."

By adopting the term *federation*, the government appeared to have accepted the doctrine of Houphouet-Boigny and of the RDA. The result was more verbal than real, however. The text, in any case, did not satisfy the defenders of the opposing thesis. If the draft denied the member countries of the federation the character and the title of states, they were acknowledged as autonomous states nevertheless and retained the name of territories.

The federation was an inegalitarian organization. It brought together an independent state, the French Republic, and the autonomous collectives, the member territories of the federation. If, in the order of affairs that was left to them, the territories were free, the power of the federation remained considerable, not only in the domain of external relations and defense, which was normal, but also in the economic, academic, and judicial domains.

On this point, de Gaulle's appearance before the Consultative Committee marked a decisive stage in the evolution of the text and, without a doubt, in de Gaulle's own thinking. Until that moment, de Gaulle seemed to have doubted that most of the Francophone countries of Africa were developed sufficiently to justify their recognition as states. From the start, he had thought of Madagascar in this way. When he examined the draft before the Consultative Committee, he realized that the question of independence could no longer be avoided. The right of independence would be recognized and prepared for.

The countries that were to be members of the Community would enter it by an act of their free will. In the same way, they would have the power of leaving it.

As the review of the text entered its last stage, these ideas were clarified and reinforced. They were stated more and more strongly by de Gaulle during his visit to Madagascar and Africa in the last days of August 1958.

At Tananarive, Brazzaville, Conakry, and Dakar, the prime minister clarified his thought. The creation of the Community would not be imposed; it would be the expression of free choice. At the time of constitutional change, the populations of the overseas territories would have the power to choose independence. They would do so by rejecting the draft of the Constitution. The referendum would have a different meaning in the overseas territories than in continental France.

If they approved the Constitution, these overseas territories would have the choice of their status and could choose to be a member state of the Community. But the Community would not be a prison. The member states would be able at any moment to leave the Community and take the risk of independence.

Articles 1 and 86 of the draft examined these principles. Article 1 of the draft of the Constitution stated that the Republic and the peoples of the overseas territories, by a free act, could adopt the present Constitution instituting a Community. This article explicated and signified that the rejection of the draft, at the moment of the referendum, by a majority of the electors of a territory would mean the independence of that territory. Article 86, section 2, recognized the liberty of every member state of the Community to become independent by a resolution of its legislative assembly, confirmed by a local referendum.

Starting from a federalist perspective, the government had ended by giving almost entire satisfaction to the demands of those arguing for independence. The problem now was not to discourage the defenders of the federalist point of view, if it was desirable that interested countries finish a stage of apprenticeship in autonomous statehood before confronting the world as independent nations.

From that moment, the government and its head would work to impress on all concerned that French aid would be tied to continued membership in the Community. De Gaulle insisted on this tie on several occasions before the Consultative Committee; during his trip to the overseas territories; and, finally, before the public of continental France. France must reserve the most aid for those former overseas territories that would remain associated in the Community. Of these territories, only Guinea chose independence; and, when it did so, the rule was applied. It could not have been otherwise: The peoples and the leaders of the countries that had ratified the Constitution would not have understood a different reaction from the French government.

The constitution of the Community. Being freely accepted by each member state and holding open the possibility of a later choice of independence, the Constitution gave the Community a flexible organization. Although the Constitution was inegalitarian, the inequality, which was susceptible to change, was accepted.

The draft submitted to the Consultative Committee was a general outline. It referred everything to organic laws. The final text was a little more precise, but it still contained references to the organic laws on questions of prime importance.

In the institutional Community, and today we must speak in the past tense, a fundamental distinction was made between the domain of the states and that of the Community. The distinction was a principle and a limited series of expectations. The member states were autonomous and thus were competent in all matters not attributed to the Community. These last matters would include obligatory powers and other powers imposed on a state only insofar as they were not excluded by a particular agreement. Such was the starting position. Particular agreements could subsequently enlarge the domain of common powers or transfer a specific power from the Community to one of its members.

In 1960, all the states of the Community chose their independence by this second procedure.

In its final organization, the Community retained the characteristics presented by the federation in the draft: the union of an independent state and autonomous states. The president of the Republic was president of the Community, but the powers of the Community were exercised by the organs of the Republic. The organs of the Community, other than the president and a court of arbitration (which has never met), would receive only the attributions of a consultative nature. The Executive Council and the Senate of the Community were to be similar to those of the former French union.

In a final stage of the preparation of the Constitution and of the organic laws, however, a few developments permitted an evolution that would have separated the government of the Community from that of the Republic. In the first version, the Executive Council of the Community included the prime minister of the Republic, the heads of government of each member state, and the ministers responsible for matters of mutual concern. These ministers were obviously those of the government of the Republic. At the request of Mr. Houphouet-Boigny, this statement was accepted to mean the ministers responsible for the Community on matters of mutual concern. This subtle formula signified that, later, these ministers could not all be members of the government of the Republic. The organic law concerning the Executive Council stated that the decisions of the president of the Community would be formulated and presented without a ministerial countersignature. In these provisions were the germs of a presidential government superimposed on the parliamentary government of the

Republic. In this sense the Constitution would be applied to the Community during its first and only year of effective application.

Was the Community viable? In the referendum of September 28, 1958, all the territories gave the constitutional proposal their massive approbation. The vote was seven to one in favor, except in Guinea, which seceded. The Community was born by the will of the great majority of the overseas peoples. The defection of a single people very shortly condemned the Community.

Short Responses to Various Issues

The Role of Religion. The text of 1958 reproduces that of 1946, according to which the Republic is secular. This phrasing signifies the separation of the state from any religion. During the last examination of the draft, the government clearly defined the notion of secularity by writing that citizens are equal without any consideration of religion and that the Republic respects all beliefs. This addition conferred on the notion of secularity the sense of tolerance that had been desired (or asked for?) by the Catholic episcopate.

The Importance of the Army. The French Republic is not a military state. The Constitution confers on the president of the Republic the title of head of the army and the presidency of the councils and superior committees of national defense. These provisions were borrowed from the constitution of 1946.

The Consultative Committee added to article 21 that the prime minister is responsible for national defense. This position is greater than that over the army, but the text does not try to emphasize its importance.

The Different Levels of Nationality. The different levels of nationality disappeared in 1958 by the institution of a single constituency. From then on, all nationalities enjoyed the same rights and the same liberties. The difference in civil status has no consequences concerning civil rights. The conservation of civil statutes of local law in the overseas territories or in other parts of the national territory depends exclusively on the will of those concerned. Nobody suggested any modification of this condition of law.

Possession of the Power to Levy Taxes. Fiscal law belongs by its nature to the domain of law. It was quickly decided to limit the legislative domain. Then the rules concerning the basis for taxation, the rate and the modes for collecting taxes of all kinds, were placed in the domain of the law (article 34). No discussion took place on this point.

The enabling power accorded by the Parliament to the government had the effect of using ordinances for measures that are in the domain of law (article 36) and extending them to fiscal law.

The assemblies of the territorial collectives, which are freely administered, have the power of taxation; but they are not generally in control of the rate of taxation. The rules for the basis of taxation and for collection remain, in this case, fixed by the law. The situation is different only in the overseas territories where the status stipulated in article 74 can confer fiscal power. These provisions are not innovative, and they were retained without discussion.

Concerning the state, Parliament has the power not only to fix the rules for taxation, the rates, and the collection of taxes but also to authorize annually the receipt of taxes through application of the laws in force. This authorization is the object of article 1 of the finance law. A new rule was written into article 47, section 3. It concerns one of the provisions suggested by the minister of France, who was at that time Premier Antoine Pinay. If Parliament did not decide on the proposal for finance law within the time established by the Constitution, the provisions of the proposal could be put into effect by ordinance.

Commentary

François Luchaire

The Quest for Institutions Adapted to Modern Times

It is true that both Marshal Henri Pétain and General Charles de Gaulle considered the institutions of the Third Republic in great part responsible for the dramatic situation in which France found itself in 1940. Because both wanted to endow France with a made-to-order constitution, it was necessary to discredit the Constitution of 1875 in the eyes of the public. Yet the institutions of the Third Republic had been able to overcome the tests of the First World War. The reasons for the weakness of France are indicated by Jean Foyer: the immense bleeding that France suffered during the war of 1914–1918 and the disappearance of a great part of its elite. Moreover, before the rise of authoritarian and fascist regimes, all reform tending to increase the powers of the government vis-à-vis Parliament was looked upon with mistrust by the parties of the left.

It is not true, however, that the president of the Fourth Republic had a more obtrusive role than the president of the Third Republic. President Vincent Auriol was able to take a certain number of initiatives, particularly as president of the French Union or of the Supreme Court. President René Coty was known to have forced the return to power of de Gaulle in 1958.

Moreover, the Fourth Republic had reconstructed France (thanks to the aid of the Marshall Plan); since 1950, by taking the initiative in creating the European Coal and Steel Community, it had brought France and Germany together and brought about the political evolution of black Africa. Through the authority of Pierre Mendès-France it had ended the Indochinese War and withdrawn from South Vietnam, Cambodia, and Laos, which had by no means been defeated by communism. It had brought about the independence of Tunisia and Morocco. Without a doubt, it stumbled over the problem of Algeria, which for more than a century had been seen as a wholly French land. Certainly, governmental instability did not facilitate resolution

47

of the Algerian problem; this instability was essentially a consequence of the end of an alliance between the Communist members of Parliament and the Gaullist members, who united their voices to disrupt the government and to hinder every effort at negotiation.

Certainly, if de Gaulle had been able to take power in 1958, it would have been through constitutional procedures. But Coty, president of the Republic, threatened the National Assembly with his resignation if it did not block "the most illustrious of Frenchmen." An intervention by the French army was also threatened, a threat to which the dissidence of Corsica lent some credence. Certain commentators have said that during those days of May 1958 de Gaulle played with the Republic as a cat plays with a mouse.

The Major Problems to Resolve

Although almost all the French saw de Gaulle as the only person capable of settling the Algerian problem, they wished for different solutions. In fact, he required nearly four years to achieve a solution.

Algeria was certainly important to de Gaulle, but it was secondary to institutional reform. He had confidence in French institutions—as an author has confidence in his lines—when he made his first trip to Algeria soon after his investiture. He knew well, in fact, that without a profound change in institutions, the French politicians would be rid of him as soon as the Algerian war was over. That is why the first task of his government was to endow France with a new constitution before ending the war.

Foyer is right to emphasize that the constitutional proceedings were marked by the influence of former presidents of the council Guy Mollet (Socialist), Pflimlin (MRP), and Antoine Pinay (Independent), Minister of State Louis Jacquinot (Independent), and Minister of National Education Berthouin (Radical). All of them, instructed by the difficulties of the Third and Fourth republics, sought to establish relations between the government and Parliament that would ensure the stability of the government.

The Basis of Constitutional Reform

To the list of opponents with whom de Gaulle clashed must be added François Mitterrand, Mendès-France, and several Socialist delegates. Their reasons for opposition were twofold: on the one hand, military pressure appeared to them to sully the regularity of constitutional processes; on the other hand, they understood that the elimination of Parliament from these processes led to recognition of de Gaulle as a personal power. Certainly, there was a difference from the processes used by Marshal Pétain in 1940, since the new constitution should immediately have been submitted to a referendum of all the French. But a constitution presented to the French by a prestigious general would remind them of Napoleon Bonaparte.

Mollet, secretary general of the SFIO (the French division of the Labor International), thought that his party had everything to win by participating in the renovation of French institutions—that is, in preparing a constitution that the French would certainly approve.

The Central Themes of the Constitutional Debate

The Choice of Political Regime. Foyer had good reason to say that the constituent assembly ought to have reconciled two tendencies, both of which would increase executive power. One tendency concentrated the increase to the benefit of the president of the Republic (the idea held by de Gaulle), the other to the benefit of the government (the idea held by the ministers of the Fourth Republic).

Finally, however, the members of the assembly did not choose between the two concepts; they combined them. They held that power is inseparable from responsibility and from the means of using it. For some, the chief of state should be accountable to the people; being able to demonstrate his accountability through a referendum and the dissolution of the assembly, he would thereby have the power. For others, the power should be given to the government, which is accountable to the National Assembly, and should be retractable. They held this view all the more because the chief of state would be elected by a limited vote and the National Assembly by a universal, direct vote.

Title 5 of the Constitution, which too often allows the government to be harassed and even overturned by Parliament, easily created more of a consensus concerning political spheres than of legal spheres, which would have benefited from the immunities of a presidential system.

The Separation of Powers. The incompatibility of ministerial functions and parliamentary mandate was widely recognized, except among the members of Parliament, who tried to extricate themselves from it. They were unsuccessful because of opposition from the Constitutional Council.

Foyer justifiably emphasizes that the separation of powers has not achieved the objective of seeing that the Parliament member-become-minister continues to hold his district (each district elects two representatives; one is an alternate who replaces a deputy appointed

49

to the government). Many senators (who are elected to nine-year terms) have been prevented from holding ministerial office. In effect, a senator cannot accept a ministerial position that he would occupy at the end of his senatorial term; if he is reelected senator, he may remain in the Senate and abandon his ministerial post.

Since the Constitution of 1958 was implemented, numerous persons have become ministers before becoming members of Parliament. Thereby, they have first studied the electoral mandates and the paths generally taken in preceding republics, which they have then reversed (Georges Pompidou, Raymond Barre, Jacques Delors).

Bicameralism. The Senate of the Fifth Republic can be understood only by remembering that the minister of justice during the period of constitutional proceedings, Michel Debré, was a senator; he urged de Gaulle to renounce the powerless tripartite, second assembly that de Gaulle had conceived. The renunciation was temporary; in 1969 de Gaulle had to take on a similar project, the failure of which brought about his resignation.

Foreign Policy: Treaties and International Agreements. In international law, reciprocity plays no role in the application of humanitarian conventions under multilateral treaties. In protecting human rights Chile or Poland may not differ in the treatment of its nationals from France in the treatment of French nationals or of Chileans or Poles; the conditions of reciprocity can be invoked only under a bilateral treaty of a contractual nature.

The condition of reciprocity nevertheless served as a vehicle for the Constitutional Council, to refuse to censure a law contrary to a treaty because of its contingent and variable character and its superiority; in its application in time and place, this condition therefore appeared prejudicial to international agreements.

A ratified and published treaty is superior to all internal law, even constitutional law. No treaty predating the Constitution (such as the Treaty of Rome) and no subsequent treaty not subject to the Constitutional Council can be ruled unconstitutional.

Laws, Regulations, and Regulatory Power

Articles 36 and 37 of the Constitution have lost their main point of interest as a result of rulings of the State Council and of the Constitutional Council.

The State Council has determined that (1) these articles limited the powers of the legislature, not those of the government; the government has therefore maintained previous delegations of power; (2) the decrees issued by the government for the execution of a law should enter the legislative domain; and (3) the decrees taken up in the legislative domain—with the permission of the legislators—should be applied.

It is important to remember that one of the reasons for the rejection of the first constitutional proposal in 1966 was precisely the absence of bicameralism. That was the reason the French twice responded negatively to referendums that proposed to suppress the Senate. This shows how much the French were attached to this institution.

Foyer is correct in thinking that Debré perceived a risk that the National Assembly would be hostile to the government, which would then benefit by relying on the Senate. The situation was reversed as often with Mitterrand as with de Gaulle.

The powers of the Senate appear more important than Foyer has indicated. Certainly the Senate has not been able to prevent the chief of state from addressing himself directly to the people; in this respect, the National Assembly is scarcely better situated than he is.

In the relations between the government and Parliament, however, the role of the Senate is far from negligible. Under article 89, the Constitution cannot be revised without the Senate's agreement. Certainly, for other texts, the government cannot have the last word over the National Assembly. The Senate can prolong the discussion of a text, and the government cannot interrupt the discussion, as it can in the National Assembly. Finally, the fact that a text can first be examined by the Senate increases the authority of the Senate. Moreover, the president of the Senate—or, since the constitutional reform of 1974, sixty senators—can refer a law to the censorship of the Constitutional Council.

Protection of Individual Rights

As Foyer explains, no one in 1958 thought that those rights and liberties named in the Constitution permitted the constitutional judge to oppose the will of the legislature. The provisions concerning them thus appeared, like so many declarations of intent, to orient Parliament but not to restrain it. It is only since 1971 (and, above all, since 1976) that constitutional protection has appeared effective enough. It has, however, caused several difficulties.

First, the provisions of the Declaration of the Rights of Man and those of the preamble of 1946 express philosophical conceptions more than rules. Second, the first issues derive from an individualist conception of human relations, whereas the second come from a much more social ideology. Certainly, according to the preamble, the latter complete the former (and thus do not contradict them), but this affirmation is not always exact. Third, the Constitutional Council, which ensures this protection, was created not for this purpose but essentially to oversee the distribution of power between the executive and the legislative branches. If the members of the constituent assembly had been aware of the council's new mission, they might have given it a different composition.

Article 66, which made the judicial authority the guardian only of individual liberty, is the only statute that does not respect the Constitutional Law of June 3, 1958, concerning the preparation of the Constitution. According to this law, the mission of the judicial authority ought not to be limited to individual liberty but should extend to all the "essential liberties, such as they are defined by the Preamble of the Constitution of 1946, and by the Declaration of the Rights of Man to which it refers." Interpreted literally, this sentence would have the French adopt the practice of the United States, that is, give judges the power to question the constitutionality of laws contrary to personal rights and liberties.

Problems of Judicial Organization

The Appearance of Constitutional Jurisdiction. For the first commentators on the Constitution, the Constitutional Council appeared as a "cannon trained against Parliament." The expression was not wholly inaccurate. Because it was feared that Parliament might overstep the limits of its powers, a guardian was assigned to it. That is why the Constitutional Council automatically controls the organic laws and internal statutes of the assemblies and, when they are misunderstood, the common laws. Its other powers are added to these. Since it was created, it is necessary to use it. But, recognizing itself as competent to oppose laws contrary to rights and liberties, the Constitutional Council has taken on a new dimension.

The Constitutional Council comprises three persons named by the president of the Republic, three designated by the president of the Senate, and three designated by the president of the National Assembly. Former presidents of the Republic are members by law (this clause was introduced to compensate President Coty, who waited— in vain—to be named president of the Constitutional Council by de Gaulle). The former presidents of the Fourth Republic are already seated; those of the Fifth (de Gaulle, Valéry Giscard d'Estaing) refused the position. Nevertheless, they very likely voted for the Constitution.

Judicial Authority. The courts of justice are well entrenched in France; this results from article 16 of the Declaration of Human Rights of 1789, as the Constitution of 1791 indicates.

The clauses regarding the judicial system are the most faulty in the Constitution. The independence of the judicial authority appears only in the clause that entrusts its safety to the president of the Republic. It is understandable, then, why it is he who appoints and promotes all the magistrates, as well as all members of the Supreme Court, over which he himself presides except when it rules on disciplinary matters. This court is not elected. A magistrate is the only public agent who, in case of error, is judged by a council that includes no one elected by his peers.

That is why de Gaulle could say, on January 31, 1964, that "the indivisible authority of the State is granted entirely to the President by the people that elected him, that there exists no other authority— ministerial, civil, military, or *judicial—that was not granted and maintained by him.*"

High Court of Justice. Foyer interprets the Constitution as he does the Court of Cassation, considering that if a minister commits a misdemeanor in the performance of his duties, he can be prosecuted only before the High Court of Justice.

Such an interpretation, which gives ministers a curious privilege in relation to other public agents for a state that places equality in its motto, should be avoided. We should read the text more carefully and affirm that a minister can be tried in a court of common law only in cases of conspiracy against the security of the state. For a political infraction, a minister may be judged only under a political jurisdiction.

Centralization or Decentralization

Decentralization—that is, the "free administration" of local or territorial communities—is affirmed twice in the Constitution. It therefore has constitutional status.

Article 16 and the Emergency Powers

The mandatory publication of the advice of the Constitutional Council increases its authority. I am all the more anxious to say that it was at the instigation of Foyer and me that the obligation to publish was inscribed in the common law.

Amending the Constitution

"The Republican form of Government cannot be the object of a revision"; but no one asked himself what was meant by "Republic."

Napoleon was Emperor "by the grace of God and the Constitution of the Republic."

A Sketch for a Federal Structure

The overseas territories were invited to vote for or against the Constitution, having been warned that rejection of it would imply secession. When New Guinea voted "no," the French government, within forty-eight hours, published a unilateral declaration that the exercise of French sovereignty thereby ceased in that territory. This procedure of abandoning a territory had no historical precedent.

To invite a territory to remain French by accepting a constitution or to free itself from France by rejecting it is to recognize at that moment the independence of its population. From then on, its ultimate evolution is inevitable. Furthermore, de Gaulle never admitted that overseas populations could participate in French sovereignty.

General Considerations

The paper by Foyer is discreet regarding the relations of the president of the Republic with the prime minister as well as with the government, but it justly recalls de Gaulle's declaration that the prime minister would be accountable not to the president but only to the National Assembly. On January 31, 1964, de Gaulle ought to have affirmed that the chief of state was able to end the mission of the prime minister, and this, in effect, was the result. But between 1958 and 1964 came the referendum of 1962, which decided that the chief of state would be elected by direct, universal vote.

The Constitution was interpreted differently in 1958 by de Gaulle and his ministers of the Fourth Republic. For the ministers political life was based on a dialogue between Parliament and the government that was responsible to it. The president of the Republic was elected by a limited electoral body of noteworthy people comparable to that responsible for the election of senators. Mollet hoped to become the first prime minister of the new regime. His party's banners affirmed that the Socialist party constituted the leadership of the Fifth Republic.

De Gaulle viewed political life as a direct dialogue between the chief of state and the people. He by no means considered that his authority came from his nomination by these noteworthy electors. He considered himself directly supported by the French people who, in the referendum of September 28, 1958, approved the Constitution that he presented to them.

Now, this direct contact between the people and the chief of state renders entirely secondary the dialogue between the government and

Parliament. How can Parliament be opposed to the will of a government that emanates from a chief of state who himself commands uninterrupted popular support? But this dialogue between the president of the Republic and the voters requires the repeated use not only of referendums but also of the universal, direct election of the chief of state.

In 1958 it was too soon, but by 1962 the use of the direct-election procedure was necessary to recognize and accept the fact that de Gaulle had formed the Constitution.

Discussion

ROBERT A. GOLDWIN: George Washington, presiding at the Constitutional Convention of 1787, is known to have said nothing on any substantive point until the last day, when he proposed some small concession that would make it easier for some of the delegates to agree to the final version of the Constitution the delegates were to propose to the people. But he did have an influence. Some even argue that the design of the presidency in the Constitution of the United States was affected by the presiding presence of George Washington at the convention—that the framers of the American Constitution were designing an office fit for that man. I mention this example to put before you the factor of a great man, a towering figure, influencing, if only by his presence, the writing of a constitution.

Further, the Constitution of the United States, proposed in 1787 and put into effect two years later, would not have even been considered ten years earlier. I mention this to put before you the factor of present problems; that is, certain things can be done only at certain times and under certain circumstances.

Reading the accounts of Mr. Foyer and Mr. Luchaire, one is struck by the presence of a towering figure, General Charles de Gaulle, as well as the unusual circumstances of the moment—the conflict in Algeria—during the writing of the Constitution of France in 1958. At the same time, very important constitutional principles and ideas were developing, which had both support and opposition among the French people.

What were the relative weights of these three factors—the constitutional ideas and principles, the personal stature of General de Gaulle, and the Algerian situation? Was one of them dominant? What were the interrelationships of these factors, and how important were they relative to each other?

JEAN FOYER: It is absolutely clear that the French Constitution of October 1958 was the result of a concatenation of circumstances. These

56

included the influence of a very strong personality, General de Gaulle, who for several decades had held very clear and precise ideas about the constitutional problem, as well as other circumstances present in May 1958. For quite some time, there had been institutional malaise in France; there was instability, and governments changed constantly. This instability was not due only to the Constitution; it was made much more serious during the Fourth Republic, in my opinion, by an electoral system that emphasized proportional representation. Proportional representation has been a cancer on democracy in Western Europe. There are too many parties, the parties fight among themselves, and they arrive at precarious political agreements, all of which make overcoming problems faced by the state very difficult, if not impossible.

Before the Constitution of 1946 was adopted, General de Gaulle had undertaken widescale reform. Between 1946 and 1958 he constantly repeated and stressed his criticism of the existing system, but the politicians and the political parties were used to the system and strongly supported it. At the end of the regime, when the Algerian war was going very badly, there was a revolt in the army, but it was too late to undertake institutional reform, even if proposals made by the government of the Fourth Republic had been adopted by the National Assembly.

In May 1958, the last president of the Fourth Republic considered that the only possible solution was for General de Gaulle to take the reins of power. When the General returned, he concluded an agreement with the national representatives on a proposal for constitutional reform. This reform was carried out in two phases. First, the representatives voted in one day on a constitutional law changing the process of constitutional revision; then, according to the new procedure, the new constitutional text was worked out in a little under three months and was published a month later. The whole process took four months.

The text of the Constitution contains some of the ideas General de Gaulle had worked out in a speech in June 1946, and that had been inspired by the collapse of the Third Republic and, unfortunately, of France in June 1940. General de Gaulle was given the opportunity to apply his constitutional ideas when he took power, and the circumstances outlined in my essay explain to a great extent the writing of the 1958 constitutional text.

These factors do not explain everything, however, because even though the text was closely marked by the personality of General de Gaulle, it is a "hybrid animal," and we can identify some other influential factors as well.

FRANÇOIS LUCHAIRE: The ideas of General de Gaulle with regard to the Constitution of France were well known to all. These ideas constituted a general framework, but within that framework those who drafted the Constitution obviously had freedom of action. It is for this reason that portions of the Constitution derive from different sources. The procedure that led to the Constitution of October 1958 was not typical—usually one either draws up a constitution for a new state, as happened in the United States, or a *coup d'état* or revolution overturns a previous regime, making a new constitution necessary. In 1958, however, neither occurred; it was with respect to the provisions of the former constitution that France enacted a new system for revision in order to draft a new constitution. So there was legal continuity between the old and the new constitutions.

This procedure was original in drafting constitutions—the constitution would be offered by one man, General de Gaulle, and would be submitted for acceptance to the electorate. The influence of General de Gaulle was considerable, but there also is a series of revisions in the Constitution that are not the brainchild of General de Gaulle, though neither are they contrary to his general line of thought.

HARVEY MANSFIELD, JR.: I must protest somewhat against the distinction that seems to have been made here between personality and principle, because a towering personality also can have an impressive mind. The French Constitution of 1958, more than other constitutions, seems to have been the product of one mind, especially by comparison with the American Constitution, in respect to which we habitually speak of Founders or Founding Fathers.

That a constitution is the product of one or primarily one man's mind, however, need not make it idiosyncratic. We have the notion of the classical legislators from Greece—Lycurgus and Solon—who made their constitutions by themselves. In modern political philosophy—for example, in Rousseau—the notion reappears of the classical legislator who legislates by himself for everything. General de Gaulle intended the French Constitution of 1958 not merely to cure institutional malaise or narrow constitutional problems, but also to cure a moral malaise in the French people.

MR. LUCHAIRE: I believe General de Gaulle supported a new constitution because he thought that new institutions were essential for him to govern as he saw fit. It is very common, whether a political party or a coalition of parties draws up a constitution, for constitution writers to try to make governing easier. Therefore, General de Gaulle was thinking first and foremost of how he would exercise power.

Once he gained the provisions that allowed him to have a direct dialogue with the people through the right of dissolving Parliament and holding referenda, and also the means to exercise almost complete sovereignty in emergency situations, his aim was fulfilled.

The portions of the Constitution having to do with the relationship between the government and Parliament were not the result of de Gaulle's input into the constitutional process. Those parts of the Constitution have been informed by subsequent proposals and, politically, the result has been that the dialogue between the head of state and the people has undermined the purpose of the dialogue between the Parliament and the government.

The Constitution of 1958 is not a compromise between the ideas of General de Gaulle and those of others. It is, in fact, an interim constitution. To solve the Algerian problem, the Constitution had to grant General de Gaulle the necessary powers to do it; then, everyone hoped that the Constitution would work in a certain way for General de Gaulle—to the benefit of the head of state—and the politicians of the Fourth Republic hoped that the system would work as a parliamentary regime, stressing the importance of the relationship between the government and Parliament.

MR. FOYER: I disagree with François Luchaire's comment that General de Gaulle wanted an interim constitution. I do not think this is correct at all, and I also do not think General de Gaulle was concerned with the idea of making a constitution that was personally his own. At the time, de Gaulle was almost seventy years old, and he did not think he was going to be in the seat of power for thirty more years. What was most important in 1958, as he himself repeated on many occasions, was that the president be elected by universal suffrage. While de Gaulle may have had a certain personal interest in this reform, it was quite obvious that his successors would not have the same historical role that he had. Now, the Constitution has not developed in the way we perhaps foresaw in 1958, but I think that is due more to the electoral system than to the institutions created by the Constitution.

I think we can say that the French people and General de Gaulle were convinced that his principal mission as president would be to solve the Algerian problem. The National Assembly at the time had much more confidence in the president than in his government for solving the Algerian problem. In 1958 we wanted to resolve the problem of instability in the government, which was due to the almost total absence of any coherent, homogeneous majorities in the National Assembly, and we had made a constitution that gave the president

59

the right to dissolve the Parliament and that allowed the government to govern provided that there was no majority against it. This was the main philosophy of the Constitution of 1958.

In 1962 General de Gaulle obtained a majority in Parliament that would not pose an obstacle to his point of view. This situation continued and the French people, reflecting a change in their political habits, consciously or unconsciously decided not to send to the National Assembly a majority whose political stripe differed from the president's. Therefore, in the constitutional system the president of the republic remains the dominant figure. The burning question that remains today is what will happen if by chance the legislative elections resulted in an assembly majority hostile to the president of the republic? We still have not solved that problem.

TERENCE MARSHALL: Mr. Foyer indicates in his essay that the framers of the Fifth Republic had two broad aims: to establish national unity and to ensure governmental stability. I wonder, though, if some of the constitutional provisions create a tension between these two aims. The provisions for separation of powers, for example, are designed to overcome the *regime des partis* and to establish executive authority in such a way that the majority forming the government will prevail over the parties. To achieve this aim, articles 6 and 7, having to do with electoral procedure, require an absolute majority to win an election. This does lead to the formation of stable governments based on majority will, but it also leads to a system of two-tiered elections in which, not surprisingly, parties on the left and right form alliances against each other. Given the Fifth Republic's provisions for executive-legislative relations, this practice perpetuates a profound national division in France. Once an electoral majority has established its authority, there is no need for a government to negotiate with the minority. Subsequent deliberation occurs not on a national basis, but only within the majority group itself. As a result, the electoral losers are excluded from further political influence for five years, and governmental stability under majority rule is achieved at the price of increasing national disharmony. When the constituents discussed articles 6 and 7, did they consider the problem that these provisions would pose for national unity in relation to governmental stability and party divisions?

DIOGO FREITAS DO AMARAL: I would like to stress two points: First, it is not frequent that a country decides to replace one constitution with another through the due process of law. In many cases only some articles of the original constitution are changed. In France, one constitution was replaced by another. That is, the 1946 Constitution was legally abrogated. It was what we could call the "legal suicide" of a constitution. What I would like to ask is whether the initial idea was to *review* the Constitution of 1946, while maintaining it as the Constitution of France, or to *replace* the Constitution of 1946 with a new one.

Second, Mr. Foyer said that we do not yet know what will happen when the parliamentary majority is different politically from the presidential majority. Of course, we do not know what will happen in France, but I can say what has happened in Portugal where the constitution is very much like the French one. The 1976 Constitution of Portugal provides for a president of the republic elected by universal suffrage, and the government is responsible to Parliament as well as to the president. As it happens, Portugal has had a right-wing majority in Parliament and in government for three years and a president elected by a left-wing majority (mainly Socialists and Communists). What is the result? The result is permanent conflict between president and parliament, and this is what in Portugal is called the "institutional guerrilla." The president makes public statements against the government or against the parliamentary majority, and the government makes public statements against the president.

My conclusion is that, in France, reinforcing the powers of the president was a solution meant to produce a stronger and more stable executive, but the same solution will instead produce a weak government and a weak state if and when the parliamentary majority is of a political color different from the presidential majority.

GERALD STOURZH: What were the relative roles of experts in constitutional law, on the one hand, and politicians, on the other, either on the side of General de Gaulle or on the side of the parties? This question will also concern us when we examine other constitutions.

We know that the constitutional jurisdiction of the Constitutional Council developed in a way that was different from that foreseen in 1958. What were the reasons for creating the Constitutional Council, and what was its composition at the time of the origin of the constitution?

MR. LUCHAIRE: Dr. Marshall asked whether, in 1958, we had predicted that the election of the president with an absolute majority would cause division in the country. I would remind you that, in 1958, the chief of state was not elected by universal suffrage; he was elected by an electoral college of about 80,000 persons, comparable to the college that elects senators. As a result, this concern was not raised in 1958, but it was expressed in 1962 when General de Gaulle changed the system so that the chief of state would be elected by universal suffrage. At that time, the danger of division was well known, which is why some were against this reform. It might have been more acceptable if it had been accompanied by other more balanced measures and, quite notably, if there had been the introduction of proportional representation for the elections to the National Assembly.

On this point I disagree with Jean Foyer, who believes that proportional representation is the cause of all malaise and evils. I would remind him that if this became apparent to those of the Fourth Republic it was because de Gaulle, in 1945, imposed proportional representation while, I believe, most of the ministers were opposed to it. Furthermore, in some countries of Western Europe the proportional representation system works extremely well. The Constitution of the Federal Republic of Germany, for example, was established precisely to provide stability in government even if there is not perfect agreement between the National Assembly and the government.

I am convinced that when de Gaulle supported the reforms in 1962 he was thinking of himself because he thought he could be elected more easily by universal suffrage than by the 80,000 electors; he exercised authority over the Parliament, and he feared that there would be a revolt in the nation. He felt much more secure being judged by the French people themselves, and this was the reason for the reform. General de Gaulle had three or four referenda addressed directly to the people. How could he admit that his authority could be debated even further by 80,000 electors?

In response to Mr. Do Amaral's question, in 1958 the intention was to draft an entire constitution, not to modify the 1946 Constitution. General de Gaulle stated that he was opposed to the 1946 Constitution, and he characterized the regime as one of malaise. So we needed a new constitution. Concerning the composition of the presidential majority and the majority of the National Assembly, the circumstances in Portugal are not the same as in France; and history is always different. There might be some points of similarity, but the conditions in the two countries were different.

Professor Stourzh asked about the role of constitutional experts. I will answer in a personal way. Thinking of my own role in devising technical solutions concerning the relations between the government and Parliament, I can say that experts played a big role. For instance, I helped put a certain article in the Constitution that I am very sorry about, one that gives the government the right to amend a bill when it is before Parliament. Before 1958 I was assistant to the last president of the council of the French government. At that time, the government did not have the right to amend a bill, so when the government introduced a bill to the Parliament, in order to obtain a majority vote it would have to be modified a bit. In my position, I was obliged to find a friendly deputy and prevail upon him to present the amendment the government wanted. But every time I did that, other deputies would tell me I had chosen the worst person to present it and that they could have found someone better. It was quite embarrassing for the government to have to fish for people to introduce amendments, so when we discussed the new Constitution, I thought the government should have the right to offer its own amendments.

I am very sorry for it now for the following reason. When a bill is introduced by the government it is first studied by the Council of State, which gives its opinion of it; then there are deliberations by the Council of Ministers, so all the ministers interested in the bill may contribute; the ministers then send it to the Parliament. At the time of debate in the Parliament, the minister with jurisdiction over the matter at hand may introduce a new amendment that has not gone to the Council of Ministers or to any other ministers interested in it. I have seen a minister take advantage of this right of amendment by the government to get the recognition of other ministers. From my own experience, therefore, the experts did play a role in the constitutional debates, and this example shows that they are not always the best people to do so.

MR. FOYER: I do not agree with Mr. Luchaire on the question of the 1962 reform. I do not believe that General de Gaulle, in those circumstances, worked for his own benefit. It is not clear that in the autumn of 1962 he was soliciting a second mandate. In 1965 he hesitated a long time before deciding to announce his candidacy. He was very much struck, as he said to me many times, by the thought that a system with a president elected only by the electoral or senatorial college could not be maintained. But it was very difficult to get this accepted by the public policy makers as long as decolonization had not been achieved. By July 1962, it had been achieved. I was there at the time, and it was in these circumstances that de Gaulle introduced the idea of electing the president of the republic by popular vote.

Since we cannot elect the president by proportional representation, unless we cut him in pieces, so to speak, and since we have only one president of the republic, it is desirable that he be elected by the greatest number of French citizens. Because of the number of parties in France, the president will never be elected by a single party or a coalition. Furthermore, in the profound philosophy of General de Gaulle, the president should not be elected by the parties; his

63

election should take place above the parties. The truth is, however, that it has not always happened that way.

MICHAEL DECLERIS: I think we should distinguish between the concept of a constitution as a document—that is, a master plan with abstract provisions applicable to future contingencies—and the actual constitutional process by which that master plan is applied, thereby becoming a "living constitution." A constitution gains real meaning through its application, by the constant constitutional process. In this sense, we should distinguish between the document of the French Constitution of 1958 and its actual meaning.

Having made that distinction, I would like to ask a question. Now, after thirty years of constitutional application and three presidents—Pompidou, Giscard d'Estaing and Mitterrand—it is well known in the study of the institutional presidency that each president has his own political style. Assuming that the French Constitution of 1958 was, in a sense, tailored to suit the personal views of General de Gaulle in 1958, how do you explain the survival and the actual working of the French Constitution of 1958, after de Gaulle, under different presidents who acted in different political ways, each with his own political perspective? Have the constitutional provisions devised in 1958 worked in the desired way or have they taken on different meaning? I personally believe, for instance, that autonomous presidential rule making has failed. In reality, the main rule maker in France today is the Parliament. There are also some indications of an increasing role for the Constitutional Council of France. Is this correct?

MR. LUCHAIRE: If successive presidents of the republic have been able to govern even a little bit in the style of General de Gaulle, with each one still having his own peculiarities, this is due to the concordance that has existed between the presidential and the parliamentary majorities. I believe that if we did not have this concordance the constitution would be applied in a different way.

Concerning the Constitutional Council, it is true that the council was not instituted to protect individual liberties. It was not instituted as in Germany and Italy where constitutional limitations were created; we created the council in France so that Parliament would not exceed its authority. The Constitutional Council has now asserted the right to adjudicate according to constitutionally guaranteed rights which refer to the Declaration of Rights of 1789. France also has permitted members of Parliament to contest the constitutionality of laws, and many laws have been deferred to the Constitutional Council for this reason. Under General de Gaulle the opposition had a right to contest the constitutionality of laws, but at the time there were no great conflicts between Parliament and the government. Quite notably, there was some conflict concerning extraordinary sessions of Parliament, but since de Gaulle's time we have not had major conflicts between the governmental powers; the Constitution has worked, and the council has intervened to protect the prerogatives and the rights of the opposition.

MR. FOYER: I would like to go back to Mr. Decleris's question—What is the great difference between the institutional system described in the Constitution and the way the Constitution has been applied, especially since 1962? The Constitution of 1958 was drafted, as almost all constitutions are, by men and women who reflected on their recent experiences, that is, their experiences with fragile governments forced to depend on varying governmental and parliamentary majorities. Many thought that there would never be true majorities in the French National Assembly, and all the constitutional provisions that were drafted were aimed at overcoming this problem, this lack of a substantial majority to avoid carnage in the assembly, the fall of ministers almost weekly, and the instability of government generally. So we gave the president of the republic certain powers, such as the discretion to dissolve Parliament and the power to submit to referenda certain questions that otherwise would poison the relations among the parties making up the majority. We also tried to enforce regulations concerning the vote of no confidence, the pledging of government responsibility, and so on. These changes provided for the formation of a substantial majority up until 1962, but it was undermined somewhat by the Algerian affair. From 1974 to 1978, the president of the republic was Mr. Giscard d'Estaing. We found in the National Assembly at this time a compact majority that was elected on the name of the president because it claimed that its job was to support his policy. At that point, the president of the republic did what he liked, and we foresaw a system through which the government would be run by a prime minister who would represent the parliamentary majority and to whom the president of the republic would give a certain amount of support.

The prime minister would do what he could with his majority depending on its strength. Under the procedures of rationalized parliamentarianism in which a parliamentary majority may ask the elector to vote for it because it plans to support the policy of the president of the republic, and the prime minister appears as chief of staff of the army whose general is the president, the prime minister's majority can be strong. But this is no longer the case.

This is the question: What would happen if there were no political agreement between the president and the parliamentary majority? Although I have no crystal ball, I think it is possible that the president could find a prime minister who would be conciliatory and who would try to keep the system moving. If, however, there really were a strong disagreement between the president and a parliamentary majority elected against the president, I do not see how the regime could go on working as it does. The president of the republic would have few possible options. He could announce that he would no longer be the head of the government, provided that the members of the parliamentary majority say that they do not want to communicate with him. In that case, he would be forced to resign. Or he could try to solve the problem of opposition between himself and the National Assembly by dissolving the National Assembly. But if the National Assembly were reelected against him, he still would have to resign.

MR. LUCHAIRE: In the United States, there has frequently been a Republican president and a Democratic Congress, and they always succeed in getting through the difficulties of opposition by compromise. Why? Because Republicans and Democrats share in a common consensus and belong to the same political world. On the continent— in Portugal, in France, maybe in Greece—the differences between the political parties run deeper. Each party has a different philosophy, so compromise is much more difficult. The problem of opposition is solved in the United States in a very smooth way, but on the continent it cannot be solved without this "institutional guerrilla" Mr. Do Amaral mentioned, and the problem will arise in France if the right wing holds a majority in the next Parliament. What will be the president's political situation then? The problem is that the Constitution of France, like many other constitutions in the world, has roots in a strong personality, the personality of de Gaulle, a strong man with immense prestige in France and throughout Europe. Although the man is not there now, the Constitution still bears the imprint of his personality.

MR. GOLDWIN: If the parties are of different "political worlds" (to use Mr. Luchaire's phrase), is there the possibility of a constitutional solution?

MR. LUCHAIRE: When there are two different majorities, one in the National Assembly and the other with the president of the republic, the political solution is very simple. We are a democracy, and therefore the supreme will is the will expressed by the people as they most recently have been consulted. If the parliamentary majority is absolutely clear after the election of the president, its will must be supreme. That is, the president will resign and go cultivate his garden, and that way, I think, the question is solved by itself.

With regard to General de Gaulle (and here I do not concur with Jean Foyer), as de Gaulle himself frequently said, if he never had any predecessors, can we imagine that he would have thought he could have any successors?

MR. FREITAS DO AMARAL: In view of the Portuguese experience, I do not believe that we can always give preference to the most recent expression of the will of the electorate to solve the opposition between the Parliament and the president. In Portugal, we had two elections, a presidential election and a legislative election, within two months, and they produced opposite political results.

In my view, either the president agrees not to act any longer as the leader of the executive branch and to confine himself to the role of a parliamentary head of state, in which case things can work, or he does not agree to reduce his powers to the model of a parliamentary president, in which case we will have a kind of executive branch with two heads. This produces the bad result I had emphasized before, the "institutional guerrilla."

Of course, it is possible to govern with that system. But while it does not bring democracy down, it very much weakens the efficiency of government because, for example, the president can refuse to sign government decrees, or he can make statements against the policies of the government and thereby undermine the authority of the government to rule the country.

MR. FOYER: I agree with Mr. Luchaire that the most recent general expression of universal suffrage should be considered supreme. Moreover, in France, we have experienced the problem in reverse. When the current president of the republic was elected on May 10, 1981, one of his first acts was to dissolve the National Assembly elected in March 1978 with a majority that turned out to be his opposition. If legislative elections have been more recent than the presidential election, he can try one more thing as an alternative to submitting to the opposition or resigning; he can dissolve the assembly that refuses to collaborate with him and then allow the electorate to decide. I do not see any other possible solution if we are to remain true to the ideals of democracy.

NAJDAN PASIC: This discussion shows how difficult and even dangerous it is to try to reduce the number of factors that determine the

67

drafting of a constitution to only one or two—in the case of the French Constitution, for example, to the personal influence of a very prestigious political leader and the exceptional external situation. What is most characteristic of the French Constitution of 1958 is the persistent search for new formulas governing the relationship between Parliament and the government. The French constitution makers made an interesting effort to solve that problem, and General de Gaulle certainly influenced the solution. Many other countries, in completely different social and political circumstances, have conducted or are conducting the same search for new solutions to this problem. I have in mind, for example, the recent cases of Portugal, Greece, Yugoslavia, Sri Lanka, and other countries. It is interesting, for example, to compare the constitutions of France and Yugoslavia in this respect.

Of course, the next question would be, how will a constitution be applied in different social, economic, and political contexts? A solution to the structural problem that is very successful in one country may be only partly successful in another. Obviously, objective needs inspire similar endeavors in different countries. It is not by chance that so many countries have tried to find a new formula for regulating relationships between the executive and the legislative powers. One cannot attribute all that has been included in the French Constitution of 1958 only to the personality of General de Gaulle and to the Algerian crisis. Many countries, in which circumstances differ greatly, have the same need to find some new formula, some new solution to a basic structural problem.

3
Making the Constitution of Greece

Constantine D. Tsatsos

To understand the present Constitution of Greece, one has to bear in mind the evolution of its political life. In the fifteenth century a state with a Greek character ceased to exist, and most of the territories to which Hellenism had extended were held by the Ottoman Empire. Nevertheless the Greek nation kept its national consciousness, even though it did not form a free state, thanks to the following factors:

• The people's devotion to the Greek Orthodox Church, which was dependent on the patriarch of Constantinople. For four centuries this church was for the Greeks what the Jewish religion was for the Jews in the Diaspora.

• The government of local affairs by competent elders and notables. Such strong local government was possible because of the lax organization of the Ottoman central administration in the provinces, especially in matters of taxes and justice.

• The fast growth and the flowering of Greek communities in many countries outside the Ottoman Empire (for example, Italy, Russia, and Austria).

• The domination by the Venetians of certain islands where the Greeks easily preserved their economic and, mainly, their spiritual identity.

• The trading ability of the Greeks, who had advanced beyond the agrarian period. Trade put the Greeks in contact with other ethnic groups, who did not, however, assimilate them. Consciousness of Greek ethnic identity was thus further cultivated.

At the beginning of the nineteenth century, when the idea of rebelling against the Ottoman Empire—an idea that had its origins in the revolutionary movements of France and the United States—had taken root in the souls of thousands of Greeks, two courses of action were discussed. One course was to rise up immediately; the other course was to allow the Greeks who were living under the Turkish yoke to become culturally prepared before the uprising. The former idea prevailed. The revolution broke out in the spring of 1821, although the Holy Alliance—which was then at its height with Metternich at its head—opposed all revolutions against any establishment. Such revolutions were sparked in opposition to the principle of the legality of monarchy, which Metternich had imposed.

The revolution was fought by two kinds of people. On the one hand were the warriors from the rural communities—the notables, the simple farmers, and the shepherds who were mainly from the mountainous regions—who either lived under the direct administration of the Turks or had made some arrangement with them. On the other hand were the intellectuals, mainly those who were living in France, southern Russia, the Moldavian principalities, the Ionian islands, and Italy. The former formed the military wing, while the latter made up the political wing in the struggle.

The first independent Greek state in modern history was formed after 1821. From the outset the political wing wanted an independent state with a constitution for the recently liberated country. The liberal and democratic climate in Greece compared more than favorably with that of the existing regimes in the countries of the Holy Alliance. It was not surprising, therefore, that the Greeks drew up several of the most liberal and democratic constitutions, taking for their inspiration the U.S. Constitution and the French 1789 Declaration of Human Rights.

In addition to proclaiming the liberty of the Greeks, the constitutions of 1822 and 1823 founded a republican regime which guaranteed human rights. The Constitution of Trisina (1827) was a model legislative text at the time. This Constitution, which was firmly based on the sovereignty of the people, established a republic with a governor as head of the state, elected by parliament for seven years.

After the assassination of the first governor, John Kapodistrias (1831), the people felt the need for a more stable form of government. Thus a monarchy was established in Greece, after an agreement with Great Britain, Russia, and France (1832). In 1843 the king, after a revolt, had to grant the people a constitution. Thus the Greeks arrived at a form of government that was a constitutional monarchy.

In 1862 there was another revolt. The king, Otto of Bavaria, was expelled and a convened national assembly elected a new king, George of Denmark. At that time, France was an empire, the German states were monarchies, Italy was politically unripe, and Great Britain, though a parliamentary democracy, had no written constitutional law. Belgium, however, possessed a new, written, parliamentary, democratic constitution that could be used as a model. This time the Greek people demanded a written constitution that would consolidate human rights, judicial independence, and parliamentary authority and procedures. One must not forget, as I have pointed out, that such tendencies existed not only among the common people but even more among the intellectual elite, dating from before the revolution of 1821 and deeply rooted in the conscience of the nation.

By 1875 the principle was established—incidentally without any legal basis—to oblige the king in the future to appoint a government that had a vote of confidence from Parliament. This basic change should not surprise us because a similar situation had developed in this very way in Great Britain. As the king of Great Britain was compelled to abandon his right to choose the prime minister, it became a tradition for the king to ask the person who had the majority in Parliament to form the government. Therefore parliamentary democracy was instituted in Greece through usage, just as it was in Great Britain and the other European countries. Most of the basic provisions of the 1862 Constitution, which was revised and modernized in 1911, exist in the present Constitution.

After the Balkan Wars, which were followed immediately by World War I, Greece was sorely troubled with political instability. At times the Greeks had a parliamentary democracy with a king at its head, and at other times a president, as is now the case. From time to time, however, they had dictatorships that suspended the power of the constitution. After World War II, in 1946, the parliamentary democracy was restored, with a king at its head, because a monarchy was considered to be more stable. In 1967, however, a junta of colonels overthrew the monarchy.

Whoever studies the constitutional history of this country with care will see that despite constitutional disruptions and changing regimes—and always taking into consideration the strong reactions of the people each time the democratic regime was abolished—there is a deeply rooted faith in the soul of the Greeks that the people are the source of political power. The Greeks believe, furthermore, that the fundamental principles that define the function of the state come from the people and should be expressed in a charter that is the exclusive expression of the people's will.

The majority of Greeks considered the dictatorships that occurred—one year in 1925, almost five years from 1936 to 1941, and seven years from 1967 to 1974—to be out of tune with their historical tradition. To understand this contradiction between the democratic feelings of the Greeks and the turmoils that lasted for more than fifty years after the end of World War I, one must consider some facts that were unknown outside of Greece.

After the defeat of 1922 and the expulsion of the Greeks (approximately 1.5 million people) from Asia Minor and Thrace, a democracy without a king was established in Greece (1924). It functioned most irregularly until 1927, and only from 1927 to 1933 did it follow a regular course. Further irregularities led to the fall of this democracy and to the overthrow of the Constitution of 1927, with the result that the Constitution of 1911 became valid again in 1935.

For the short time between 1928 and 1935, in contrast to the long periods of democratic rule with a king, Greece was a republic and had a senate. In 1935 the Senate was abolished and was followed by a democracy with a king and a unicameral legislative structure, just as in the Constitution of 1862. The discord among the Greeks had nothing to do with individual liberties, parliamentarianism, or democracy. The discord was over the question of whether a king or a president should be at the head of the state. In 1923 Greeks voted for a republic, and in 1935 a referendum favored a king. The elections that took place in February 1936 showed that the parties representing the two prevailing opinions were equal in strength; they received almost the same number of votes. The stalemate that developed was a direct result of the government's failure to obtain a decisive majority.

One of the effects of this impasse was the arousal of passions so strong that a group of royalists, within a year of the return of the king (and with his approval), suspended the Constitution of 1911 and established a dictatorship on August 4, 1936. In Europe at the time there was not as much opposition to totalitarianism and dictatorships as at present. The Metaxas dictatorship lasted until the Greeks were defeated by the Axis forces. The Greeks contained, and would have continued to resist, the Italians if German and Bulgarian forces had not come to their assistance. After the death of Metaxas in February 1941, the king appointed other prime ministers, forming a government in exile in Cairo. On April 16, 1941, the dictatorship came to a formal end.

On October 12, 1944, the exiled Greek government, led by George Papandreou, the father of the present prime minister, came back. The king, however, did not return because, in the meantime, the government had agreed to hold a referendum to enable the Greeks to decide whether the king should return. A vote against his return would mean a rejection of democracy with a king. Greeks of all political persuasions discussed this crucial matter of whether they would have a republic or a democracy with a king.

The continuing disruption, which was a result of the outbreak of the civil war between the official government and the military organization of the Communists, delayed progress toward a return to normal constitutional rule. At last, on March 31, 1946, elections were held in which the Communist party did not take part. The Parliament that came to power was charged with revising the Constitution of 1911 in part. The provisions regarding the kind of regime were to be determined after a referendum for or against the king, which took place on September 1, 1946. The referendum, by a wide majority, favored the king. The Communists, held responsible for slaughtering civilians opposed to them, which had been ascertained by international committees, had completely lost their popular basis. The referendum was against communism, and the king was the anti-Communist symbol.

At the same time, a forty-member committee started drafting the new constitution. The Parliament, during the four years it lasted, failed to pass the draft of the constitution, though it had had the draft in hand since June 1948 and though it was without Communists or proponents of any kind of totalitarianism (the parties were all moderate, with slight ideological differences). Thus the Parliament that was elected to revise the constitution was dissolved, and the Constitution of 1911, which had been adopted provisionally in 1935 when the king returned, remained in force. In March 1950 elections were held for a Parliament that did not have a popular mandate to draft a new constitution. Then the king and the leaders of the parties in the Parliament decided to dissolve this Parliament. They considered the whole situation irregular and wished to elect a new body that would have a mandate to complete the revisionary work of the Parliament of 1946. The new elections took place on September 9, 1951. The Parliament then voted for the new constitution, which was published and became valid on January 1, 1952.

Although the 1952 Constitution contained some improvements of provisions from the 1911 Constitution, the basic principles were unchanged and have remained unchanged, as we shall see, to the present. (I discuss these basic principles later in my analysis of our present constitution.)

The 1952 Constitution was outdated from the moment of its conception. It might have been acceptable in 1946 or even before World War II, but it lacked the style of modern constitutions. It established a democratic and liberal state that bore, however, the characteristics of a state of law (*Rechtstaat*) at a time when the social state (*Sozialstaat*) had already been realized. The social state protects not only classical individual rights but also other established values—that is, the freedom to work, the importance of the family and of the social and natural environment, and the social significance of property. New constitutions of the Federal Republic of Germany, of France, and of Italy had been published following World War II. In comparison with these constitutions, ours was inferior in expression. Ours was also inferior in relation to the Greek social reality, which had progressed further than the constitution that served it.

For this reason, procedures for revising the constitution began in 1962 under the government of Constantine Karamanlis. Once more government changes took place. Elections in which Karamanlis was defeated and political irregularities after June 1965 postponed all progress on the revision of the constitution.

When the colonels came to power in April 1967, they understood that public opinion favored progress toward this goal of constitutional revision. I do not think it worthwhile to concern ourselves with moribund constitutional drafts, which they announced every now and then to buoy up the hopes of the people, with the aim of delaying their own overthrow. The fact is that immediately after the downfall of the dictatorship in July 1974 the constitutional impasse emerged in full. The problems of 1946 were repeated.

In 1974 the constituent power was again bisected. By a plebiscite, the people decided that the future regime should not have a hereditary head of state. By a vote of approximately 70 percent they chose to have an elected head of state. The rest of the governing power they entrusted to a parliament with constituent competence to draw up a new constitution, which has remained in force in its original form to the present.

The first government, which held elections on November 17, 1974, and won 216 of the 300 seats in Parliament, drew up a first draft, which was submitted to the house. The Parliament appointed a committee of thirty-seven regular and fourteen alternate members, on which all the parties were represented in proportion to the seats they held in Parliament. The committee was charged with drawing up a final draft of the constitution, which was to be voted on in Parliament. The committee presented the draft in installments to Parliament, and on January 8, 1975, discussion of the constitution, article by article, began. Several modifications were proposed, and many of these were accepted.

Parliament worked on the draft from January 8, 1975, until June 7, 1975. The opposition took part in the debates of all the articles and voted on them. When the proposed constitution in its entirety was finally put to the vote, the opposition left the chamber and abstained from voting. Their main objection was that the president of the republic had been given excessive power.

The government, with its parliamentary majority, voted for the constitution. The provisionary president of the republic, appointed by the Parliament, published the constitution in the *Government Gazette*, after which it immediately took effect.

The first act of Parliament, according to the rules of the new constitution, was the election of the president of the republic. On June 20, 1975, the election took place, and the chairman of the committee that drafted the constitution was elected as the president of the republic. Thus the constituent authority completed its tasks by establishing all the constitutional powers.

Although the opposition abstained from voting on it, the constitution's legality has not been disputed politically or legally by either side; it has been in force with full constitutional powers from the day that it first became valid.

To understand these developments, one must refer to events of World War I. The great Greek politician Eleftherios Venizelos, prime minister at the time, wanted to bring Greece into the war on the side of the Allies because the two main enemies of Greece, the Turks and the Bulgarians, were allied with Germany and Austria-Hungary. Constantine I, who was then king, opposed this policy, since he believed in the victory of the Germans and in the Kaiser's assurance that Greece would not be harmed if it remained neutral. Venizelos, however, was convinced that such a policy would destroy Greece. He insisted on his own policy; and when he finally saw, in the winter of 1916, that the German propaganda for neutrality had influenced public opinion, he led a rebellion with the help of the Allies. The greatest part of the Greek navy and army followed him. They supported the formation in Salonica of a new revolutionary government, which proclaimed general mobilization in those regions under Venizelos's control and entered the war on the side of the Allies. Within a few months King Constantine was forced to abdicate under pressure from the Allies. His second-born son, Alexander, ascended to the throne; and Venizelos returned to Athens, united Greece, and mobilized the remaining regions. This experience of "national schism," in spite of Venizelos's triumph and in spite of the extension of Greece to Thrace, caused such a profound psychological division among the people that nobody can interpret political developments in Greece since then without reference to it. These feelings were still alive in the hearts of many Greeks when the 1974 dictatorship collapsed and a new constitution had to be drawn up.

For this reason the issue of the monarchy had to be settled first, separately, by referendum. The government and the whole state apparatus remained absolutely neutral so that the people could express themselves freely. Only after that decision could the draft of a new constitution proceed normally.

The second experience that one must take into account to comprehend the constitutional history of Greece and the essence of its contemporary constitution is the role of the Communist party during World War II. Communism first appeared in Greece shortly after the October Revolution of 1917. Communists, however, were an unimportant minority, consisting mainly of certain intellectuals and a few tobacco workers. When Metaxas's dictatorship prevailed, communism was apparently annihilated; but, unobtrusively, Communists learned the art of going underground and acquired more fanatical followers and a remarkable clandestine network.

Thus, when World War II broke out and when, after six months of resistance, Greece surrendered to the Germans, those who were best prepared for the tasks of the Resistance, which was naturally encouraged by the Allies, were the Communists. In October 1944, when Athens was liberated and the Germans left, most of Greece was occupied by the Revolutionary Communist Army, which recruited, either willingly or unwillingly, many non-Communists. Then, with the help of Great Britain and after great bloodshed, Athens avoided capture by the Communists. But one year later, communism re-emerged, and the second phase of the civil war began, ending in 1949 with the defeat of the Communists.

The Communists' disruptive behavior, wherever they had prevailed, was such that the great majority of the people, ignoring the old dissension, demanded in a genuine referendum the restoration of the monarchy. In reaction to the left, the people turned to the right—that is, to the king—creating the impression that the old World War I dissension had been forgotten. Unfortunately, clumsiness on the part of the court, on the one hand, and on the part of the political world, on the other, revived the old dissension. And so, after the 1967–1974 dictatorial interlude, which young King Constantine did not manage to overturn, the problem of the monarchy had to be solved by means of a referendum. And this problem has been solved. But communism, thanks to the seven-year dictatorship of the colonels, revived and found many sympathizers among those who were not Communists.

Such was the general political atmosphere when the discussion of the constitution began. It was most fortunate that Constantine Karamanlis, with his imposing presence, his moderate policy, and his rejection of both communism and totalitarianism, helped to draw up a liberal constitution completely in accordance with the French Declaration of Human Rights. It is a constitution that, as in Great Britain, gives complete power to those having the majority in Parliament and grants only restraining authority to the head of state, authorizing him to refer to the people if he judges that the Parliament or the government are not in harmony with the will of the people. If he resorts to those measures and the people reaffirm their support for the same parliamentary majority, this vote amounts to the president's political annihilation.

Greece does not have two parties whose disputes develop in the same spirit or over specific issues as in the United States. The basic philosophies of U.S. parties do not differ because they share the spirit of those who drew up the U.S. Constitution and who wrote *The Federalist Papers*. In Greece we have two *worlds*, completely different and opposed: totalitarian communism on one side and democracy as conceived in the Western world on the other. The differences in these worlds manifest themselves in the considerable differences in the two groups of parties that exist. On the one side there are Marxist parties, or parties inclined to Marxism, and on the other there are parties subscribing to the principles of Western European liberalism, be they Christian Democratic, Liberal, or Social Democratic.

When the present constitution was being drawn up, this cleavage was not so tense; common experiences under the military dictatorship were still fresh in everybody's mind. Nevertheless, the dispute, although latent, had always been smoldering, and it influenced the debates that preceded the voting on the constitution. What fueled this dispute most powerfully, however, was the refusal of the minority at that time to vote on adoption of the constitution in its entirety. This refusal is characteristic of this part of the Greek political spectrum. Those inclined to Marxism have not made a constitutional revision because their objectives can be met within the framework of the existing constitution. But if dogmatic Marxism were to prevail within the parties of the left, the Communists quite possibly might revise the constitution, after gaining either control of a parliamentary majority or the means of controlling without a majority. In many cases, they have already reached the limits prescribed by the constitution. Several demands for the repeal of decrees or of acts of the administration, as unconstitutional, are now pending before the Council of State.

In July 1974, however, these cleavages were still latent because the 1967–1974 dictatorship had persecuted, without discrimination, all parties of the left and right. The dictatorship had persecuted and dethroned the king as well. This is why, after the collapse of the

77

dictatorship, there was a feeling of solidarity among all those who had been subjected to persecution, regardless of their different political views. All the Greeks were united against a dictatorship that had but a small number of supporters and had been humiliated by the Turkish invasion of Cyprus. So when the Greeks appealed to Karamanlis, who had been exiled in Paris and in whose person they found a true rescuer, to take over the government of the country, everybody welcomed him in an atmosphere of national unity. Under the circumstances Karamanlis realized that the country had a unique opportunity to settle two critical political issues: (1) to provide a lasting solution to the problem of the monarchy and (2) to provide a constitution relevant to the social needs of the country.

Because of this unity, the voting of a constitution that was both up-to-date and in accordance with our national tradition was uneventful. Comparatively few difficulties had to be faced in spite of the dramatic gestures of the left at the end of the six months of voting by all delegates on the individual articles of the constitution. In light of this unity, it should be obvious that at the opening of the debate on the drafting of the new constitution there was remarkable unanimity on many points. Only on a few occasions was there any sort of disagreement.

Actually, the following general ideas prevailed among all political parties:

- *Everybody* agreed that after a dictatorship of seven years a new, up-to-date constitution should be drawn up.
- *Everybody* agreed—since a preceding referendum had done away with the idea of a parliamentary republic with a king—that we should form a parliamentary republic without a king.
- *Everybody* agreed that we should create a social state in the fashion of the latest German Constitution and not just a state of justice (status juris).
- *Everybody* agreed that we should protect human rights according to the internationally established rules.
- *Nobody* thought of establishing the American system of a strict division or separation of powers (legislative-executive).
- On the contrary, we *all* agreed on the system of the British or Belgian parliamentary republic, valid in our state since 1864, and, with some variations in its detail, in the whole of continental Europe, with the exception of the new constitution of France.

As for human rights, there appeared to be two trends in opinion. The left insisted that human rights should be so strongly protected that the state would be powerless before the individual, their insistence applying especially to the right to strike. The other, more conservative view of human rights, was the one that prevailed as stated in the Constitution as I have analyzed it.

There were also two views regarding the authority of the president of the republic. One view, supported by the left, was that the president should have no authority at all and should have no right to refer to the people within thirty days to call for either new elections or a referendum. The majority in Parliament, however, should have absolute authority during the four-year term for which it had been elected. The other view, the one that prevailed, I analyze below. Mainly because of this difference, the opposition abstained when the constitution as a whole was put to the vote. The left wished for a weak state in every matter; the right wished for a moderate solution and, being then in the majority succeeded in imposing one.

Thus the majority party then in power, desiring to pass a constitution that would eventually enjoy general public acceptance (except by the Communists—as has been confirmed in practice in the past eight years), agreed to the following:

• Moderate solutions, especially regarding the authority of the president of the republic; nothing was left out that had become part of the common conscience of the people. This desire for moderation explains the similarity between the Constitution of 1975 and that of 1864.

• The need to state certain principles that express the new idea of the *Sozialstaat*, taking a considerable number of elements from the new German Constitution. That constitution provides guidelines to the legislator rather than rules of justice (for example, that property creates obligations, the family, the arts are protected).

• Certain concessions to the opposition, as, for example, in the most lenient formulation of the article on strikes.

• Certain formulations—without changing the essence of the constitution—asked for mainly by the left for the protection of individuals and inspired by the arbitrary actions taken against them by the recent dictatorship.

When de Gaulle asked Karamanlis why he had not drawn up a more austere constitution as he himself had done, the Greek leader answered: "You came to power after a parliamentary chaos and your people wished for a strong government. I came to power after a dictatorship and my people wished for freedom."

In the following discussion of the articles of the new Constitution of 1975, I shall note those articles that in the drafting debates provoked differences of opinion and discussions and those that present some-

79

thing original, different from all other Western Europe constitutions. I shall omit the examination of articles that are identical or almost identical with corresponding provisions in the constitutions of almost all the European nations of the Western world. These articles comprise all the detailed provisions pertaining to human rights.

The Form of Government

The constitution begins with the structure of the regime. Article 1, paragraph 1, states that the "form of government of Greece is that of a parliamentary republic." This statement means the following:

1. The regime is democratic, and every form of totalitarianism is excluded, as well as any form of government that abolishes the principle of popular sovereignty. Thus, this provision excludes the creation of a regime that might bear the name "democratic people's republic" but that abolishes the expressed will of the majority of the people, at regular intervals, as the last and final criterion of political life.

The meaning the Greeks give to the word *democracy* is confirmed, first, by paragraph 2 of the same article, which states that "popular sovereignty is the foundation of government" and, second, by paragraph 3 of the same article, which states that "all powers are derived from the people and exist for the people and the nation. They shall be exercised as is specified by the constitution." It is also confirmed by a whole series of other articles.

2. The principal agent of the state is the Parliament and not the president of the republic. This statement means also that direct democracy is excluded at least as far as the usual evolution of political life is concerned. The statement refers to a regime that Alexander Hamilton calls representative democracy, in which popular sovereignty is exercised through Parliament by representatives of the people. Under present conditions, direct government as practiced in the Athens of classical times is not possible. Even if direct government were possible, it creates other problems, which were noticed by the drafters of the U.S. Constitution.

The term *parliamentary* means that the popular sovereignty is expressed in Parliament; and, therefore, as in Britain a government cannot be in power without the declared vote of confidence of Parliament. The government governs, but the Parliament determines who shall govern. The president has power to take the initiative only under extreme circumstances, as we shall see, and only provisionally.

3. A democracy headed by a king, as in Great Britain or the Scandinavian countries, is excluded. The head of state is elected for

office; he does not inherit the office.

To those three features should be added a fourth: "The Greek State would be a state of law [*Rechtstaat*]." This feature is confirmed in article 26, which says that legislative power is vested in Parliament and the president of the republic. The executive power is vested in the president and the government, and the judicial power is vested in the courts of law (the decisions of which shall be executed in the name of the Greek people) but also in the totality of the articles of the constitution.

In a state of law the political sovereignty is self-binding. The legislative power is bound by the constitution, and the executive by the legislative authorities. Thus, the whole structure of government is responsible to the public in general for what it is permitted to do and for the way it will function. If the agents of the government do not exercise self-control, the injured parties may have recourse to law and claim restitution of their rights. The judiciary is an independent power.

In article 26 the legal form of the division of power is defined as set out in our constitution. From now on I shall distinguish between the legal form and the political act. Although apparently the president and the Parliament have an equal part in the exercise of legislative power, in reality, as we shall see, the power of the president is very limited. Although the president appears to perform the executive power through the government, here, too, his power is limited. In Greece, as in many other democracies of Europe, such as, Great Britain, the Scandinavian countries, and the Federal Republic of Germany, the government that has a majority in Parliament performs both these functions.

Although according to the letter of the law of the constitution every member of Parliament can take the legislative initiative, in practice the government performs this role. Although members of Parliament frequently propose new laws, this action is nothing more than a declaration of the attitude of the opposition. All laws are a result of the initiative of the government.

These basic structural principles, which I mentioned earlier, are specified in the constitution by a series of articles that will be mentioned in the discussions of the separate functions of the state. It is evident that the clear division or separation of legislative and executive powers as they exist in the United States is not a feature of the Greek regime. Since 1862 Greece has insisted on the principle that the government, which is based on a majority in Parliament, constitutes the essential expression of popular sovereignty; it legislates, and it governs.

The President

The Election of the Head of State. The president of the republic is selected by Parliament. In the 1974 debates this provision provoked lengthy discussion. It was first proposed and contested that the president should be elected, as in France, directly by the people. An alternative was to have an electoral body—elected by the people—added to the total number of members of Parliament to elect a president.

Election by Parliament prevailed, however. If having a senate had not been rejected, two houses would have elected the president. But, since Greece has no upper house (senate), a two-thirds majority of the total members of Parliament is required (article 32, paragraph 3).

Thus we avoid the disruption direct elections would create. In Greece such elections would be fought along the lines of party politics. If a president were selected contrary to the wish of the majority of the members of Parliament, the government would fall and Parliament would dissolve. If, however, the candidate of the government were elected, the election could be seen as a vote of confidence in the government.

All the disruptions of an election would be justified if the president had a decisive vote in the government as have the presidents of France and the United States. The powers of the president, however, are formal during regular political procedure; only in extreme crises does he acquire powers that he may exercise at the risk of losing his office. These restrictions on the president's powers justify his election by Parliament.

The presidential term in office is five years; the president may be reelected only once. To be eligible for election the candidate must have been a Greek citizen for at least five years, be a descendant of a Greek father, be at least forty years old, and be entitled to vote.

The candidate who receives two-thirds of the votes of the total number of members of Parliament is elected. If this majority is not attained by any of the candidates, the election must be repeated in five days. This situation would rarely apply in Greek politics. Should the second ballot fail to produce an acceptable result, the procedure is repeated as before. Should the third ballot still not produce the two-thirds majority, the candidate having three-fifths of the votes of the total number of members of Parliament is elected. If the three-fifths majority is not attained, Parliament shall be dissolved in ten days and new elections announced within thirty days.

As soon as the new Parliament has convened as a body, it shall proceed by secret ballot to elect a president requiring a three-fifths majority of the total number of members of Parliament. Should there not be a clear majority, the balloting shall once more be repeated after five days between the two persons with the highest number of votes, and the person receiving the greater number of votes shall be the president of the republic.

The Powers of the President. "No act of the president of the republic shall become operative nor be executed unless it has been counter-signed by the competent minister and unless it has been published in the *Government Gazette*" (article 35, paragraph 1). This essential provision reflects the spirit of the Greek Constitution. In principle the president is obligated to act in unison with the government. No act of his is valid without the approval of the government.

This rule has certain exclusive and limited exceptions:

• The president appoints the prime minister. This provision does not mean that the president appoints whomever he wishes as prime minister. As is pointed out in article 37, the president must appoint as prime minister the leader of the party that has the absolute majority in Parliament. If no party has an absolute majority in Parliament, the president of the republic shall assign to the leader of the party with a relative majority an exploratory mandate to ascertain the possibility of forming a government enjoying the confidence of the Parliament. If such a government is not formed, the president of the republic may assign a new exploratory mandate to the leader of the second largest party in Parliament, or he may appoint as prime minister, after consulting with the Council of the Republic (article 37), a person who may or may not be a member of Parliament and who shall try to get a vote of confidence from Parliament. Should this attempt also fail, the solution is to dissolve Parliament and call within thirty days for new elections.

It thus becomes evident that the powers of the president of the republic are very restricted. By following a strictly defined procedure, the president does only what is necessary to ensure that the country will have a government enjoying the approval of Parliament. These provisions disclose that the president only regulates the functions of the institutions of the republic (article 30, paragraph 1). The president, in appointing the prime minister, acts alone as this appointment is prior to the formation of a government.

• Furthermore, the president under extraordinary circumstances may convoke the Cabinet under his chairmanship. This right is significant only in certain cases. The president has no need to preside over the

Cabinet if he agrees with the government. If he disagrees and if the government is formed by one party only, then his action might prove to be futile. The presence of the president may prove useful with a coalition government. The president takes part in the meeting of the Cabinet without having the right to vote on its deliberations; and, acting as a mediator, he has a stabilizing effect.

• The president has some restricted legislative power. He may send back a bill passed by Parliament, within one month of its having been voted on, stating the reasons for not sanctioning it. The bill that has been sent back shall be introduced to a plenary session of Parliament; and, if it is passed again by an absolute majority of the members, the president of the republic shall be bound to sanction it or step down.

Under this provision, too, the president acts as the regulator of the functions of the institutions of the republic. In the event of parliamentary dissidence or government obduracy, the president endeavors to marshal Parliament into collaboration, and the government into performing its function, in accordance with the will of the majority in Parliament (article 42).

• The president may, by decree, proclaim a referendum on crucial national issues without the cooperation of the government. The result of the referendum must be put into practice. If the government agrees with the proclamation of this referendum, there is no political problem.

The president and the government together decide that the people are to be consulted and are ready to accept the outcome. When the president proclaims a referendum on a crucial national issue and the government is not in agreement, then the people become the arbitrators between the government and the president, and the result of the referendum will have decisive consequences either for the government or for the president.

Hence, the president will dare to announce a referendum alone either when he suspects that the people will disapprove of the government policy on a crucial issue or when he does not want to link his name with a policy of which he disapproves. If the people do not support him, he will have to resign. Although resignation is not legally imposed, it is a dictate of honor.

• The president, furthermore, has the power, under exceptional circumstances, to address political messages to the people independent of the government. These messages shall be published in the *Government Gazette* to make their communication completely responsible. The constitution does not rule out the possibility that these messages may not be in agreement with the policies of the government. If they are not in agreement a political crisis to be faced by the president, as in a referendum, would likely result.

• The president may, without the cooperation of the government, convoke the Council of the Republic. Such convocation is obligatory in certain cases that I shall enumerate, but it can be done in any critical circumstance that the president deems to justify such action.

The Council of the Republic shall be constituted of a democratically elected former president of the republic, the prime minister, the speaker of Parliament, the leader of the parliamentary opposition, and the former prime ministers who have been members of the Parliament or who headed governments having received a vote of confidence by Parliament (article 39, paragraph 2). Since 1975, until the time of this writing, this council has met only once and then only for the purpose of determining how the council was to function.

According to the intent of the legislation, this council, which is a purely advisory body, has two functions. First, it expresses its opinion on crucial problems that the president must face. These opinions carry great political weight because they come from people who belong to all, or at least to the main, parties. Second, through its decisions the council restricts the president when he makes decisions on crucial problems such as the dissolution of Parliament, the dismissal of the government, or the appointment of a prime minister when such appointment is not dictated by a majority in Parliament.

• The president may dissolve Parliament in two instances: first, if in his judgment Parliament is out of step with public feeling on crucial matters, and, second, if the composition of Parliament does not ensure governmental stability (as, for instance, when many members of Parliament are vacillating). In such cases the president can dissolve Parliament after having taken into consideration the opinion of the Council of the Republic. He is then obliged to announce elections within thirty days and the convening of Parliament to occur in another thirty days.

In essence, the president only regulates the function of the institutions. He does not violate the principle of the people's sovereignty, but he protects the functions of the constitution and refers to the people when he proposes to dissolve Parliament. He promptly ascertains whether or not the people want a change of parliamentary composition.

The dissolution of Parliament by the president is certainly an act against the majority of the Parliament, and such an act will create a breach between them. After thirty days the electorate will either endorse the president's decision or reinstate the former Parliament. In the event that Parliament is reelected, the president's judgment is proved erroneous. As a result, his political position becomes not only weak but also problematic.

• The president may dismiss the government but only after consulting with the Council of the Republic and assigning a mandate to form a government to a member of Parliament or to a person who may not be a member of Parliament. Whoever accepts the mandate is obliged to request a vote of confidence within fifteen days. If the president fails to obtain a vote of confidence, then he can dissolve Parliament and announce elections within the decreed time limit. A government without a vote of confidence from Parliament can exist but only for the purpose of having elections.

Even in this case the people will judge the correctness of the president's action. It is clear what his political position will be if the people do not endorse his decision. The president will exercise this right only in matters dictated by principle and conscience or if he foresees that the people will support his decision.

Surprisingly some political parties did not consider it undemocratic for the Parliament to remain in office after losing the confidence of the people and did consider it undemocratic to ask the people whether they want a change in the composition of the Parliament. This line of reasoning confers a greater value on Parliament than on the sovereignty of the people. Parliament, however, is simply an instrument elected by the people.

When a parliament cannot form a stable government and, as a result, the state is unable to function, why should it be considered undemocratic for the president to dissolve Parliament and give the people the opportunity to elect within thirty days a new one that may be able to form a stable government? Fortunately the opposition's concepts, which would not strengthen democracy but, conversely, would increase the power of the deputies, did not prevail. I consider those concepts circumstantial: they were based on the opposition's fear that a president of great prestige, who would be able to influence the people and overthrow weak parliaments, might be elected.

All these suspicions have proved to be unfounded. More than a year has passed since a revision as provided for in the constitution might have been proposed. In 1974 the party now in government severely criticized these provisions; however, they have not yet proposed any revisions. Many of the former critics may have realized, as they observed the functioning of the regime over the years, that the provisions concerning the powers of the president have a logical basis and, furthermore, that they guarantee the harmonious coexistence of the people's will and the will of political authority.

• The president of the republic, by means of a presidential decree countersigned by the Cabinet, may suspend the functioning of certain provisions that concern individual liberties. He may do so in case of war or of mobilization to meet external threats. In the event of internal disturbances that seriously threaten public order and the security of the state, the presidential decree shall be signed only by the prime minister, thus putting into effect the law pertaining to a state of siege. The president may issue decrees of legislative content without restriction throughout the duration of this period.

"The presidential decree issued as specified in paragraph 1 shall, if not revoked at an earlier date by similar decree, be lifted *ipso jure* in the case of war as of the termination of the war, in all other cases thirty days after its publication, unless its operation has been extended beyond thirty days by a presidential decree issued with the prior consent of Parliament" (article 48, paragraph 3).

The Senate

The Constitution of 1927, which established a republic in Greece and was valid until 1935, had decreed the institution of the senate as a second house. This second house functioned successfully. Those who study the history of Greek regimes may well wonder why we did not bring it back in 1975.

The more progressive members of the committee were afraid that the senate would be a very conservative body, little influenced by public opinion. The conservatives were concerned about a more practical complication, the fear that the legislative process would become very dilatory. Usually one house of Parliament moves slower than the executive power would like. If a second house were added, matters would become more cumbersome. In a country that is developing, the state machine must move fast, and this speed is possible only in a system with one house. The instituting of a senate was rejected by almost unanimous agreement. Therefore legislation is composed by one house, the Parliament.

The Parliament

The constitution determines some matters that concern Parliament; it leaves others to be settled by the regulations of Parliament and still others by common law.

The electoral system is determined by law not by the constitution. A law defines the constituencies. A law specifies the total number of members of Parliament within the limits defined by the constitution. At present the law limits this number to 300.

For a country with fewer than 10 million inhabitants this number sounds too big. Experience has shown, however, that as the number of representatives decreases, so their individual power proportionately increases. This situation creates political instability because, by withdrawing their support from the government, a proportionately smaller number could cause its overthrow.

In Greece we tend to settle everything by law. This kind of settlement is justified by the growing number of cases that need to be settled by law because of technical changes and state intervention. Apart from this reason, the Greeks' traditional distrust of civil servants and judges also creates the need for legislation on every issue. This mentality will take years to change. Thus Parliament at present is burdened by a disproportionate volume of work.

According to article 51, paragraph 3, "the members of Parliament shall be elected through direct, universal, and secret ballot." By "direct ballot" we mean that nothing interferes between the elector and the parliamentary candidates. By "universal" we mean that "the law cannot abridge the right to vote except in cases where minimum voting age has not been attained or in cases of legal incapacity or as a result of irrevocable criminal conviction for certain felonies."

Elections are always general—that is, they are held simultaneously throughout the state. "Members of Parliament shall be elected for a term of four consecutive years, commencing from the day of the general elections" (article 53, paragraph 2). They come from certain specified constituencies with the exception of the state deputies and are provided for in the constitution.

Parliament-Government Relations. The provision of article 84, paragraph 1, of the Constitution is essential: "The government must enjoy the confidence of Parliament. The government shall be obliged to request a vote of confidence by Parliament within fifteen days of the date the prime minister shall have been sworn in and may also do so at any other time. If at the time the government is formed, Parliament has suspended its work, it shall be summoned within fifteen days to resolve on the motion of confidence."

This is the provision that qualifies our regime as a parliamentary democracy. When a new government does not obtain a vote of confidence, it must resign. In this case the president proceeds according to the provisions made in the constitution that I have already examined.

> Parliament may decide to withdraw its confidence from the government or from a member of the government. A motion of censure, however, may not be resubmitted before the

lapse of six months from the most recent rejection by Parliament of such a motion.

A motion of censure must be signed by at least one-sixth of the number of members of Parliament and must explicitly state the subjects on which the debate is to be held.

A motion of censure may, by exception, be resubmitted before the lapse of six months if it is signed by the majority of the total number of members.

A debate on a motion of confidence or censure shall commence two days after the motion was submitted, unless the government, in the case of a motion of censure requests immediate commencement; the debate may not be prolonged for more than three days from its commencement. . . .

A motion of confidence cannot be adopted unless it is approved by the absolute majority of the members present, which, however, cannot be less than two-fifths of the total number of members. A motion of censure shall be adopted only if it is approved by the absolute majority of the total number of members (article 84, paragraphs 2, 3, 4, and 6).

This distinction is made because the government must lose the confidence of the majority of the Parliament in order to be overthrown. For a government that has already obtained a vote of confidence, however, the constitution leaves the decision whether to continue its duties to the discretion of the members of Parliament. If they want to overthrow the government, they have only to attend a session and overthrow it; but a government shall not be lightly overthrown merely because of the absence of several members from a sitting. This provision, and the further prohibition of successive motions of censure, indicate that the constitution writers aimed to ensure the protection and stability of governments that, on a former motion of no confidence, nevertheless obtained a vote of confidence.

The first time that the government appeals for a vote of confidence is when the prime minister outlines to Parliament the general domestic and foreign policy of the government, which is quintessentially what it proposes to implement.

The Judiciary

"The high courts are divided into (a) administrative and (b) civil and criminal courts, and they are organized by special laws" (article 93, paragraph 1). Each group is formed by courts in a hierarchical structure headed by the highest court. The civil and penal courts have a common apex, the Supreme Court, the highest court for cases of penal or civil law. The administrative courts have as their head the Council of State.

The Council of State, being the supreme administrative court, has the following jurisdiction: the "annulment upon petition of executive acts of administrative authorities for abuse of power or violation of the law" (article 95, paragraph 1a). The Council of State annuls presidential decrees and ministerial decisions, acts, and omissions of any agent of the executive power if he abuses the power given to him by law or if he violates the law.

In all these cases the Council of State shall judge whether the administrative agent has employed his authority justly or whether he has abused it. This power is based on article 25, paragraph 3: "Abusive exercise of rights is not permitted." The Council of State also has the power to obtain the "reversal upon petition of executive acts of administrative authorities for abuse of power or violation of law" (article 95, paragraph 1b).

The Council of State examines those disputes with the administration that have been put under its jurisdiction, whether by the constitution or by the law (article 95, paragraph 1). Besides these administrative responsibilities, the Council of State is also liable for "the elaboration of all decrees of a regulatory nature" (article 95, paragraph 1d). That is to say, it is responsible for those decrees that do not simply make the laws but that set new special rules in the general scheme of the existing laws. The statements about these decrees have a simple advisory character. Quite frequently, however, the influence of these statements is very important because this same court, with its power of annulment, may, if a citizen requests, later annul the decree that it had judged as unconstitutional or illegal during its deliberations. "The administration shall be bound to comply with the annulling judgments of the Council of State. A breach of this obligation shall render liable any responsible agent as specified by law" (article 95, paragraph 5).

The Supreme Special Court. A Supreme Special Court has also been established by the Constitution (article 100). Its jurisdiction is the "settlement of any conflict between the courts and the administrative courts on the one hand, and civil and criminal courts on the other, or between the Comptrollers Council and any other courts"; and the "settlement of controversies on whether a law enacted by Parliament is fundamentally unconstitutional, or on the interpretation of provisions of such law when conflicting judgments have been pronounced by the Council of State, the Supreme Court, or the Comptrollers Council" (article 100, paragraphs 1d and e). This court is composed of the three presidents of the highest courts, four members of the Council of State, and four members of the Supreme Court; the members of this court are elected every two years. The Supreme Special Court, a constitutional court with no permanent character, functions only when there are cases that fall under its jurisdiction.

Revising the Constitution

The people, who are the source of all authority, may vote for a Parliament that will have the authority to draft a new constitution. The same Parliament may also revise the constitution and make laws; that is, it has constituent and legislative powers. According to the Greek Constitution, the form of the established regime cannot be touched so long as the continuity of political and constituent power is unbroken. This stipulation is also valid for certain principles that are an integral part of this kind of regime, as is clearly designated in article 110, which concerns the revision of the constitution.

Therefore, certain provisions may not be revised: provisions that determine the basis and the form of the regime as a parliamentary republic; provisions that ensure the inviolability of individual liberty and the freedom of religious conscience; and provisions that determine the distinction between the three powers, legislative, executive, and judicial.

> The need for revision of the constitution shall be confirmed by a resolution of Parliament adopted, on the proposal of not less than fifty members of Parliament, by a three-fifths majority of the total number of its members in two ballots held at least one month apart. This resolution shall define the provisions to be revised.
>
> Upon a resolution by Parliament on the revision of the constitution, the next Parliament shall, in the course of its opening session, decide on the provisions to be revised by an absolute majority of the total number of its members.
>
> Should a proposal for revision of the constitution receive the majority of the votes of the total number of members, but not the three-fifths majority specified in paragraph 2, the next Parliament may, in its opening session, decide on the provisions to be revised by a three-fifths majority of the total number of its members (article 110, paragraphs 2, 3, and 4).

Thus, we need two parliaments to revise constitutional provisions (except the basic ones, which cannot be revised). The first Parliament votes for revision with an absolute majority of its members, and the second one votes with a reinforced majority of three-fifths of its members.

The constitution writers, by allowing for revision after such a long procedure, show that they demand mature thought and insistence from the Parliament and the people in their wish for a revision, so that the constitution is protected against superficial aims and the periodical capriciousness of a changing majority.

Conclusion

Regimes must correspond to the cultural level of the people. There is no ideal form of government for all people.

In Greece we do not have two authorities. The government governs, supported by a majority in Parliament. The people, however, must be in accord. The president, who does not govern, has the right to ask the people whether they agree with the government; if not, the government is overthrown by proclaiming elections or by a referendum.

Certain values and principles are essential to a people that has reached the cultural level of modern Western civilization, and the regime must correspond to these. The absolute value of the human personality; moral, social, and political freedom; the respect of one's fellow human beings; and the contribution to the community—all these principles form the basis of the regimes that suit the countries of the Western world. These principles are realized in the best way in some form of democracy, in which the people always determine, in a way, the course of their destiny. These principles are rooted in the soul of the Greeks. They have been especially precious since their emergence 160 years ago after 400 years of Ottoman oppression. The Greek does not lack the love of freedom. He lacks the will to discipline this love so that it does not risk disturbing social order.

I believe that the Constitution of 1975 corresponds both to the cultural level of the Greek people and to the balance between freedom and social order. This is the reason I believe that it is a good constitution for Greece. It establishes a constitutional ideology that is very broad and that offers much potential for evolution within the framework of democracy and individual liberty.

I believe, too, that every American citizen will appreciate this spirit of freedom in the same way that the Greeks have appreciated · the spirit of freedom that permeates the American regime. Greece has, as a national anthem, the "Hymn of Freedom," written by one of its greatest poets, Dionysios Solomos. The anthem contains the following lines:

> Joy filled the heart
> of Washington's earth

and remembered the shackles
of bondage past.

A hundred and fifty years ago the Greeks' love of freedom saluted the love of freedom of the American people and responded to it.

Commentary

Michael Decleris

The writing of the Greek Constitution of 1975 may be classified as the kind of constitutional change called restoration. Defined in modern terminology, restoration is a process of constitutional change whereby the political system resumes an earlier structure following the failure of the subsequent structure to evolve into a viable pattern. The restored structure is usually an updated version of the earlier one. The important element in restoration, however, is the return to the old structure, not its updating. The Constitution of 1975 restored constitutional democracy in Greece following the breakdown of the military regime that had abolished it in 1967. The military regime produced its own constitution (1968/1973) but eventually failed to evolve into a novel constitutional order.[1] Following the restoration process, the Constitution of 1975 reproduced and revised the Constitution of 1952, which had been abolished by the military regime. Still, the primary concern of the constitution makers was the urgent return to the Constitution of 1952 and not an elaborate study of its improvement. The 1952 Constitution, too, had followed the classical model of constitutional democracy, which has been deeply rooted in Greece since 1864. Its basic features include a comprehensive list of individual rights, a unitary state, popular sovereignty, the separation of powers, an independent judiciary, a unicameral parliament, and the parliamentary system generally (1875). The multiplicity of Greek constitutions since 1864 indicates a discontinuity in the constitutional process. The high frequency of crises did not, however, result in significant structural changes of the classical model. This lack of significant structural change is also true for the making of the Constitution of 1975.

The writing of the Constitution of 1975 was part of the broader process of transition from military to constitutional rule. This transition, which lasted about one year (July 24, 1974, to June 11, 1975), took place peacefully and smoothly. Another quite different attempt at transition had failed in 1973. The transition of 1974–1975, therefore, deserves a theoretical study, which is the subject of this commentary. It is important to note that the military regime was not overthrown by a revolution. Divided and weakened by long inertia, the regime rather broke down after a national crisis over the Cyprus issue. The coup in Cyprus (July 15, 1974) and the ensuing Turkish invasion of this island (July 20, 1974) were the precipitating events for the return to civilian rule. Faced with a national emergency, the ruling military elite became conscious of its inability to handle the crisis and consequently handed over power to the politicians.

Willingness in the transfer of power under such circumstances did not make the normalization process an easy task. The transition from a military dictatorship back to constitutional democracy is generally acknowledged to be a delicate process, one that is usually threatened from two opposite directions: by the resistance of the military extremists and by the overreaction of resentful politicians or violence-prone radicals. The makers of the Constitution of 1975 managed to avoid both such dangers. Their strategy consisted of (a) an immediate conversion of the power entrusted to them into authoritative rule through the provisional reestablishment of the Constitution of 1952, (b) the gradual building up of their supremacy over the military, and (c) a speedy and controlled constitutional process whereby the Constitution of 1975 was put into effect in less than a year after they assumed power.

The transition period can be divided into two phases. During the first phase (July 24–November 17, 1974) succession to power was implemented through a de facto coalition government, which consolidated civilian rule. This consolidation paved the way for the second phase (November 18, 1974–June 11, 1975)—the making of the new Constitution by a national assembly.

More specifically, the military kept its man (General Gizikis) as president of the republic. Gizikis, after consulting a national council composed of selected politicians, authorized a senior political leader (Constantine Karamanlis) to form a coalition government. The president acted formally on the basis of the Constitution of 1968/1973; however, as indicated in the preamble of the decree of July 24, 1974, whereby Karamanlis was invested with the power to form a government, the change was deeper and was, in fact, *constitutional*. The "Government of National Unity," composed of politicians and other personalities of a wide political spectrum, took power "by the unanimous decision of the military and political leadership" to handle the national emergency and reestablish constitutional democracy in Greece. According to Greek constitutional theory, such a government, presumably holding authority by reason of its mission and having the effective control of the country, was a de facto government invested with constitutive power [Council of State, Decision No. 3700/1974]. By its first constitutional act of August 1, 1974, the Government of National Unity promptly reestablished the Constitution of 1952 and committed itself to the task of calling a National Assembly to decide on the issue of the definitive constitution. Because the Constitution of 1952 provided for a king as the head of the executive, relevant constitutional provisions were suspended to accommodate the existing president in the provisional constitutional order.

By the immediate revival of the Constitution of 1952, the Government of National Unity meant to emphasize the continuity of constitutional democracy in Greece. As was solemnly stated later in the preamble of the constitutional act of January 15, 1975, the philosophy of the constitution makers was that "democracy was never abolished by law." For them the military regime was an illegal interval, and the coup of April 21, 1967, an act of treason punishable by law (constitutional acts October 3, 1974, and January 1, 1975).[2] The leading politicians involved in the restoration process were men who had grown up in, and were educated under, the system of constitutional democracy. Since the military regime had failed to mobilize political support and to create a new political elite, the restoration of the Constitution of 1952 was more than simply symbolic; it was, in fact, the only feasible solution at hand. The real need felt by the pragmatic politicians was a speedy return to the familiar constitutional order. In this way the politicians avoided the political risks inherent in prolonged constitutional uncertainty or in a novel experiment.

Having established its authority on the solid basis of the familiar constitutional model, the Government of National Unity also took care to build up its supremacy over the military. It had to consolidate its power before starting an effective constitutional process. Circumstances were favorable in this respect. Owing to the national emergency, the army was kept in the barracks. The hard-core elements of the fallen military regime, discredited and dispirited after their failure, also experienced severe measures. In this way potential military opponents were discouraged from interfering with the policies of the Government of National Unity. Still, some fear of the military persisted.

Conditions were now suitable for beginning the constitutional process. The constitutional act of October 3, 1974, clarified the policy of the Government of National Unity: elections were to be held for a National Assembly vested with constitutive power. Such power was intended to be extensive, since the National Assembly could amend even fundamental provisions of the Constitution of 1952. The issue of the form of government, however, and more specifically of the hereditary or elected head of the executive, was excluded from the power of the assembly. For this issue a referendum was to be held. The constitutional act of October 3, 1974, provided also for the procedure to be followed by the National Assembly in the making of the new constitution: It should proceed on the basis of a draft constitution prepared and made available to it by the government to be formed after the elections. The National Assembly was not bound by the draft, but it had to make a constitution out of the draft within three months after its convocation. If it failed to do so, the government was authorized to hold a referendum on its own draft. Such provisions indicated the unwillingness of the Government of National Unity to embark upon constitutional innovation and its determination to streamline the constitutive process toward a limited revision of the Constitution of 1952. The urgent need at the time was to consolidate constitutional democracy as quickly as possible. Karamanlis considered forming a committee of specialists for a thorough study of the constitutional problems, but he quickly abandoned this idea when he was informed that such a study would require six months of work.

Remarkably, the two main constitutional conflicts that had bedeviled the Greek political process for many years were not resolved by the constitutive work of the National Assembly. These conflicts, over the fate of the Crown and the legal status of the Communist party, were settled by the Government of National Unity through other means. The form of government provided by the restored Constitution of 1952 was that of a "crowned democracy"—a Greek-coined term traditionally used instead of "constitutional monarchy" to stress popular supremacy over royal prerogatives. During the de facto Government of National Unity, that constitution's provisions concerning the Crown were suspended, and the president of the late military regime exercised the royal powers and functions. There had been recurrent constitutional conflict over the issue of the Crown since World War I. National calamities and staunch republicanism undermined the authority of the king, who had to leave the country four times in fifty years. The Government of National Unity referred this problem to a national referendum held on December 7, 1974. The government thereby repeated an old practice by which the fate of the Crown had been decided four times in this century (1920, 1924, 1935, and 1946). By a majority of 69.18 percent, the Greeks now chose a republic. The king and his supporters (30.82 percent) acknowledged defeat.

The problem of the status of the Communist party had been

created by the protracted Communist rebellion that seriously challenged constitutional democracy in Greece in the 1940s. The interlude
of the military regime weakened this conflict, which in the past had
been so acute it ended in the virtual banning of the Communist party
from political life. Communists were now granted legitimacy by the
Government of National Unity through a law (59/1974) authorizing
free activity for any party officially disclaiming violence. In this way
the Communist party was able to participate in the elections for the
National Assembly.

The election for the National Assembly, held on November 17,
1974, marked the end of the first phase of the transitional period.
Karamanlis's rightist party (New Democracy) was the beneficiary of
the policy of the Government of National Unity and won by a clear
majority (54.37 percent). Karamanlis's personality and policies dominated the first phase. Trusted by the loyal military elite and respected
by other politicians and by the people, he rose to the stature of the
sponsor of restoration. Of the other main parties, the Union of Center
(Liberals) took 20.42 percent of the vote, and the Socialists (PASOK)
only 13.58 percent. Communists were relegated to 9.47 percent. Thus
the Government of National Unity was succeeded by a strong government of the victorious party, presided over by Karamanlis and
supported by a monolithic majority in the National Assembly. Also,
following the provisions of the constitutional act of October 3, 1974,
a provisional president of the republic (M. Stassinopoulos) was elected
by the National Assembly to succeed General Gizikis.

The provisional constitutional order now had an enhanced
legitimacy. The making of the Constitution of 1975 went as scheduled
by the constitutional acts of October 3 and December 24, 1974. The
new government prepared and made available to the National Assembly a draft of the proposed constitution (January 8, 1975). This
draft provided the basis of the constitutive work by the assembly.
The assembly chose thirty-seven of its members, selected proportionally from the parties represented, to form a constitutional committee.[3] No one contested this procedure, established on December
24, 1974, by a special constitutional act of the National Assembly;
there was a consensus that the making of the new constitution was
an urgent task. A forty-day limit was placed on the committee to come
up with its own draft. This limit was subsequently extended, but the
committee managed to present its draft to the National Assembly on
March 28, 1975. The committee worked in two subcommittees: one
held nineteen meetings, the other sixteen meetings. Discussions seemed
to be constructive, since the government accepted 140 amendments
proposed by the opposition. Time did not, however, allow for the

deep analysis that characterized constitutive work in the past. Still, owing to bitter memories from the military regime, the constitution makers showed an excessive concern for matters of individual rights and took often unrealistic positions on them. In a general assessment, the committee did not depart essentially from the government draft.

Given the effect of the governmental draft on the making of the Constitution of 1975, our study should include the sources of inspiration of this draft. The draft largely reproduced the text of the Constitution of 1952, which was modified in view of the experience acquired from its application. Among the foreign constitutions that influenced certain provisions of the draft were the French Constitution of 1958 (presidential powers and functions) and the German basic law of 1949 (individual and social rights). The authors of the draft were experienced politicians of the ruling party (C. Papaconstantinou, C. Tsatsos, C. Stefanakis), not professors or visionary theoreticians.[4] The governmental team drew heavily from Karamanlis's constitutional proposals of 1963 as expanded later in the "Project Maniatis-Papaconstantinou" (1967). Three main areas of proposed improvement were identified: (a) the need to strengthen the executive to counterbalance the often paralyzing influence of the Parliament under the cabinet system (in this context a more extended rule-making power was claimed for the government); (b) the need to increase the efficiency of the rule-making function of Parliament; and (c) the need to introduce so-called social rights.

No matter how constructive the cooperation between the government and the opposition in the making of the new constitution, it was bound to stumble on controversial issues. There were mainly two: the powers and functions of the president of the republic and the regulation of certain individual and social rights. After seven years of autocracy, the opposition was sensitive on both emotionally loaded issues. Liberals and Socialists were obsessed by the fear of a strong president dominating the political arena, and this fear aggravated traditional Greek distrust of state power. Also, memories of the state encroachment upon individual rights during the recent military rule intensified the individualism that has been a permanent feature of Greek political culture since ancient times.

The opposition would have preferred a rather ceremonial president dependent on Parliament instead of a strong chief of the executive equipped with sufficient powers of his own. The governmental view explicitly stated in the report accompanying the draft was that the president, being elected by the Parliament, should be given "the powers and functions necessary for the creative performance of the state machinery and for the requirements of exceptional circumstances too." The opposition's stand was not motivated simply by an old-fashioned nostalgia for the supremacy of Parliament as the true guarantor of individual rights; Liberals and Socialists did not conceal their specific fear that by proposing "super-powers" for the president, Karamanlis was in fact paving his way to an unrivaled position of power for the future.

The position of the president in the Constitution of 1975 is somewhere between the French model of 1958 and the classical continental model. Among the powers entrusted to him alone—that is, those not requiring the countersignature of any minister—by article 35, paragraph 2, are appointing the prime minister, convoking the cabinet under his chairmanship, vetoing, dissolving Parliament, holding a referendum, issuing legislative decrees, and giving messages to the nation. Most of these powers—for example, dissolving the Parliament and appointing the prime minister—should be exercised in the context of the cabinet system, which requires the government to have parliamentary support. The other powers, involving high political risk, could seldom have been exercised by a president wise enough to avoid conflict with a strong government. Today, eight years after those acrimonious discussions in the National Assembly, none of the above powers has so far been exercised, since all these powers presuppose a multiplicity of small parties in the Parliament. Thus distrust of state power rather than actual danger of autocracy explains the controversy about this issue. The cabinet system has remained the main feature of Greek government.

The regulation of some individual rights became the other controversial issue of constitution making. Except during crises, Greeks have always enjoyed individual rights. During restoration after the interval of autocracy, however, Liberals and Socialists looked with suspicion upon any proposed regulations in the public interest. There was consensus on expanding the traditional list of rights by the addition of social rights, a euphemism for the guidelines given to the legislator to cover such modern issues as protection of family, health, and environment. But when such matters as the right to work, to form associations, and to hold meetings came to discussion, it became clear that the opposition refused to accept traditional regulation by law or by the courts in the name of the public interest.

Though accepting many of the opposition's demands, the government was unable to meet extreme claims on matters related to public order such as the prohibition of public meetings in cases of serious threat to public security (article 11, paragraph 2), the administrative restrictions in case of emergency (article 5, paragraph 4), the regulation of general working conditions by law (article 22), and the right of civil servants and employees of local government, public corporations, or public enterprises to strike (article 23, paragraph 2). The conflict between the government and the opposition on these issues culminated during the discussions in the National Assembly, which started on March 23, 1975, and were ruled by a speedy procedure. As the opposition became increasingly frustrated, intransigence succeeded constructive dialogue. Though none of the issues was of fundamental importance (in comparison with the other matters settled by agreement), the opposition made the decision to abstain from the last meetings of the National Assembly (May 21 to June 7, 1975) and even from the final vote on the integral text of the Constitution, which took place on June 7, 1975. This behavior, however, should be interpreted in the context of Greek parliamentary tactics: in the past, the opposition had also abstained from the final vote on the Constitution of 1952. Such abstention, motivated by unconcealed bitterness, was meant to convey strong disapproval and not to question the legitimacy of the constitution, which has never been disputed by anyone.

The Constitution of 1975 was put into force by a special act of the National Assembly on June 11, 1975. This date marked the end of the transitional period. The National Assembly was divested of its constitutional power and retained a normal legislative function. A new president (C. Tsatsos) was elected on June 9, 1975, and a new era of constitutional democracy in Greece began. In general, the Constitution of 1975 has stood the test of time. It has even accommodated (at least so far) the policies of a Socialist government elected in 1981. Because the focus of this commentary has been the writing of the constitution, particular institutions have, of necessity, been left out of the discussion.[5] A detailed study of the Constitution of 1975, like the one undertaken by President Tsatsos, should confirm the conclusion that the constitution is an updated version of the classical model for constitutional democracy suitable for Greece. Greek constitutional problems usually originate not from imperfect constitutional provisions but from the particulars of the Greek political culture and social processes, which are beyond the scope of this commentary.[6]

Notes

1. The Constitution of 1968/1973 provided for a kind of "guided" democracy.
2. This law was given, in fact, retroactive effect.
3. The committee was presided over by C. Tsatsos, professor of law and leading member of the party.

4. All three members were lawyers by training. C. Tsatsos also had a distinguished career as a law professor.

5. Among other significant innovations of the Constitution of 1975 should be mentioned the following: (a) article 2 §1, stressing the duty of the state to respect and protect the value of man (taken from article 1 §1 of the German basic law); (b) article 28, placing international law above the domestic statutory law (§1) and allowing for the cession of state functions to agencies of international organizations (§2); (c) articles 43, 44, and 48, expanding the rule-making power of the executive both in normal and exceptional circumstances; (d) article 70 ff., simplifying the legislative procedure; (e) article 150, setting up a Supreme Special Court for solving conflicts in the rulings by the supreme courts on constitutional issues.

6. The full text of the Constitution of 1975 and that of the constitutional acts mentioned in this paper were published in an official edition by the Parliament in 1975. English, French, and German translations of the constitution were also printed by the Parliament in 1975. The texts of all Greek constitutions before 1952 have been collected in E. Kyriakopoulos, ed., *The Constitutions of Greece*, 1960.

The proceedings of the constitutional committee and of the National Assembly were published in four volumes by the Parliament in 1975. Both the governmental draft and the draft of the constitutional committee were included in the first volume. In the same volume Karamanlis's "Proposals for the Revision of the Constitution" (1963) has also been reproduced.

The making of the Constitution of 1975 stimulated several publications by Greek politicians and scholars, mainly in the form of articles printed in reviews and newspapers. Most of the articles are biased and heavily influenced by the political climate of the period.

A reliable constitutional history of Greece is still missing. Historians have proved ill-equipped for this task, while relevant chapters in the various textbooks on Greek constitutional law usually lack adequate analysis. For the period under study foreign readers may draw information from N. Alivizatos, *Les institutions politiques de la Grèce à travers les crises* (Paris: L.G.D.J., 1979), and A. Pantelis, *Les grands problèmes de la Nouvelle Constitution Hellénique* (Paris: L.G.D.J., 1979). They should be cautious, however, about the analyses provided therein. For background study, useful information is provided in N. Kaltchas, *Introduction to the Constitutional History of Modern Greece* (N.Y.: 1940) and K. Legg, *Politics in Modern Greece* (Stanford: Stanford University Press, 1969).

Discussion

ROBERT GOLDWIN: In his paper President Tsatsos emphasizes that there was an opportunity not only to restore the Constitution of Greece in 1974 but to modernize it, to add new ideas that would bring it up to date. Judge Decleris argues in his paper that the major impetus was restoration, not the development of new ideas. I pose this difference in emphasis because Greek constitution making is a striking example of a desire to return to something that was a fundamental part of the character of the nation and the people. Why, then, if the inclination to liberal democracy is so powerful in the Greek character, has it been lost so frequently? That raises the question of why a new constitution was required. Was it primarily to restore something old, or was it primarily to strike out in the direction of something new in addition to the restoration?

PRESIDENT CONSTANTINE TSATSOS: This is a crucial question you pose. I think that my colleague Mr. Decleris is right: the main problem in 1974 was to restore parliamentary democracy, and I shall try to explain why. Modern Greece became a free nation in 1821. It was a very poor country at that time. The Greek revolution was the first during the period of the Holy Alliance, a period when revolution was not allowed anywhere in the world. Our main enemy at that time was the Holy Alliance. Five months after the beginning of the revolution, in January 1822, when a small part of the south of the country was free, the Greeks made their first constitution—a constitution framed in the manner of the Constitution of the United States.

Later, and during the revolutionary war, the Greek people wanted a new constitution, a more perfect constitution, but always in the spirit of the philosophy dominating the Constitution of the United States and with certain articles emulating the French Bill of Rights. The people, although mostly illiterate, always wanted a *written* constitution. This was a political objective of all parties and, indeed, of the nation as a whole during the nine-year period. A year after the

103

end of the revolution, however, Russia, Great Britain, and France installed the absolute monarchy of King Otto, without any written constitution. Twelve years later (1843), the army rioted, and the people of Athens again demanded a constitution. This riot resulted in the Constitution of 1844. Then the arbitrary rule of King Otto resulted in a new revolution in 1862 and yet another constitution. The new constitution was modeled on the 1830 Constitution of Belgium. It provided for a unicameral legislature, many parties, sovereignty of the people, and human rights, as is usual in the constitutional monarchies in Europe. After that, we had no reason to change our constitution until 1923. Why in 1923?

As a result of the defeat by the Turks and five years of war (1917–1922), more than 1½ million Greeks were compelled to abandon Asia Minor and Thrace, where they had lived for centuries, and come back to Greece, a state of 3,500,000 people at that time. So more than one-third of our population were immigrants, who considered the royal regime responsible for their catastrophe. They demanded deep changes, among them the abolition of the dynasty of Glucksburg. This change did not occur smoothly or quickly. Between 1923 and 1935, after many upheavals, we achieved an unsteady democratic regime. But in 1935, after a riot in the army, the constitutional monarchy was reestablished.

Therefore, for reasons mainly internal to Greece, the Greek nation was obliged to frame several constitutions between 1830 and 1935. In recent history (1935–1974), the reasons were more external. First came World War I and the dictatorship of Metaxas. Why did the dictatorship of Metaxas come to power? At that time in Europe, there were three dictatorships: Germany, Italy, and Spain. There was also a crisis of the democratic regime in Austria. Dictatorship was more accepted then than now. The atmosphere was different then in all of Europe. After World War II, we had two problems to solve: who will be the chief of state, a president or a king, and who will be the predominant force, the resistance of the left or the army fighting in Egypt and Italy with the king? These critical problems converged, forcing us to make a new constitution. We began to frame it in 1946. I was a member of the committee that conducted long discussions for three years—1946, 1947, and 1948. The Parliament was dissolved; the constitution was not yet ready. Then we had to go back and write a constitution in a few days, in 1952, and we did so, before the framing of the new German Constitution, which presented new ideas and new problems. Greece came under the dictatorship of the colonels from 1967 to 1974. In 1974 the dictatorship ended. We had the tragedy concerning the island of Cyprus, about which the Greeks are very sensitive, and we needed yet another constitution. The result was a restoration of the old constitution, with changes adopted after thirty years of experience and with a view to the German, the Italian, and other new constitutions.

In spite of the Greeks' preference for a written constitution of the Western type that favors democracy, we suffered from many interruptions. The question posed is a good one, because it is the first one every person who reads the Greek Constitution asks: Why have the Greeks made so many constitutions? Why have they made so many changes? The reasons are not only internal to the constitution but also arise externally from historical facts. That's the reason we have this Constitution today. I think it is more or less accepted by all the parties—not the by Communists, but by all other parties.

MICHAEL DECLERIS: Mr. Goldwin asked, Why have there been so many Greek constitutions, and why was there a case for restoration? Then there was another question: if the Greeks are democratically minded, why was the earlier, deeply rooted constitution destroyed, and why was there an interim of military rule? First, I would make the distinction between a constitution as a document and a real or "living" constitution. As a document the constitution provides the model of the political system. The living constitution is rather a continuing process that is stimulated by environmental demands and aims at maintaining the stability of the political system. The regulatory function of the living constitution is limited by the capacity of the political system to process the environmental demands. If the volume of demands from the social, including the international, environment is within the capacity of the system, then the system will manage to work somehow. But if the demands from that environment exceed the capacity of the system, then the system suffers partial or total catastrophe. Even the best constitution presupposes a smooth flow of environmental demands. It cannot cope with abrupt changes.

The Americans, the Scandinavians, and the British may be happy that they have gone through the process of more or less orderly change, but in other parts of the world—for instance, in Greece— the demands of the environment sometimes exceed the capacity of the system. Therefore, the system suffers a partial or total collapse and needs to be restructured. It is in this context that we should understand abrupt constitutional changes. In Greece, there is no question that the political will since the very beginning has aimed at democracy. The first Greek state, however, was a small state within a much larger nation, and the process of national unification lasted more than one hundred years. Each involvement in war creates demands on internal security and on the capacity to conduct war. In

105

this century catastrophes for Greece have exceeded the capacity of the system. With problems of such magnitude the ordinary constitutional process could not hold up. Each new constitution emerged in response to a major crisis. The successive crises—the process of national unification, the involvement in major wars, and social upheavals—produced the discontinuity that explains the multiplicity of Greek constitutions. It is in this context that the framing of the constitutions of 1864, 1911, 1927, 1952, and 1975 are to be explained.

Why was there a case for constitutional restoration in 1975 specifically? I believe that two main conflicts put great demands on the Greek constitutional system. The first was the involvement in World War II, creating a situation, well understood, in which Greece was occupied by Germans, the free government was in exile, and loose public order in the interior favored the rise of the Communist rebellion. There was major social change at the time. The formal government of Greece was a constitutional monarchy. These events, however, undermined the authority of the king, forcing the question of the future of the constitutional monarchy to be settled. The defeat of the Communist rebellion and the reaffirmation of constitutional monarchy by the Constitution of 1952 did not eliminate bitter republican opposition. Constitutional conflict over the powers of the king continued, and this was one of the reasons that the 1952 Constitution eventually proved fragile.

The second reason was that, in reaction to these crises, the system had to resort increasingly to deviations from its ordinary process. The crisis was suffocating, even before the military involvement in government in 1967. Even as early as 1963, Karamanlis had urged constitutional reform. The military intervention in 1967 can be seen as the culmination of this crisis and was very different from any in the past: as the military regime sought unsuccessfully to restructure the system, it triggered instead a major national crisis over the Cyprus issue. The military seemed to be unable to cope with it. Therefore, when the regime collapsed in 1974, the need was urgent for a return to the familiar constitutional order. In this way the Constitution of 1975 settled conflicts originating from World War II.

Even though restoration signifies a return to the old structure, experience acquired in the meantime usually leads to a modification of the system in view of new needs and new demands, as in Greece. Democracy does not necessarily ensure stability. An essentially open political system is necessarily a dynamic one. In times of catastrophe, the system that worked well as a constitutional government has to return to the old, familiar structure, which is usually further developed. This is what happened in Greece.

J. CLIFFORD WALLACE: I was struck, in reading President Tsatsos's paper, that the experiences of Greece seem somewhat similar to those of the United States 200 years ago. I refer to the contention in America between the Federalists and the Antifederalists. Both groups were attempting to achieve a democratic system for the United States, but the Federalists asserted that we could not have a democracy in its purest sense because the country needed greater stability. It seems, I suppose, from our experience and that of Greece, and perhaps from other nation-building efforts, that sometimes tension exists between a theory of democracy and the desire to have stable government. I gathered from President Tsatsos's paper that, indeed, this was the case in Greece. My question is, How strong was this tension during the period when the Greek Constitution was being drafted? That is, was there open tension between those who desired a more democratic approach with direct election of leaders, as there was in France, and those who desired more stable government? What factors led to the ultimate decision on which was to prevail?

PRESIDENT TSATSOS: There was tension during the framing of the Constitution, but I must be more precise. The major tension was with the Communists, who wanted a completely new form of constitution, a new form of the Greek state. Among the others, there was minor tension, because all the political parties were democrats and had suffered in common from the dictatorship for seven years. All the former politicians were either in jail or exiled from political life for those seven years. When the dictatorship collapsed in July 1974, we all came out of the same jails, came back from the same islands where we were exiled, or returned from isolation in our homes. So there was no tension at the beginning. We were united against dictatorship. That was the first phase, but it did not last very long.

Just as the honeymoon lasts for some time before the first quarrel between man and wife, so we had, after the constitutional honeymoon, an increase in the tension, which was concentrated in two areas. The first was the breadth and importance of human rights; the second, and more important, was the power of the man who was the leader and the leading personality at this time, Karamanlis. Everybody wanted democracy; everybody agreed, as Mr. Decleris said, to continue to be a Western democracy, but we also wanted to fix the power of the president in a new way. Some of us—not I, but some of us—wanted a very strong president to keep order during the reconstruction of the country. Others wanted a very weak president. The tension between these two groups produced quarreling during all the months of intense debate in the Parliament about the constitution. On all

107

other points, there was agreement to restore the old order, but on this point, having decided through a referendum that the king would not return, we had to decide what the powers of the president would be.

The opposition was reluctant to accept any change. They wanted a president with unchanged powers, while we wanted the French solution. I mentioned in my essay a dialogue that took place between de Gaulle and Karamanlis, in which de Gaulle asked Karamanlis why he did not put in his constitution a stronger executive as de Gaulle had done. Karamanlis answered, "My dear president, you had parliamentary instability, and the people in France were fed up because of it, because of this weakness of the government, and they wanted the power and discipline necessary for strong government. So you made a strong constitution. I came out of a dictatorship, which was strong and severe, and the people wanted freedom. So, I was obliged to accept that. Starting from that point of view, I had to compromise, and our Constitution is a compromise in which the Parliament remains the last resource with all the power, deciding on everything, and the government is always drawn from the majority of the Parliament." That was the point of origin for this restoration. We said the president has the right to dissolve the Parliament, to dismiss the government, to call for a referendum, but—and this is what the president usually forgets—he is obliged to call for elections after thirty days, and if in the elections his point of view is rejected by the people, though he legally can remain president, he is not president with the same prestige.

So we gave the president power, not to change the government because he wants a change, but to ask the nation, to ask the people whether they want a change; and if the answer is no, he is finished as president. If the answer is yes, the government is finished. Our solution to this problem of who has the ultimate power is quite different from the solution in France.

WILLIAM T. COLEMAN, JR.: I am intrigued by President Tsatsos's suggestion in his essay that among the sources of law from which the Greek Constitution is derived the emphasis is on international law and on the precedent of the German Constitution. I am intrigued that in a country that relied on the tradition of the Greek Orthodox Church (and President Tsatsos points out that the Ottoman Empire was not able to suppress the Greeks because of the church and because of the tradition that Greeks have had since ancient times in expressing the rights of men) the emphasis in the sources of the Constitution is on international law, including the Treaty of Rome and the Charter of the United Nations and that President Tsatsos indicates that there was great reliance on what the German state did. In his essay, the only reason for that emphasis seems to appear in the section on social rights where it is indicated, as it is in the international documents, that the state has the responsibility to provide for health, youth, old age, and the like. Does the provision of social rights in the Greek Constitution mean the Parliament does not act in those areas and that the people cannot bring a law suit to make it act?

This leads me to ask about the special court that resolves fundamental constitutional issues. President Tsatsos indicates that this court changes, or is elected, every two or three years. It seems to me that if a continuing struggle exists between the Parliament and the people there ought to be an institution of government that has great continuity. In the United States, for example, only 102 persons have sat on the U.S. Supreme Court during its existence, so I am interested in knowing about the special court in Greece.

In the parliamentary democracies it is the people who finally govern, and the leaders can be turned out whenever they are not in sympathy with the will of the people or when the people are not in sympathy with them. But in the history of the United States, our great leaders have been able to take actions and lead the country even though, if it were put to a vote at some times, the leaders would have been voted out of office. I was impressed when the Chief Justice of the United States mentioned at the opening of this conference that the framers of the American Constitution left the issue of slavery unsettled because they would not have come up with a constitution if they tried to resolve the issue. I would assume that in a parliamentary system during the 1830s, if any president had said he planned to abolish slavery he would not have been around for thirty days. I certainly believe that if, when the United States came to grips with ending racial segregation, it had been put to a vote a majority would not have voted to end it, even if the vote determined the fate of a parliamentary leader. I would also suggest, since it touches close to home in Greece, that when President Truman decided to send aid to Greece to help defeat the Communists, if that had been put to a vote in this country in a parliamentary way, I do not think President Truman would have survived in office for thirty days. I could give many other examples. In the countries that have really tough, divisive political issues, how do you expect the parliamentary system to work when the vote of the people at a particular time would be contrary to what a great leader of the country would ultimately have his people do?

MR. DECLERIS: First, I would like to answer Mr. Coleman's question concerning international law. There was a slight modification in the Constitution, mainly to enable Greece to join the European Community. Other than that, our position on international law has remained the same. International law has always been part of the law of the country. Moreover, the list of human rights in the Constitution is the same list that is in the United Nations Declaration of Human Rights and in the Convention of Rome.

On Mr. Coleman's second point, the question of social rights, I assume you will agree that there is something of a manifesto in every constitution. In addition to strictly legal rules there is also the source of the constitution's authority. In the nineteenth century, the slogan was individual rights. At that time, the American Declaration of Independence and the French Declaration of Human Rights were the sources of inspiration. In this century, the German Constitution of Weimar of 1919 has been the source of inspiration. Constitutionalists have moved from the position that a constitution is a system for limiting government to the position that, more dynamically, a constitution should promote social welfare. There is a great difference between constitutional rhetoric and constitutional reality. And there is much constitutional rhetoric in the matter of social rights.

There was a demand in Greece, as in all countries, to include certain social rights in the Constitution, since, in practice we applied them anyway. We have had a system of social insurance since the 1930s, for example. As far as I am concerned, therefore, there is not much difference in the new articles. I see them only as guidelines for the lawmakers, to streamline the legislative process toward achieving social welfare. But this is different from a strictly legal meaning of these articles. Anyway, we now have explicit guidelines in our Constitution for protecting health, family, environment, work, and the rest.

As far as Mr. Coleman's question about the special court is concerned, I must point out that this is a Special Supreme Court in Greece. Following the French model, we have a duality of jurisdiction—a hierarchy of administrative courts and a hierarchy of ordinary courts. It sometimes happens that the solutions to legal problems, or even constitutional problems, by the administrative courts and ordinary courts may differ. Therefore there was a need for a special court, which is now mainly assigned the task of coordinating jurisprudence between the highest ordinary and administrative courts.

I agree with Mr. Coleman's last comment that some hard issues cannot be solved by the parliamentary system. That some issues cannot be solved is exactly what creates strains in the system and sometimes causes catastrophes. It is true that issues may be solved more easily under a strong presidential system, but I am not sure whether they can be decided safely. Under the parliamentary system, information about what all portions of the population want and, therefore, what the system can or cannot do, is always available. This system sometimes makes decisions difficult or even impossible, but I believe it is safer.

AFONSO ARINOS DE MELO FRANCO: I would like to discuss the transition from military power to the restoration of constitutional democracy. Mr. Decleris and President Tsatsos spoke of the military dictatorship from 1967 to 1974 and the return to constitutional democracy. Such a transformation is happening in my country, Brazil, although the military rule is not collapsing since it is very hard for such a collapse to occur. In Brazil, it is rather a progressive weakening of the military power due to the failure of government to meet the objectives of economic development vis-à-vis the world economic crisis, which is extremely grave for Brazil, and also due to almost unanimous national opinion in support of the return to democratic traditions. In my opinion, the government of Brazil will not collapse, but we will have a rather long transition period because the president will complete his term in office.

I would like to know how the transition from military dictatorship occurred so peacefully in Greece. It is not a juridical question or a legal question so much as a political question, because the problem of military intervention is quite different from country to country.

A. E. DICK HOWARD: President Tsatsos mentions in his essay that the 1952 Constitution was outdated by the time of its adoption because it was a throwback to rather more traditional, liberal-democratic constitutions that did not anticipate, and did not conform to, social aspirations as they had been developed as a social fact of life in Greece. This suggests a general question that I think can be asked about a number of constitution-making experiences. Two important constitutional models stand out among the others. One is a more eighteenth- or nineteenth-century liberal constitution emphasizing one's Lockean individual rights—rights of life, liberty, and property; rights of due process of law; rights that are typically and traditionally enforced in court by individuals as claims against government. They are essentially atomistic or individualistic rights.

The other important model is one in which twentieth-century constitutions partake of social obligation—that is, claims of a more organic kind, such as housing, education, old-age benefits, maternity

111

benefits, social welfare, and so on, may be made upon the state. Typically, a modern constitution, especially one drafted since World War II, includes provisions dealing with both kinds of rights. It has a declaration of rights or a bill of rights enumerating free speech, free exercise of religion, and so on; but it also has a list of aspirations or obligations upon the state to provide certain benefits for the state's citizens.

It seems to me that there are two ways to enforce, or speak about the enforcement of, rights of a more social nature. One can go in the direction Mr. Coleman suggested, looking to a court to enforce social rights as one looks to a court to enforce the more traditional atomistic rights. In a few American states, for example, state supreme courts have forced state legislatures to fund school districts and equalize school expenditures among rich and poor districts. Such actions suggest the social welfare right is enforceable. The other direction is implied by Mr. Decleris's comments that the enumeration of social rights is essentially declaratory or aspirational, and they are not really meant to be read legalistically as being enforceable claims one can take to court and upon which one might found a cause of action.

The concern I have is that either one of those directions raises problems. If one seeks to make a declaration of social obligation, enforceable in court, one is asking judges to do that which judges are not very good at doing, and that is to make decisions about the allocation of social resources. That decision is better made, in my judgment, by legislative bodies, given the existence of finite social resources and economic opportunities. If, instead, one reads the social claims simply as aspirations or prophecies, then one blurs the distinction between enforceable constitutional rights and those that are merely rhetorical. So I am concerned that the approach that says rights are not enforceable would lead to a dilution of the rather important distinction between fundamental law and that which is simply statutory—the distinction between the bedrock of superstatute, which one thinks of as a constitution, and the ordinary conventional code of laws. I wonder, therefore, whether that second approach doesn't lead to a dilution of constitutional rights across the board—that is, the Constitution no longer represents something fundamental that is beyond the reach of ordinary day-to-day legislation.

NANI A. PALKHIVALA: I am much impressed by two points about the amending procedure in the Greek Constitution and I want to comment on them. The first is that certain parts of the Constitution cannot be amended at all; the second is that two successive parliaments must approve an amendment before it can become effective. I would like to refer to the experience of my own country, India, on these points. The experience of my country shows the great wisdom of having the first of these provisions. Our Constitution, which does not have such an express provision, came into force in 1950. By 1980 the Constitution had been amended forty-five times. Three of the amendments were struck down by the Supreme Court of India as being unconstitutional on the grounds that the amending procedure, while it extends to all parts of the Constitution, does not extend to altering or destroying its basic structure. The court held that before 1950 India never was one country, but as a result of a compact, a contract between various parts of the country, in 1950 it became one political entity. That compact cannot be altered by the whim of one party to the detriment of others who may suffer, or are likely to suffer, as a result of the amendment.

The court also held that in every constitution what is left unsaid is as important as what is said. What is left unsaid in our Constitution is, in fact, said in the Greek Constitution. We merely say Parliament shall have the right to amend the Constitution. The court said that one meaning of the word "amend" is to alter or change for the better, but amending does not mean changing the Constitution in a way that destroys its basic structure. Our free republic cannot be converted into a totalitarian state or into a monarchy, for example. Therefore, the Supreme Court held that Parliament, when it was given this power to amend the Constitution, could not arrogate to itself the role of the official liquidator of the Constitution. In short, the judgment was that such a provision for amendment cannot operate as a provision for the legal suicide of the Constitution. I think that it is perhaps the Indian Republic's greatest contribution to jurisprudence.

But the advantage of having an express provision for preserving the sanctity of certain parts of the Constitution, such as exists in the Greek Constitution, is that while the rulings of the Supreme Court can be reversed by subsequent rulings of the same court, the Constitution cannot be changed in that way.

President Tsatsos points out that in the Greek Constitution there is no prohibition against appointing a person to the cabinet even though he does not happen to be a member of Parliament. This is a very sensible provision. The Japanese Constitution provides that the number of ministers shall not exceed twenty-one, so that pressures may not be brought to bear on the prime minister to enlarge the cabinet to accommodate more people who want the benefits of office. The Japanese Constitution also provides that a minority of the ministers may be from outside the Diet, the Japanese parliament, so that as many as ten ministers can be technocrats who are not professional politicians. In India the Constitution provides that, though you may appoint any man to be a cabinet minister, he has to become a member of Parliament within six months of his appointment. If within six months he does not become a member of Parliament, he ceases to be a cabinet minister. The Greek Constitution seems to say that he never need get elected; he can be a professional man, he can be a technocrat, and never enter politics as a professional politician. This strikes me as a very sensible provision. I have been pleading for an amendment to the Indian Constitution to allow people who are not and do not want to be in Parliament to get into government, to act as members of the cabinet, and to continue in that office. These provisions would be very beneficial in third world countries, and I believe the experience of India is significant in this respect.

MR. DECLERIS: I want to address several questions that have been raised. Ambassador Arinos de Melo Franco from Brazil asked how it is possible to speak of the collapse of the military regime, since the military willingly handed power to the politicians. The last discontinuity of the Greek constitutional process was a national crisis, not simply a constitutional crisis. There was a national crisis *before* there was a constitutional crisis. This explains the fall of the military regime. The military regime was not overthrown by revolution; it reached the limits of its capacity when it faced the national crisis over the Cyprus issue. The military was unable to cope with that situation in the sense that it felt unable to assume the responsibility involved in the settlement of such a major national issue. The system could not work as before, and that began the transition period. The military decided to hand over the government to the politicians, so the politicians assumed responsibility over the national crisis. This is the fundamental point that one should consider when asking why the military willingly handed power to the politicians. In my paper I explained why the transition from the military to the constitutional regime was peaceful in 1974–1975. Hard measures were not avoided altogether, however. On the basis of a special constitutional enactment with retroactive force the leaders of the fallen military regime are still in prison.

In this period, Karamanlis probably played about the same role in this transition that de Gaulle played in France in 1958. De Gaulle, in a sense, prevented the major crisis in France. Had it not been for de Gaulle, the French army might have taken over after the national crisis over the Algerian issue. Karamanlis played a similar role. He appeared as a guarantor, as a sponsor of the delicate transition, and he managed to take advantage of favorable factors to ensure a peaceful transition.

On the issue of social rights, the question seems to be whether guidelines for social rights can be enforced in certain situations. President Tsatsos and I use a term, guidelines, which is accurate, but which, to a certain extent, is too simple. Other rights, individual rights, started out as guidelines. In the beginning, for example, the principle of equality was interpreted by many courts in European countries as a guideline to legislatures, but in due time it acquired the status of a legal rule. The same may happen with the so-called social rights. The section of the Constitution concerning protection of the family, for instance, serves as a strong reminder to the legislator. It is a guideline, but you can imagine a situation in which you discover a fundamental rule under this guideline, as happened in the Supreme Court concerning the provision for protection of the family: there was a taxation system on property, under which the husband, when he submitted information about his property, had to add the property of his wife to his own. That meant that he would be taxed at a higher percentage. The court agreed that it could not advise what laws should be enacted to protect the family, but it could find an underlying rule that prevents damage to the family. The court said, in effect, that if it is bound to take measures to protect the family, then it cannot take a measure that is, in fact, against the family. In my estimation, this was the beginning of a legal rule. In fact, this was the beginning of a new interpretation of this article. One can see, therefore, that such a guiding provision in a constitution is not devoid of legal meaning, but may well serve as a basis for protecting social rights.

Before the updating of the 1952 Constitution, the constitutional model in Greece had been basically unchanged since 1864, and reproducing constitutions did not significantly alter the initial model. Modifications were made in each restoration, and some modifications updated the model, but did not bring to it a new, advanced stage of development. We worked under the Constitution of 1952 for a long time and discovered no shortcomings in it. But that Constitution came under attack politically because it was still in the fashion of a nineteenth-century constitution, limiting the role of the state and not calling for the provision of social rights. The demand was for an active approach, using the state and the constitution to transform society.

CHIEF FREDERICK ROTIMI ALADE WILLIAMS: Under the Nigerian Constitution, we describe social rights as fundamental objectives, as "directive principles of state policy." I am not sure that these rights can ever be elevated to legally enforceable rights, because all of them depend on the availability of resources. It is meaningless to talk of educational, housing, or other rights in the same way one talks about the rights that are usually included in a bill of rights; they differ fundamentally. Exercising one's freedom of speech, the liberty of the press, and so forth does not require any resources.

There is another point of difference between what I call fundamental liberties and social rights. Judges who are trained in the legal profession are not necessarily trained for the enforcement of social rights, and I think, therefore, that ultimately the electorate or the legislature should be the guardians of these rights. Under the Nigerian Constitution, the National Assembly—that is, the federal legislature—is vested with the power to propose means for enforcing social rights. The makers of the Constitution recognized that, within the time at their disposal, it was not possible to devise any method for enforcing these social rights, so it was left to the National Assembly. The National Assembly has not been able to make any proposals, but, speaking broadly, I do not think that these rights can be enforced by courts of law; they will continue to serve as guidelines to the legislature and to the government.

FRANCISCO RUBIO LLORENTE: How can we reconcile the principle of religious liberty with the existence of a dominant church in Greece? How was this question resolved in the constitutional debates, and what were the historical and sociological justifications for resolving it?

I also want to raise a question concerning academic freedom in Greece under the Constitution. There are constitutional provisions concerning the condition and status of university professors but also prohibiting private universities. It seems at first glance that the Constitution puts on the same level the principle of academic freedom and the prohibition of a system of private universities. What is the theoretical basis for the provisions on universities, and what was said during the constitutional debates on these subjects that led to this apparent contradiction?

MR. DECLERIS: I would like to address the two issues raised by Mr. Rubio, one concerning the position of the Greek Orthodox Church, and the other the issue of academic freedom under the Constitution. It is true, first, that Article III of the Greek Constitution, which has been the same since the first Constitution of Greece, seemingly confers a special status on the Greek Orthodox Church. This does not mean in any sense, however, that it is at the expense of other religions. Another article in the Constitution, Article XIII, states that freedom of religious conscience is inviolable; all religion shall be free and the right to worship shall be unhindered. The first article, Article III, is

116

included for historical reasons. The Church of Greece played a sig-nificant role in the national liberation movement, and only in this sense has the status of the church been preserved. Otherwise, its privileged position has nothing to do with the privileged position of the Catholic Church in the past. The privileges of the church are very few and do not even bring into question its equality with other reli-gions.

With respect to the issue of academic freedom that Mr. Rubio raised, I must admit that he pointed out a very important problem. There are no absolute rights granted by any constitution; however, all rights acknowledged by a constitution are qualified in the sense that they are subject either to explicitly stated limitations or are re-served for qualification by the legislature. In the United States, higher education is the responsibility of states or of private institutions. For various reasons, in Greece the academic freedom that Mr. Rubio refers to is not the same as in the United States because every university has to be a state university; nonetheless, academic freedom still exists in Greece. There is a special status for professors: they are autono-mous, they are chosen by their peers, and they have freedom in their research and in their teaching. They do not have the right to institute their own universities, which is a limitation that has been imposed by the constitutions of Greece since the very beginning.

JEAN FOYER: I want to go back first to the distinction that was made between traditional rights, which are recognized by declarations, and the new social rights. Certain social rights—for example, the right to strike—are in fact clear; the state must abstain from interfering, and if it violates that right it can be challenged by a private individual whose right has been trampled on, and the judge can sanction the challenge. There is also the question of the state's shouldering a pos-itive right, but the objective of doing so is not sufficiently clear and, if we were to carry our thought to its logical conclusion, we would have to transform the judge and make him into a legislator. I think that we must, therefore, raise this question of the two categories of law.

President Tsatsos wrote in his paper that the Greek Constitution gives no place to direct democracy. This is stange in a country that witnessed the birth of democracy, and I do not completely understand the position democracy currently has in Greece. The present Hellenic Republic, with its small number of citizens, has no place for direct democracy; how, in fact, can this be in its constitution? Although there are several modern forms of direct democracy, or at least some-what direct—popular initiatives, popular vetoes, referenda—why are these ideas not reflected in the modern Greek Constitution? Why has this idea of direct democracy been totally rejected?

PRESIDENT TSATSOS: To reply to your question, Mr. Foyer, I would like to say that we are more American than European on this particular point. We believe in democracy, of course, but we consider that the present population no longer permits *direct* democracy; of course, it was ideal in other times. Why did we eliminate all reference to direct democracy? We need to have recourse to direct democracy only when we confront issues requiring decentralization. If we look at the direction of the present government with its socialist bases and the spirit that animates it, we see that there are certain units in the villages where there is, in fact, direct democracy. They are more like Swiss cantons, which still have rational, direct assemblies. So, like the Swiss, we also have direct democracy on the village level in Greece.

4

The Writing of the Constitution
of the United States

Walter Berns

The frequency with which the process has been repeated should not be allowed to conceal the fact that in 1787 the writing and formal adoption of a constitution of government was a novelty. This was well understood by Americans when they were asked "to deliberate on a new Constitution for the United States of America"[1] and even better understood by the fifty-five men who assembled in Philadelphia to write it.

The Constitution they wrote and were instrumental in having adopted was not, however, the first to be written or to be adopted by Americans. In the period immediately preceding 1787, each of the states making up the United States (with the qualified exceptions of Connecticut and Rhode Island) had adopted, and was governing itself under, a written constitution.[2] Some of the men assembled at Philadelphia had played an active part in this process at the state level.

The Constitution of 1787 was not even the first national constitution. At the very time the convention was deliberating and debating in Philadelphia, there was a Congress of the United States meeting and debating national policy in New York, a Congress that derived its authority from an agreement—the Articles of Confederation and Perpetual Union—entered into by delegates of the thirteen states in November 1777 and declared formally ratified by the states in March 1781. It was, in fact, at the call of this Congress on February 21, 1787, that the convention met in Philadelphia.

Thus the Constitution of 1787 was neither the first to be written nor the first under which the American nation was governed; nevertheless, as its framers knew very well indeed, they were engaged in what was still a novel enterprise, an experiment, and one for which history provided little guidance. They also understood its significance. As one of them wrote, "the subject speaks its own importance," and

119

not only for Americans. He and many of his colleagues thought they were setting an example for the whole of mankind.

> It has been frequently remarked that it seems to have been reserved to the people of this country, by their conduct and example, to decide the important question, whether societies of men are really capable or not of establishing good government from reflection and choice, or whether they are forever destined to depend for their political constitutions on accident and force.[3]

One other feature of this Constitution deserves mention here: though written by delegates representing the particular states, it claimed to derive its authority from "the people of the United States," an assertion that gave rise to a good deal of controversy. "What right had they to say, *We, the People*," demanded Patrick Henry, one of the heroes of the American Revolution; "who authorized them to speak the language of *We, the People*, instead of *We, the States?*"[4] Henry was not being merely querulous; he and the scores of others who made similar objections had legitimate cause to complain. The country was governing itself under a constitution—the Articles of Confederation and Perpetual Union—which, by its own terms, could be altered or amended only with the consent of "the legislatures of every state." The amending provision was wholly compatible with the governing principle of the Articles, namely, the quasi-sovereignty of the individual states, and that sovereignty was not recognized in the new Constitution. Furthermore, Congress had called the convention

> for the sole and express purpose of revising the Articles of Confederation and reporting to Congress and the several [state] legislatures such alterations and provisions therein as shall when agreed to in Congress and confirmed by the states render the federal constitution adequate to the exigencies of Government & the preservation of the Union.[5]

But everyone acknowledged that the Constitution that came out of the convention was much more than a revision of the Articles of Confederation; it was wholly new, in its principle as well as in its provisions. It recognized the sovereignty not of each individual state but, rather, of the people of the United States, and, Patrick Henry to the contrary notwithstanding, its framers could argue, as they did argue, that they were fully justified in having it do so.

To understand the making of the Constitution of the United States, it is necessary to appreciate the extent to which the process (as well as the document that emerged from it) was informed and influenced by these two not necessarily compatible principles, popular sovereignty and state sovereignty. They were part of the political theory and the history that went into it.

Popular Sovereignty

Writing toward the end of his long life to Nicholas Trist, James Madison, the Constitution's principal author, explained the nature of the compacts that lay behind American government:

> Altho' the old idea of a compact between the Govt & the people be justly exploded, the idea of a compact among those who are parties to a Govt is a fundamental principle of free Govt.
>
> The original compact is the one implied or presumed, but nowhere reduced to writing, by which a people agree to form one society. The next is a compact, here for the first time reduced to writing, by which the people in their social state agree to a Govt over them.[6]

No precise date can be fixed to the original compact according to which the American people came into being. They had been separated into thirteen distinct groups of colonials and joined formally only by a common allegiance to the British Crown, but that one formal connection may have been broken when, with the taking up of arms, the allegiance was renounced. It is possible, however, that the agreement to take up arms and join in a common struggle against the king's armies was also understood to be an agreement to form a new civil society. In any case, it was as "one people" that, in 1776, they declared the right formally to "dissolve the political bands which [had] connected them with another [people], and assume among the powers of the earth, the separate and equal station to which the laws of Nature and of Nature's God entitle[d] them." The implication of this is that they had become one people before casting off "their British colonial dependence," as Lincoln was to say many years later.

But this formal renunciation of allegiance to one political authority (the British Crown) did not, and in principle could not, by itself institute a new political authority or a new government. That much is suggested in Madison's letter and is clear on the face of the Declaration of Independence itself. There it is said to be self-evidently true that all men are created equal insofar as they all possess the natural rights to life, liberty, and the pursuit of happiness and that "to secure these rights, Governments are instituted among Men, deriving their just powers from the consent of the governed." And there it is also said that, whenever any government becomes destructive of these ends, it is the right of the people "to alter or abolish it, and to institute new Government, laying its foundation on such principles and organizing its powers in such form, as to them shall seem most likely to effect their Safety and Happiness." This is followed by an indictment of George III listing his "usurpations" of power and the "repeated injuries" he had inflicted on the people of the United States, all, it was alleged, with the purpose of establishing "an absolute Tyranny over these States." The Declaration then concludes with a renunciation of "all Allegiance to the British Crown." In short, by declaring independence the people of the United States exercised their right "to alter or abolish" a government that had become destructive of the proper ends of all government, but they did not exercise their right to "institute new Government." The Declaration speaks of the necessity of consent, of the withdrawal of consent and the reasons for that withdrawal, but it does not pretend to be a compact in which the people give their consent to a new government.

A necessary condition of legitimate government, consent must be given formally; as Madison put it, it takes the form of a compact that is "reduced to writing." The reasons may not be self-evident; after all, Americans had never formally consented to the government of George III, but, by declaring their independence when, in their judgment, his government had become tyrannical, they implied that they had consented to it, if only tacitly. Besides, if the first compact— that by which individuals agree to form one society—can be unwritten, there would seem to be no necessity for the second to be written. It might be written, but as John Locke himself acknowledged, it might also be "tacit" and no less valid for that.[7] Nevertheless, for reasons that can be traced back to Locke, Madison was correct in suggesting that the constitution of government should take the form of a written compact.

If, as Locke wrote[8] and the Declaration repeated, all men are by nature free and equal, then no man has a natural right to rule another. A man may be stronger, more intelligent, handsomer, or better connected, but the unequal possession of these attributes or qualities does not entitle him to rule. Attributes may endow him with political influence, but in the matter of entitlement to rule, what is decisive is the *fact* that no one has any because all are equal. George III claimed to be king by the grace of God—*Dei gratia rex*—but Locke and the Americans who, with Jefferson, joined in the Declaration of Independence denied this claim. If all men are by nature free and equal, then no man may rule another without that other's consent. It is consent alone that makes an individual a member of a civil society, and only by or with the consent of that society may it be justly governed. The power to govern society comes from the people constituting that society—as free and equal individuals each yields his right, or power, to govern himself to the government they collectively institute—and it is exercised at their pleasure. This is what is meant by popular sovereignty.

On the occasion when government is instituted, however, that sovereignty will be exercised by a majority; as Locke makes clear, on that occasion the majority rules.[9] Given the improbability if not the impossibility of unanimity on the great issues to be determined, this is as it must be; with everyone casting an equally weighted vote, authority goes with the greater number. Acting, therefore, on behalf of the whole society, the majority is charged with the heavy responsibility of determining the form of government that will best secure the rights of all.

It should be understood that men might be in complete agreement on the right of the people to institute government and the ends to be served by the government instituted and yet have sharply divergent views on the best form of government. (That was surely the situation in the United States in 1787.) It is in this situation that the majority is authorized to act for all, and it is no derogation from the principle of popular sovereignty if the majority decides to institute a nonmajoritarian form of government. Popular sovereignty does not necessarily lead to popular or democratic government; it may even lead to monarchical government.[10] This is clear from the Declaration of Independence, which speaks of "governments"—governments in general—deriving their just powers from the consent of the governed, not only of a particular form of government. Then, too, it speaks of "any form of government" becoming destructive of the ends of government, which suggests not only that a democratic as well as a monarchical government might misgovern, or even become tyrannical,[11] but that a nondemocratic government is capable of governing properly. In short, the principles associated with popular sovereignty cover the authorization, the ends, but not the forms of government. Aware of this and of society's inability to agree on the best form, and aware as well of the propensity of those who govern to misgovern under whatever form, those charged with the responsibility of instituting government will act with great circumspection, leaving as little as possible to chance. Entering into a compact according to which each of them gives up his natural right to govern himself in favor of a government whose purpose is to secure the rights of all, they will see the necessity of reducing that compact to writing.

They are not, after all, creating a sovereign with the unrestricted authority "to make laws for the Peace, Order, and Good Government" of the country;[12] the people themselves retain the sovereign authority.[13] The government they are instituting will have the limited purpose of securing their rights—including emphatically their right to pursue a happiness each of them defines for himself—and otherwise leaving them alone. They will, therefore, specify the powers granted and the powers withheld and, to guard against the misuse of the powers granted, will organize them in a certain way. It is conceivable (but not likely) that they themselves might tacitly agree to all the detailed provisions of the compact each is making with all the others, but, because that compact is binding on their posterity as well as on themselves, they have an additional reason to embody it in a written document. Besides, even the immediate parties to a compact sometimes forget their obligations under it, especially when it is to their advantage to do so. As Madison also said, "the legitimate meaning of the Instrument [of government] must be derived from the text itself,"[14] and that meaning can be confidently ascertained only when the text can be read and not merely recalled. For all these reasons, popular sovereignty requires or leads to a written constitution.

State Sovereignty

Even the motto of the United States—*e pluribus unum*—lends some plausibility to the state sovereignty argument. In the beginning there were indeed "many," and much of the early history of the United States was dominated by a dispute over the effort to make from, or of, or out of the many, one. No one disagreed that in the very beginning there were many colonies. The issue disputed was whether those colonies became states before there was a United States, and that was not resolved until 1865, when the self-styled Confederate States of America were defeated on the battlefield.

In the name of state sovereignty, the eleven states of the confederacy had "seceded" from the Union and fought what they were pleased to call the War between the States. As sovereign powers (or so they claimed), they had been parties to a contract in 1787–1788, which, as sovereign powers (or so they claimed), each of them was entitled to revoke, thereby ending its association with the others. Here, for example, is South Carolina's Ordinance of Secession of December 20, 1860:

> We, the people of the State of South Carolina, in Convention assembled, do declare and ordain, and it is hereby declared and ordained, that the ordinance adopted by us in Convention, on the 23rd day of May, in the year of our Lord 1788, whereby the Constitution of the United States was ratified, and also all Acts and parts of Acts of the General Assembly of this State ratifying the amendments of the said Constitution, are hereby repealed, and that the union now subsisting between South

Carolina and other States under the name of the United States of America is hereby dissolved.[15]

Four days later, in language strikingly similar to that used in the Declaration of Independence,[16] the state announced that with the ordinance it had resumed its "separate and equal place among nations."[17] Here, in a phrase, is embodied the essence of the state sovereignty argument: it was not as "one people" but as thirteen discrete peoples—as "free and independent states," to cite the phrase that appears three times in the last paragraph of the Declaration of Independence—that independence was declared in 1776.

More than anyone else, Abraham Lincoln was responsible for the defeat of this Confederate project. It was he who challenged its pretensions—ultimately, the right of its people to enslave black people and carry them into the territories of the United States—he who forged a political coalition that captured control of the national government from its representatives in Washington, he who refused the compromise that might have precluded the war, he who sustained the cause of freedom throughout the four terrible years of that war, and, as president, he who was charged with the responsibility of countering its argument of sovereign right.[18]

His argument was that the Union was older than any of the states and had created them as states. Before that they had been "dependent colonies," and in this capacity they had created the Union that "threw off their dependence for them." Not one of them had ever been a state "out of the Union." What the Declaration of Independence declares to be "free and independent states," he pointed out, were described as the "United Colonies"; and the plain object of the men who issued it "was not to declare their independence of one another, or of the Union, but directly the contrary, as their mutual pledge, and their mutual action, before, at the time, and afterwards, abundantly show."[19]

In response the Confederates of 1860 could point to the Articles of Confederation. Though written in 1777 by the "Delegates of the United States in Congress assembled"—a point for Lincoln—they were agreed to in 1778 by the "undersigned Delegates of the States" and, of course, during the subsequent three years, ratified by the legislatures of the states. Furthermore, the Articles flatly declare that "each state retains its sovereignty, freedom and independence"—a point for the Confederates. Beyond that, in the Congress, after as well as before the Articles, voting was done by states. (A plan prepared by Benjamin Franklin that provided for voting by individuals was rejected by the Congress.)[20] And, finally, the Articles could be amended only with the consent of the "legislatures of every state."

On the basis of such textual evidence, the Confederates of 1860 concluded that the states existed before the United States,[21] that the states first constituted the United States when they ratified the Articles of Confederation and Perpetual Union, and that any state was free at any time to withdraw from the Union. On the basis of the same evidence, the "confederates" of 1787 opposed the new Constitution. They did not, of course, succeed in preventing its adoption, but they did succeed in putting their mark on it.[22]

Try as they might, the advocates of popular sovereignty and consolidated government—the nationalists—learned that they could not ignore the states and the political authority they had accumulated. This fact was driven home to them by William Paterson, one of the New Jersey delegates to the 1787 Constitutional Convention. On the floor were two constitutional plans, one providing for a strong national government and the other, introduced by Paterson himself, providing for a system under which the states would have retained much of their power. In this context he issued the following almost defiant challenge to the nationalists:

> If we argue the matter on the supposition that no Confederacy at present exists, it cannot be denied that all the States stand on the footing of equal sovereignty. All therefore must concur before any can be bound. . . . If we argue on the fact that a federal compact actually exists, and consult the articles of it we still find an equal Sovereignty to be the basis of it.[23]

This, as Herbert Storing once wrote, was the dilemma the proponents of the states challenged the nationalists to resolve. Within the Articles or outside, the states stood on a footing of sovereign equality. "The equality could be relinquished only with the consent of the states concerned, a consent which the states were under absolutely no obligation of any kind to give, and which the small states did not propose to give." Their position was strengthened by the fact that in the convention, as in the Congress, voting was done by states.

In their opposition to a strong national government there was, undeniably, an element of parochialism and perhaps a lack of vision. (Some historians have accused them of being "men of little faith.") But there was more to their opposition than a selfish desire to hold on to their local offices or a fear of being overwhelmed by men of greater talent. And they certainly could not be justly accused of a hostility to republican government. On the contrary, with the support of some of the greatest names in political philosophy—Aristotle, for example, Montesquieu, and Rousseau—they could argue that republican government could not be exercised over a territory so large as that comprehended by the thirteen states. As one of them wrote, so extensive and various a territory "cannot be governed in freedom" except in a confederation of states. Within each state, "opinion founded on the knowledge of those who govern, procures obedience without force. But remove the opinion, which must fall with a knowledge of characters in so widely extended a country, and force then becomes necessary to secure the purposes of civil government."[24] Their view of the American situation and what might safely be done about it is reflected in the letter by which the Continental Congress transmitted the proposed Articles of Confederation to the various state legislatures:

> This business . . . has . . . been attended with uncommon embarrassment and delay, which the most anxious solicitude and persevering diligence could not prevent. To form a permanent union, accommodated to the opinion and wishes of the delegates of so many states, differing in habits, produce, commerce, and internal police, was found to be a work which nothing but time and reflection, conspiring with a disposition to conciliate, could mature and accomplish.[25]

If the size and diversity of the country made it difficult to unite under the Articles of Confederation, where Congress was charged mainly with providing the means of defense against possible foreign enemies, how much more difficult—and, indeed, hazardous—it was to unite for the purpose of domestic governance.

In laying such stress on the diversity of the various peoples and economies, as well as on the great distances involved, these early proponents of state sovereignty—who, to do them justice, are better described as proponents of small republics—may have exaggerated the difficulties of union. Leaving aside the African slaves, Americans were all, or nearly all, of British origin and spoke a common tongue; they were nearly all Christians (the vast majority of them Protestants); and, as Tocqueville would later point out, they had all "arrived at the same state of civilization."

> I do not know of any European nation, however small, that does not present less uniformity in its different provinces than the American people, which occupy a territory as extensive as one half of Europe. The distance from Maine to Georgia is about one thousand miles; but the difference between the civilization of Maine and that of Georgia is slighter than the difference between the habits of Normandy and those of Brittany. Maine and Georgia, which are placed at the opposite extremities of a great empire, have therefore more real inducements to form a confederation than Normandy and Brittany, which are separated only by a brook.[26]

He was, of course, writing of an America that had been living under the Constitution for almost fifty years, but it is doubtful that, in these cultural respects, it had changed very much during that time. In the important respects, the Americans were one people living in thirteen states. They were united in their opinion that government was instituted to secure the rights with which all men are equally endowed and, in 1787, divided only on the question of the form of government that would best secure these rights. What would divide them later on, and would threaten to divide them permanently, was the slavery issue. The framers of the Constitution had reason to believe—or, at least, they chose to believe—that that problem would be resolved with the passage of time.

A More Perfect Union

The Americans of 1787 may not have agreed on the character of the Union or on when it was constituted, but they agreed that the Articles under which it was being governed were in need of revision. Even the state sovereignty men—soon to be given the name Antifederalists—were willing to concede that under the Articles the powers of Congress were inadequate to the "exigencies of the Union."

With the concurrence of at least nine of the thirteen states represented, Congress had the authority to borrow money and "emit bills on the credit of the united states," but it had no sure source of revenue out of which to repay the loans or redeem the bills. For revenue it had to rely on the willingness of the individual states to pay the assessments levied on them; it had no way to enforce payment. It was empowered by the Articles to discharge the debts incurred during the War of Independence, but, in the event, it lacked the funds to pay the soldiers who had fought that war. It could— again with the concurrence of nine states—enter into treaties with foreign nations, but it was unable to compel the British to honor certain provisions under the Treaty of Paris ending the War of Independence. It could regret what Madison called the "trespasses of the states on the rights of each other" but do nothing to prevent them. It could do little by way of promoting commerce among the states or protecting the means by which it was carried on with other nations. It could do nothing to compel, or even to induce, the attendance of delegates and, as a result, frequently lacked the quorum that would enable it to carry on its business. Thus, for example, aware of the powers it lacked, it might compose amendments to the Articles with a view to increasing its authority, only to be frustrated by the absence of the quorum required to bring them to a vote. With such evident displays of its impotence, it risked becoming an object of open contempt, not only to Europeans but, with more pernicious consequences, to Americans of "weight and understanding," state sovereignty men and nationalists alike.

The former, while acknowledging the desirability of alterations to the Articles, were ever fearful of embarking on the course that would produce them. Richard Henry Lee, for example, agreed that Congress ought to be able to ensure state compliance with its fiscal requisitions, but he was reluctant to concede the means by which it might be done. The difficulty, he wrote to George Mason, is "how to give the power in such manner as that it may only be used for good, and not abused to bad, purposes. Whoever shall solve this difficulty will receive the thanks of this and future generations."[27] Meanwhile, especially to a government not under the immediate and close control of the people, it was better to withhold than to grant powers. "I think Sir," Lee wrote to Samuel Adams, "that the first maxim of a man who loves liberty should be, never to grant to rulers an atom of power that is not most clearly and indispensably necessary for the safety and well being of Society."[28] Beyond this, he was of the opinion that mere structural changes would not solve the problem. "I fear it is more in vicious manners, than mistakes in form that we must seek for the causes of the present discontent."[29] And the cure for vicious manners could be prescribed only in the small republic in which the people would (in Rousseau's sense) be forced to be free and forced to be virtuous. As one New Yorker put it, government should rest on "a substantial yeomanry" because they are "more temperate, of better morals, and less ambition, than the great."[30] Anyone harboring such sentiments was certain to distrust a government empowered to promote foreign commerce and become an active force in the world of nations.

The nationalists were united in the judgment that political salvation was not to be had in the small agrarian republic depending on the "substantial yeomanry" (whose existence in substantial number they tended anyway to doubt). It followed that, for them, the remedy lay not in amendments conceding a few additional powers to the Congress but, rather, in the replacement of the Articles with a wholly new constitution of government. As early as 1778 Alexander Hamilton was calling for radical measures; in due course he was joined by Robert Morris, Rufus King, John Jay, James Madison (who, characteristically, prepared a careful draft of the "vices of the Political System of the United States"), and others, including, most significantly, George Washington.

By the summer of 1786, Washington was describing the reluctance to admit the need of national powers for national purposes as "popular absurdity and madness"; the country was faced with a "crisis," and means had to be found to meet it.[31] He was especially impatient with anyone who hesitated to recognize the country's dependence on foreign commerce and to yield the powers required to promote and control it.

> It has long been a speculative question among Philosophers and wise men, whether foreign Commerce is of real advantage to any country; that is, whether the luxury, effeminacy, and corruptions which are introduced along with it; are counterbalanced by the convenience and wealth which it brings with it; but the decision of this question is of very little importance to us: we have abundant reason to be convinced, that the spirit for Trade which pervades these States is not to be restrained; it behooves us then to establish just principles; and this, any more than other matters of national concern, cannot be done by thirteen heads differently constructed and organized. The necessity, therefore, of a countrouling power is obvious; and why it should be withheld is beyond my comprehension.[32]

Still, the state sovereignty people hesitated. They could point to some solid advance by the country under the Articles (and the greatest achievement of Congress—the Northwest Ordinance—was to come in 1787 even as the convention was meeting), and it was only natural that they should be apprehensive of a general convention charged with proposing constitutional amendments. (Have we not heard our own contemporaries express fears that a constitutional convention called on the application of two-thirds of the states would be a "runaway convention?") And perhaps the most difficult task faced by the nationalists was convincing their opponents that free republican government could be established in a country the size of the United States. Conventional wisdom had it that that was impossible. Thus, while there was a general agreement on the need for changes to render the Congress "adequate to the exigencies of the Union," the contending parties disagreed on the sort of union they wanted to build.

The attempts at union building began in 1754 when, at the instigation of Benjamin Franklin, commissioners representing eleven of the thirteen colonies drew up the Albany (New York) Plan of Union. Designed to promote a common and more effective defense against the French and Indians, as well as to foster further colonization under British auspices, the plan would have provided a measure of popular self-government combined with royal government in the person of a president general appointed by the Crown.[33] The extent of the disunity then existing among the colonies is reflected in the decision to submit the plan to Westminster, asking it to be established by act of Parliament. As Franklin explained, the jealousy and distrust then prevailing among the colonies persuaded the commissioners that nothing would induce the colonies to agree to a common plan of action, let alone a common government.[34] In the event, in Franklin's words, "the Crown disapproved it, as having plac'd too much Weight in the democratic Part of the Constitution; and every [colonial] Assembly as having allow'd too much to [royal] Prerogative. So it was totally rejected."[35]

A somewhat similar proposal was drawn up by loyalist Joseph Galloway in September 1774, after the outbreak of hostilities. Taking the form of a petition by the Continental Congress, it asked the King-in-Parliament to establish a political union, "not only among [the colonies], but with the Mother State."[36] But by a vote of 6–5 the Continental Congress (voting by colonies) rejected the plan; and, with that rejection, the die was cast for war and the formal declaring of independence. The time had passed when a union could be forged—peaceably, at least—under the auspices of the Crown.

It was by no means certain, however, that a union "more perfect" than the one achieved under the Articles of Confederation could be forged even under the auspices of dire necessity. Somehow—British military ineptitude and the assistance of France had a lot to do with it—the war with Britain was won; but within less than a year after the last engagement of that war, Washington (still commander in chief) was warning the states of the impending crisis. Unless they could agree to forgo their jealousies and institute a proper national government, the Union, he predicted, could not be of long duration. "For, according to the system of Policy the states shall adopt at this moment, they will stand or fall, and by their confirmation or lapse, it is yet to be decided, whether the Revolution must ultimately be considered as a blessing or a curse: a blessing or a curse, not to the present age alone, for with our fate will the destiny of unborn Millions be involved."[37]

Although Washington's word carried a weight greater than that of any other American, not everyone was persuaded by it. Some remained irresolute. Others, including men who were later to become enthusiastic supporters of the new Constitution, had well-founded doubts about the feasibility of a more perfect union of continental proportions and wondered whether the solution for the country's problems did not consist in regional confederations. "Some of our enlightened men," wrote Benjamin Rush in the fall of 1786, "who begin to despair of a more complete union of the states in Congress have secretly proposed an Eastern, Middle, and Southern Confederacy to be united by an alliance offensive and defensive."

> These confederacies they say will be united by nature, by interest, and by manners, and consequently they will be safe, agreeable and durable. The first will include the four New England states and New York. The second will include New Jersey, Pennsylvania, Delaware, and Maryland; and the last Virginia, North and South Carolina, and Georgia. The foreign and domestic debt of the United States they say shall be divided justly between each of the new confederations. This plan of a new continental government is at present a mere speculation. Perhaps necessity, or rather divine providence, may drive us to it.[38]

This theme was to be sounded again during the 1787 convention, as well as during the ratification debates, when Hamilton suggested that a man would have to be "far gone in Utopian speculations" to doubt that these "partial confederacies" would have "frequent and violent contests with each other."[39]

Washington's efforts began to be rewarded in 1786 when nine states accepted Virginia's invitation to convene at Annapolis, Maryland, ostensibly to consider problems of interstate commerce. Only five states (New York, New Jersey, Delaware, Pennsylvania, and Virginia), represented by the small total of twelve "commissioners," were actually present when the convention met in September; but among those twelve were Hamilton and Madison. Working together and undeterred by the apparent lack of interest on the part of the states or the real lack of legal authority from the Congress, they contrived to have the commissioners adopt a report (written by Hamilton) that called upon the legislatures of the five attending states (and by implication all the states) to appoint delegates to meet "at Philadelphia on the second Monday in May next, to take into consideration the situation of the United States, to devise such further provisions as shall appear to them necessary to render the constitution of the Federal Government adequate to the exigencies of the Union." The report ended with an acknowledgment that the "Commissioners could not with propriety address these observations and sentiments to any but the states they [had] the honor to Represent," but they concluded nevertheless that it would not be improper to transmit "copies" of the report, not only to the executives of the other states but to the Congress.[40]

This démarche produced the desired result. In February 1787, on a motion by Massachusetts, Congress resolved that it was "expedient" that there should be a convention of the states "for the sole and express purpose of revising the Articles of Confederation and reporting to Congress and the several [state] legislatures such alterations and provisons therein as shall . . . render the federal constitution adequate to the exigencies of Government & the preservation of the Union."[41] The convention would exceed the authority given it—by the Congress as well as by the twelve states (all except Rhode Island) that appointed delegates—but there could be no denying that it was authorized to meet and to do *something* on behalf of union. This was to have happy consequences.

The Philadelphia Convention

There was no dispute concerning the principle governing the selection of delegates to the convention. Except in South Carolina, where the legislature authorized the governor to make the appointments, the delegates were chosen by the state legislatures, which, in almost every instance, specified the number required to constitute a quorum of the state's delegation at the convention and, thereby, to cast its vote.[42] The delegates represented their particular states; their number was determined by the states—the smallest being New Hampshire's (two) and the largest Pennsylvania's (eight)—they voted as states; and their expenses, when paid at all, were paid by the states, not the Congress.[43] Yet, with all that, many of them came to Philadelphia determined to diminish the political force of the states.

Some were unknown (and remained so), but most of them came not as strangers to one another. The more distinguished among them especially had worked together in the Congress or the army, and, even when that was not the case, knew one another by reputation. They were a remarkably learned and talented group of men. Even Richard Henry Lee, who did his best to prevent the ratification of the Constitution, acknowledged that "America probably never will see an assembly of men of like number more respectable." Their average age was forty-three, but Franklin at eighty-one and two members of the Connecticut delegation—Roger Sherman at sixty-six and William Johnson at sixty—were largely responsible for making it that high. Four of them were not yet thirty, and fully a third—including four of the most distinguished (James Madison, Alexander Hamilton, Gouverneur Morris, and Edmund Randolph)—were in their thirties.

All being of British stock and native speakers of English, they had no need of simultaneous translation of speeches or materials. Their discourse was further facilitated by their having read the same books, lived under and, in many cases, practiced the same law, and shared in a common political tradition. Without exception, they respected the rules or forms of doing business, which was altogether to be expected because they were assembled to write a constitution. By secret ballot (but, as it turned out, unanimously) they elected George Washington presiding officer (or president) of the convention, and, it being a custom or formality with which they were all familiar, two of them—Robert Morris of Pennsylvania and John Rutledge of South Carolina—"conducted" him to the chair. They elected a secretary, who would keep the official journal, and "appointed" a messenger and a doorkeeper. On formal motion, they ordered that a committee be appointed to draw up the rules of order and then, by ballot, named Hamilton of New York, George Wythe of Virginia, and Charles Pinckney of South Carolina to that committee. Drawn up over the weekend and, after debate and amendment, adopted on Monday and Tuesday, the rules governed the forms both of behavior and of doing business.

In the first category were rules such as these: members wishing to speak shall rise and address the president (and, when another is speaking, they shall not hold discourse with each other "or read a book, pamphlet, or paper, printed or manuscript"); and "When the House shall adjourn every Member shall stand in his place until the President pass him." With such rules the delegates demonstrated a respect not for one another as individuals or for George Washington the man (although they did mostly respect one another and unanimously and greatly respected Washington) but for the dignity and importance of the enterprise in which they were engaged. As they saw it, they were engaged in demonstrating the truth of what was then only an untested proposition, namely, that it was possible for men to govern themselves, or to be governed, by rules of their own devising. Formal rules serve as restraints on behavior, and, because it depends on such restraints, constitutional government is government according to formal rules.[44] The men gathered in Philadelphia to write a constitution acted formally because they had an important example to set.

In the second category were rules of procedure designed in part to promote deliberation (but with an eye on the need for decision) and in part to permit compromise. Prominent among these were rules guaranteeing the privacy and, indeed, the secrecy of their deliberations. Separated from their constituents by the exclusion of the public and the press (to say nothing of the television cameras), the delegates were free to speak frankly and, when appropriate, tentatively rather than definitively—with no galleries to play to, delegates had little reason to score debating points against other speakers—and to listen carefully. It was understood that they might change their minds, and the rules made it easy to do so.[45] It was also understood that it might be desirable to reconsider matters, even those decided by majority vote, and the rules permitted that as well.

These rules were adopted on May 29, after little debate and remarkably little disagreement,[46] and they were to serve the convention well throughout the almost four months of its meetings. They helped to ensure deliberations that were serious—the record is free of any evidence of persiflage—and, what is more important, efficacious: the convention produced a constitutional document to which Washington and thirty-eight delegates (at least one from each of the twelve states present) affixed their signatures.

Although the rules required secrecy—even the official journal was not printed until 1818—they did not forbid the members to take notes of the deliberations. It is to these, and especially to Madison's, that we owe knowledge of what was said and done in the convention. Because he was impressed by the significance of their enterprise, Madison, working at night from notes compiled during the course of each working day, accomplished the herculean task of transcribing the debates, accurately and fully. In an unfinished paper written many years later, he explained what led him to do this:

> The curiosity I had felt during my researches into the History of the most distinguished Confederacies, particularly those of antiquity, and the deficiency I found in the means of satisfying it more especially in what related to the process, the principles—the reasons, & the anticipations, which prevailed in the formation of them, determined me to preserve as far as I could an exact account of what might pass in the Convention whilst executing its trust, with the magnitude of which I was duly impressed, as I was the gratification promised to future curiosity by an authentic exhibition of the objects, the opinions & the reasonings from which the new System of Govt. was to receive its peculiar structure & organization. Nor was I unaware of the value of such a contribution to the fund of materials for the History of a Constitution on which would be staked the happiness of a young people great even in its infancy, and possibly the cause of Liberty through[ou]t the world.[47]

Madison did not explain why, in his judgment, future writers of constitutions could find instruction in an account of the proceedings of the 1787 convention, but Herbert Storing suggests that it could be found in the members' awareness of the need for decision. It was this that made compromise possible, and clearly compromise was required if there was to be a constitution. The contending principles—popular and state sovereignty—were each represented in the convention, but, as Storing writes, an unyielding pursuit of either principle would almost certainly have resulted in its irretrievable loss.

> The two sides found the grounds of compromise in their common desire to "form a more perfect union," though their ideas of a perfect union differed. The debates leading to the Great Compromise yield insight into a great question of principle lying at the heart of the American political order. They also yield an example of how such questions are properly approached in political life.[48]

It is to the debates culminating in that Great Compromise that we must now devote our attention.

The rules adopted, the delegates turned immediately to the substantive business of the convention. On behalf of the Virginia delegation, Edmund Randolph (the state's governor as well as a member of its delegation), after outlining what he described as the defects of the confederation, formally proposed a set of fifteen resolutions that together amounted to a comprehensive plan of government. Prepared mainly by the indefatigable Madison, the so-called Virginia Plan called for the establishment of a strong national government to replace the Congress of states, a government with a national executive, a national and independent judiciary, and a national bicameral legislature with the power to legislate "in all cases to which the separate States are incompetent" and, most significant, the power "to negative all laws passed by the several States, contravening . . . the articles of Union."[49] Its first branch was to be elected directly by the people of the several states—a significant departure from the principle of the Articles of Confederation—and its second branch by the members of the first, "out of a proper number of persons nominated by the individual [state] legislatures." In each branch the number of representatives to which a state would be entitled would depend on its quota of "contribution" or the number of its free inhabitants. It was this provision that gave rise to the dispute that occupied the convention for an entire month.

For the first two weeks after its introduction on May 29, however, the Virginia Plan dominated the debates, and by June 13 it had been substantially adopted by the convention, thus illustrating the importance of being first in the field with a plan of action. Even the provision respecting the proportioning of representatives was "generally relished" and would have been adopted as early as May 30 had not George Read of Delaware moved that consideration of it be postponed. Reminding the convention that "the deputies from Delaware were restrained by their commission" from assenting to any such rule of representation—an instruction for which he was himself partly responsible—Read explained that, if the rule were adopted, he and his Delaware colleagues might have "to retire from the Convention."[50] This threat marked one of the low points of the convention. By the time (June 9) debate on this rule was renewed, the number of delegates of Read's persuasion had grown to the point where they were able to offer effective resistance to what, up to then, had been a strong nationalist tide. Their state-sovereignty motion—according to which states would be equally represented in the second branch of the legislature—failed by a single vote. By the same margin (6–5), the nationalists' motion calling for proportional representation in the second (as well as in the first) branch was adopted.[51] But so wide a disagreement could not be settled by a majority so narrow, not on so fundamental an issue. These votes were taken on June 11; on June 13 the Committee of the Whole reported the Randolph proposals as amended, and the house (that is, the convention) postponed consideration of them until the following day. On June 14, however, on a motion by William Paterson of New Jersey, significantly seconded by Randolph, consideration was put off until June 15, and the house promptly adjourned. On June 15 Paterson introduced what came to be known as the New Jersey (or small-state) Plan. The convention now had two plans before it, and the issue was fairly joined.[52]

Offered as a series of amendments to the Articles of Confederation, the New Jersey Plan would nevertheless have increased the powers of the general government in significant respects. Congress would have been authorized, for example, to levy duties on imported goods, thus providing the government with a source of income independent of the requisitions on the states; to coerce payment of those requisitions; and to make rules regulating foreign and domestic commerce and assess fines against anyone found to be in violation of them. Finally, the plan called for the establishment of a federal judiciary and a plural executive empowered to enforce federal law and to appoint "all federal officers not otherwise provided for."[53] If adopted, these amendments would have gone some distance toward remedying the defects of the Articles, but they would have left the principle of state sovereignty or quasi-sovereignty intact. Their chief advantage over the Virginia Plan consisted in their "legality"; by adopting them, the convention would not be exceeding its authority. Paterson made much of this point.

Before going on to discuss the resolution of the conflict between these sharply different plans, it is necessary at least to mention other items on the convention's agenda. These included the method by which the chief executive was to be chosen, the length of his term of office, and, of course, the powers he was to exercise; the characteristics of the judiciary (one supreme court or, in addition, a complete system of federal courts); the qualifications of electors for the popular branch of the legislature; the size of the second branch and the qualifications of its members; the extent of the legislative powers, including the power to regulate the slave trade; and the methods of ratifying and amending the Constitution. These and other items provoked spirited and, in some cases, prolonged debate, but in none of them was the disagreement one of principle. Everyone agreed, if not in every case on the superiority, then at least on the appropriateness, of a republican form of government. "No other form would be acceptable to the American people." But they also recognized the temporary necessity to accommodate the southern states on the slavery question. When debating the Virginia Plan, they agreed on the need to provide for legislative, executive, and judicial powers and to separate them one from another; in that context they also agreed that the legislature should consist of two houses. In addition to the slavery "interest," there were commercial, agrarian, small-state, large-state, and a variety of other "interests," but none that could not somehow be accommodated.

The one issue that embodied a difference of principle was that of representation. So grave were the differences on this issue, and so seemingly obdurate were the parties disputing it, that, as if in desperation, Franklin suggested daily "prayers imploring the assistance of Heaven." That was on June 28. Two days later Gunning Bedford of Delaware delivered a long and bitter attack on the large-state delegates, proponents of the Virginia Plan. "The little States," he said, "will meet the large ones on no ground but that of the Confederation." Referring then to the argument that this was America's last opportunity to establish good government, he indicated that he was under no apprehensions on this score. The large states, he said, dared not dissolve the confederation. "If they do the small ones will find some foreign ally of more honor and good faith, who will take them by the hand and do them justice."[54]

This speech marked the lowest point of the convention. Yet, by openly threatening a course of action that the other delegates had long feared as a possibility, Bedford, by his very recklessness, may have served the cause of compromise. At any rate, the compromise was not long in coming. Its terms are familiar and readily comprehended—one branch of the legislature would represent the people of the United States and the other the states as states—but its elements deserve to be elaborated.

It is not sufficient—to some extent it may even be inaccurate—to describe the dispute as a clash of "interests." What, besides large (or small) numbers, did the large (or small) states have in common that caused them to act in concert? "We might say, for example, that the 'interest' of the small states was to maintain a degree of influence in the affairs of the Union disproportionate to the number of people they contained; and that the 'interest' of the large states was to use their greater population to dominate the Union."[55] As Madison was to point out, however, and as our subsequent history attests, the states (and, indeed, the regions) were more divided by material interests than they were by the size of their populations; and an interest that divides some states may unite others, regardless of their size. Besides, the debate was not carried on in those terms. The delegates did not speak of maintaining or acquiring political influence; they spoke the language of political principle, and there is no reason to believe that they were speaking dishonestly or disingenuously.

Roger Sherman of Connecticut (a small state) was opposed to the Virginia Plan, but not for selfish reasons. The powers granted to the national government by that plan were far in excess of what was needed by a government whose objects, in his judgment, were very few indeed: defense against foreign danger and against internal disputes and a resort to force, treaties with foreign nations, and "regulating foreign commerce, & drawing revenue from it."[56] He firmly believed that "all other matters civil & criminal would be much better in the hands of the States." This was a respectable and venerable argument. James Madison of Virginia (a large state), the principal author of the Virginia Plan, "differed from the member from Connecticut (Mr. Sherman) in thinking the objects mentioned to be all the principal ones that required a National Govt." Those were certainly important and necessary objects, "but he combined with them the necessity, of providing more effectually for the security of private rights, and the steady dispensation of Justice."[57] He then proceeded to make the argument—which he was to repeat in *Federalist* Nos. 10 and 51—that only in the large commercial republic would it be possible to control the effects of factions[58] and, with that control, provide the desired security for private rights. What divided Sherman and Madison was a disagreement about the form of government best calculated "to secure these rights."

If, as the Antifederalists argued more cogently and fully during the ratification debates, rights could best be secured in a relatively small and essentially agrarian republic, where the government was kept close to the people by means of a fully democratic franchise, annual elections, and rotation of office, where manners would be kept simple and pure by means of moral education and the exclusion of foreigners as well as of foreign luxuries, then it followed that the principal seat of government would have to be the state. Someone of this persuasion would think of himself as first of all a citizen of his state and would stress the rights of states and the illegality of a plan depriving the states of their equal representation in the confederation; and, because the objects of the confederation were few, he would grant few powers to its government.

If, as Madison believed, rights could be secured only in a large republic, consisting of a wide variety of economic interests and religious sects, where it would be possible to prevent the formation of a majority faction, then it followed that the principal seat of government would have to be the nation. Someone of this persuasion—for example, James Wilson of Pennsylvania—would think of himself first of all as an American: "Among the first sentiments expressed in the first Congress one was that Virginia is no more. That Massachusetts is no [more], that Pennsylvania is no more etc. We are now one nation of brethren."[59] He would also argue—and Madison and Wilson did repeatedly argue—that the proponents of the New Jersey Plan were contending for a principle that was "confessedly unjust," contrary to the republican principle,[60] which required representation according to population.

But, of course, that principle was applicable only if it were true that the one nation had superseded the many colonies, and it was this that Paterson denied. "If," as he argued on June 16, "a proportional representation be right, why do we not vote so here?" Voting in the convention was by states because there was a confederation governed by Articles that recognized the sovereignty of the states. And the Congress that governed that confederation had called the convention for the limited purpose of revising the Articles. In the light of these instructions, the Virginia Plan was illegal, and Wilson's response—that the convention, while "authorized to *conclude nothing* [was] at liberty to *propose anything*"[61]—was clearly insufficient. Except that it begged the question, Randolph's response was better. He was not, he said, scrupulous on this matter of their authority. "When the salvation of the Republic was at stake, it would be treason to our trust, not to propose what we found necessary."[62] But what was it whose salvation was at stake, *the* republic or, as Paterson contended, the "league of friendship" among many republics?

This issue was presumably resolved when on June 19 the convention, by the comfortable margin of four votes (7–3, with one state divided), rejected Paterson's New Jersey Plan and resolved to continue consideration of Randolph's Virginia Plan. Undeterred, however, Luther Martin of Maryland continued to protest that on the separation from Great Britain the states were placed "in a state of nature towards each other [and] would have remained in that state till this time, but for the confederation."[63] A week later he launched a two-day harangue repeating the familiar legal objections to the Virginia Plan and warning of a dissolution of whatever union there was if the plan were to be adopted. Patiently, Madison explained that Martin's Maryland and the other small states had more to fear from dissolution than did his Virginia and the other large states:

> In a word; the two extremes before us are a perfect separation and a perfect incorporation, of the 13 states. In the first case they would be independent nations subject to no law, but the law of nations. In the last, they would be mere counties of one entire republic, subject to one common law. In the first case the smaller states would have everything to fear from the larger. In the last they would have nothing to fear.[64]

In the event, however, it was to be neither a perfect separation nor a perfect incorporation, or union. It was, however, to be a "more perfect" union than that achieved under the Articles.

Madison's speech was followed by Franklin's call for daily prayers. Then, on the next day (June 29), William Johnson of Connecticut proposed the terms from which, two weeks later, the compromise was to emerge. Just as Franklin had urged delegates to acknowledge their need of divine assistance—which is to say, to recognize their fallibility—so Johnson now asked them to recognize the facts governing their situation. "The controversy must be endless whilst Gentlemen differ in the grounds of their arguments; those on one side considering the states as districts of people composing one political Society; those on the other considering them as so many political societies."[65] Whatever the truth according to political theory or political history, in political fact the states were both districts *and* societies, and "the two ideas embraced on different sides, instead of being opposed to each other, ought to be combined; that in *one* branch the *people*, ought to be represented; in the *other*, the *States*." On that same day the convention voted (6–4, with one state divided) that the "rules of suffrage in the 1st branch ought not to be according to that established by the Articles of Confederation." Oliver Ellsworth then moved that the rule of suffrage in the second branch should be that of the Articles. Like his Connecticut colleague Johnson, he urged the convention to accept this "compromise." We were, he said, "partly national; partly federal." Wilson, Franklin, and Madison, each in his own way, contributed to the movement toward compromise, but it was at this point that Gunning Bedford made his imprudent reference to the possibility that the small states might choose to form alliances with foreign powers. What happened next is best described in Storing's words:

> On the next working day [July 2], a vote was taken on the motion to allow each state an equal vote in the second branch. The result seems to suggest that Franklin's prayer for divine providence was not altogether fruitless, though human reason also played its part. The Maryland delegation was divided on this question, Daniel Jenifer being opposed to equal representation and Luther Martin in favor of it. Providentially, Jenifer was late in taking his seat that morning and Martin was thus able to cast the vote of Maryland in favor of the motion. The consequence of this was that when Georgia, the last state to be polled, was reached, instead of the question having been decided in the negative, five states had voted in favor of the motion and five states against. Ordinarily the whole of the four-man Georgia delegation would have voted against equal representation, but it happened that two of the members were absent. One of the remaining Georgians was Abraham Baldwin, who was a native of Connecticut and is supposed to have come under the moderating influence of the Connecticut delegation. In any case, Baldwin apparently feared that the Convention would break up unless a concession was made to the small states. By chance or providence, the absence of two of his colleagues put in his hands the power perhaps to determine whether there was to be a Union or not. Voting, contrary to his convictions, in favor of equal representation in the second branch, Baldwin divided Georgia's vote, maintained the tie, and kept open the way for compromise.[66]

The question was then turned over to a committee, and the convention adjourned. Working on July 3 and reporting on July 5, this committee made the following proposals, which were to be accepted as a package: each state to have an equal vote in the second branch of the legislature; all money bills to originate in the first branch and not to be amended in the second; and, in the first branch, each state to have one member for every 40,000 inhabitants or, lacking that number, at least one member. This was followed by more discussion in the convention, and still more questions were referred to committees, from one of which came the provision that direct taxes as well as representation should be apportioned among the states according to their number of inhabitants, counting three-fifths of the slaves for both purposes. Finally, on July 16, this so-called Great Compromise was accepted, 5–4 (with Massachusetts, a large state, divided). The negative votes were cast by Pennsylvania, Virginia, South Carolina, and Georgia. In a note appended to his journal, Madison reports that the next morning "a number of the members from [these] larger states . . . met for the purpose of consulting on the proper steps to be taken in consequence of [this] vote."[67] Being unable to agree on the significance of giving the states an equal vote in the second branch—"time was wasted in vague conversation on the subject"—or on the course of action they might then follow, the large-state delegates could do little other than acquiesce in the outcome.

Another two months were spent working out the details of the other provisions, but with this vote on July 16 the crisis was reached and passed. The constitution that came out of the convention was partly national, partly federal, but without question it was more national than federal. It provided for a national government modeled, on the whole, on the Virginia Plan; that is why Luther Martin and Lansing and Yates of New York refused to sign it. Paterson, Bedford, and Read (all of whom did sign) got their way on second-branch representation, and there was to be no national legislative negative on laws enacted by the states, but they won little else. (It can be doubted that they would have signed had they known that the national judiciary would possess such a negative.)[68] Ultimately, the small states had to admit that a more perfect union was a necessary condition of their continued existence as self-governing societies; they needed union more than the nationalists needed the states. Although the nationalists, in turn, denied that constitutional change required the unanimous agreement of the states (the Articles of Confederation to the contrary notwithstanding) and their plan of a large commercial republic in no way depended on the continued existence of the states, they had to recognize their need of something close to unanimity if, as Storing puts it, they were to establish the principle for which they contended, which was, after all, *union*.

The point should be made again that the delegates were in complete agreement that government is instituted to secure the rights of man; they disagreed merely on how those rights might best be secured. Strangely, perhaps, there was almost no discussion whatever in the convention of the necessity of a bill of rights;[69] for all we know, everyone agreed with what Hamilton was to say in the ratification debates, namely, that the Constitution was itself a bill of rights.[70] If so, they then agreed that rights are best secured in the very structure of a government that provides a "republican remedy for the diseases most incident to republican government."[71] The opponents of the Constitution—Patrick Henry prominent among them—seized on the absence of a bill of rights and exacted a promise from Madison to remedy this defect at the earliest opportunity. Madison honored this promise in the First Congress when he introduced the amendments that became the Bill of Rights in 1791, after ratification by the required three-fourths of the states. In this connection, it should be mentioned—if only to indicate one of the ways in which this oldest of written national constitutions differs from those written in the twentieth century—that not even the Bill of Rights refers specifically to political parties or to the rights to organize, strike, or work. Nor is there anywhere a reference to a ministry of culture, and considering what is sometimes done by governments under the label of "culture," Americans can probably be thankful for this omission. Standing as they did at the beginning of the modern constitutional era, the framers had a better opportunity, and perhaps a better reason, to weigh the advantages of classical political institutions. Thus, during the discussion of the structure of the second legislative branch, there were references to the institution of mixed government, or mixed regime. Why not, it was suggested by some delegates, add "weight" to the legislature by adding an element of aristocracy in the second branch, making it an American version of the British House of Lords? To which Charles Pinckney of South Carolina replied, because America does not have an aristocracy—"the materials for forming this balance or check do not exist"—and there is no prospect of its springing up out of a merchant class or, more generally, a commercial society.[72] If there was to be "weight" in the legislature, it would have to come not from great families but, as Madison made clear, from the smaller number of senators combined with the greater authority lodged in them.[73] The framers knew they were constituting government for an egalitarian people; their problem was to devise institutions making equality compatible with liberty.

Because of the states and their functioning governments and societies, the convention was able to avoid making decisions on matters that are usually thought to be of a constitutional nature. Foremost among these was religion. Except for including a provision (Article VI) forbidding religious tests as a qualification "to any Office or public Trust under the United States," the convention left religious matters to the states. The fact that, to one degree or another and in one or another of the Christian varieties, over half the states had an established religion undoubtedly made it easy, if not necessary, to ignore the matter. Another was education. It was proposed that the new Congress be empowered to establish a national university and "seminaries for the promotion of literature and the arts and sciences," but nothing came of this proposal, and to this day higher education remains under the control of the states and private institutions. As for elementary and secondary education, not only was the subject not discussed in the convention, but, to the extent to which such education existed at that time, it was a private matter. In his *Notes on the State of Virginia*, Jefferson elaborated a plan for free public education, but it was to be years before any state established such a system.

Still another subject was the qualifications of voters. These varied from state to state, and, in the one case where specification was necessary, the convention simply turned the matter over to the states; the electors in each state of members of the House of Representatives "shall have the Qualifications requisite for Electors of the most numerous Branch of the State Legislature." Senators were to be chosen directly by the state legislatures. As for the president, some delegates favored election by the legislature; others favored election by the states (by way of the governors, the legislatures, or electors chosen by governors or legislatures); but only Pennsylvania favored election by the "people at large." A long time was consumed before the convention settled on the electoral college system. Judges and other federal officers were to be appointed to office by the president with the consent of the Senate. Finally, the military, which plays so prominent a role in the politics of many countries, was conspicuously absent from the Philadelphia convention. The president was made commander in chief of the army and navy of the United States, but at the time the United States had not much of an army and very little of a navy. There were, in principle at least, state militias, and the president was given command of them "when called into the actual Service of the United States." As mentioned earlier, a variety of "interests" were represented in the convention, but not one of them could be described as military.

A brief word now on the convention's mode of procedure: the resolutions debated in the committee of the whole and, after being reported, adopted by the "house," were turned over to a five-man Committee of Detail; from these resolutions the committee produced a constitutional draft, printed copies of which were furnished to each member on August 6.[74] The finished draft of the Constitution was the work of the Committee of Style, particularly Gouverneur Morris; printed copies of its report were furnished to members on September 12.[75] Several days were spent debating various provisions in the committee's draft, and a few significant changes were made in it. One of these had to do with the amending clause (Article V). As drafted, this clause provided for amendments to the Constitution to be proposed by the Congress, either on its own initiative or on the application of two-thirds of the states. Because some delegates feared that Congress might not respond to an application from the states, this provision was changed to require Congress, on such an application, to call a convention for the purpose of proposing amendments. To the clause was also added a provision prohibiting amendments depriving a state, without its consent, "of its equal Suffrage in the Senate."[76] This took place Saturday, September 15. Then, on September 17, after an eloquent speech of Franklin (read for him by James Wilson) appealing to the delegates to overlook whatever they regarded as its faults, the engrossed Constitution was approved by a unanimous vote of the states (but not by a unanimous vote of the delegates).

The convention then resolved that "the preceding Constitution be laid before the United States in Congress assembled, and that it is the Opinion of this Convention, that it should afterwards be submitted to a Convention of Delegates, chosen in each State by the People thereof . . . for their Assent and Ratification."[77] The significance of this lay in the decision to seek the "approbation" of the people ("the foundation of all power," as Madison put it when the question was being debated on August 31) and not of the Congress. The convention further resolved that, in its opinion, upon the ratification of (any) nine states, the Constitution should be considered in force among them. It then, after almost four months, adjourned sine die.

To James Madison goes the honor of pronouncing the authoritative judgment on the work of the convention:

> But whatever may be the judgment pronounced on the competence of the architects of the Constitution, or whatever may be the destiny of the edifice prepared by them, I feel it a duty to express my profound and solemn conviction, derived from my intimate opportunity of observing and appreciating the views of the Convention, collectively and individually, that there never was an assembly of men, charged with a great and arduous trust, who were more pure in their motives, or more exclusively or anxiously devoted to the object committed to them, than were the members of the Federal Convention of 1787, to the object of devising and proposing a constitutional system which should best supply the defects of that which it was to replace, and best secure the permanent liberty and happiness of their country.[78]

Ratification

The draft of the Preamble to the Constitution prepared by the Committee of Detail began with the words "We the people of the States of . . . ," followed by a list of all thirteen states. But the decision to have the new government begin operation upon ratification of the

Constitution by at least nine states necessitated a change in this formulation. Who, in August 1787, could have predicted which states—
or which nine states—would ratify? So the exordium was changed
to read "We the People of the United States." Once again the proponents of the states yielded to necessity what they would not concede in principle.

Both principle and the peculiar (confederal) condition of the United
States in 1787 required ratification to be by the people rather than by
the state legislatures. Madison made this point in a letter to Washington just before the convention. "To give a new system its proper
validity and energy," he wrote, "a ratification must be obtained from
the people, and not merely from the ordinary authority of the Legislatures. This will be the more essential as inroads on the *existing
Constitutions* of the States will be unavoidable."[79] In conformity with
this, the convention suggested that the Congress submit the Constitution to specially convoked conventions in the several states, and
the Congress, in turn, sent it on to the states with instruction that it
be submitted "to a convention of Delegates chosen in each state by
the people thereof."[80] This congressional resolution was adopted, in
the absence of Rhode Island and over the opposition of New York,
on September 28, eleven days after the convention adjourned in Philadelphia.

Historians dispute the number of eligible voters as well as the
number who actually participated in the elections in which convention
delegates were chosen. As one might expect, hard evidence is hard
to come by. Nothing better demonstrates the "popularity" of the
Constitution, however—that is, its origins in the people—than the
debates outside and preceding the various state ratifying conventions.
This is especially true of New York, in whose newspapers Hamilton,
Madison, and John Jay combined under the name of Publius to write
the eighty-five papers soon collected under the title of *The Federalist*.
Like their counterparts elsewhere, as well as the papers written by
the Antifederalists (as they were now called), these were addressed
to the *people*. In whatever numbers, it was the people who elected
the delegates, and it was therefore the people on whose judgment
everything ultimately depended. The significance of this may be
glimpsed by comparing it with the Canadian confederation debates
leading to the British North America Act of 1867, the Canadian Constitution. In the parliament of Upper Canada (Ontario), the objection
was raised that members ought to consult opinion "out-of-doors," to
which the response was that a decision respecting a constitution of
government was not one for the people to make. (Thus the enacting
clause of the British North America Act read, in part, as follows: "Be

it therefore enacted and declared by the Queen's Most Excellent Majesty. . . . ") It was otherwise in the United States, in principle and, as well, in practice: the source of legitimate government was understood to be the people.

Beginning with Delaware on December 7, followed closely by Pennsylvania and New Jersey on December 12 and 18 respectively, the people of the United States in their various state conventions began to ratify the Constitution. The process continued in 1788, when, on June 21, New Hampshire became the ninth state to ratify. (None had voted to reject the Constitution.) But no one had any illusions that the new government could now begin its operations, not so long as New York and Virginia remained outside. (North Carolina and Rhode Island were not seen as essential, and, indeed, the new government had been in operation for over a year before Rhode Island ratified on May 29, 1790.)

The debates in the Virginia and New York conventions were probably the most spirited and surely the most interesting. On June 2, 1788, 170 delegates convened in Richmond, Virginia's capital, and began the debate, which went on for over three weeks. The Federalists, as they were now called, were led by Madison, George Wythe, John Marshall (one day to become chief justice of the United States), Henry Lee, Edmund Pendleton, and, once again, Edmund Randolph (who had refused to sign the Constitution). Their opponents were, at that time, equally famous and equally distinguished, especially George Mason and Patrick Henry. The June 27 vote to ratify was very close, 89–79, with "recommendations" that Henry and his associates would have preferred to look upon as conditions. (These had mainly to do with adoption of a bill of rights.)

In New York it was a contest between Alexander Hamilton and the followers of Governor George Clinton, joined by a group of principled Antifederalists led by Melancton Smith. Hamilton was brilliant in debate, but Smith and company were able to respond with arguments well known to their classical republican predecessors in England.[81] They ended up voting for ratification, not because they were persuaded by Hamilton's substantive arguments but, more likely, because they knew there was substance to his argument that if New York did not ratify, its southern counties and its principal city would secede from the state and join the larger union. Hamilton saw to it that the news of Virginia's favorable vote reached Albany, the capital of New York, even as the convention was meeting there. Yet, with all these factors in favor of ratification, the July 26 vote margin was very narrow indeed (30–27).

Upon being informed that the ninth state had ratified the Constitution, the Congress appointed a committee to "report an Act to Congress for putting the said constitution into operation." (This was on July 2, 1788, after Virginia's action had made it the tenth state to ratify.) On September 13, 1788, Congress resolved that "the first Wednesday in Jan.ⁿ next be the day for appointing [presidential] Electors in the several states [and] that the first Wednesday in March next be the time and the present seat of Congress [New York City] the place for commencing proceedings under the said constitution."[82] Washington took the oath as president on April 30, 1789, and in due course the new government was organized.

There have been many changes in the Constitution since 1789, changes both formal and informal, but the basic structure remains intact. It is probably true to say that the men who framed it would have little difficulty recognizing it as their handiwork.

Notes

1. *Federalist* No. 1.

2. New Hampshire was the first to act. Its constitution was adopted on January 6, 1776, six months before the Declaration of Independence. It is said to be the first written constitution "drawn up by an English colony without consultation with or the approval of the crown or Parliament." Massachusetts, the last state to act during this period, adopted its constitution in 1780. Connecticut and Rhode Island governed themselves until 1818 and 1842 respectively under their royal charters but "stripped of their monarchical components and reinterpreted as republican constitutions." See Willi Paul Adams, *The First American Constitutions: Republican Ideology and the Making of the State Constitutions in the Revolutionary Era*, trans. Rita and Robert Kimber, with a foreword by Richard B. Morris (Chapel Hill: University of North Carolina Press, 1980), pp. 5–6 and passim.

3. *Federalist* No. 1.

4. Patrick Henry, Virginia Ratifying Convention, June 4, 1788, in Herbert J. Storing, ed., *The Complete Anti-Federalist* (Chicago: University of Chicago Press, 1981), vol. 5, p. 211.

5. Charles C. Tansill, ed., *Documents Illustrative of the Formation of the Union of the American States*, 69th Congress, 1st session, House Doc. No. 398 (Washington, D.C.: GPO, 1927), p. 46.

6. James Madison to Nicholas P. Trist, February 15, 1830, in *The Writings of James Madison*, ed. Gaillard Hunt (New York: G. P. Putnam's Sons, 1900–1910), vol. 9, p. 355.

7. John Locke, *Treatises* II, sec. 119.

8. Ibid., sec. 4.

9. Ibid., secs. 96–98, 132.

10. Ibid., sec. 132.

11. This point is made explicitly in *Federalist* No. 47.

12. This phrase is taken from section 91 of the British North America Act of 1867, 30 & 31 Victoria, c. 3.

13. "The great and penetrating mind of Locke seems to be the only one that pointed towards even the theory of this great truth [namely] that the supreme, absolute and uncontrollable authority, *remains* with the people." James Wilson, Pennsylvania Ratifying Convention, December 4, 1787, in John Bach McMaster and Frederick D. Stone, eds., *Pennsylvania and the Federal Constitution, 1787–1788* (Lancaster, Pa.: Historical Society of Pennsylvania, 1888), p. 316.

14. James Madison to Thomas Ritchie, September 15, 1821, in *Writings of James Madison*, vol. 9, p. 72.

15. James Morton Smith and Paul L. Murphy, eds., *Liberty and Justice: A Historical Record of American Constitutional Development* (New York: Alfred A. Knopf, 1958), p. 215.

16. "and to assume among the powers of the earth, the separate and equal station to which the Laws of Nature and of Nature's God entitle them."

17. Smith and Murphy, *Liberty and Justice*, p. 215.

18. See Harry V. Jaffa, *Crisis of the House Divided: An Interpretation of the Issues in the Lincoln-Douglas Debates* (Garden City, N.Y.: Doubleday, 1959).

19. Abraham Lincoln, Message to Congress in Special Session, July 4, 1861, in *Abraham Lincoln: His Speeches and Writings*, ed. Roy P. Basler (Cleveland and New York: World Publishing Co., 1946), pp. 603–4.

20. Worthington C. Ford, ed., *Journals of the Continental Congress* (Washington, D.C.: GPO, 1904–1937), vol. 2, pp. 195–99.

21. Even though he is a Republican, President Reagan shares this opinion. See his inaugural address of January 20, 1981.

22. In a recent and excellent study of the politics of the Continental Congress, Jack N. Rakove points out that the debates on the Articles of Confederation failed to provoke in Congress a great discussion of the nature of the Union. Yet, as he demonstrates, there was at least an implicit agreement that the Union existed before the Articles. In 1777, for example, Thomas Burke of North Carolina proposed a bicameral legislature for the confederation, thereby acknowledging the existence of an American nation (to be represented in one house) as well as the states (to be represented in the other house). See Jack N. Rakove, *The Beginnings of National Politics: An Interpretive History of the Continental Congress* (New York: Alfred A. Knopf, 1979), p. 173 and passim.

23. Max Farrand, ed., *The Records of the Federal Convention of 1787* (New Haven, Conn.: Yale University Press, 1911, 1937), vol. 1, p. 250 (hereafter cited as Farrand, *Records*).

24. Richard Henry Lee to ——, April 28, 1788, in Storing, *The Complete Anti-Federalist*, vol. 1, p. 17.

25. Continental Congress, "Letter Transmitting Proposed Articles of Confederation," in Jonathan Elliot, ed., *The Debates in the Several State Conventions on the Adoption of the Federal Constitution* (New York: Burt Franklin, n.d.; reprint of 2d ed. published in 1888), vol. 1, p. 69.

26. Alexis de Tocqueville, *Democracy in America* (New York: Vintage Books, 1945), vol. 1, p. 176.

27. Richard Henry Lee to George Mason, May 15, 1787, in *The Papers of George Mason*, ed. Robert A. Rutland (Chapel Hill: University of North Carolina Press, 1970), vol. 3, p. 877.

28. Richard Henry Lee to Samuel Adams, March 14, 1785, in *The Letters of Richard Henry Lee*, ed. James Curtis Ballagh (New York: Macmillan, 1911–1914), vol. 2, pp. 343–44.

29. Lee to Mason, May 15, 1787, in *Papers of George Mason*, p. 877.

30. Melancton Smith in the New York ratifying convention, in Storing, *The Complete Anti-Federalist*, vol. 1, p. 18.

31. George Washington to John Jay, August 1, 1786, in *The Writings of George Washington from the Original Manuscript Sources, 1745–1799*, ed. John C. Fitzpatrick (Washington, D.C.: GPO, 1931–1944), vol. 28, p. 502.

32. George Washington to James Warren, October 7, 1785, ibid., p. 290.

33. Albany Plan of Union, July 10, 1754, in *The Papers of Benjamin Franklin*, ed. Leonard W. Labaree et al. (New Haven, Conn.: Yale University Press, 1959–), vol. 5, pp. 387–92.

34. Franklin, "Reasons and Motives for the Albany Plan of Union," ibid., p. 400.

35. Ibid., p. 417.

36. Ford, *Journals of the Continental Congress*, vol. 1, pp. 49–51.

37. Washington, "Circular to the States," June 8, 1783, in *Writings of George Washington*, vol. 26, p. 486.

38. Benjamin Rush to Richard Price, October 27, 1786, in *Letters of Benjamin Rush*, ed. L. H. Butterfield, memoirs of the American Philosophical Society, vol. 30, 2 parts (Princeton, N.J.: Princeton University Press, 1951), pt. 1, p. 408.

39. *Federalist* No. 6.

40. Tansill, *Documents Illustrative of the Formation of the Union*, pp. 39–43.

41. Ibid., p. 46.

42. Ibid., pp. 55–84. The relevant sentence in the Virginia statute reads as follows: "BE IT THEREFORE ENACTED by the General Assembly of the Commonwealth of Virginia that seven Commissioners be appointed by joint Ballot of both Houses of assembly who or any three of them are hereby authorized as Deputies from this Commonwealth to meet such Deputies as may be appointed and authorized by other states to assemble in convention in Philadelphia. . . ." (Ibid., pp. 69–70.)

43. On September 5 the convention voted unanimously to request Congress to pay "the Secretary and other officers of this Convention such sums in proportion to their respective times of service, as are allowed to the secretary & similar officers of Congress" (Farrand, *Records*, vol. 2, p. 510). The officers referred to, presumably, were Nicholas Weaver, messenger, and Joseph Fry, "Door Keeper" (ibid., vol. 1, p. 2).

44. See Harvey C. Mansfield, Jr., "The Forms and Formalities of Liberty," *The Public Interest*, no. 70 (Winter 1983).

45. "Mr. King objected [to a proposed rule that was not adopted] authorizing any member to call for the yeas & nays and have them entered on the minutes. He urged that as the acts of the Convention were not to bind the Constituents it was unnecessary to exhibit this evidence of the votes; and improper as changes of opinion would be frequent in the course of the business & would fill the minutes with contradictions" (Farrand, *Records*, vol. 1, p. 10).

46. The rules are printed in ibid., pp. 8–10, 17.

47. Madison, "Preface to Debates in the Convention of 1787," ibid., vol. 3, p. 550.

48. Herbert J. Storing, "The Constitutional Convention: Toward a More Perfect Union," in Morton J. Frisch and Richard G. Stevens, eds., *American Political Thought: The Philosophical Dimension of American Statesmanship*, 2d ed. (Itasca, Ill.: F. E. Peacock, 1983), p. 68.

49. Farrand, *Records*, vol. 1, p. 21.

50. Ibid., p. 37.

51. Ibid., p. 193.

52. On the Monday following Paterson's Friday speech, Alexander Hamilton of New York presented to the convention still a third plan, for a "high toned" government on the British model. Under it both the executive and the senators would serve during good behavior, and the governors of the states would be appointed by the "General Government" and would have a negative over all laws enacted by the states (ibid., pp. 282–93). Hamilton's plan was given no consideration whatever, and by introducing it he succeeded in depriving himself of further influence in the convention's deliberations. But he also succeeded—and there is no way of knowing whether this was his intention—in making the New Jersey Plan appear to be extreme (the opposite of his own) and the Virginia Plan appear to be moderate.

53. Ibid., pp. 242–45.

54. Ibid., p. 492.

55. Storing, "The Constitutional Convention," p. 54.

56. Farrand, *Records*, vol. 1, p. 133.

57. Ibid., p. 134.

58. "By a faction I understand a number of citizens, whether amounting to a majority or minority of the whole, who are united and actuated by some common impulse of passion, or of interest, adverse to the rights of other citizens, or to the permanent and aggregate interests of the community" (*Federalist* No. 10).

59. Farrand, *Records*, vol. 1, p. 166.

60. Madison "entreated the gentlemen representing the small states to renounce a principle wch. was confessedly unjust, which cd. never be admitted, & if admitted must infuse mortality into a Constitution which we wished to last forever" (ibid., p. 464; see also pp. 49, 134, 446, 527).

61. Ibid., p. 253.

62. Ibid., p. 255.

63. Ibid., p. 324.

64. Ibid., p. 449.

65. Ibid., p. 461.

66. Storing, "The Constitutional Convention," pp. 65–66. The facts are taken from Luther Martin, "Genuine Information," in Farrand, *Records*, vol. 3, pp. 187–88.

67. Farrand, *Records*, vol. 2, pp. 19–20.

68. The so-called supremacy clause (Article VI) reads, in part, that the Constitution, the laws made pursuant to it, and all treaties made or which shall be made "shall be the supreme Law of the Land; and the Judges in every State shall be bound thereby, any Thing in the Constitution or Laws of any State to the Contrary notwithstanding." It is not clear that the state-sovereignty delegates appreciated that this would lead to judicial review by the Supreme Court of the United States.

69. On September 12 Elbridge Gerry of Massachusetts moved the appointment of a committee to prepare a bill of rights, a motion seconded by George Mason of Virginia, but the motion was defeated, 0–10 (Farrand, *Records*, vol. 2, pp. 587–88). Significantly, neither Gerry nor Mason signed the Constitution.

70. *Federalist* No. 84.

71. *Federalist* No. 10. See also Walter Berns, "The Constitution as Bill of Rights," in Robert A. Goldwin and William A. Schambra, eds., *How Does the Constitution Secure Rights?* (Washington, D.C.: American Enterprise Institute, 1985), pp. 50–73.

72. Farrand, *Records*, vol. 1, pp. 399, 401.

73. Ibid., p. 152.

74. Ibid., vol. 2, pp. 177–89.

75. Ibid., pp. 590–603.

76. Ibid., pp. 629–30. It is interesting in this connection to note that the amending provision embodies elements of both popular and state sovereignty. An amendment becomes part of the Constitution when ratified by a majority of the people of the United States (acting either through state legislatures or through state conventions), but that majority must be an extraordinary one, expressed as three-fourths of the states.

77. Ibid., p. 665.

78. Madison, "Preface to Debates," p. 551.

79. Madison to George Washington, April 16, 1787, in *The Papers of James Madison*, ed. William T. Hutchinson et al. (Chicago: University of Chicago Press, 1962–1977), vol. 9, p. 385.

80. Tansill, *Documents Illustrative of the Formation of the Union*, p. 1007.

81. See Zera S. Fink, *The Classical Republicans: An Essay in the Recovery of a Pattern of Thought in Seventeenth Century England* (Evanston, Ill.: Northwestern University Press, 1945).

82. Tansill, *Documents Illustrative of the Formation of the Union*, p. 1062.

Commentary

Jack N. Rakove

Among the many celebrated quotations that the founders of the American republic transmitted to later generations, few are as revealing of their sense of mission as the exclamation with which John Adams closed his influential pamphlet of 1776, *Thoughts on Government.*

> You and I, my friend, have been sent into life at a time when the greatest lawgivers of antiquity would have wished to live. How few of the human race have ever enjoyed an opportunity of making an election [that is, choice] of government, more than of air, soil, or climate, for themselves or their children! When, before the present epocha, had three millions of people full power and a fair opportunity to establish the wisest and happiest government that human wisdom can contrive?[1]

A decade later, when the movement that led to the writing of the federal Constitution was getting under way, few Americans still felt the sense of exultation that John Adams had so characteristically failed to restrain. The political mood of the 1780s lacked the enthusiasm and optimism that the colonists had discovered when they declared independence and wrote the first state constitutions as avowed republicans. Yet, as Walter Berns aptly notes at the opening of his paper, the framers of the federal Constitution "knew very well indeed [that] they were engaged in what was still a novel enterprise, an experiment, and one for which history provided little guidance." A sense of novelty and possibility had outlasted the discouraging developments of the last years of the revolutionary war and the early years of peace. Indeed, a few candid observers were even prepared to admit that the Americans now enjoyed a better opportunity "of considering and debating the subject [of government], and of making a deliberate choice" about it than had existed even during the heady days of 1776, when "the confusion of the times put it out of the power of the people, to pay that attention to the subject [which] its nature and importance required."[2]

In a sense, this awareness of the possibility that governments may be reconstituted on new principles at any time is the great legacy of the Age of Revolution that reached one climax in America in 1787 and another in France in 1789. Yet such opportunities are more easily missed or lost than safely secured; and the familiar comparisons that are made between the outcomes of the revolutions in America and France testify to our belief in the fragility of the process. Opinions of the genuinely revolutionary character of the American Revolution are known to vary widely, but whenever the comparison with France is pursued, the framing of the Constitution makes for a far happier conclusion than the Terror, Thermidor, or the Napoleonic accession. The conviction that the writing of the Constitution was the proper and justly celebrated culmination of the revolutionaries' experiment in republicanism has been shaken only on rare occasions—for example, by nineteenth-century abolitionists and twentieth-century Progressives; it has never been overturned.

Professor Berns is certainly one who would cast his lot with the celebrants of the Constitution. As a distinguished political theorist, his concerns diverge somewhat from those of historians, who generally focus their attention on the motives of the men who framed the Constitution and the characteristics of the social and political groups that struggled for and against its ratification. He is, perhaps, more deeply interested in the underlying issues that the convention had to resolve or the great principles that it had to vindicate than in the political process that led to their resolution. Even so, few scholars would take serious issue with his account of the writing of the Constitution, as far as it goes.

In presenting what might be called a complementary view of the framing of the Constitution, I would like to table, for the time being, consideration of such ideas as state or popular sovereignty or the fundamental Lockean premises under which Professor Berns sees the framers operating. My concern will instead be with the political dynamics of the convention, that is, with the conditions that both led to its assembling and shaped the character of its debates. As my opening remarks indicate, an awareness of the self-consciousness with which the framers undertook their enterprise is indeed critical to understanding how their deliberations proceeded. At the same time, we must appreciate that few if any of the participants were optimistic about their prospects for success, either in framing a constitution or in making it acceptable throughout the thirteen existing states. The hegemony that the Constitution so rapidly acquired after its ratification in 1788 stands in sharp contrast to the fluid and unstable situation that existed in the spring of 1787.

The sequence of events that led the delegates to gather in Philadelphia is familiar to all students of American history, but the meaning and intentions underlying these developments are often misperceived. Reviews of the background to the convention usually focus on the catalogue of political ills that James Madison summarized so thoroughly in his memorandum on "The Vices of the Political System of the United States."[3] Here I shall ask instead how the deteriorating state of national politics in the 1780s affected the delegates' calculations about the likely outcome of a federal convention.

Criticism of the existing framework of federal government, the Articles of Confederation, had been raised literally from the moment the Articles belatedly took effect in March 1781. None of the modestly drawn amendments that were periodically debated in the Continental Congress and less frequently proposed to the states was ever ratified, however. All such proposals foundered on the difficulty of securing either a consensus within Congress or the unanimous approval of the states. By early 1786 it was apparent that any amendment formally proposed by Congress (as the Articles required) would never be approved by the states. Congress itself had fallen into such low esteem that its acts were inherently tainted. At the same time, the successful conclusion of the war and the emergence of new (and sectionally divisive) problems of foreign policy in the mid-1780s had revealed that there was no longer one identifiable national interest to which all the states could readily defer.[4]

One might suppose that the existence of all these obstacles to the reform of the Articles would have had a liberating effect on the thinking of that small group of national politicians who were most deeply troubled by the "imbecility" of the confederation. In fact, the result was exactly the opposite. Far from inspiring efforts to rethink the nature of the federal system, the frustrations of the mid-1780s kept constitutional thought—at least at the national level—confined within narrow bounds.

The calling of the Annapolis convention of September 1786 illustrates this point nicely. The rationale for this meeting was twofold. A meeting called under the authority of the states, rather than Congress, might not be exposed to the same suspicions that had greeted every amendment Congress had proposed since 1781. At the same time, a convention whose agenda was confined to matters of commerce might succeed in endorsing a single proposal whose acceptance and implementation would, over time, pave the way for additional, though still incremental, reforms.

The weakness of this strategy became evident when only a dozen commissioners from five states actually appeared at the appointed time. No substantive amendment proposed by such a body could carry any weight. Yet if the meeting adjourned in abject failure without taking any action, the bankruptcy of all efforts to amend the articles would finally have to be acknowledged. It was this dilemma that made possible the bold and desperate measure the commissioners adopted: to issue an appeal to the states (again, rather than Congress) to call a second convention for the following spring and to recommend that its agenda should be "to devise such further provisions as shall appear to them necessary to render the constitution of the federal government adequate to the exigencies of the Union."[5] Historians have sometimes cast the commissioners' recommendation in a Machiavellian light, seeing it, that is, as an adroit attempt to steal a march on the opponents of a more vigorous union. It would probably be more accurate to say that the call for a second convention was the act of men who, having exhausted all prudent measures, realized there was nothing left to do but go for broke.

Why is it so important to stress the political background of the federal convention? Because neither the intellectual nor the political dynamics of the convention can be understood unless one considers the context within which the delegates were acting. Several points deserve particular emphasis. In the first place, the wide-ranging and open character of the convention's deliberations was a function of the narrowly delimited way in which the problem of *federal* government had been considered before 1787. Previous discussions of the debilities of the confederation had focused on its failure to vest Congress with the power to regulate trade or raise its own revenue. But many of the issues that would preoccupy the convention—most notably those coming under the broad heading of separation of powers—had never become promising subjects for discussion for the simple reason that the additional authority sought for Congress was not so extensive as to warrant a fundamental restructuring of the federal government.[6] Within the states, of course, there had been growing discussion of the utility of an independent executive and judiciary, the dangers of legislative tyranny, and the collapse of popular deference to duly constituted authority. But before 1787 none of these concerns had seemed relevant to the existing problems of the confederation, where all authority was lodged in the Continental Congress, a constitutional anomaly.[7]

Even in the early spring of 1787, it was very difficult to anticipate the scope of the convention's deliberations. Save for a handful of private letters, few surviving documents from these months show any great foresight into the convention's imminent agenda. Thus when the convention assembled in May 1787, such issues had to be considered candidly and thoroughly in large part because they had never been viewed from a federal perspective. This lack of prior discussion had one further implication. It meant that the delegates journeyed to Philadelphia unencumbered by the kinds of restrictive instructions that could easily have made agreement even within the secrecy of the convention's chambers much more difficult to achieve. Lacking either rigid instructions or *cahiers* of their constituents' grievances, they were free to define their agenda as broadly or narrowly as they chose.

Where Professor Berns would stress the importance of certain sources of intellectual influence on the framers' thought—for example, underlying notions of government by consent—a practicing historian might prefer to identify the circumstances that permitted debate to take the shape it did. Such an approach, with its emphasis on specifically political factors, seems particularly necessary for an additional reason: it helps to explain why the convention was able to see its work through to a harmonious conclusion marred only by the idiosyncratic dissents of Elbridge Gerry, Edmund Randolph, and George Mason and the opposition of a handful of other delegates known to be unsympathetic to the entire enterprise. Few of those who gathered in Philadelphia in the spring of 1787 would have predicted that so high a level of agreement would prove possible.

That the delegates were willing to spend the better part of four months at work on a constitution is itself not the least important sign of their seriousness (and also of their independence from the personal cares of less affluent men). In an era when politics was still far more an avocation than a career, not a legislature in America could have maintained a quorum for so long a period; and in the midst of some of its worst crises, the Continental Congress had had to scrape by with far fewer members than the convention mustered.

A willingness to accept election to the convention thus suggests that a member already grasped the premises that had led the rump session at Annapolis to gamble on its proposal. During the intervening months a conviction had taken hold, at least within the elite circles concerned with national issues, that the convention would truly mark the last chance not only to strengthen but even to preserve the union. And once the delegates assembled at Philadelphia, they could only have felt an enhanced commitment to their mission, particularly after the presentation of the Virginia Plan, with its expansive redefinition of the purposes of the meeting, had revealed just how widely their work would range.

158

The great test of attitude came, of course, with the protracted struggle over representation in the upper house of the legislature. This was the one issue whose manifest importance every delegate understood from the opening session. The question whether the states were to be represented equally as identical corporate units or proportionally as aggregates of population was literally the oldest problem of American federalism, being the first issue of substance raised at the First Continental Congress of 1774.[8] Much of the ease with which the convention quickly worked its way through the other features of the Virginia Plan may have been a reflection of the delegates' awareness that unless and until this issue was somehow resolved, all their other decisions would go for nought.

Professor Berns suggests that this problem of representation was "the one issue that embodied a difference of principle" and then goes on to note that "it is not sufficient—to some extent it may even be inaccurate—to describe the dispute as a clash of 'interests.' " He rightly notes—as James Wilson had heatedly argued during the original debates over the Articles of Confederation—that the only "interest" large and small states shared with those within their class was size. This could be an interest only within the convention; its significance once a new national government actually went into operation could be described only in vague or fantastic terms.

Even so, it is far from clear that the contending delegates saw the problem of the composition of the upper house as a test of two different principles of representation. True, in the heated debates of June and July, advocates of proportional representation in both houses did imply that the retention of an equal state voice even in the Senate alone would deter the larger states from approving any substantial addition to the powers of the federal government. And when the spokesmen for the smaller states submitted the New Jersey Plan, with its closer adherence to the model of the existing confederation, they seemed to confirm that representation was the key to the solution of all other issues. But more than a little posturing went into giving this debate its increasingly bellicose tone. Threats escalated as the deadlock deepened, and the tendency to treat the problem as a matter of high principle grew accordingly. Yet the evidence that the spokesmen for the small states really were contending for a principle of state sovereignty is weak. It was George Read of Delaware who was prepared to entertain the possibility that the states should actually be annihilated, and once the Great Compromise was secured, other delegates from the small states supported the creation of a vigorous national government. Charles Pinckney may well have been right to imply that the whole New Jersey Plan was merely an elaborate device to secure the principle of equal representation in the Senate. "Give New Jersey an equal vote," he scoffed, "and she will dismiss her scruples, and concur in the national system."[9]

Nor do the convention's subsequent actions involving the Senate demonstrate that principles of state sovereignty, rather than state interest, were the essential source of dispute. The lengthy and fixed terms that senators would enjoy left them essentially independent of state control, while the additional "executive" powers with which they would be vested led some of the delegates—and later many opponents of the Constitution—to fear that the Senate would become the most powerful and least accountable branch of the new government.

However one assesses the balance between interest and principle on this least tractable of questions, its centrality to the dynamics of the Constitutional Convention cannot be overestimated. The deadlock of June and July had raised the emotional temperature of debate more than a few degrees; and well into August and early September, resentment of the compromise continued to be expressed in some of the maneuvering that led to the enhancement of the power of the president. For our purposes, however, the critical point is that the convention was able to withstand the divisive pressures that this one issue had exerted. It was not at all clear, at first, that it could. The threats and accusations that were exchanged during the debates preceding the compromise may have owed something to rhetorical habit and calculations of bluffing and bargaining, but they seemed real enough at the time to make fears of a premature adjournment legitimate. For a brief moment the delegates from the large states did contemplate folding their tents. The possibility of an adjournment sine die was discussed immediately after the compromise was finally sealed, but in the end debate was resumed after less than a day of soul searching.[10] A few members were willing to see the convention dissolve; but the others took a deep breath and decided that they could live with a decision they could hardly have considered a compromise even in name.

This resolution can be explained only by the political assumptions that the delegates had carried with them to Philadelphia, assumptions that rested on the hard experience of national politics during the mid-1780s. They knew, quite simply, that this might indeed be the last opportunity any of them would enjoy for some time to make that "election of government" in which John Adams had rejoiced a decade earlier. There was no practical alternative to carrying on with the task, even if many of them privately believed that the charter they would ultimately produce would be critically, if not fatally, flawed. An appeal to their constituents that explained why the convention had dead-locked would be of no value even if a second meeting could be assembled. The prospects for a second convention could hardly be viewed favorably, if only because public knowledge of what had already been in dispute would lock later delegations into positions from which they could never escape, making effective bargaining on any substantive issue next to impossible.

Most recent scholarship on the founding of the American federal republic has centered on the intellectual and ideological sources of the institutions that took their definitive form at Philadelphia in 1787. But the Constitution was also the outcome of a political process whose details and nuances need to be mastered before the actual decisions that were reached can be fully understood and also before the magnitude of its framers' achievement can be fully appreciated.

Notes

1. [John Adams], *Thoughts on Government* (Philadelphia, 1776), p. 27.

2. Edmund S. Morgan, ed., "The Political Establishment of the United States, 1784," *William and Mary Quarterly*, 3d ser. vol. 23 (1966), pp. 288, 300, 304. Perhaps the best-known expression of this attitude came from the pen of Benjamin Rush, who in 1786 criticized the prevailing tendency "to confound the terms of the American Revolution with those of the late American war. . . . It remains yet to establish and perfect our new forms of government, and to prepare the principles, morals, and manners of our citizens, for these forms of government, after they are established and brought to perfection." It is often forgotten that the remainder of this essay focused specifically on the problems of the confederation. Rush (writing as "Nestor"), in the Philadelphia *Independent Gazetteer*, June 3, 1786.

3. Reprinted in *The Papers of James Madison*, ed. Robert A. Rutland et al. (Chicago and Charlottesville: University of Chicago and University of Virginia Presses, 1962–), vol. 9, pp. 345–58.

4. This and the following paragraphs draw heavily on the argument in Jack N. Rakove, *The Beginnings of National Politics: An Interpretive History of the Continental Congress* (New York: Alfred A. Knopf, 1979).

5. The address of the Annapolis convention is reprinted in *The Papers of Alexander Hamilton*, ed. Harold C. Syrett and Jacob Cooke (New York: Columbia University Press, 1960–1978), vol. 3, pp. 686–90.

6. Rakove, *Beginnings of National Politics*, pp. 360–88.

7. See especially Gordon S. Wood, *The Creation of the American Republic, 1776–1787* (Chapel Hill: University of North Carolina Press, 1969), chaps. X, XI. Still valuable is Edward S. Corwin, "The Progress of Constitutional Theory between the Declaration of Independence and the Meeting of the Philadelphia Convention," *American Historical Review*, vol. 30 (1924–1925), pp. 511–36. A

recent book that should greatly influence our understanding of the theoretical complexities of early American federalism is Peter S. Onuf, *The Origins of the Federal Republic: Jurisdictional Controversies in the United States, 1775–1787* (Philadelphia: University of Pennsylvania Press, 1983).

8. Rakove, *Beginnings of National Politics*, pp. 139–41; and see the general account in J. R. Pole, *Political Representation in England and the Origins of the American Republic* (London: St. Martin's, 1966), pp. 344–48.

9. Max Farrand, ed., *The Records of the Federal Convention of 1787* (New Haven, Conn.: Yale University Press, 1911 [rev. ed., 1937]), vol. 1, pp. 255, 136–37.

10. Ibid., vol. 2, pp. 15–20.

Discussion

ROBERT GOLDWIN: A number of things about the Constitution of the United States are unique and striking, among them that as a written national constitution it was, at the time it was framed, a novelty. That there were certain explicit principles guiding it, especially as expressed in the Declaration of Independence, was also a novelty for the founding of a national system. The arrangement of what is now called federalism was a novelty. Perhaps the most striking thing about the U.S. Constitution, of course, is its durability; it is almost 200 years old in a world where most constitutions are only about twelve years old. These are some of the things that we can talk about when we discuss the Constitution of the United States.

To begin, therefore, I refer you to the passage that Professor Berns quoted in his essay, from the beginning of *The Federalist*:

> It has been frequently remarked that it seems to have been reserved to the people of this country, by their conduct and example, to decide the important question, whether societies of men are really capable or not of establishing good government from reflection and choice, or whether they are forever destined to depend for their political constitutions, on accident and force.

My question is, Has that question been decided? That is, did they then, and do constitution makers now, really establish government from reflection and choice, or are we all destined forever to be subject to accident and force?

WALTER BERNS: We are about to celebrate the bicentennial of the U.S. Constitution; I suppose that in itself is a partial answer to your question. As I wrote at the end of my essay, I am fairly well convinced that if James Madison, James Wilson, Gouverneur Morris, Alexander Hamilton, and others were to come to Washington today, they would be astonished by many things, but they would recognize the government that they established. The structure of that government is still

163

in place. We sit in a building where the Supreme Court of the United States does its work; it is an independent judiciary; it was established as such, and it is separate from the other branches; it is across the street from the legislature, which was supposed to be separate and which itself embodies the notion of a separation of powers, with one wing of its building occupied by one branch of the legislature, the Senate, and the other wing occupied by the other branch, the House of Representatives.

The men who framed the U.S. Constitution would be astonished by the number of office buildings used to house our senators and representatives and their 20,000-odd administrative assistants, but they would recognize the structure of the government in the buildings that house it, and they would recognize our government today as having its origin in the Constitution they wrote. Of course, down Pennsylvania Avenue is the White House, the home of a separately established executive, and they would recognize that branch of government as well. This supposed recognition by the founders of our government goes a long way toward answering Mr. Goldwin's question.

JACK RAKOVE: As a person who spends most of his waking hours in the eighteenth century, I am a bit puzzled to know how to respond to a question that requires me to pass judgment on events in the twentieth century. Taking Mr. Goldwin's question literally, the evidence of this conference itself demonstrates how the question of choosing reflection and choice over accident and force in establishing government has been decided. The pervasiveness of the written constitutions that Professor Albert Blaustein and his colleagues around the world are so busily compiling suggests that one of the striking legacies of the U.S. Constitution is the notion that constitutions can be compiled and written and rewritten and revised with what seems to be astonishing rapidity.

The response to the tradition of British constitutionalism, of the unwritten constitution, indicates that the American example has prevailed even if constitution writers in other countries have not been particularly attracted by many features of our separation of powers structure. The contemporary idea—that to constitute or reconstitute a state one has to establish or revise some formal, legal, written document rather than rely on the mixture of precedent, custom, tradition, and law that the British tradition entails—suggests that the experience of modern generations has been, at least in this sense, a vindication of American principles.

VAKUR VERSAN: The writing of the U.S. Constitution illustrates that no group of persons assigned the writing of a constitution, whether they start from scratch or are to rewrite a previous one, feel entirely free to accept principles or institutions of government of their liking. We all are affected by the political, social, and economic conditions of our societies and also by the merits—and perhaps the demerits and defects—of previous constitutions and governmental systems. We took note of this fact in discussing the French and Greek constitutions, and the two most recent constitutions of my country, Turkey—the Constitution of 1961 and the present Constitution, which came into force in 1982—may also be seen as examples. I understand that this is also true of the U.S. Constitution. In other words, it cannot be said that the U.S. Constitution was entirely based on the philosophical principles of John Locke and others; it is also a result of political and social conditions in the United States at the time it was written.

The U.S Constitution reflects two preoccupations of those who wrote it: first, to replace the integration of functions and organs previously supplied by the British Crown, especially in matters of commerce and defense, with something more forceful than the arrangements under the Articles of Confederation; second, to guarantee to citizens the limitations of government and the common-law freedoms that the colonists had asserted. As far as the first is concerned, the task was to create a federal government encompassing the already established thirteen states, each with its own constitution, legal system, and political institutions. That is why the Constitution devotes itself almost exclusively to federal machinery and powers and says almost nothing about the form of state governments except that they shall be republican. The second preoccupation, the limitation of governmental powers, determined the design of the Constitution insofar as it explicitly led to the establishment of three separate branches of government with checks and balances regarding each branch's operations.

One other point that strikes this foreign observer is the agreement among the founders about what they considered the essentials of good government. Apart from the two opposing doctrines of "states' rights" and "national sovereignty," the most fundamental political and constitutional issues—such as representative government, elections at fixed intervals, separation of powers, checks and balances, a bicameral legislature, and a single, strong executive—were accepted by the founders without debate or were discussed very briefly. The principles behind these provisions could have been taken for granted in no other country in the eighteenth century, and the combination of them could be accepted without discussion in no other country today. What may be the cause of this? Why were the founders able to agree so easily on such basic principles in constituting a new state?

MR. BERNS: I would like to elaborate on my answer to Mr. Goldwin's question. If constitutionalism has something to do with legitimacy and finding a new basis for legitimacy, clearly the Constitution of the United States has been a success for almost 200 years. At times, however, people have questioned its legitimacy. When slavery existed in this country, the abolitionists from the North went so far as to say that the Constitution was a "covenant made in Hell." That sort of statement has been rare in our history. To an astonishing extent, Americans identify what is constitutional with what is good; that is, they believe that if something is constitutional, it is thereby good.

On at least one occasion Supreme Court Justice Felix Frankfurter, who served from 1939 until 1962, complained of this tendency of Americans to identify constitutionality with wisdom. I think he was mistaken in that criticism because there is a great deal to be said for the habit of a people of identifying wisdom, goodness, probity, and the like with constitutionality. That was one of the purposes of the men who wrote the Constitution. It is a condition for the success of this enterprise, and it has existed in the United States to an astonishing extent.

JOSEPH A. L. COORAY: Some of the principles of democratic government that are basic features of the U.S. Constitution, written by fifty-five men who assembled in Philadelphia in 1787, are still of great relevance to those of us concerned with drafting suitable democratic constitutions for developing third world countries. They certainly were relevant to us in Sri Lanka when we were drafting our new republican Constitution in 1978. That relevance is closely related to the question about the establishment of good government through reflection and choice. There was a considerable amount of reflection and choice when we sat down after twenty-five years of independence to draft a constitution suited to our own requirements and with due regard to the economic, social, and political conditions prevailing on our island. At that time we thought we should profit from the experience of democratic countries, such as the United States, whose Constitution was the first existing written constitution to be drafted. The authors of *The Federalist*, whom Professor Berns cites in his essay, seem to have visualized the importance of the decisions they were making and the constitutional principles they were laying down, not

166

only for future Americans but for future citizens of other nations as well.

I would like to comment on the separation of powers embodied in the American Constitution. Professor Berns states that when the framers of the Constitution were debating the Virginia Plan, they agreed on the need to provide for legislative, executive, and judicial powers but to separate them from one another and especially to provide for the independence of the judiciary. They instituted checks and balances to prevent tyrannical government.

When we in Sri Lanka drafted our new republican Constitution, we also took note of the view expressed by Madison in *Federalist* No. 47: that when the great French jurist Montesquieu, in *The Spirit of the Laws*, urged the adoption of separation of powers, he did not mean to suggest what some of his more enthusiastic followers thought he did. I quote from Madison, that Montesquieu did not mean to suggest "that these departments ought to have no *partial agency* in, or no *control* over the acts of each other." Madison's view was that "where the *whole* power of one department is exercised by the same hands which possess the *whole* power of another department, the fundamental principles of a free constitution, are subverted."

Accordingly, we in Sri Lanka did not think we were departing from the principle of separation of powers when we provided in our Constitution for a considerable measure of cooperation and coordination between the executive and the legislature. Our Constitution establishes a presidential executive freely elected by all the people, along with a cabinet of ministers that is appointed by the president (who is its head), is composed of members of Parliament, and is collectively responsible and answerable to Parliament. As we understood Montesquieu's doctrine and the view of the framers of the American Constitution, the most important element of the doctrine of separation of powers is the complete independence of the judiciary. It is even more important than the relationship between the legislature and the executive, although we thought there should be some formal separation there too and vested the executive power in the president and the legislative power in Parliament.

Professor Berns writes that the delegates at the 1787 convention were in complete agreement that government is instituted to secure the rights of men and that the opponents of the Constitution, for instance Patrick Henry, seized on the absence of a bill of rights and exacted a promise from Madison to remedy the defect at the earliest opportunity. This Madison did when he introduced the amendments in the First Congress.

In 1978 we in Sri Lanka, again after reflection and choice, provided for a bill of rights in the Constitution, including the rights contained in the American Bill of Rights. We expressly made these rights justiciable and enforceable by an independent supreme court. Professor Berns has said that this oldest of written constitutions differs from those of the twentieth century since the Bill of Rights makes no reference to the rights to organize strikes, to work, and so on. In a chapter containing directive principles of state policy in a constitution such as ours, is an enunciation of economic, social, and cultural rights— not made justiciable in courts but to guide the Parliament and the executive—in accord with the universal nature of human rights? In constitutions such as those of Ireland, India, and Sri Lanka, principles of social policy are laid down for the guidance of the legislature and the executive; they are not legally binding or enforceable. I wonder whether these are in the spirit of the U.S. Constitution and the Bill of Rights or whether in the United States they are considered "glittering generalities."

Finally, I am aware that there is still controversy in the United States about whether the framers of the Constitution of 1787 intended the Supreme Court to have the power of judicial review. The first independent Constitution of Sri Lanka also provided no express power of judicial review. Our judges took the view, however, as Chief Justice John Marshall did in *Marbury* v. *Madison* and *McCulloch* v. *Maryland*, that the Constitution included such an implied power. As Marshall asked: "To what purpose are powers limited, and to what purpose is that limitation committed to writing, if those limits may, at any time, be passed by those intended to be restrained?" Our courts took the same view. Judges in both the United States and Sri Lanka have adopted the spirit of judicial self-restraint, although, in the words of Chief Justice Charles Evans Hughes, the Constitution "is what the judges say it is." Our present Constitution gives express power to the Supreme Court to determine whether any bill is inconsistent with the Constitution. This change was made after reflection and choice and after our constitutional experience as a developing democratic society. Needless to say, the democratic way of making a constitution and establishing good government is after reflection and choice by the elected representatives of the people.

GERALD STOURZH: First, Professor Berns and Mr. Goldwin have stressed the novelty of writing and formally adopting a Constitution in 1787. The term "written constitution," which has been used at least twice in this discussion, though confusing, seems ineradicable in Anglo-American constitutional terminology. In America, of course, this has much to do with Marshall's famous words in *Marbury* v. *Madison*:

"Certainly all those who have framed written constitutions contemplate them as forming the fundamental and paramount law of the nation." The term "written constitution" really encompasses, and sometimes confuses, two things: first, fundamental and paramount law, commanding a superior place in the hierarchy of norms, what French (and continental) terminology refers to as *constitution au sens formel*; and second, a written document codifying constitutional matters in a simple piece of legislation but not necessarily of paramount validity and above normal legislative amendment. These two meanings of the term "written constitution" are different but are often confused.

It is of course true that the rise of the constitution *au sens formel* in eighteenth-century America was a new development, and this was perfectly understood and expressed by the founders even before Marshall, who is quoted so often. Madison, in *Federalist* No. 53, wrote: "Where no constitution paramount to the government, either existed or could be obtained, no constitutional security similar to that established in the United States, was to be attempted." These are proud words, particularly if we reflect that they were written as early as February 1788; they reflect a great certainty about the novelty and superiority of what the founders were about to achieve. That was before ratification.

Even earlier another founder and one of the first justices of the Supreme Court, James Iredell of North Carolina, put the same idea in very impressive words. He said, in 1786, before the Philadelphia convention: "It will not be denied that the Constitution is a law of the state as well as an act of Assembly, with the difference only, that it is the fundamental law, and unalterable by the legislature, which derives all its power from it." He was speaking about North Carolina, but his point was the same, that the Constitution is the fundamental law and unalterable by the legislature, which derives all its powers from it. Looking back 200 years, I find it impressive that the idea of a hierarchy of legal norms (*Stufenbau der Rechtsordnung*), which was developed in legal theory in the twentieth century by Adolf Merbl and Hans Kelsen, can be found rather clearly adumbrated in the writings of some of the American founders. The words of Iredell seem to me particularly precise.

Second, Professor Berns has stressed the importance of rules and forms for conducting governmental business, that formal rules serve as a restraint on behavior. Max Weber once called form the twin sister of liberty—an extremely interesting formulation. I am aware that constitutional lawyers do not need to be reminded of that, but everyone outside the legal world knows how difficult a truth this is, how impatient people "with a cause" tend to become when confronted with formal rules of procedure. Contempt for rules of procedure is a permanent threat to constitutionalism.

Third, Professor Berns also refers to the issue of slavery at the time of the Constitutional Convention, raising the question whether the issue would divide the delegates later or would threaten to divide them permanently. He writes that the framers of the Constitution had reason to believe, or at least chose to believe, that the problem of slavery would be resolved with the passage of time. On my reading of the records of the federal convention and of writings surrounding it, including *The Federalist*, I believe there was a more worried and more serious awareness of the issue. Professor Berns himself very rightly points to Madison who, in an extremely moving and interesting speech on June 30 at the convention, said that

> the States were divided into different interests not by their difference of size, but by other circumstances; the most material of which resulted partly from climate, but principally from [the effects of] their having or not having slaves. These two causes concurred in forming the great division of interests in the U. States. It did not lie between the large & small States: it lay between the Northern & Southern. and if any defensive power were necessary, it ought to be mutually given to these two interests.

Madison was so strongly impressed with this important truth that he had been casting about in his mind for some expedient that would answer the purpose. The one that occurred to him was that, instead of proportioning the votes of the states in both branches to their numbers of inhabitants and computing the slaves in a ratio of three to five—that is the famous three-fifths clause of the Constitution, in which a Negro slave was counted as three-fifths of a person— Madison thought, for a while at least, that states should be represented in one branch of the legislature only according to the number of free inhabitants and in the other chamber by including the whole number of slaves as if they were free.

Madison then rejected this idea, but it is most interesting that we have it on record that the convention delegates reflected on it. If we read the debate on the three-fifths provision and on other questions related to slavery, such as whether the importation of slaves should be prohibited by the year 1800 or by 1808, we see that these issues very much moved the convention delegates. Perhaps the issue of large states versus small states, which led to the famous "great compromise," has been emphasized too much at the expense of these other necessary compromises, which were dealt with in a more subdued way but which really agitated the founders.

At the federal convention James Wilson of Pennsylvania "did not well see on what principle the admission of blacks in the proportion of three fifths could be explained." If blacks were admitted as citizens, why not admitted on an equality with white citizens? If they were admitted as property, why was no other property admitted into the computation? "These were difficulties," Wilson said, "which he thought must be overcome by the necessity of compromise." James Madison addressed this very difficult issue in *Federalist* No. 54, where he wrote:

> Let the case of the slaves be considered as it is in truth a peculiar one. Let the compromising expedient of the Constitution be mutually adopted, which regards them as inhabitants, but as debased by servitude below the equal level of free inhabitants, which regards the *slave* as divested of two fifths of the man.

It is interesting that two opponents of slavery—Wilson and Madison—not only mentioned but stressed the need for compromise. Professor Berns referred in his essay to the late Professor Herbert Storing, who said, rightly, that one motive for the founders' willingness to compromise was their awareness of the need for decision. This is a key sentence in Professor Berns's paper. It supplies a clue to understanding the successful contriving of constitutions in the face of considerable differences or clashes of interest. To some extent the impression left from our discussions of France in 1958 and Greece in 1975 is that the constitution writers were aware of a need to come to decisions by way of compromise.

MR. GOLDWIN: From what has just been said, is it not clear that the effort to establish good government by "reflection and choice" receives a kind of battering by the powers of "accident and force"? What one would do by reflection and choice seems to be greatly modified by forces that are not completely rational but that bear down on all those who have the responsibility for making a constitution.

MR. RAKOVE: When Hamilton wrote of "accident and force," I do not believe that he meant to ignore the fact that the circumstances of a society at different points in its history may diverge widely. What Hamilton meant and John Adams was alluding to when he said, "You and I, my friend, have been sent into life at a time when the greatest lawgivers of antiquity would have wished to live," was simply that the Americans had an opportunity to create a government based

171

neither on conquest nor on hereditary right residing in a monarch. They realized they could take into account the circumstances in which they lived and proceed accordingly. Americans understood this quite well, and their efforts to frame governments, first in 1776 and then in 1787, were in many ways predicated on their conception, primitive as it was in some ways, of the nature of the society in which they lived.

It is not at all clear from the debates at the convention that the framers expected the government they were attempting to impose or create in 1787 to survive 200 years. When they referred in one context or another to the issue of monarchy, my impression is that they agreed that in 1787 monarchy would not be suitable to the genius or character of the American people. This point was reiterated time and again; but on other occasions various delegates seemed to imply that in the future, when the country to be governed would be as extensive as it now is, a much more vigorous executive, on the order of a constitutional monarchy, would be appropriate.

Slavery was a central issue of which the framers were well aware, but they did not know how to come to grips with it. It is clear that Madison was troubled by it and that Rufus King and a handful of other delegates, such as Wilson, were also troubled by its moral implications, but they did not know how to get a handle on it. When Madison spoke about slavery on June 30 during the convention, the context was critical. It was during the debate over the tritest of all questions, the big state versus small state dispute concerning representation in the Senate. What Madison was trying to do was not so much to resolve the slavery issue per se as to find a solution so as to get the convention back on track from its impasse over the small state–large state question. Madison was struggling, as he was struggling in his memorandum on the vices of the Confederation, and as he struggled again in *Federalist* No. 10, to arrive at what we would recognize as a modern definition of what a society consists of. He was trying to define the interests that actually composed American society and that would be involved in the politics of the society once it got under way. He was not able to convince his colleagues that the slavery issue, or the division between North and South, was more important than the question of big states versus small states. In a sense one of the trickiest things about understanding the convention is to assess just how well the delegates understood the nature of the society for which they were trying to devise a government.

MR. BERNS: Surely part of the success of the United States has to do with the fact that its two major political parties live in the "same world," and I think Americans were of the same world at the very beginning. It is easy for Americans to exaggerate the differences that existed at the beginning. Practically everyone who was responsible for the Constitution shared the same principles, would have agreed with the description in *The Federalist* of the celebrated Montesquieu, and would have shared the opinion that government is an artifact, that it has to be brought into being by man. They refused to accept the proposition that anyone may govern by the grace of God; they believed it was contrary to the principle of equality of all men, as stated in the Declaration of Independence, which means that no man may govern another without his consent.

The Constitution of the United States is the statement of that consent. The government comes out of the people; hence, the first words of the Constitution are "We the People of the United States, in Order to form.". . . Legitimate government comes out of the people. To an astonishing extent, almost all Americans agreed with this view at the beginning. Tocqueville understood that there were fewer differences between New Englanders and Georgians, separated by a thousand miles, than between Britons and Normans, separated by a brook.

As Professor Rakove says, the framers did not know how to deal with the slavery issue; it is also quite clear that they could not have had the Constitution if they had tried to deal with that issue as a matter of principle. It is also true, however, that everyone there agreed that what they were doing with respect to Negro slaves was unjust, that it was contrary to natural right. The constitutional provision having to do with the slave trade is itself an index of that. They knew that what they were doing was improper but did not know what else to do about it. Let me stress again the extent to which Americans were united at the beginning, something that surely had to do with the success of this attempt to establish good government through reflection and choice.

When I served in Geneva as the American representative on the United Nations Human Rights Commission, I saw how the notion of the rights of man or of human rights is cheapened by the extent to which rights are brought into being by United Nations assemblies. One of the United Nations covenants, which, in its wisdom, the U.S. Senate has refused to ratify, has a "human right" to a paid vacation, as if Thomas Jefferson in the Declaration of Independence had said, "We hold these truths to be self-evident, that all men are created equal, that they are endowed by their Creator with certain unalienable Rights, that among these are Life, Liberty and a paid vacation." The absurdity of that I think needs no further comment from me.

One interesting thing about the government of the United States, which was brought into being to secure rights, is the extent to which those rights have been secured not by the judiciary but by the very structure of the government that the founders established. We in this country enjoy freedom of religion. It is not frequently understood that the first occasion on which the Supreme Court of the United States had to enforce the First Amendment—which reads, in part, "Congress shall make no law respecting an establishment of religion"—against the government of the United States was in 1971. We enjoy free speech, and the first occasion on which the Supreme Court of the United States enforced that provison against the government of the United States was in 1965. The Court has had a major role in securing these civil rights only in its capacity of supervising the states. All the great free speech cases, the great freedom of religion cases, almost without exception, have had to do with the federal structure. That, in part, is because of the failure of the states to have the kind of structured system that has secured rights at the federal level.

GUSTAVO PLANCHART MANRIQUE: Mr. Goldwin began by asking whether the system established by the U.S. Constitution was based on reflection and choice and not on accident and force. The immediate answer of the people who have commented on this question has been yes. We forget that the issue the framers could not resolve in 1787—the question of slavery—had to be resolved not by reflection and choice but by accident and force, as we saw in the war of secession. It was a very bloody war; the problem that had not been resolved in 1787 brought about the first modern war seventy years later. Therefore, we see how the Union and the Constitution are maintained not by the instruments of the Constitution itself but, as unfortunately happens in many parts of the world, by the use of force.

The U.S. Constitution conceived in 1787 is and has been, without doubt, a great success. But I believe that it is not possible to say that it is the same constitution today that the founders conceived in the eighteenth century. Professor Berns says that if the framers came back today, they would see a president of the republic; they would see an independent judiciary; they would see a senate and a house of representatives. But we can say this of practically all countries. France, which has had three constitutions since 1875, would find as well that under its Constitution today there is a president of the republic; there is a senate; there is a national assembly; there is a supreme court; there is a council of state; when all is said and done, these institutions existed during the past century, at least beginning in the year 1875. Nevertheless, the French Constitution today is very different from the French Constitution that was written in the Third Republic.

The essence of the U.S. Constitution has changed a great deal because of a complex factor—the power of the Supreme Court—as it has developed. One of the mysteries of political life in the United States is that the one power not included in the Constitution that has become a basic power is that of constitutional review by the Supreme Court. This development was a political triumph for Marshall, and we can discuss over and over whether this power is or is not in the Constitution. Without doubt, however, whatever we might decide and even though we must admire the genius of Marshall, the U.S. Constitution is different from that conceived in 1787. *Brown* v. *Board of Education* (1954), for instance, transformed the Constitution. It is a different constitution now. Formally it is the same, but there have been many changes. Quite simply, a peaceful evolution of interpretation is the secret, I believe, of the U.S. Constitution.

Something very striking about the constitutions we are to discuss in this conference is that all of them are parliamentary constitutions except those of the United States and Venezuela, which are presidential. The presidential system of government in the U.S. Constitution has not been imitated except in Latin America. The model of the United States—the *first* constitutional model—serves throughout the South American continent, but on the entire European continent and the Asian continent and the African continent, countries look for systems based on the parliamentary system of English origin. Why is presidentialism, as it was conceived by the people of the United States, not a model that has been imitated except by Latin American countries? Why have all other countries thought of parliamentary solutions?

BERNARD LEWIS: I would like to address the question about choosing "reflection and choice" over "accident and force." Perhaps after some 200 years of experience with written constitutions in a wide variety of societies and political cultures, we might reformulate the alternatives and regard the problem rather as the interplay of historical and ideological forces in constitutional development and struggles. Writing a constitution is not the only way of making one. You also can grow one, so to speak, and there are half a dozen examples of that. At first one wonders what there can be in common among Israel, Libya, Oman, Saudi Arabia, New Zealand, and the United Kingdom. But if we look more closely, they fall into two groups, one British and the other Islamic, with certain features shared by each side. "Growing" a constitution is not precisely the same as "accident and force," although both accident and force obviously have their roles; it is

175

building on the basis of the historical experience of a nation or of a society.

President Tsatsos, in the introductory pages of his essay on the Greek constitutional experience, gives us a brief but important insight into the role of historical experiences in the emergence of successive Greek constitutions—the role of the Orthodox church, the decentralization of the Ottoman Empire in the eighteenth century, and the consequent development of a provincial gentry and magistracy exercising constitutional powers.

On the other side is the ideological element, which begins, in formal constitutional enactments, with various examples both earlier and later than the U.S. Constitution. The Belgian Constitution of 1831 had many advantages for Europe and the Middle East. It was moderately liberal, it was parliamentary, it was monarchical, and it was written in French; all these characteristics made it more acceptable than the American model in many parts of the world in the nineteenth century.

Ideological constitutions, as distinct from historically developed ones, are transferable; they can be moved from one country to another. One can even trace a kind of genealogical tree of constitutions as they have developed in different parts of the world over the past 200 years. I am not a lawyer; I do not know whether this has been done; but I think it would be worth the trouble. Obviously, all sorts of difficulties arise with imported constitutions. The strength of the U.S. Constitution is that it was indigenous to one political cultural tradition. The external elements, the French ideologies, were an outcrop of British constitutional experience. Constitutions in all too many cases have simply been imported in a box with a do-it-yourself kit, often with instructions written in a language that the purchaser cannot fully understand. The application of such constitutions has raised important questions, such as, On whose reflection and by whose choice are governments established?

As we look at more recent developments, we see that the historical conditions, the facts, the realities, may be greatly modified by imported ideas, often imperfectly assimilated. But ideologies must be adapted to the realities of particular societies, or constitutions based on them will fall apart, and we shall see the familiar sight of a historical landscape littered with broken-down and abandoned constitutions. Even if they do not break, they become empty forms, of which we see many examples in the world today. A constitution, in such cases, is not a means of securing certain rights but is a substitute for them. All kinds of splendid rights and liberties are enshrined in a constitution, but a more accurate term would be "embalmed" in it. They are very safely contained in the constitution but with a purely declaratory value, and this relieves the rulers of the countries concerned from doing anything serious about them.

The unique strength of the U.S. Constitution, which has enabled it not only to last for a long time but to remain effective, is precisely in the merging of the historical and the ideological aspects of its formation. This Constitution was a result not only of reflection and choice but of the historical experiences of the American colonies and of the countries from which the Americans came.

VOJISLAV STANOVCIC: I would like to address the relation of the writing of the U.S. Constitution to the chain of events that we call the American Revolution. The very understanding of the revolution has been changing. The American Revolution was a revolution in the proper sense, and it was taken to be such by the leaders of the time—Adams, Washington, Madison, and others—who referred to the events they participated in as a revolution. It was the first anticolonial revolution, but it was not the first democratic revolution; a revolution in the Netherlands and the revolution in England were also democratic revolutions. But the American Revolution was the first in which a large number of people participated in constituting government by reflection and choice and also by accident and force. Even before the War of Independence began, popular assemblies were constituted in some colonies, and they acted contemporaneously with colonial assemblies and governors named by the British Crown. The American Revolution was a political revolution, but it also had elements of social and economic revolution, because the British government had tried to introduce the structure of British society into the colonies in America. For instance, many American farmers could not sell their lands without written permission from the legislature; their land was treated as the property of the British king or of people to whom the British king delegated it. The American Revolution had some elements of social revolution, then, but some modern political ideologies have incorrectly created a picture of it as a revolution like the French Revolution, including the bloodshed.

Fortunately, the leaders of the American Revolution succeeded in constitutionalizing their revolution. At least some of the basic ideas of the revolution were transformed into working political and legal institutions, and the Constitution was the culmination of this process. The process of making the Constitution lasted for almost twenty years; it had begun even before the Declaration of Independence was written. The question now is, When did the process end? I would say that it did not end in 1787, because, as Article 16 of the French Dec-

177

laration of Rights of 1789 says, a society in which guarantees of human rights do not exist and the separation of powers is not established has no constitution. The separation of powers, the mechanism of checks and balances, which is a contribution of the American Founding Fathers to the history of political institutions, limited the power of government; but without the first ten amendments the United States still had no constitution. I am inclined to treat the first ten amendments in quite a different way from the rest of the amendments, although they are all formally part of the Constitution.

MR. GOLDWIN: I must ask you a direct question on that, Dr. Stanovcic. *The Federalist*, which you have translated into Serbo-Croation, is a commentary on the Constitution of the United States without a bill of rights. Would you really argue that the document interpreted in *The Federalist* is not a constitution?

MR. STANOVCIC: It is *called* a constitution, and many contemporary constitutions do not guarantee human rights. But, in a proper political sense, it can also be argued that they are not constitutions. Hamilton, in *Federalist* No. 84, argued against the Bill of Rights; he thought it unnecessary. But I do not think the process of constitutionalization of the American Revolution ended in 1787. It was a promise not only of Madison but of many others during ratification that a bill of rights would be added.

MR. GOLDWIN: In that very passage you speak of in *Federalist* No. 84, in which Hamilton argued against adding a bill of rights to the Constitution, his argument was that "the constitution is itself in every rational sense, and to every useful purpose, A BILL OF RIGHTS." It was not that he was against a bill of rights; he thought they had written one, and it was called the Constitution of the United States.

HARVEY C. MANSFIELD: The question of rights in the American Constitution cannot be considered without reference to the Declaration of Independence. The relation between the U.S. Constitution and the Declaration of Independence was made especially clear for us by the most authoritative interpreter of the Constitution, Abraham Lincoln; that is that the Constitution was a "frame of silver" and the Declaration was an "apple of gold." He interpreted the Declaration as more important, or more fundamental, than the Constitution, because it contains within itself the right to consent. We are indebted to Mr. Lewis for reminding us that the success of constitutionalism is not proved by the number of constitutions in the world. He referred to ideological constitutions, which are communicable and may sometimes be communicated by imposition, by being imposed on foreign or subject peoples. The principle of the U.S. Constitution, insofar as it is inspired by the Declaration, attempts to avoid this kind of imposition by ensuring that each people that copies the American example does so with its own right of consent and its own right of choice.

ALBERT BLAUSTEIN: The American Revolution was a part of the Great Atlantic Revolution, but it was not as strong or as revolutionary as Tocqueville said. The people of America were already literate; they owned land; there was plenty to go around. By 1776 America had the highest literacy rate in the world and no feudalism. The reason why the French Revolution was greater was that the French had so much further to go. They were separating themselves from a feudal structure.

As to the necessity of a bill of rights, no one in his right mind today would think of writing a new constitution without a delineation of rights. We start with the concept that the people are sovereign and that they sacrifice certain rights to have a framework for society. They sacrifice the right to some of their own earnings and property, for example, to provide taxes to support a central government. It is very dangerous to list rights for fear of the application of the doctrine of *expressio unus est exclusio alterius.*

In America we put down a list of rights 200 years ago. These rights are found in the United Nations Universal Declaration of Human Rights. When that document became inadequate for our modern needs (as far as the United Nations was concerned), they wrote a new bill of rights. New constitutions include the right of privacy, the right to travel freely, and so on—not things that were important at the time the U.S. Constitution was written.

The listing of rights is not what gave them to the American people. It was the Constitution itself that incorporated the sovereignty of the people. I would say, with Hamilton, that the Constitution is itself a bill of rights. To please everyone, the framers spelled some rights out to make certain that we knew them. Dr. Berns was correct, of course, that we did not get around to talking about freedom of religion or the establishment clause for a hundred years. When the United States was founded, half of it was a theocracy; so what did they mean by freedom of religion? We had a good Constitution, and we embellished it with the first ten amendments.

BRUCE E. FEIN: The question was raised why the United States seemed to be peculiar in adopting an executive, presidential constitution as opposed to a parliamentary system, which has been the model for a vast number of countries. At least a partial answer is that a parliamentary system was initially established in the colonies. The state constitutions that prevailed in 1787 endowed the state legislatures with a vast amount of power. The federal Constitution of 1787 was a reaction against what was called the tyranny of the majority, which was so firmly ensconced in the structures of the state constitutions. The initial constitution building in the United States, undertaken by the states, did, indeed, reflect a parliamentary system, and we might well have begun our federal government with a more parliamentary system if we had not had an unfortunate experience with strong legislative power in the states.

I also want to address the point about how closely our Constitution today resembles that envisioned by the Founding Fathers. Hamilton remarked that he envisioned the American judiciary as "the least dangerous branch" of the three. Today, however, after a period of several decades, the judiciary in the United States is, in my judgment, far more powerful an institution than our legislative bodies. The Supreme Court entertains 5,000 cases each term; it hears issues relating to abortion, school busing, books in school libraries, and the operation of prison systems. I could go on *ad infinitum* on the number of issues that the Supreme Court entertains. It even decides such questions as whether there is a constitutional right to have a municipal utility company explain why one's water service has been terminated for nonpayment of a bill. The Constitution, as expounded by the judiciary, has crept into virtually every dimension of American life, something that the Founding Fathers never envisioned.

Moreover, the Founding Fathers clearly thought that power would move toward the legislative branch, which is one reason why they endowed the executive with more power than was the custom in the state constitutions. Today, however, the executive branch is recognized as far more powerful than Congress. Its power is due to the forces of war. During the Civil War and World Wars I and II vast accretions of power to the president occurred simply as a matter of necessity. Today we have many institutions that violate the traditional norm of separation of powers—namely, our independent agencies, which have the authority to promulgate rules, to enforce them, and to adjudicate claims of violations of them. We now merge all three functions that the Founding Fathers once insisted could not be merged if we were to obtain liberty. I do not think that they would recognize the operation of the Constitution as what they had envisioned. Indeed, they would perceive Americans today as experiencing far less freedom than they would have desired.

MR. RAKOVE: I would like to discuss Mr. Stanovcic's point about the essential character of the Bill of Rights. I disagree in part for reasons that Professor Blaustein mentioned, but also for another reason that has not been touched upon. At the time the framers met in 1787 a number of bills of rights were available to them for their use. Most of the state constitutions, which had been written in 1776, contained bills of rights. These were rather hodgepodge documents, hard to characterize. They included some of the classic common-law notions; they also included a number of other provisions that we might no longer recognize as parts of a bill of rights.

When Madison and others attempted to put their ideas together in the spring of 1787, they had the experience of constitutions of which bills of rights had been essential parts. Madison in particular had thought a great deal about the merits of bills of rights as found in the state constitutions. He himself had contributed in a minor way to the framing of the best known of these, the Virginia Declaration of Rights of 1776. It was virtually his first political act. Madison believed that bills of rights were potentially useful documents, but he did not have a great deal of faith in them, because they are rarely self-enforcing. An independent judiciary or a vigorous population or some other force is needed to make sure that a bill of rights can work, and the experience of the ten years that passed between independence and the assembly of the federal convention in 1787 had demonstrated that bills of rights by themselves were not particularly useful.

As Madison sat down in the spring of 1787 to think through the problem of federal government, he was very much concerned—indeed, we could say he was preeminently concerned—with the problems of creating a federal government capable of protecting what he regarded as the private liberties of citizens within the states and within the nation. He was thinking particularly of the rights of property, but he was also very sensitive to issues of civil liberties, such as religious liberty, an issue he had felt deeply about ever since he had been a student at Princeton in the early 1770s.

Madison's answer to the problem of rights and how to protect them is quite revealing. His own rather original proposal, in some ways the most innovative aspect of his thought, was the idea of creating in the national government a veto over the legislative powers of the states. Any law passed by the states would have had to be submitted to the national legislature for approval. His concern was principally that the greatest threat to the existence of individual liberty came from the state governments and, in particular, from the character of the state legislatures. Accordingly, he thought that to create the right kind of national government and to vest this power in it would be the most secure protection for individual liberty.

This proposal was not accepted by the convention, although it was initially received somewhat favorably. It gave way to the supremacy clause and, eventually, to the Bill of Rights, which Madison agreed to frame in 1789. It is nevertheless fair to say that when he and the framers generally were thinking about the problem of protecting liberty, they did not place the confidence in bills of rights that we do today. Their original conviction was that the best way to protect liberty is to create a well-ordered government, a government that would check itself through the various mechanisms that fall under the heading of separation of powers or checks and balances.

It is sometimes argued that the Federalists were disingenuous in making the argument that Mr. Blaustein very ably summarized, namely, that a bill of rights is not needed in a government with limited powers. One could also say that the framers saw the problem of protecting liberty as a problem of creating the right kind of government. If so, bills of rights—though nice things to have and under some circumstances more than nice things to have—in themselves would not carry much weight. The right kind of government, properly constructed and properly balanced, would provide a stable institutional setting in which liberty, given the inherent genius of the American people, could protect itself.

MR. BERNS: It was altogether proper for Mr. Planchart to remind us that the United States experienced a civil war and was affected by that violent event. Except for the Vietnam War, more Americans were killed in the Civil War than in all the other wars that the United States has fought combined. Within a few miles of where we are sitting are some of the battlefields where thousands were killed during that Civil War. We are still suffering some of the consequences of slavery, that blemish on our history that was not altogether removed by the victory of the United States over the Confederate States of America during the Civil War. When we talk about nonvoting and so forth, that is a large part of it; we are still paying a price.

I was struck by the question why the Constitution of the United States has not served as a model to the extent that parliamentary systems have for constitutions around the world. I do not know the answer, but I offer some suggestions. The U.S. Constitution was based on certain principles that were very quickly challenged by very powerful minds. The first of those challenges, issued by Jean-Jacques

Rousseau, came before the Declaration of Independence and therefore before the writing of the U.S. Constitution.

To generalize my point, the United States was very fortunate that it began after Locke and Montesquieu but before Marx—letting Marx serve as a metaphor for all kinds of other people. In that connection, surely it is visible to those who see the United States with fresh eyes that the number of Marxists on university faculties in the United States is probably ten times the number in the American labor movement. Discontent with American principles and with the Constitution of the United States is much more likely to come from college professors, who have read Marx and talk the language of Nietzsche, than from the American labor movement, whose members are probably the strongest supporters of the Constitution that can be found in this country.

As to why the U.S. Constitution has not served as a model in our democratic times, I can make my point this way: Jeremy Bentham's formulation—the greatest good for the greatest number—is, in an important respect, un-American. What the greatest number regards as their greatest good may be incompatible with the good of the minority. In the beginning, therefore, when the focus was on securing the rights of all, there was an awareness that a simple majority government can also threaten rights. Hence the U.S Constitution is a series of limitations on popular majorities and was so understood by Madison. See, for example, the last sentence of *Federalist* No. 10.

> And according to the degree of pleasure and the pride we
> feel in being republicians, ought to be our zeal in cherishing
> the spirit and supporting the character of Federalists.

I wonder whether, as the idea of democracy has spread around the world and been severed from the idea of the rights of man, the authority of popular majorities has been enhanced and the idea of constitutionalism—understood as limits on popular majorities, limits imposed to secure rights—has been undermined.

I want to comment on whether the United States had a revolution and how revolutionary its beginning was. It is, of course, true, as Tocqueville pointed out, that the United States was lucky because Americans were born equal without having to become so. That, I think, is an exact quotation, at least in the English translation. It was a tremendous advantage, of course, but that statement must be modified. Some people in this country at the beginning—"throne and altar" people—did not subscribe to the principle of equality and, because they did not, were driven out or found it advisable to leave, for Britain or for Canada.

5
The Creation of the 1974 Constitution of the Socialist Federal Republic of Yugoslavia

Jovan Djordjevic

Fundamental Principles

Since the beginning of this century, differences among mankind's economic, social, political, and cultural systems or forms have been increasing. Differences in constitutions have also been increasing. The creation and content of constitutions are influenced by the major political and social doctrines (especially today by socialism and capitalism) as well as by political ideas and religious ideologies. These areas have changed and, parallel to these changes is the development of the science of policy and theory concerning constitutional law. Scientific thought is coming closer to politics and politics closer to science. To a decreasing extent constitutions are mere proclamations and declarations; increasingly they are not only instruments of government and means for consolidating existing political orders but also acts of change and anticipation.

Under such conditions, constitutions become the object of science. Most constitutions are entrusted to scholars and experts who are also providers of the ruling ideologies that inspire the creation and passage of new constitutions. A particularly important innovation is the introduction of economic and sociocultural principles and provisions, which makes modern constitutions even more complex and necessarily links them in their formulation to science.

The first Yugoslav constitutions, passed after the Liberation War and the Socialist Revolution, were political constitutions in the sense that they were devoted exclusively to the institutionalization of new political governments and new institutions. This is true, not only of the revolutionary decrees on the establishment of supreme government organs in the federation in 1943 but also of the first constitution of Yugoslavia in 1946. The other constitutions, primarily the currently valid 1974 Constitution of Yugoslavia, changed in character, and thereby the concept and method of creating and passing legislation changed; but each constitution maintained continuity with the previous phases of the social and political development of Yugoslavia and thereby with previous constitutions. In this continuity each constitution not only extends but also surpasses previous constitutions. In this sense, the present Yugoslav Constitution is both a new and, to a considerable extent, an original political-legal act.

Yugoslavia has passed four constitutions since the end of the Second World War: in 1946, 1953, 1963, and 1974. All these constitutional changes expressed the degree of sociopolitical and cultural development of the country and the desire to confirm constitutionally the changes that had come about or that were anticipated. Between passage of the 1963 Constitution and the decision to pass a new constitution, the following occurred: in 1971, amendments were passed to define the Yugoslav federation in accordance with the desire for greater autonomy for all the Yugoslav nations and nationalities. In this period in our republic there were separatist aspirations and even a separatist movement. The amendments, however, did not go far enough in elaborating and supplementing the socioeconomic provisions of the 1963 Constitution. The 1971 amendments partially addressed the questions about the change in the structure of the federation and the establishment of the socioeconomic system based on self-management, but the need for a more coherent solution to these problems made passing a new constitution necessary. The new constitution, however, only repeated or supplemented the principles and provisions of the 1963 Constitution.

In the beginning, the following objectives were the basis for preparing the new constitution:

• strengthening the equality and community spirit of the nations (Serbian, Croatian, Slovenian, Macedonian, Montenegrin, and Moslem) and the nationalities (especially the Albanians and the Hungarians because of their large numbers);
• developing the concept of the socialist economic and social system, founded on community ownership and worker self-management; and

- democratizing political processes and the political system as a whole

In the course of elaborating these fundamental objectives, other issues were discussed and resolved in the same context, such as

- broadening the rights of the republics and decreasing the federation's jurisdiction compared with previous periods;
- transforming the previous autonomy of the regions of Vojvodina (due to its ethnic pluralism) and of Kosovo (as a result of the majority Albanian population) into autonomous provinces approaching the status of federal units;
- introducing the delegate system in forming all representative bodies to improve the representative system and prevent its alienating citizens and workers from true decision making;
- developing self-management as a principle, both in the economy and in social and cultural institutions, including the formation of residents' associations and communities of interest;
- introducing parallel heads of state, the presidency of the republic and the presidency of Yugoslavia, with the stipulation that with the death of President Tito, all attributes of the head of state would be transferred to the presidency of Yugoslavia as a collegial body; and
- decreasing executive functions in favor of representative bodies and in accordance with the general principle of "assembly government" (the principle of convention).

These changes transformed Yugoslav constitutional law for they created a new concept of Yugoslav constitutionalism. This new concept was expressed, first of all, in the 1963 Constitution and even more so in the present constitution. Once mainly a political plan the constitution has become a social plan.

This social constitution or "constitution of the society" developed because of the political and ideological emancipation of Yugoslavia and the adoption of an independent and autonomous position in the system of socialist states. Yugoslavia achieved this emancipation because it resisted Stalin's hegemony and because its people wanted to become constituted and to live in accordance with their socialist and democratic aspirations based on freedom-loving traditions. The backbone of this social constitution is self-management as a new relation between productivity and the distribution of generated income among economic and other organizations of associated labor. Thereby a new and radically changed relationship exists between one social element in society and the regulation of basic economic, political, and cultural relations. Although the state is part of this social complex, it is not the governing form. This change has also decreased the traditional, normative nature of the constitution. The Constitution of Yugoslavia contains the philosophy of one form of socialism: self-management socialism. It is not a static or positivistic document, however, for it also allows for changes that a constitution as a social and political force should ensure in recognizing new areas of socialism, democracy, and freedom on the path to communism.

Yugoslavia is a multi-ethnic community made up of nations and groups that are, in the main, ethnically close but that differ in their interests, histories, and conditions of life. From this fact alone stems (1) the phenomenon of greater autonomy, yet greater unity, in the economic structure, the result of introducing the concept of the "organization of associated labor" as an instrument to ensure the right of self-management in a direct manner; and (2) the degree of decentralization in the federal structure, which has led to the dilemma between confederalism and federalism.

These controversies and dilemmas were not political; they became manifest in the process of creating the constitution. The accepted solutions have their own constitutionally legal and practical side. The relative atomization of the economic system is solved by the constitution's stress on the coordinating functions of the federation and the republics as well as on the economic principle underlying the integral nature of the Yugoslav market. In the creation of the constitution, certain confederal problems were comprehended and solved within the concept of federalism.

Discussion on these points led logically to mainly common positions and opinions. The practical implementation of the solutions, however, opened up old difficulties that had not been solved in the "living" constitution. The fear of centralization and even of homogeneity, resulted in the maintenance of decentralized diversity, especially in the economy, and in the underestimation of the importance of common, centralized functions in the economic, social, and cultural life of the community.

The realization of constitutional solutions to these problems was initiated by questioning not only the necessity of centralizing functions (even outside the domains of national defense and foreign policy) but also the necessity of finding room for integrative forces and processes, within the scope of both the state and the "citizens' society."

The 1974 Constitution of Yugoslavia, like the previous constitution, is characterized by its division into theoretical-ideological and normative spheres. Accordingly, the constitution contains, besides the preamble, an introductory section devoted to basic principles and goals. These objectives and principles are elaborated, as much as possible, in imperative provisions in other parts of the constitution. This emphasis on constitutional philosophy causes certain difficulties, especially with respect to the boundary between theoretical and normative principles or provisions. The solution to these difficulties is that the constitution partially repeats philosophical principles in its concrete provisions.

Every constitution has its own philosophy and ideology, though they frequently are concealed. The Constitution of Yugoslavia lifts such principles and goals to a constitutional level for two basic reasons: first, it constitutes the society during a transitional period, when there is no definitive and permanent system; second, constitutional principles serve as the basis for interpreting not only the spirit but also the letter of the constitution. In this respect, there have been no controversies or problems. In the process of creating the constitution, however, Yugoslavians hoped that it would include the entire social life. Although such problems were eliminated, everything in the constitution does not represent constitutional material *lege artis*. In any case, the experts themselves, too, generally believe that the structure of the constitution is one of the heritages of the Yugoslav constitutional tradition. This structure—the introduction of principles and aims into the constitution—also has been implemented in other nations' constitutions passed after 1974 (the 1982 Constitution of the People's Republic of China; the 1975 Constitution of the USSR; and the Constitution of Portugal, among others).

From the historical point of view, this innovation in constitutional structure brings the constitutional act back to its classic sources. The constitution becomes not only the basic law but also a modern ideological-political charter.

The Creation of the Constitution

The constitution for the present, mainly democratic society in Yugoslavia, was created in two phases—the intellectual and creative phase and the politically confirming phase. The first phase refers, according to legal terminology, to the drafting of the text of the constitution, while the second refers to the process of passing the constitution in the parliamentary sense.

In the modern state, parliaments are no longer creative bodies; there are no ideological or theoretical struggles between the various ideological movements as there were in the nineteenth century. Parliaments are no longer composed of ideologically minded politicians and intellectuals. The majority are made up of technocrats, political bureaucrats, and representatives of financial and economic interests. As is shown by modern political practice, parliaments are no longer assemblies in which members conduct principled discussions on the basis of which far-reaching projects are created, comprehensive laws are made, and problems are solved without postponement or amendments. Thus creating a constitution, in the technical and creative sense, requires that the first phase take place mainly outside of parliament, that is, outside the body which "passes the constitution" legally and technically.

The implementation of the first Yugoslav Constitution in 1946 occurred in two phases. The first phase was entrusted, so to speak, to representatives of science, legal theory, and political life. This was also the procedure in the creation of the 1974 Yugoslav Constitution. Far more than in previous periods, however, the composition of the Constitutional Commission, which met from 1971 to the end of 1973 and had the task of preparing the draft for the present constitution, was based on the principle of equal republican and provincial representation.

The preparation of the constitution was carried out under the special political conditions that existed in 1970–1971. During that period a national question arose concerning the relation between the federation, on the one hand, and the republics and the autonomous provinces, on the other. The political atmosphere that surrounded that question touched upon the integrity and stability of the Yugoslav federation and affected the composition and the work of the Constitutional Commission; it thereby also affected the content of the Constitution of Yugoslavia, especially several of the relatively new principles concerning federalism.

The Constitutional Commission was mostly composed of politicians, representatives of the assemblies and of other political bodies of the republics and provinces. The majority among them supported revising the existing concept of centralized federation, centralized especially in the domain of the economy and in the exercise of federal power.

The work of the commission was organized in plenum and in subcommissions. The tasks of the plenum were to devise the constitutional draft, to arbitrate in cases of differing positions or even of conflicts in the work of the subcommissions, and to establish the final text of the constitution. The subcommissions had the tasks of examining and drafting the individual parts of the Constitution: socioeconomic relations; the political system; the rights and freedoms of the citizens; and the organization of and relations within the federation. During the work of the commission several specific questions were submitted to special ad hoc commissions, for example, those concerned with introducing a collective presidency in addition to the president of the republic and one that had the task of defining the relations in the federation—the distribution of powers between it and the republics and the relations between the legislative, executive, and judicial departments.

The ideological basis for the draft of the constitution was not to be devised entirely ad hoc. The bases for this ideology were to be found in reasonably elaborated form in the social theory developed, and creatively renewed and deepened, in 1968–1971, especially through the criticism of Stalinist dogmatism—that is, state socialism—and through the affirmation and elaboration of the principle of self-management. The outlines of the concept of self-management socialism, and increasingly of self-management federalism, were expressed in the Constitution of 1963 and in the amendments to that constitution passed between 1967 and 1971 (especially those passed in 1971). This background was mentioned in the initiative for constitutional changes addressed by the president of the republic to the Assembly of Yugoslavia.

Because of the above-mentioned character and tasks, the work of the Constitutional Commission had a dual nature. The commission conducted discussions, first, to establish positions on new, controversial questions to create the corresponding text for the final draft of the constitution. Second, in addition to discussing basic questions about the constitutional draft and its acceptance, the Constitutional Commission discussed and approved—or, rather, supplemented and changed—certain positions and formulas proposed by the subcommissions. When the commission was discussing controversial and delicate questions, certain high-ranking political officials of the republics and of the federation attended the sessions. Even President Tito attended some sessions.

Constitutional Provisions. The sessions on the text of the constitution addressed the following matters:

- *Distribution of functions among the individual branches of the government.* The basic principle behind this distribution stems from the concept of so-called assembly government, the concept that the functioning of government is centered on the assemblies of sociopolitical communities (federations, republics, autonomous provinces, and municipalities). But the constitution also delegates executive and management functions to the executive departments and the administration of justice to the judicial department.

- *The concept of unity of government.* This concept relates to the division of governmental function in accordance with the Locke-Montesquieu tradition and, therefore, can be defined as a variant of parliamentarianism. The existence of the presidency introduces elements of the presidential system, although it mainly has the functions of the head of state derived from the practice of parliamentarianism and constitutionalism.

- *The limitation of power.* First of all, the general principle is held to be valid that no person, nor any department of power, has more rights than those delegated by the constitution. Other instruments for limiting power are (a) the self-management mechanism, which has its own sphere of functional jurisdiction to keep all others, including the law itself, from interfering; (b) human and citizen freedom and rights, which are contained in the constitution; (c) constitutional courts that control the constitutionality of all regulations and general acts and are autonomous in the constitutional system; and (d) public opinion on and scientific assessment of all cases in which problems arise concerning constitutionality and legality.

- *Competence in foreign policy.* This competence requires the establishment and conduct of foreign policy in the federation by a special body (Secretariat for Foreign Affairs). The socialist republics and autonomous provinces, however, do have the right to participate in the realization of international relations, in accordance with the principles of foreign policy as established by the federation, including international contracts, which only the federation can conclude.

- *The role of religion.* Yugoslavia is a lay state in which exist many religions, including the Orthodox, Catholic, and Moslem religions, which have the most followers, in addition to several smaller sects. The status of religion is defined in the following constitutional terms: (1) freedom of religious choice and conscience; (2) separation of church, state, and school, with the right of the religious communities to organize religious teaching and to perform religious business freely; and (3) equality of all religions and churches, barring the establishment of a "state" or other privileged religion.

- *The role of the army.* The army is characterized in the constitution as basically the defensive force of the country, with no right to interfere in political life. The Constitution of Yugoslavia devotes several provisions, more than any other constitution, to national defense and the armed forces in accordance with the principle that the defense of the country is the right and duty of all citizens and that surrender to an enemy is prohibited.[1]

- *The role of the judiciary.* There are three judicial departments: constitutional courts (federation and republic or province), regular courts, and courts of associated labor. The constitutional courts have jurisdiction over all laws and other regulations and general self-management acts, while the regular courts are administrative, civil, and criminal. The courts of associated labor protect the implementation of self-management and social ownership. The courts are independent in their work and are subject only to the constitution and the law. Their decisions can be changed only by higher courts.

Within the organization of the judiciary are also the public prosecutor's office, the office of criminal prosecution, and the social defender of self-management (the protector of the practice of self-management and behavior in social ownership). All these offices have certain executive jurisdiction: prior to verdicts, the courts can issue executive orders that prevent serious breach of the constitution and the laws.

• *The nature of the legislative bodies.* The legislative power lies exclusively in the assemblies of the sociopolitical communities, with the stipulation that the executive offices have the right to propose legislative acts. The Assembly of Yugoslavia has two chambers: the first chamber is the Federal Chamber and the second is the Chamber of the Republics and Provinces.[2] The Federal Chamber is made up of delegates of self-management organizations and communities, and the Chamber of the Republics and Provinces is made up of delegates from all the republics and provinces with an equal number of delegates from each. These chambers have both independent functions and functions that both perform equally, even at joint sessions. The division of powers between them is based mainly on the following principle: Everything concerning social, economic, or cultural matters belongs to the Federal Chamber, and all other business, mainly political in nature, belongs to the Chamber of the Republics and Provinces.

• *Measures for the development of unity.* The federation was conceived and, in part, functions with the aim of realizing brotherhood and unity among national groups, a type of self-management in a democratic community. All endeavors to form national unity by older national groups are alien to the constitution and to practice. This community, in its present stage and within the scope of the existing constitution, honors the identity of the nations and, in equitable unity, permits the expression of national cultures and national particularities.

• *The unified federal structure.* The political system of Yugoslavia is ideologically and structurally centered on the federation. Yugoslavia is a federal state of united and associated nations and their republics

with specific autonomous provinces that together compose a type of federal unity to implement the principle of equality of nations and nationalities. This form of federalism is decentralized, with its sovereign basis in the nation, that is, in the republics as the nearest expression of that sovereignty, bringing the republics closer to a constitutional definition as states.
(All the provisions above show that decentralized federalism has been established and is practiced in Yugoslavia.)

• *Provisions for the protection of civil rights.* These provisions, expressed in the developed declaration on human freedoms and rights, stress the priority of people in the political system.

• *Provisions for the protection of religious, ethnic, and regional minorities.* These are as follows: Every ethnic, religious, and other kind of minority enjoys autonomy and the right to cultural self-expression; and ethnic minorities in the regions where they are numerous are constituted as autonomous provinces.[3]

• *The status of ownership and management of the economy.* Besides social ownership as the basic status of man in associated labor, the constitution also recognizes associated ownership as a type of social ownership; private ownership in agriculture and the personal use of one's own resources; and the personal ownership of consumer goods. The management of the economy is founded on self-management by commercial producers over organizations and planning, which is *mainly ensured* by the federation and the republics or provinces and by municipalities. The management of the economy falls under the laws and measures passed by executive offices and especially by the Federal Executive Council, which performs the function of government within the framework of the federation.[4]

• *The status of education.* Education is a social function that is performed by schools having self-management status. The purpose of education is to prepare people for work in society and to teach citizen virtues. The latter requires education in ethics devoid of coarse individualism or selfishness.[5]

• *Provisions for political parties.* In the section devoted to principles, the constitution contains principles referring to political organizations (League of Communists of Yugoslavia [LCY], Socialist Alliance, Trade Union Confederation, and citizens' associations). All these organizations are autonomous and are legal under the constitution. The constitution does not provide for a monopoly position of any one of them and, therefore, does not so provide for the LCY.

• *Provisions for the media.* The constitution provides for freedom of the press and freedom of information and communications. In accordance with this provision, mass media are not a "fourth authority," but they do considerably influence public opinion and the work of the state machinery.[6]

• *The several types of citizenship.* Each person is a citizen of a republic and of the federation. Every republican citizen is automatically a citizen of Yugoslavia, however, which makes Yugoslav citizenship general and basic. This provision is relevant not only for international relations but also for the free circulation of ideas and goods within the country itself.

• *Criteria concerning the enjoyment of human rights.* The constitution confirms, as its basic principle, the equal rights of all citizens; and therefore it bans all discrimination on the basis of religion, sex, nationality, or other such criteria.

• *Taxing power.* This power resides in federal, republican, and provincial law. The federation defines this power in accordance with its constitutional power, and the republics and provinces enjoy the same right.

• *Status of international law.* The constitution provides for the priority of international law and the binding nature of international contracts into which Yugoslavia has entered. On this basis, too, Yugoslavia upholds the relation between national law and international law, especially that passed by the United Nations.

• *Suspension of the constitution in extraordinary circumstances.* The constitution contains a stipulation that the president of Yugoslavia may suspend certain of its provisions in the case of war and other extraordinary circumstances, although that suspension can last only as long as the emergency persists. The act of suspension must be submitted to the Assembly of Yugoslavia for confirmation.[7]

• *The process of passing amendments.* Amendments are passed under the same conditions and according to the same process as the constitution itself. There is no specific or shortened process for the passing of amendments.

• *Process of ratification.* Once passed and voted upon, the constitution is subject to ratification by each republican assembly. The deadline for ratification is not stipulated, but in practice it is effective directly after passing of the constitution in the federal assembly. The proclamation of the constitution takes place at the federal assembly, at a joint session of both chambers.

• *Principle and forms of self-management.* A considerable portion of the constitutional principles and provisions is devoted to the nature and, especially, the forms of self-management. This concept makes the Constitution of Yugoslavia unique. Self-management means the right of, and the possibility for, associated workers to manage resources, products, and the conditions of their common labor. The constitution guarantees self-management with several principles, especially the following:

—the elimination of all forms of socioeconomic or political relations and organizations founded on class exploitation and monopoly of ownership;

—the right to work with socially owned means the founding of economic, social, political, cultural, and scientific enterprises and other organizations, all through self-management elements in all structures of government and management;

—the free and equitable organization of mutual relations and the adjustment of common and general interests with the passing of such acts of nonstate or autonomous law, such as self-management agreements and social compacts;

—the right to choose delegates to the assemblies of sociopolitical communities;

—the right to obtain information on all questions on which qualified decision making depends;

—the public nature of the work of all organs of government and the self-management and the creation of an open society;

—collective decision making, and collective and personal responsibility of all bearers of self-management functions;

—the social control of self-management jurisdiction over work and the functioning of the entire self-management and state system;

—the realization and protection of constitutionality and legality; and

—free and complete activities of individuals and collectives.

In addition, the normative section deals with organizational and legal questions and the status of each of the forms of self-management. The constitution, therefore, contains several provisions of an economic character, which is unusual, as well as organizational solutions. Besides the fundamental principles, the normative section also contains 403 other provisions, which makes it the most voluminous section of the constitution.

All these individual problems of constitutional regulation were the subject of comprehensive and frequently controversial discussion. This discussion did not lead to any essential ideological or political differences, however. The relative unanimity is the consequence of two factors: First, the country had a reigning political culture; second, for the most part the drafters had already accepted the constitutional heritage confirmed and expressed both in the 1963 Constitution and in the 1971 amendments. Accordingly, the differences and controversies primarily concerned constitutional formulas and the structure of the constitution.

The Constitutional Commission was mainly an expert, creative body that interpreted the general consciousness regarding constitutional questions and the scope of individual constitutional innovation, especially from the point of view of comparative constitutional law and the rational concept of socialism. Such creation is, at the same time, a political act, but only under the condition that it is not reduced to formalism and verbalism. In this sense, the participation of the Constitutional Commission in the creation of the constitution was both creative and political. This statement is confirmed by the fact that the chairman of the commission was Edvard Kardelj, the late leading Yugoslav theoretician and politician.

In this process of creation, certain accepted positions were more ideological and political than rational and realistic. This situation was justified by the absence of historical precedents. The creation of an original constitution of socialism and democratic federalism, structured by the objective circumstances of the place and the time of its preparation and passage, helped make the constitutional process possible. In the discussions, however, and in individual positions and solutions—especially in the subcommissions—extremism was noted concerning bureaucratic centralism versus human spontaneity, federalism versus confederalism, and the right of nations to self-determination versus a unitary state.

The distances between these positions widened because of still unclarified concepts and confusion about the differences between centralism and centralization, unitarism and centralism, and federalism and confederalism, as well as between federalism and autonomy, state- and self-control, freedom and self-will, law and responsibility. Certain members of the commission and subcommissions in their speeches and interventions markedly endeavored to clarify these concepts and differences, which, in the case of the acceptance of scientifically justified solutions, contributed to the original and coherent character not only of the draft but also of the final text of the Constitution of Yugoslavia.

Influences on the Yugoslav Constitution

Viewed historically as a political and legal act, the constitution was gradually created through a struggle between autocracy and democracy, a struggle to limit political absolutism and to provide certain human freedoms and rights, such as the right to social conditions that allow respect for the human personality. The first elements of what was later to be called a constitution are to be found in the history of almost all countries of the world. The constitutional history of England, for instance, has had the greatest influence on the gradual creation of political, ideological, and legal concepts found in documents that, since the eighteenth century, have been instruments establishing and limiting the authority of the sociopolitical organization. This is the sense in which I use the term "constitution."

Influence of Foreign Constitutions. The constitution as a model, from the eighteenth century until the present, has been accepted throughout the world, regardless of differences in social or political systems or in the degree of development and civilization of particular regions and countries. Although constitutions are mainly national and specific ideological instruments, the constitutions of certain countries have exerted influence on other constitutions having similar aspirations and political commitments. As a result of this influence, countries have ranged from accepting basic principles and institutions to imitating a constitutional text completely. Such influence was especially characteristic of the constitutions passed after the American and French revolutions. The two constitutions of France, passed at the end of the eighteenth and at the beginning of the nineteenth centuries, were especially used as constitutional models, but after them the Belgian Constitution was so used. After the First World War the 1919 Constitution of the German Reich and the 1931 republican Constitution of Spain exerted special influence. In the establishment of socialist countries to the present, the 1936 Constitution of the USSR has been the accepted model both in and outside Europe (for example, it was the model for the first Chinese and Vietnamese constitutions).

In addition to imitating the characteristics of other constitutions, certain constitutions try to express the specific nature of a nation's social system and its new political objectives and institutions. This attempt applies especially to constitutions passed after a country's revolution, expressing essential social and political changes and, thereby, even the desire to free itself from the influence of imposed or, sometimes, accepted constitutional models. The current Constitution of the Socialist Federal Republic of Yugoslavia finds a special place among these constitutions.

No historical or modern constitutions have had any direct effect on the structure and fundamental provisions of this Yugoslav Constitution, as has been shown. The contrary could even be said: The Constitution of Yugoslavia, as is true of all constitutions in history, has begun a new dialectic. According to dialectical law, conservative political regimes uniformly create conservative constitutions. The desire to create democratic and progressive constitutions, however, results in differences among them or, rather, results in some constitutions' being original. Such an original one is the Yugoslav Constitution.

To say that the Yugoslav Constitution is original does not mean that certain existing constitutions exerted no influence on Yugoslavian constitutional principles and forms. The Constitution of the Swiss confederation and the U.S. Constitution, for example, inspired constructive solutions for Yugoslav federalism. The U.S. Constitution inspired the introduction and development of constitutionality and the rule of law as well as the mechanism for maintaining constitutionality within the scope of the Yugoslav Constitution. The Yugoslav Constitution was also directly influenced by international constitutional acts, especially the Universal Declaration on Human Rights and Freedoms.

The 1936 Constitution of the USSR indirectly influenced the Yugoslav Constitution concerning autonomy of republics and provinces and concerning the differentiation between self-management and state socialism, between state ownership and state planning, and between social ownership and self-management planning. In all political creativity, and therefore in the creation of constitutions as well, influence can be derived from criticism of certain unacceptable solutions found elsewhere. Such influence can be felt, first, through discovering the essences of various approaches to sociopolitical relations and, second, through criticizing these approaches as existing solutions. Such criticism influenced the creation of many of the institutions and provisions of the Constitution of Yugoslavia. In this way both the old creative constitutions and the modern democratic constitutional acts had their influence.

The Influence of Creative Thought. Crucial influence is exerted on the creation of constitutions that aim to be original, and on original acts of new systems, by creative political theory. This statement is especially true of the Constitution of Yugoslavia, which reflects both the criticism of statism and the effort to explain the priority of socialist society vis-à-vis the state and the establishment of self-management. This influence was felt in the critical and constructive phase of the development of Yugoslav social science during the past four decades, especially since the introduction of self-management and the emphasis on the democratic, humanist variants of socialism in Yugoslavia. Besides the social sciences, in which both the older and the younger generations in all Yugoslav nations and nationalities are learned, of special interest in the creation of the constitution was the general theoretical and creative political thought that went into it.

Many individuals, especially those who were members of the Constitutional Commission and those of rank and renown in social science and politics, influenced the creation of the constitution. Although the constitution is basically a collective act, two individuals—President Tito and Edvard Kardelj, president of the Constitutional Commission—made particular contributions to its creation. Their contributions can be defined in two ways. The first can be described as ideological and theoretical creativity, while the second lies in concrete solutions to disagreements over the formulation of the constitution.

New ideas and support for the principles and orientation of the constitution can be found in the works of both Tito and Kardelj, but their original form is in the theoretical and political works of Tito. His work was influenced by his personality and by the reigning views and ideas that inspired the creation and development of Yugoslavia from the Liberation War and Socialist Revolution until the creation of the constitution. Tito followed the work of the Constitutional Commission closely and injected his own publicly expressed opinions on controversial questions. He also was called upon to serve on the Constitutional Commission itself.

In this way, Tito helped resolve several problems concerning federalism and confederalism. By stressing the former, he helped settle questions in favor of exclusive federal functions, for example, concerning the army and foreign policy. Tito also supported introducing the presidency of Yugoslavia in addition to the office of the president of the Republic, which remained in the constitution while Tito was titulary ruler. Tito also urged ensuring the equality of national groups and nationalities in the organization and functioning of the federation. A year later he called for consolidating the principle of collective decision making and rotation at all upper levels of the state.

Edvard Kardelj, known as a leading theoretician of self-management and the "indefinite" institutions of socialist democracy, made a special contribution to the preparation of the constitution, especially in stressing new and effective ideas in economics and in the general social system. He contributed his lucid and critical thought to virtually all theoretical formulas, especially to the concept of the "self-management organization of associated labor" and its introduction into the constitution as the foundation for the self-management of society. Kardelj also urged recognition of the principles of responsibility and of new human rights (including ecological rights, which, thanks to him, for the first time appear in a modern constitution and thereby protect the natural and social integrity of the environment in which people live and work).

Tito's participation in the creation of the constitution did not subjugate the role and influence of his collaborators nor those of the experts, especially in political and legal areas. Kardelj, although an uncontestable authority in political theory, maintained open discussion and allowed open confrontation when doubt existed as to whether a problem had been well defined or when agreement could not be easily and quickly achieved. He also listened to others though he disagreed and changed his opinion when proof was no longer on his side. This method of thought and conduct enabled the constitution to be accepted without any major dispute among the members of the Constitutional Commission or in public forums.

Mutual tolerance among the politicians and theoreticians, especially among the legal experts, also contributed to easing the debate. This tolerance meant respect for knowledge, influence, and the contributions of the participants, whether groups or individuals, but did not lead to predominance of influential groups or persons. This respect was facilitated by the absence of open class and ideological conflicts. Differences did exist, however, and they were defended frequently with emotion and conviction, although they touched mainly upon the adequacy of constitutional formulation or logic and the systematic nature of the thinking behind it.

The creation of a constitution in such circumstances shows that achieving solutions and agreement is frequently more difficult if there are no prior confrontations between propositions and criticisms of them. Without such prior confrontations a constitution could not be created—only regulated and approved—especially in societies that are not pluralistic.

Scientific creation of a constitution by a pluralist group in a pluralist society shows that the process of collective examination and creation is one way of seeking and acquiring truth, but only if relations of rule are replaced by relations established to conduct, to channel, and to lead. Such a change can both alter the methodology of collective scientific research and create a new relation of politics (especially concerning party and ideology). Politics can be creative and democratic only if the new class and its vanguard lead rather than just rule. In the same way that collective, scientific thought does not allow for ruling groups or individuals, so politics is not collective if it is not founded on leadership and does not exclude rule or the role of ruling groups. This kind of Socratic thought, which arose in ancient Greek political culture, returns to politics through the concept of hegemony reintroduced by Antonio Gramsci and through the concept of leadership developed in psychoanalysis and group psychology. The methodology of collective discussion and group creativity, especially in the social sciences, ensures and protects scientific theory and practice and extension of political horizons and knowledge.

Science has the task, on the special basis of collective discussion and work, of defining the concepts of ruling and of leadership. Ruling is the act of making one submit to another under conditions of inequality; leadership is the act of channeling under conditions of closeness, alliance, and community. Ruling aims at alienating and eliminating; leadership at lifting and expanding. Ruling, contrary to political tradition and legal formality, divides and breaks, while leadership links and unifies. The former seeks and gives birth to power, the latter to authority and renown. Ruling is based on the concept that the group, and the society in general, is the mechanical sum of isolated and alienated individuals. Leadership establishes centers that presuppose and create new relations of unity among people. There can be no collective decision making or creativity—cultural or political—if differences between ruling and leadership are not comprehended and overcome. Self-management practice and thought seek and, as a rule, make possible these radical new processes.

In the creation of all important, original, and democratic constitutions, so-called great men have played special roles as major thinkers and revolutionaries. According to the terminology of the nineteenth century, these men were "demi-gods." Today, instead of great personalities, collectives create the new political systems, and the truly great men are those who lead and inspire those collectives. This change is confirmed by the creation of the Constitution of Yugoslavia. The difference between individualist and collective creativity explains the form of participation of Emmanuel-Joseph Sieyes in the creation of the French Constitution after the revolution; of James Madison in the creation of the U.S. Constitution; and of Josip Broz Tito in the creation of the Constitution of Yugoslavia.

The Influence of Josip Broz Tito

Tito did not narrow his thought and action into dogmatic Marxism. He knew that theory does not contain "the key to all doors" of the unknown; in general, the idea of an all-embracing theory was foreign to him. This viewpoint stemmed not only from his awareness of the limited and relative nature of even the most efficient scientific theory but also from his conviction that theory can and must be refreshed and perfected with creative thought. Creative thought, he knew, is the path to discovery of new truth and to such knowledge that critically surpasses earlier, even Marxist, theoretical knowledge. Creative activity of the mind surpasses even the best theoretical knowledge. Creativity does not reject theory, but it presupposes the existence of an examining and inventive mind and a comprehensive and critical sense. It also involves creative and revolutionary intuition.

The true, active thinker unifies theoretical knowledge, historical intuition, and creative and concrete thinking. Hegel stated that only thought is concrete. This concrete nature, he found, is consistent with the general philosophical concept of spiritual control of the world and history. Class struggles, the social and conceptual development of mankind, the great revolutions in the course of the last three centuries, show that concrete thought is founded on creativity and criticism, not only on philosophy and abstract theory. Without a relation to creative thought, theory can become barren and nonproductive, as thought transformed into fact can become isolated empirical data. The unity of theoretical knowledge and the ability for critical creativity are the conditions for comprehensive, modern thought. Without this unity there are no modern influential thinkers, who discover new truths and trace new and previously unknown paths for human activity and thought.

As a thinker, Tito united the nondogmatic Marxist theoretician and the original, creative thinker. In this he was exceptional, and his thought was current and daring. He was not a theoretician and thinker shut off "in an ivory tower." He did not think only of himself or only for the development of knowledge and truth; as a revolutionary strategist and as the builder of new institutions of a socialist society, he viewed his function with respect for the organization he directed and for the people or the class whose aspirations, interests, and needs he articulated and whose collective wisdom he personified.

Tito's meditative personality was also expressed in an individual, particular way. He did not think in terms of others' formulas or in a complicated way. His thought was simple, comprehensive, and popular. Only a man who is a true thinker and who is close to the masses and understands their desires and potential can have such thought.

In the course of the revolution in Yugoslavia, Tito introduced two principles into revolutionary theory and practice. The first links national liberation with social revolutionary elements. Tito was the first to realize and stress that without liberation of nations and nationalities from hegemonist multinational communities ("national prisons"), there can be no social liberation, no social revolution. The importance of this national principle for social and class transformation is one of the original thoughts which were to influence the success of the revolution in Yugoslavia and gradually change the picture of the world. The second principle, a contribution to modern political theory, links national and class principles for the process of establishing and developing socialist society with the political system ("state") itself.

Under conditions of mainly agrarian and industrially under-developed society, the class principle covers not only the place and leading role of the industrial proletariat but also the role of the rural population and other working strata, including the intelligentsia and youth. The introduction of the rural population into the revolutionary front changed the nineteenth-century concept of revolutionary power that had been colored in industrial tones.

Furthermore, this thought represents the first concept of de-mocracy and revolutionary associations as the conditions necessary for progressive change, especially in countries where the village and the rural populations play an important role. This concept extends the concept of class, liberates Marxist thought, works through class limitations and sectarianism and thereby opens up new possibilities for revolution, victory, and leftist influence in the struggle to change old societies and place them on the path to socialism. Democratic associations of class still have various forms, from national fronts to so-called historic compromises. According to Tito's concept, class as-sociations are organic in character, created and realized on the foun-dations of society, on the unity of towns and villages.

The twentieth-century revolutions have been mainly social rev-olutions. Having specific social, political, and ethnic structures, these revolutions become realistic but have a successful outcome only if they also comprehend and solve national contradictions and differ-ences that arise in the course of historical development (the solution of the national question).

Tito's concept of the national question not only stressed the ele-ments for solving the social question but also recognized the national identity of individual, previously suppressed, even denationalized, ethnic groups. This recognition presupposes the adoption of Lenin's formula, "the right of each nation to self-determination," but also includes something more, something crucial and original: the estab-lishment of a political system in which self-determination of nations is guaranteed within the framework of socialist democratic commu-nities. The political system, or the framework for achieving national identity and equality, Tito stressed, is not and cannot be the state in the traditional sense—that is, a centralized and enforced machinery of government. The framework should be set up on the side of national unity and state centralism, on the basis of the attempt of the bourgeoisie in Yugoslav nations to create a "united Yugoslav state" and a "united people."

According to Tito's concept, community can and must be a social and political environment in which nations and nationalities enjoy and achieve their national and cultural identities in conditions of equality and freedom. Such a community is inseparable from the idea and the practice of socialism and social progress. On the basis of these concepts, the practice of a new type of federalism was created in Yugoslavia. That type of multinational, equal, self-managing, and cooperative federalism is today more important and of greater significance than classic unitarist federalism.

These concepts had, and still have, crucial importance for the framework within which socialist society—and the working class, as its hegemon—is evolving. One path in this direction is statist, while another is the social-cultural form of socialism. The first is founded on the glorification of the role of the state and of violence in history; in the creation of the socialist state, dependence on these factors often is recommended. This was the source of "state socialism," and of "socialism of the state" but not of "socialism of the masses and classes of the people." The second path is sociological and puts socialism in the forefront, not only as the solution to international difficulties but also to those of intersociety and interhuman relations. This path is the way to realize unity, equality, and brotherhood of peoples and men; it stresses the primary importance of society and class as compared with state and government.

The primary importance of society in modern sociopolitical transformations requires a role for a free and self-organized working class, the creation of a society of solidarity founded on the freedom of initiative and action, and commitment and decision making by the masses. In Tito's thought, and in the practice inspired by it, the creation of a sociocultural form of socialist society was important for the further development of socialism and freedom, not only in Yugoslavia but also in those countries that desired to create and build a new society. This is one of the new and crucial ideas behind the forces for overcoming crises, contradictions, and conflicts in the modern world.

The Role of the Constitution

All revolutions have their evolution and regression, their ebb and flow. The transformation of a revolution into institutions reveals its course and realization. Continuity not only refers to the movement of history but also to the way a revolution is realized. The continuity of the revolution that Tito expressed, defended, and, according to existing possibilities, implemented can be seen both in the decrease of statism and in the expansion and strengthening of relations among institutions in which revolutionary change takes a leading role and becomes the subject of socialism. In this way Tito supplemented the idea of the *Communist Manifesto* that after the revolution "the working class will be constituted as a state." On the contrary, the working class, in association with other active, democratic forces of socialism, has increasingly become the subject of the revolution as well as the vehicle for managing the common business of society. Thus self-management becomes the basis for the new political system, transforming the state and opening it up for a democratic political system.

This universalist thought produces a new basis for humanity in two ways. First, it may stimulate new and better thought while not being monopolized by one country, one working class, or one personality. It gives rise to creation and to the discovery of new truths and new frontiers of humanity. Second, it is available to all people struggling for true social progress. It is universal also in that it can be claimed and realized within both the objective conditions of the historical movement and the subjective conditions of the capabilities of individuals.

In a democracy, the constitution and institutions have a special role. Unlike the instruments of punishment and impersonalization, the constitution and other institutions must take on a Promethean role in the sense comprehended by the ancient Greeks: the rejection of all gods but one, man in freedom; the overcoming of all religions except the service of truth, justice, and humanity. Everyone who is authorized to implement the constitution and the law, including the courts, must be neither a soulless bureaucrat nor a vengeful Lucifer who drives out evil and therein seeks purgatory for the liberation and redemption of man.

Democratic legal ideology and the Promethean concept of morals both stress the fulfillment of the human personality through work, practice, and culture, not through repression and the expulsion of guilt. Instead of seeing evil as a ruling idea in society and man, the democratic and humane constitution undergirds and implements the good in society and the good in man's personality. Society and man are not projections of eternal institutional and religious dogma, for they change in practice, become transformed and improved. In this way they overcome both outmoded institutions and old and new forms of evil and prevent hindrances to constitutions and laws becoming new Promethean institutions and values. Because of this, guilt is essentially a relative and time-limited tendency. Although it is true that no guilt exists without man, neither man nor guilt exists without a specific social structure and political rule.

This philosophical and constitutional ideology is based on the idea that man is a being that is created and that creates, that predicts events around him and thereby can become different and better. The idea of guilt is a twisted strand of a frightened, morally repressive society. In this context, the state is not a form of life. It should rather serve to fulfill and change man, institutions, and rights. The life of a man—his needs and his desires—cannot be fulfilled if his qualities and potentialities become subject to control and judgment outside of man. Everything that gives rise to fear does not necessarily give rise to respect. Everything that is unjust creates hatred and conflict. A constitution not founded on these postulates is incapable of ensuring state legitimacy and authority or justice with true decision making. In such a situation, a constitution cannot realize its political and ideological function as fundamental higher law.

An active and creative constitution, especially one created on a self-management and humane basis, must be capable of discovering and overcoming everything which slows it down, brings it into question, and negates it. It must overcome, especially, the fetishes of statehood; the static concept of man; the instrumental concept of law; and traditional, bureaucratic, and falsely ascetic morality. Only if these objective relations are discovered and only if bureaucratic subjective conduct is eliminated, can the contradictions of a constitution be resolved in favor of its function. Only then can the practice of law be liberated from its arbitrary positivist and formalist nature, behind which are self-will and the tendency to subjugate others. This is the case everywhere, even in Yugoslavia.

The historical development of law has been composed of the democratization of legislation, the creation of law, and, in the process, the establishment of various legal forces contrary to absolutism, and monopoly over these forces in the form of monarchy, feudalism and, later, the state. Theoretically, in the modern period of pluralism of interests and rights, this background is necessarily changing. The fundamental issue is not the creation of law, not normativism, but the realization of rights, the life of the constitution. The constitution, then, is not just what it intends but what it does. This concept enables a change in a civilization from one of symbols to one of acts and reality. The experience of the socialist world shows that law changes and begins to die, not by becoming simpler but by reproducing itself. In a socialist society certain phenomena and tendencies can lead not only to the weakening of the legal system and of unity in society but also to various forms of discretionary power, to localism and particularism. The elimination of these phenomena, which we find not only in old but also in existing societies, requires a firm and strict constitutionality, the ideological and functional unity of the legal system and the role of justice. All those values that link the individual act with the social system—that is, to correct the normative and abstract nature of the law—decrease self-will, nationalism, particularism, and excesses of all kinds. All this must be done both conceptually and ideologically in the constitutional and legal system, and, especially, in the judiciary.

In this way alone can the still existing phenomena of differences between "important" and "ordinary" people, between those "up there" and those "down there" be eliminated. Besides the immorality of these differences, the consequences of them reflect the constant renewal of inequality among people and the illusion that equal standards ensure equal status and rights and that, therefore, the law is in itself just and fair. Not only the function but also the essence of a constitution consists mainly and even primarily in the realization and the life of the constitution and the law. The realization of the constitution is what correctly distinguishes modern constitutional theory from traditional theory. The creation of a constitution is inseparable from the form and the environment of its realization or from the ways the conflicts of norm and fact, which accompany the social contradictions of each modern society, are overcome.

Notes

1. The army is an institution of the federation. The supreme commander of the armed forces of Yugoslavia is the president, who may entrust certain tasks to the secretary for national defense.

National defense, a broad concept, encompasses civil defense, the police, and, in general, the organization of national defense in which both organizations and citizens take part. The constitution stipulates, "The defense of the country shall be the inviolable and inalienable right and the supreme duty and honor of every citizen" (Article 172).

2. "The assembly is a social, self-managing body and the supreme organ of power within the framework of the rights and duties of its sociopolitical community" (Article 132, paragraph 1).

Working people in basic self-managing organizations and communities, and in sociopolitical organizations, come from delegations to exercise their rights directly and to organize participation in the performance of the functions of the assembly.

All assemblies, from the local community (municipality) to the federation, have the same nature concerning their constitutional authorizations. They are delegate institutions whose members are elected according to the delegation principle. In the sociopolitical communities, they are the highest organs of government and self-management, which means that the constitutional system of Yugoslavia does not recognize the division of government: The executive function, although in a separate body, arises in the assembly and is under its control. The presidency (which exists in the federation, republics, and provinces) has only one dimension of executive power; it is the collective head of state.

3. "Citizens shall be guaranteed the right to choose their nation or nationality, to express their national culture and to use their language and alphabet freely" (Article 170).

"Members of nationalities shall, in conformity with the constitution and statute, have the right to use their language and alphabet in the exercise of their rights and duties and in proceedings before state agencies and organizations exercising public powers. Members of the nations and nationalities of Yugoslavia shall, on the territory of each republic and/or autonomous province, have the right to instruction in their own language in conformity with statute" (Article 171).

4. "Social ownership is neither state nor collective ownership." This name is for ownership that no longer implies ownership rights of the classic type. Social ownership does not give a basis for power even to the state. It is the basis of associated labor and the condition for the acquisition of personal ownership.

With respect to personal ownership and private ownership, the following provisions are characteristic: "Citizens shall be guaranteed the right of ownership of movable property used for personal consumption or for the satisfaction of their cultural and other personal needs."

"Citizens may own residential houses and apartments for their personal and family needs. Residential houses, apartments, and movables, which serve personal needs and which are subject to the right of ownership, may be used as means for earning income only in ways and under conditions spelled out by statute" (Article 78).

5. Freedom of thought and choice is guaranteed. Primary schooling for at least eight years is compulsory. Citizens have the right to acquire knowledge and professional training in all types of schools and other educational institutes under equal conditions as set out in statute.

6. "Citizens shall be guaranteed the right to be informed of events in the country and in the world that are of concern to their life and work as well as of questions of concern to the community."

"The press, radio, television, and other media of information shall be bound to inform the public truthfully and objectively and to make public the opinions of and information about bodies, organizations, and citizens of concern to the public" (Article 168, paragraphs 1 and 2).

7. "During a state of war or the event of an immediate danger of war, the presidency of the SFRY [Socialist Federal Republic of Yugoslavia] may, on its own initiative or at the recommendation of the Federal Executive Council, pass decrees with the force of law on questions falling within the power of

the Assembly of Yugoslavia. The presidency of Yugoslavia shall submit these decrees to the assembly of the SFRY for approval as soon as the assembly is in a position to meet."

"Individual provisions of the present constitution relating to the adoption of statutes, other regulations, and enactments, to the taking of measures by federal agencies in agreement with the appropriate agencies of the republics and autonomous provinces, to individual freedoms, rights and duties of citizens, and the rights of self-managing organizations and communities, or to the composition and powers of executive and administrative agencies, may—during a state of war—be suspended by a decree with the force of law for the duration of this state and, if so required, by the country's defense interests."

This suspension of the constitution is limited and refers only to the duration of the extraordinary circumstances. While the presidency may, by means of a decree with legal force, make decisions on questions over which the assembly has jurisdiction during the state of war and in case of danger of war, its authority to suspend certain provisions of the constitution is limited only to the state of war.

The suspension of certain provisions of the constitution has the aims of continuing constitutionality during extraordinary situations and of the armament of the country for efficient action in those situations. The provisions on suspension were not contained in previous constitutions and, as far as the present constitution is concerned, they reflect the time when the present constitution was adopted.

Commentary

Najdan Pasic

The writing of a constitution is a significant political process. Studying a practical example of such a process "from inside" (as a direct participant in it) provides one with a unique opportunity to observe concisely the relations among the political forces involved in it. The process represents an organized effort of a society (that is, a state) to find a rational and acceptable basis for its existence. For several reasons, pointed out by Professor Djordjevic in his essay, the work on the preparation and passage of the Constitution of the Socialist Federal Republic of Yugoslavia was of a specific character and particular importance. This event shows a significant, but as yet unclarified, side of the political history of the new Yugoslavia. To explain this statement, I make the following observations.

During the war of national liberation and socialist revolution (1941–1945), the former Yugoslav quasi-parliamentary system of multiparty pluralism fell apart and was rejected. But the system of one-party monolithism, such as the one developed under the influence of the Soviet model in Eastern Europe, was also deemed an unworthy goal.

With the development of self-management, relying directly upon the revolutionary and democratic experience of the war of national liberation, a new type of pluralism (that is, a "self-management pluralism of interests") developed. Under such pluralism, free and direct expression of different interests of working people and citizens, organized on a self-management basis, is linked with the leading ideological and political roles of the League of Communists and other sociopolitical organizations, which try to determine, with full awareness and in accordance with their programs, the basic lines of social development. The processes for creating the previous constitutions of socialist Yugoslavia, as well as, particularly, the Constitution passed in 1974 and currently in force, were characterized by the recognition of and respect for the pluralism of the interests of self-management subjects (individuals and social groups) combined with a unique ideological and programmatic conception as the basis for social development.

The character of the constituent process in Yugoslavia has been greatly influenced by the fact (given particular emphasis in Professor Djordjevic's essay) that Yugoslav constitutions, especially the 1963 Constitution and the present Constitution, are not only legal-political documents by which the governmental structure and organization of political power are normatively determined but are also comprehensive social charters (that is, they indicate the "constitution of society"). They are supreme legal and political documents meant to organize and express all the basic aspects of the material and spiritual well-being of the society and the individual. Therefore these constitutions encompass not only the political but also the socioeconomic and the cultural spheres of life. Because of this purpose, the constitution, which includes both introductory principles and detailed, normative parts, is extensive. The comprehensive political philosophy expressed in the introductory principles serves as a theoretical and ideological base for the detailed, normative regulation of the socioeconomic relations of self-management and its corresponding political structure. Full equality among six nations and numerous nationalities within the Yugoslav federation, as well as the self-management status and rights of the individual, as both a worker and a citizen, are thoroughly determined and protected in terms of constitutional law. Several new institutions (such as "public property," which is neither governmental nor private; "self-management interest community"; and "delegate system," which replaces the classical system of political representational institutions) unknown in other legal systems have been introduced and specifically defined.

The creation of the constitution—which sought to introduce revolutionary changes into the entire organization of state and society and to regulate thoroughly the relations within both the political sphere and the material production and distribution sphere—required enormous work in terms of expertise and theory. It also required coordinating the numerous interests in social life, each of which tried to impose its own interpretation of the officially declared and adopted self-management concept of the social organization. This great effort, which lasted several years and endured through several stages, is documented by thousands of pages of stenographic notes from the meetings of the Constitutional Commission of the Federal Assembly and from the assemblies of all the republics and autonomous provinces; it is confirmed also by announcements in the press about this work and about the results of the wide public debate on the new constitutional draft.

The changes that resulted from a series of constitutional amendments (1–42) and the creation of the entire text of the new constitution that followed have long been the focus of attention of the political community. The importance of this broadly conceived elaboration of constitutional changes was manifold. In one of its stages, this elaboration strongly motivated the development of an original constitutional-legal and political theory in Yugoslavia. Discussions on constitutional changes, conducted partly within the circles of experts and politicians and partly on a broader scale in the community, opened the door for discussions on different approaches to issues such as the reorganization of the Yugoslav federation and the further development of self-management within the concept of social development, already accepted and included in the program of the League of Communists of Yugoslavia (1958). The public debate on the new constitutional draft, organized by the Socialist Alliance as the political organization with the widest membership, also was significantly propagandist in its function. It undoubtedly was a powerful instrument of mass political socialization in the spirit of self-management and its democratic and human values.

The post–1945 Yugoslav constitutions, the 1963 Constitution and the 1974 Constitution in particular, were only partly political and legal means of consolidating existing relations. They also were instruments for changing social relations further, toward realization of the vision of self-management society. That is why the 1974 Constitution has several elements of so-called social engineering, that is, the normative solutions and organizational forms that go beyond the mere reflection and legal form sanctioning the status quo. They contain elements of planning; they anticipate further development; and they act to direct desirable social trends. Constitutions of this kind contain an enhanced risk of creating discord between the normative act and reality, between that which is proclaimed by the constitution and that which really exists.

The extent to which the constitution is an efficient representation of real relations, as opposed to a system of normative fictions, is the result of the planning included in the constitutional norms relying on accurate scientific evaluations and on perceptions of the objective tendencies and laws governing social trends. That is why, in the process of creating the constitution, scientific analysis and prediction and the general, theoretical conception of social development were given particular importance.

As with earlier constitutions, in the work on the 1974 Constitution not only many legal experts but also scientists and researchers of various disciplines (such as economists, political scientists, and sociologists) were involved. Particularly significant was that the late Edvard Kardelj, the prominent revolutionary leader who was rightfully considered the greatest theoretician of socialist self-management and who had a leading role in the creation of previous constitutions (1946, 1953, 1963), headed the committee that coordinated all of the work on the new constitution.

Why the Constitution Was Changed

The creation of the new constitution was preceded by a series of constitutional amendments that were passed on three occasions (1967, 1968, and 1971). It had been long believed that by passing amendments to the 1963 Constitution the creation of a new constitution might be avoided. Even immediately after 1971, when the move to integrate numerous constitutional amendments into a new constitutional entity began, it was emphasized that this process would end in an "innovated text of the constitution" not in a new constitution. The desire to emphasize the continuity of the constitutional-legal structure and general social development was strong, particularly because the constituent bodies were headed, for the most part, by the same people who had leading roles in the writing of the program of the League of Communists of Yugoslavia in 1958, as well as of the 1963 Constitution. During the work on the innovated text of the constitution, however, it became clear (with regard to the extent and significance of the changes made) that the document, in fact, was going to be a new constitution. What caused this evolution from the original commitment?

The 1963 Constitution, passed only ten years after the 1953 constitutional law, sought to express, confirm, and make final, in constitutional-legal terms, the results of highly dynamic developments and far-reaching social changes that occurred in Yugoslavia the preceding decade. Self-management, initiated by a law on yielding the management of state-owned economic enterprises to workers (June 1950), experienced an incredible expansion, strongly supported by an entire range of legislative measures. Self-management organization was expanded into the sphere of social services as well: schools, hospitals, scientific and cultural institutions—all were reorganized on self-management principles, in the same way that other, economic enterprises were.

In the 1950s, local self-management was reborn. Municipalities—the basic units of the territorial organization of authority—and communities organized on the self-management principle gained much greater economic and political independence than in the postwar period of centralized state management and planning. Far-reaching decentralization in all spheres of social life (which was both a cause and a result of the development of self-management) provided room for freer expression of pluralism as well as more conflicts among various local, national, professional, and class interests. The illusion of a conflict-free, monolithic interest was thus shattered.

Although the 1963 Constitution without a doubt contained a progressive democratic vision of further self-management development, it did not sufficiently take into account the social forces already developed in the heart of society and themselves liberated by the constitution.

The drafters of the 1963 Constitution did not anticipate any substantial changes in the structure of the multinational Yugoslav federation, changes that would correspond to the degree of self-management development achieved. By these changes, some principles of self-management (primarily the principle of self-managed disposal of income) would be transferred to the level of relations among (Yugoslav) nations, in terms of the right of federal units (that is, republics and provinces) to greater influence in the making and distribution of income in their territories.

The economic rights of workers, organized on the self-management principle, to make decisions on the income they create, however, were considerably limited by still-persisting dualism in the general organization of society. Self-management was more or less developed on a microlevel—that is, in enterprises and other basic cells of social organization—but not on the macrolevel where disposal of the means for expanded reproduction (disposal of "social capital") remained in the hands of the state. These means were still concentrated in state investment funds, primarily in federal funds and central banks. Although the 1963 Constitution had a logical and theoretical consistency, and was praised as a lasting and stable foundation for the development of a comprehensive system of socialist self-management, the above-mentioned social aspirations, which were initiated but not satisfied, soon prompted the first changes in that constitution. In 1967 and 1968 the first two series of constitutional amendments (1–6 and 7–19) were passed.

Even a superficial glance at the content of these amendments clearly reveals which social forces and tendencies became dominant on the constitutional scene and acquired crucial influence on the planning of further trends in social development. Most amendments dealt with relations within the federation. All the changes were aimed at strengthening the position of republics and provinces and limiting the centralism of the federal government. So began the process of relatively swift transformation from a centralized Yugoslav federalism to a federalism that—according to the standards of classical constitutional-legal and political theory—had traits of confederal organization.

In the beginning of the seven-year period (1967–1974) of constitutional transformation, the federal units (republics and provinces) achieved a decisive influence on the process of constitutional change. The National Council of the Federal Assembly, till then a "sleeping council" included in the structure of the federal council, was separated and transformed into a "council for general jurisdiction." Composed on the principle of equal representation of republics (twenty delegates from each republic and ten delegates from each autonomous province), this council passed all laws, either on its own or together with four other councils. It thereby gained the leading role in the process of constitutional change. The principle of parity for the republics "and corresponding parity for provinces" was accepted in the federal Constitutional Commission as well as in its subcommissions and working groups. Constitutional commissions in republics and autonomous provinces were working parallel to the federal Constitutional Commission, preparing individual constitutions for each federal unit. This organization of the entire mechanism involved in the creation first of the constitutional amendments and then of the new constitution also influenced the behavior of all the participants in the constitutional process, not only of the politicians but also of the scientists and experts, who felt like members of the corresponding teams of the republics and provinces.

In his essay, Professor Djordjevic writes of the role of politicians and the role of scientists and experts in the creation of the constitution and points out that the situation and climate in which the constitutional amendments and the 1974 Constitution were created differed from the situation and climate in which the previous constitutions were prepared. The main difference rested in that, in the process of the creation of the new constitution, republics and provinces had a recognized status as principal organized agents of decision making. They endeavored to keep this process under as direct control as possible and to include in the entire constitutional system as many guarantees and instruments as possible for protecting their independence and complete equality, particularly on the economic level. That is how original solutions, characteristic of the Yugoslav federation only, were reached; decisions on a range of vital economic issues could be made only if all the republics and autonomous provinces reached a consensus. Such guarantees of economic equality and independence of federal units are not to be found in the constitution of any other federation in the contemporary world.

The extremely strong positions gained by the republics and provinces in the process of creating the 1974 Constitution can serve as a basis for interesting historical analogies and contrasts. The substantial change in the ratio of forces in the Yugoslav federation, which resulted from the far-reaching process of self-management decentralization and other specific historical circumstances, created a situation analogous to a situation in which many states or social communities, formerly fully independent or only loosely connected, voluntarily enter into a firm and lasting union creating a common state or federation. In this union, each member state retains a degree of independence, transferring to the federation part of its original sovereign right. The republics and provinces that form the Yugoslav federation prepared, on a voluntary and agreed-upon basis, the new constitution by which relations in the federal union would significantly change. This process is analogous to the way in which the thirteen states in North America, adopting a joint Constitution in 1787, founded the United States of America to replace the former confederate union. The concrete historical experiences and preoccupations of each of these two constituent acts, which served as their respective documents' starting points, however, were in many ways opposite.

The founding fathers of the American federal system, the authors of the Constitution, were guided by the need to eliminate weaknesses in the loose confederate organization established after liberation from British colonial rule. As the authors of the famous *Federalist Papers* believed, the confederation did not appear capable of ensuring a rational organization of state authority, optimal economic development, or political and legal security with civil liberties. For these reasons they demanded that the confederation be transformed into a federally organized union.

In contrast, the authors of the 1974 Yugoslav Constitution had in mind, first of all, the negative and weak points of unitarism and administrative centralism. The former kingdom of Yugoslavia was a unitary monarchy, a country where oppression of one nation by another was typical. In the late 1940s, the new federal order, established during the war of national liberation, was constrained by an administrative-centralist economic system based on state ownership of the means of production and on centralized economic planning. Because the self-management decentralization, begun in the early 1950s, was not followed by adequate changes in the structure and in the functioning of the federation a revival of national frictions appeared possible. That is why the theoreticians and authors of the Yugoslav Constitution of 1974 accepted, as one of the basic objectives of constitutional reform, the transformation of centralized federalism into decentralized federalism.

The desire to change relations within the federation toward a greater independence of republics and autonomous provinces was not the sole motive for constitutional change, nor did this change deviate from the theoretical-programmatic goals and framework for further development of the socialist self-management system. The people who previously exerted the greatest influence on the strategy of social development were aware that radical limitation of functions and independent jurisdictions of the federal state would not weaken (or even call into question) the firmness of the Yugoslav federal union if these changes were combined with further self-management transformation of economic relations and free association of self-management enterprises throughout the Yugoslav economic system. Only a self-management integration, motivated by the interests of associated labor itself, could provide new cohesive forces that would develop instead the forms of centralization of a mostly administrative character. This is why the constitutional debates constantly focused on interconnections and complementarity between the greater independence of republics and provinces, on the one hand, and greater rights of workers, on the other, organized on the principles of self-management in enterprises, to dispose of the material means of production (social capital) and to associate these means freely in a unified Yugoslav market.

These efforts resulted in the so-called workers' amendments, which guarantee the right of workers in basic organizations of associated labor and work organizations (enterprises reorganized on the self-management principle) to have discretion over the total income they realize by their own work, through sale of goods and services and through associating their earnings with other self-management enterprises. In an expanded and systematized form, these regulations, the object of great discussion, also were included in the new constitution. The constitution guarantees equal status and free activity for organizations of associated labor throughout Yugoslavia, regardless of boundaries between the republics and provinces. The constitutional regulations dealing with the socioeconomic order and guaranteeing the status of associated labor are included in identical language in the constitutions of all the republics and provinces.

The third motive for constitutional change concerned the election, status, and constitutional power of the head of state. In the late 1960s and early 1970s, the question was raised as to how to ensure a normal, adequate change in the office of the head of state when President Tito could no longer perform this function. This question was particularly difficult to answer and had great political significance because it dealt with replacing an exceptional historical personality who enjoyed enormous personal authority. This question of succession was raised by President Tito himself.

As pointed out by Professor Djordjevic, the solution was to introduce the institution of a collective head of state, which began functioning during Tito's lifetime and under his leadership. In the solution of this question the equal influence of all republics and autonomous provinces was strictly and fully observed.

After the Constitutional Commission reached the decision to create a new, comprehensive constitution, it made great additional effort, both intellectual and political, to find original solutions to the organization of the political system and the protection of the status and rights of the worker and citizen. These solutions would be possible on the basis of changes already achieved or anticipated in normative form within the structure of socioeconomic relations and the development of self-management in general. In supporting such generally accepted ideological and programmatic structures, however, various specific interests and aspirations became involved in creating the constitution and to a great extent shaped its final form. Behind the numerous, ultimately accepted, solutions, as well as behind the theoretical and ideological explanations of principle, were sometimes factual compromises, achieved after long discussion and persuasion among advocates of the various positions. In the beginning these compromises seemed remote. Each institution, defined and confirmed by the constitution, therefore has its own history, which in most cases is only partially known. Part of the usefulness and importance for political theory and practice of studying the history of the creation of the constitution is that some aspects of the process of political decision making can be better clarified.

Constitutional Development

Looking retrospectively at almost forty years of history, one may conclude that the constitutional changes that have taken place in Yugoslavia have reflected and sustained gradual, both willed and unwilled, departures from the system of party-state monolithism toward a system based on a specific self-management pluralism of interests. This change is the single example of a peaceful transition from the one system to the other. Studying the background to this process is, therefore, of special interest and of broad importance.

The history of Yugoslav postwar constitutional development can be summarized briefly around three topical problems: the problem of continuity and discontinuity; the problem of the division of power; and the problem of cohesive forces ensuring basic unity in the Yugoslav federation (with conditions for far-reaching decentralization).

The people of Yugoslavia live under the fourth constitution since 1945; promulgated in 1974, it was amended in 1981. Is this frequency of change a sign of constitutional and political instability? Before jumping to a conclusion, one must recognize several features of Yugoslav postwar development. First, all the constitutional changes during those forty years were implemented under the same political leadership and by the same dominant coalition of social and political forces. Second, all the successive constitutions and constitutional amendments (1946, 1953, 1963, 1967–1971, 1974, and 1981) have been ideologically and politically justified as necessary steps forward in the same historical direction. The basic goal of building a socialist society and a federal community of free and equal Yugoslav nations has not changed. Third, after protracted discussions, drafting, and redrafting, which sometimes lasted for years, and after months of broadly organized public debate within the Socialist Alliance and in the mass media, the Federal Assembly always unanimously accepted a final version of a new constitution (or of constitutional amendments). An appearance of full unity has thereby always been preserved.

At the same time, the following statements are also true. First, constitutional changes by no means were mere arbitrary creations imposed by any center of unrestricted political power. Second, constitutional development did not go smoothly along straight lines. Some real problems and conflicts of interest (among factions that asked for far-reaching changes) had been recognized only gradually and reluctantly after prolonged "tugs-of-war." Beneath the surface of basic ideological and political unity, a plurality of interests gave substance more and more to the democratic political process. But that plurality also meant that keeping this process under the control of one political center was becoming more and more difficult.

In conclusion on this point, then, Yugoslav constitutional development has been a peculiar mixture of continuity and discontinuity. As a result of this development, during the past thirty years the political system has been deeply and substantially changed. A new type of pluralism has emerged.

During the prolonged period of constitutional changes, the principle of "unity of power" was tacitly abandoned, and different forms for dividing power were introduced and gradually developed. This change was not simply a free option of the most influential people

219

in the party leadership; it had to be made to adapt the political system to the situation of extensive decentralization, to the development of autonomy among publicly owned enterprises such as commodity producers for the market, and to the much freer economic and political expression of a general plurality of interests. Changes brought about under the constant pressure of these forces have been numerous. I mention just a few of them as most important for the changed character of the political system.

1.   The evolution of the Yugoslav federation from a centralized organization to a highly decentralized one has brought about a more extensive division of power on a territorial basis. Appropriate powers of the federal union have been enumerated in the constitution and in that way have been separated from the appropriate powers of the federal units that perform all functions other than those entrusted to the union. The Yugoslav Constitution of 1974 has gone further than any other federation's constitution in the direction of abolishing the hierarchy among the basic levels of federal organizations.

2.   The new constitution contains elements of the separation of powers and of "checks and balances" between the legislative and executive branches of government. The president and now (after Tito) the collective presidency of the Yugoslav federation shares responsibilities and powers with the Federal Assembly in controlling the Federal Executive Council (the government). The presidency appoints the "mandator" (the future prime minister) who forms the government "which must enjoy the confidence of the assembly." The president of the presidency can preside at a meeting of the government. The presidency also can ask the assembly to take a vote of confidence in the government. The conflict between the presidency and the Federal Assembly over foreign or domestic policy, if not solved through the procedure of reconciliation, may lead to dissolution of the assembly and termination of the mandate of the presidency. New elections of both bodies must take place within a brief time as prescribed by the constitution.

3.   In the constitution, special emphasis is given to the independence of the judicial function. Courts are obliged to apply nothing but the law. Judges are elected and reelected to their posts by respective assemblies for the periods of their offices.

4.   The constitution provides for the establishment of a constitutional court at the levels both of republics and autonomous provinces and of the federation. These courts have the power of judicial revision of all enactment, including statutes passed by respective assemblies as supreme legislative bodies. The decisions of the constitutional courts are final and cannot be revised or contested by anyone.

The very existence of institutions with such power and position is incompatible with the principle of unity of power. Yugoslavia is the only so-called socialist country to have the institution of constitutional courts.

Yugoslav federalism has evolved in the direction opposite to that characteristic of the overwhelming majority of federations. In no other federation do federal states have such strong positions and such possibilities to control directly all decisions made at the level of the federal union. How, in these circumstances, has a necessary degree of unity been preserved? What are the actual forces of cohesion in the general society? To answer these questions, two factors are of crucial importance. *Economic integration*, based on a free interplay of self-management enterprises, can operate and pool resources throughout Yugoslavia regardless of the boundaries of republic and autonomous provinces. Economic concentration and centralization achieved in this way increasingly replaces administrative centralism. *The integrative role of sociopolitical organizations* (such as the League of Communists, the Socialist Alliance, trade-unions, and the Socialist Youth Organization) with the same or with similar programmatic orientation operate on the principle of democratic centralism. These two factors are the main countervening powers that check the strong centrifugal tendencies that may emerge from a highly decentralized federal organization. The main strategic goal in the writing of the 1974 Constitution was to strike the right balance between these opposing tendencies. The stability and smooth functioning of the Yugoslav federation depends on the extent to which this basic goal is achieved in practice.

Discussion

ROBERT GOLDWIN: When the U.S. Constitution was written, the nation moved from confederation to a federal union. When the Yugoslav Constitution was written, the nation moved in the other direction, from federal union to confederation. In the United States the movement was in part due to a concern that the union might not hold together unless something were done about its very loose form of federation. In Yugoslavia it was by reflection and choice that the nation moved the other way. Why did it decide to so do? What now holds that union together? Those are the questions I suggest we begin with.

NAJDAN PASIC: I shall try to give you a concise and precise answer. First, however, I would like to stress that we cannot understand Yugoslav federalism if we do not take into account the introduction of self-management in Yugoslavia in publicly owned enterprises and later as a general pattern of socioeconomic and political organization. That was of crucial importance for the development of the country. By introducing and consistently developing self-management, Yugoslavia departed from the system of state-party monolithism; the state ceased to be the universal owner of the means of production, the universal employer, even the universal manager of the economy. In that way the main source of state power and party bureaucracy was, if not abolished, at least reduced, and the conditions were created for the emergence of a pluralistic society. The backbone of the new pluralism, which allows for the democratic development of our constitutionalism and of our political and social order, was the self-managed, publicly owned enterprises as independent, autonomous commodity producers for the market. Since that very important element of pluralism was brought into Yugoslav society, the system has not been the same.

We have discussed at some length the problems of peaceful transition from a military to a civil regime. It is also interesting to discuss

222

the problems of peaceful transition from a system of state-party mono-lithism to one of self-management pluralism as in Yugoslavia. I know of no other examples of this kind of peaceful transition. When I speak about pluralism in Yugoslavia and how it is reflected in the political structure, the first point I stress is that its best expression is in the nature of Yugoslav federalism or, better, in the *development* of Yugoslav federalism during the past twenty years. That is, when we allowed for different interests to be articulated in the society, we also had to allow for the expression of different *national* interests. These interests in the Yugoslav political, social, and economic structure had been suppressed by a system of strict administrative centralism. When we introduced self-management, we opened the door for different interests to be voiced, and among others the national interests came to the fore. That is why the Yugoslav federation moved from a rather centralized federation—where the rights of the states were limited—to a rather loose federation that gave great rights to republics and autonomous regions.

Self-management by definition means very far-reaching decentralization. Formerly centralized powers have been transferred partly to the workers (or rather to all employees) of publicly owned enterprises and partly to territorial political centers, mainly in the republics and autonomous regions. The decentralization, however, did not always substantially reduce the influence of the government in economic matters. Many rights in these matters have simply been transferred from the central government to the governments of republics and autonomous regions. A new balance of forces has thus been established in the Yugoslav federation—this time in favor of the federal units. As for the "associated labor" (publicly owned, self-managed enterprises), the process of free economic integration covering the whole Yugoslav territory has been slower than expected. That has also strengthened the position of republics and autonomous regions. In the process of writing a new Constitution in 1974 the leaders of republics and autonomous regions obtained strong direct influence and control. That was ensured by the composition of the Constitutional Commission and of all its bodies. All were composed on the basis of full parity among republics and autonomous regions, so that their representatives behaved not only as independent thinkers, or experts, but as representatives and advocates of their federal units.

People hoped that two cohesive forces would develop inside Yugoslav society. One was free economic integration on the basis of the self-managerial rights of workers, ensuring a free flow of labor and capital inside Yugoslavia. Workers should be in a position to pool

223

the resources at their disposal according to the economic interests of their enterprises regardless of territorial boundaries and thus provide for the economic integration and unity of the country. The other cohesive force was the social-political organizations, such as the League of Communists, the Social Alliance, and the trade unions, which are organized partly on the basis of so-called democratic centralism. These two forces of cohesion should counterbalance the great individual powers of the republican states. The hopes for this cohesion have only partly been fulfilled, however, and that is why many problems persist in the functioning of the Yugoslav federation.

VOJISLAV STANOVCIC: I want to confirm Mr. Goldwin's statement that in the United States the movement at the time the Constitution was written was from confederation to federal government whereas in Yugoslavia the movement was from federal or unitary government to a confederal arrangement. We were not aware of it at the beginning, but the aim was similar—to preserve the union.

Yugoslavia is a very small country with a population of about 22.5 million, but it is very complex. It consists of six republics and two autonomous provinces; that is, it has eight federal units—six nations and two "nationalities" (national minorities). We do not use the term "national minorities," because Albanians living in Yugoslavia, for instance—there are about 1.7 million of them—are not a national minority at all. There are fewer than half a million Hungarians; they are not a national minority either. We have three main religions—Eastern Orthodox, Roman Catholic, and Moslem.

Because parts of our country were ruled for centuries by foreign governments, the historical and cultural background of our population is quite varied. The levels of development in the country are very different too. Twenty years ago the poorest county in Yugoslavia had a per capita income one-fortieth the per capita income of the richest county. The poorest parts of Yugoslavia are poorer in comparison with the richest parts than the poorest countries in the world are in comparison with the richest countries. We have two alphabets, three main Slavic languages, and two other languages, Albanian and Hungarian. They are all equally used in the federal Parliament, even though all the deputies can speak Serbo-Croatian, the language spoken by the majority of the population. It is still very difficult to keep all these diversities together as "a group concern of interests."

In a little more than fifty years, Yugoslavia has changed constitutions six times, twice during the Kingdom of Yugoslavia and four times since World War II. We experienced centralization before World War II, and the result was the collapse of the country in 1941; we experienced a centralization after the war that was very similar to the Soviet system. The Yugoslav Constitution of 1946 was written—or, better, rewritten—along the lines of the Soviet Constitution of 1936. Since Yugoslavs are eager to preserve their independence, they opposed subjection under Stalin's dictatorship, and that caused the great break in 1948 between Yugoslavia and the Soviet Union and the Communist movement.

After that the Yugoslav leaders realized that to deal with the diversity in Yugoslavia, we had to accept a policy of decentralization; that was one of the basic theoretical statements or attitudes of Yugoslav leaders. Another was their belief that the main thrust of socialism had been authoritarian and bureaucratic. A third belief was that instead of having the government management and interference in all fields of social life that were leading Yugoslavia to a totalitarian state, we should have social services, enterprises, and so on free from government interference, and self-management as a part of that concept. The democratization of relations in society was the fourth cornerstone of the building the Yugoslav leaders were erecting. The program of the League of Communists stated that the happiness of an individual is the basis on which government fulfills its mission. It also stated that a leader or the government or the party or the state cannot make a man happy but that every man has a right to pursue happiness.

The Constitution of 1963, which was based on the concept of functional democracy in all areas of social life—education, culture, social services, the economy, and so on—omitted, among the five houses of the federal Parliament, a house of nationalities, although a house of nationalities was included in the so-called federal council just in case it was needed. During the 1950s Tito declared that the nationality question in Yugoslavia had been satisfactorily solved. But by the middle 1960s, because of democratization and the development of plural interests, tensions and conflicts among the nationalities began to reappear. The process of writing a new constitution, hardly four years after the previous one was enacted, began again.

What were the basic features of the constitutional changes that took place from 1966 to 1974? In my view the changes had three aims. The first was to decrease the control of government over the economy and over worker self-management. This has not yet been successfully accomplished; although the federal government has lost power, the governments of the republics and provinces have strengthened their powers to the same degree.

The second aim of constitutional change was to reframe the Yugoslav federation. In my view we have gone too far in this respect.

We have approached a system that could properly be called a *con-federation*, because on most important questions all eight units have a veto power over the federal government. For decisions to be made, to change the Constitution, and so on, all eight have to agree. It is very difficult to reach an agreement among them in the face of the religious, cultural, historical, and economic diversity of the country.

The third aim was to provide a constitutional solution for the problem of succession to power, especially since President Tito was the unchallenged leader for such a long time. This problem, in my view, has been satisfactorily solved; since Tito's death the government and the political system have continued to function normally.

DANIEL ELAZAR: Reading Dr. Djordjevic's essay and Dr. Pasic's commentary reaffirms and strengthens several thoughts I have had about constitutionalism for a number of years. First of all, I am struck by the very centrality of federalism in the constitution-making process of Yugoslavia—in the deliberations, in the debates, and in the compromises. We recognized this centrality of federalism in our discussion about the American Constitutional Convention as well.

Second, self-management and federalism are closely related. In a sense self-management is an adaptation of the Althusian model of federalism—that is to say, federalism as a comprehensive means of organizing civil society, as developed by Johannes Althusius nearly 400 years ago. It bears some relation to what is called, in Western Europe and particularly in France, integral federalism. It would have been very difficult to develop so elaborate and articulate a system of self-management unless there were a federalist perspective that informed the entire body politic.

Third, the movement in Yugoslavia from federation to confederation opens up various possibilities for consideration with regard to trends in constitution making, state building, and polity building and for consideration of the differences between the modern and postmodern eras. One could argue that federation was a response to modern state building, which required some consideration of, or some commitment to, the principle of a consolidated, homogeneous nation-state with an overarching structure. In the postmodern era, where the idea of the consolidated nation-state has had to undergo modification, we see the revival of confederation as a federal form to accommodate multinationalism. Yugoslavia is a prime example of this, and to some extent Canada is another. In the supernational arena, the European Community is yet another. But the Yugoslav constitution-making experience speaks to us more clearly than any other in this respect.

Fourth, Yugoslavia is a good example of how a polity, once committed to federalism, can use a variety of federal arrangements. In Yugoslavia the provinces constitute a third form of federal arrangement. The distinction between the republics and the provinces is increasing. What is characteristic of federalist constitutions is their ability to accommodate such overlapping arrangements, which we can find in almost any functioning federal constitution. Once a polity is committed to the federal road, it can be extended in various directions.

We can contrast the French Constitution of 1958, with its traditional emphasis on the centralized unity of France, with the Yugoslav Constitution of 1974 to see the sharp differences between them, although both were designed to foster many of the same values, each in its own particular way for its own particular people. The French Constitution of 1958 was initiated by a strong leader, the Yugoslav Constitution by principal forces—"elites" in political science terminology—scattered through the republics. The French Constitution was drafted by experts, the Yugoslav Constitution of 1974 by politicians. The French Constitution was ratified by referendum (that is to say, a plebiscitarian kind of ratification with a minimum of deliberation), the Yugoslav Constitution through an elaborate process of deliberative forums. This contrast is generally true among constitutions based on the Jacobin model as distinct from the federalist model, and these two patterns recur in all constitution-making experiences.

I would like to conclude with three general points about contemporary constitution making. As we have seen even in our discussion of the French and Greek constitutions, a federal dimension is creeping into many of the constitutions in the postmodern era, even those that are far removed from any federalist perspective in their intention. That is because of a recognition of the transformation of the ideal of the nation-state in the face of pluralism—the existence of enduring groups within a single state or polity. Our colleague Ivo Duchacek has suggested that some 90 percent of the internationally recognized independent states have substantial permanent minority groups within their boundaries and that most of the other 10 percent are only segments of larger national entities that overlap the boundaries of other polities. Somalia, for example, consists entirely of Somalis, but a high percentage of Somalis also live in Ethiopia.

Two universal concerns in constitution making are the issue of human rights and the question of the executive, legislative, and judicial powers of government and how they are treated. The first of these has been much considered in recent years. The second is deserving of closer scrutiny. No modern constitution fails to address

227

the issue of rights directly. The U.S. Constitution tried not to address it but was quickly brought to heel in the ratification process, which I consider as much a part of the process of constitution making through reflection and choice as the drafting in Philadelphia. The question of executive, legislative, and judicial powers has increasingly become a question of separation of powers, whether the original intentions of the constitutional framers were in that direction or not.

That constitutions are more than frames of government, that in an older, Aristotelian way they also reflect socioeconomic distributions of power and the moral or ethical bases of polities, is also a universal concern. We can identify five contemporary constitutional models. The Yugoslav Constitution impresses me as a revolutionary manifesto constitutionalized—what Professor Djordjevic referred to as a social charter or a social plan. The U.S. Constitution emphasizes its function as a frame of government. The French and Greek constitutions regulate and redirect long existing institutions. Latin American constitutions, like most third-world constitutions, are designed to state accepted political processes and actions. Islamic constitutions, the British Constitution, and the Constitution of Israel are, in a sense, modern adaptations of traditional codes: the Koran, the rights of Englishmen, and the Torah. Every constitution must be understood in the context of the model it represents.

DAVID CAMERON: It is fairly evident that some kind of crisis usually precipitates constitutional reform. Certainly in Canada desultory and sporadic efforts to alter the Constitution continued for an extensive period but never brought about successful change. One reason was that there was never a sufficient sense of urgency attached to those efforts by the population or, indeed, by the participating politicians. The social impetus for the latest round of constitutional discussion in Canada, which ultimately led to a successful conclusion, was the rise of nationalism in Quebec. The government of that province mounted what was essentially a secessionist movement and held a referendum on the question of secession. Though obviously more complicated than that, this was the broad social context in which the latest round of constitutional discussion got off to its start. What is obvious from the essays we have discussed is that constitution making arises from some social tension or crisis. Such internal constitutional or governmental crises vary substantially with the countries and the particular circumstances concerned.

Clearly, an instance where there is a nonconstitutional, dictatorial regime and an effort is made to construct a constitutional order has certain characteristics. In unitary states certain other features attend constitutional discussion, often related to questions of the class and social composition of a society. Among federal states, typically, one of the major animating social factors is the cultural pluralism of the society or the regional tensions that often exist in federal-state relations, to which the federal order is a response. We see this certainly in Yugoslavia, and we see it in Canada as well. There may also be differences between states that fall within the liberal-democratic framework and those that are Marxist in orientation; the differences there seem to relate more to the view of history and the question of historical evolution and progress, of whether the role of the government is to lead or to follow the society. A related issue is whether the constitution is to be understood essentially as a framework of law or as the enunciation of a social project.

My second point has to do with the nature of constitutional change. One can ask whether a new constitution is being created or an old one amended, whether the process is one of reconstituting a country in a fundamental way or of adjusting the assignment of power and the structure of government in the light of changing social circumstances. The way in which the participants in constitutional change describe their activity with respect to this issue is very significant. Yugoslavia has had four new constitutions in the past four decades: 1946, 1953, 1963, and 1974. Will there be another in the 1980s? What would that signify, compared, say, with Canada where the same constitution has been in effect since 1867? It points to different political assumptions behind the constitutional changes and different views about the nature of the political culture and the way in which the society chooses to define itself and sees its relationship to its past.

The third point I would like to make concerns the role of the people in constitutional change. We have talked about the role of leadership; that is something that can be singled out for particular attention. In Canada Prime Minister Trudeau, who was rich in years and experience, lost an election but unexpectedly returned to power just in time to lead the opposition to Quebec's referendum on secession. When he said on his return to power that he did not intend to run in another election, this put him, in a sense, beyond politics. Although he was not in the position of the classic lawgiver who declines political power, he was clearly at the end of his political career, and his hands as a consequence were untied.

The role of citizens in the constitutional process is important, however. The population can be involved in a variety of ways, for example, through the constituent assembly or the referendum, which was used in France. In my country's experience, opinion polls were often referred to in developing a proposal for constitutional change.

229

The constitutional question was fundamentally viewed as a conflict between the federal government and the provincial governments, and the major theme running through the struggle for power was whether the federation should be more decentralized. The object of the prime minister was to arrange for "constitutional patriotism," as it is called in Canada, an amending formula, and a charter of rights. The provinces, on their side, were concerned about increasing their authority vis-à-vis the central government. The strategy of the federal government was to suggest that its proposals were the people's proposals. In other words, it claimed that a charter of rights is not an issue about which governments should contend. The federal government advanced the proposition throughout the federal-provincial debate that the proposals it was defending served the interests of Canadian citizens and were not the proper subject of a struggle for power between federal and provincial governments.

When the federal government, in the teeth of provincial opposition, took its proposals to the national Parliament, the people were not seriously involved one way or the other. It was a governmental affair and a spectator sport for everyone else. A joint commission of the Senate and House of Commons was established to hold hearings to review the constitutional proposals before Parliament, and, to the amazement of the central government, the opinion polls were confirmed. The people did, in fact, want a charter of rights; they did want patriation; they did want to see the Constitution brought home; and the charter was ultimately strengthened as a result of popular pressure, for example, from native people and from women's rights groups.

A. E. DICK HOWARD: I offer my remarks this afternoon as a kind of bridge between the discussion of the U.S. Constitution and the discussion of the Yugoslav Constitution. A fundamental theme was sounded in the remarks of Professor Lewis and implicitly in the comparison of the essays of Professor Berns and Professor Rakove on the writing of the U.S. Constitution. That is the merging or competition, as the case may be, of ideological forces and the forces of history, the place of ideas on the one hand and of circumstances on the other. In the formation of the U.S. Constitution in 1787, several forces informed the work of the delegates: first, the delegates' understanding of political theory, particularly the writings of John Locke and other Enlightenment theorists; second, their understanding of the British constitutional experience and in particular the developments of the seventeenth-century struggles in England between king and Parliament; and third, the colonial experience itself, ranging from the adoption of the colonial charters through the drafting of state constitutions. That third force was, of course, distinctly an American experience for over a century and a half.

The result of this process in America was a kind of eclecticism. In the pamphlets and statements of Americans between about 1765 and 1775, the proclamations and declarations against British crown policy, the natural rights of the British Constitution and the American experience are inextricably combined. The result was that the drafting of a U.S. Constitution was distinctly grounded in an American appreciation of several strains of both history and ideology.

In Yugoslavia an interesting effort was made to accommodate once again ideas and circumstances, ideology and history. The ideas, of course, were of Marxist philosophy: the principle of social ownership of the means of production, the role of the party, and others. The effort was to accommodate those ideas to the peculiarities of the Yugoslav circumstance, especially the place of nations and nationalities. On the surface both the United States and Yugoslavia were dealing with a common problem, federalism: how to strike some balance between the rivalries and interests of regions on the one hand and the need for some kind of sufficient central authority to maintain a unitary state on the other.

I am awestruck by the attempt by Yugoslavia, a country of such regional diversity, to write a constitution and make it stick. It strikes me that the viability of a constitution may turn on an examination of whether those regional differences are, at root, economic or have a deeper, cultural base. I suspect they may take both forms in Yugoslavia. There is an obvious economic difference, for instance, between the far more prosperous north in Slavinia and the far less developed south in Corasha. Of course, that leads northerners to prefer decentralization so that they may keep the fruits of their labor and the south, by and large, to prefer a more centralized collection, distribution, and equalization of the national good.

If the differences are cultural and not simply economic, however, they may reflect something more intractable, a kind of classical nationalism. Many modern states have tended to come apart at the seams on cultural, religious, and ethnic grounds quite apart from matters of economics. If, for example, education in Yugoslavia is a province of the republics and the autonomous regions and if education pursues nationalism—that is, by instructing the youth of a region or a province in the language and culture and history of that region— that makes it more difficult to achieve Yugoslav nationality. I understand that the 1971 amendments to the Yugoslav Constitution were the starting point for transferring much authority to the republics and provinces on the condition of prior consultation. The 1974 Constitution seems to have crystallized the process, at a time of crises—for example, in Croatia—in which the party leadership was much more aware than it had been before the problems incurred by excessive devolution of the functions and authorities to the regions.

In the Yugoslav Constitution one finds many efforts to accommodate this tension between centrality and decentralization—in the operation of the collective presidency, in the federal executive council, in the chamber of republics and nationalities. What puzzled me, as a Western layman approaching the subject, was how to account in a Marxist country for the use of such a bourgeois idea as federalism. Lenin had an inherent distaste for multinational states, an idea that federalism was obviously a regressive feature. I suspect that Tito believed he had stumbled on a new political concept for Yugoslavia, one that would accommodate the needs of the regions through the Constitution and at the same time secure some kind of unitary control by way of the party. If that is so, it may have been a misbegotten venture, because even as the Constitution of 1974 was coming into being, the party had already devolved power from the central party in Belgrade to the regional parties.

If the party is not the vehicle by which Yugoslav federalism holds together, we must turn to some other aspect, in particular self-management. That is a concept I find elusive, but Article 1 of the Constitution maintains an organic link between the notions of self-management that constitute the democratic conditions of labor on the one hand and the rights and the equality of the nations and nationalities on the other. It is quite clear that the framers of the Yugoslav Constitution proceeded from the premise that if the several nations, nationalities, provinces, and republics of Yugoslavia, disparate as they are, were somehow to hold together, it would be through some counterbalancing feature, namely self-management.

Further perusal of the Constitution reveals the concept of social ownership of property (again, for me, a rather elusive concept), probably uniquely Yugoslav. Questions emerge about the precise role of law in Yugoslavia. The classical Marxist notion of state and law is that they are tools of the working class through which programs are to be implemented. I get the sense that in Yugoslavia legal controls play a greater part than in some socialist countries in which there are extralegal forms of control, such as the Communist-Soviet Comrades Court in the Soviet Union. In Article 153 of the Yugoslavia Constitution the notion of individual rights is linked to responsibilities and duties—neither exactly a Western model nor exactly an Eastern model. There is a constitutional court; I take that to be unique among East

European nations. This constitutional mixture makes it difficult for me to say Yugoslavia owes its constitutional development to any other state. The Constitution reflects a bit of Western thinking, a bit of Marxism, but an awful lot of Yugoslav experience.

I would conclude by posing some questions about the future. Looking at a country in which there have been four post–World War II constitutions, I wonder whether that suggests an inherent instability in the search for some kind of viable and lasting system. The length of the Constitution—the longest in the world, with 403 articles—suggests some search for definitude that has so far proved elusive. The Constitution uses words of art, such as self-management, social ownership, and other concepts, that have no clear grounding in the system of any other country and that suggest a search for some kind of lasting solution.

In addition, we may ask questions about influences that were simply internal. Do the stability and coherence of Yugoslavia depend as much on what happens outside the country as inside? The Soviet invasion of Czechoslovakia in 1968 rallied Yugoslav opinion as few other events in post–World War II Yugoslavia have done; yet three years later a crisis arose in Croatia. The Afghan invasion by the Soviet Union might once again raise nationalist feelings in Yugoslavia, but how long will those feelings last? Another external force would be that of international organizations. The International Monetary Fund has obliged Yugoslav banks to operate in a more centralized fashion than the Yugoslav republics would have preferred. Finally, there is the question of political socialization. Surely, to devolve functions as Yugoslavia has done, to approach confederation instead of classic federation, presupposes not only certain structures that keep the country together but some kind of national spirit. There we must turn not so much to the pure economic facts of life as to the various cultural aspirations, the system of education, and the ethos that is created throughout the country.

MR. PASIC: I want to address the question of continuity and discontinuity in the development of the Yugoslav Constitution. A really deceptive picture is given by the fact that we now live under the fourth postwar constitution. Before coming to any conclusion, remember that all the changes in our constitutional order have been implemented under the same political leadership and under the same dominating social and political forces. The man rightly considered the architect of our present Constitution is the late Edward Kardelj, the chief man in the drafting of all four constitutions. In our theory and in our political thinking, we look at these successive constitutions

233

as steps in the same direction. Each one brings us further and makes the same principles more concrete. We are continually moving in the same direction, toward the same basic goals. That might be questioned, because there are also elements of discontinuity in our development, but on the whole it is true. Bear in mind also that after discussions that lasted for years each of those constitutions was adopted more or less unanimously and on the basis of consensus.

What should also be said is that no great constitutional changes are intended in the future. This worries me because, in my view and that of some of my colleagues and a large part of the Yugoslav population, we might need more changes. The problem is how to achieve them in a constitutional way, because the existing Constitution provides that it may be amended only if there is prior consensus among all the republics and autonomous regions. Without that consensus we cannot even begin the process of rewriting any part of the Constitution. A recent example would be the constitutional amendments adopted in 1981 concerning the length of term for presidents in collective bodies, such as the League of Communists of Yugoslavia and the Federal Assembly. President Tito proposed that the term be shortened to one year, and his authority stood behind the proposal. It was nevertheless very difficult to reach an agreement. It might not be considered crucial whether the term for a president in a collective body is one year or four years, but it was difficult to reach an agreement. Finally an arrangement was agreed to whereby the republics and autonomous regions have the right to settle this problem each in its own way.

The many changes in the Yugoslav Constitution and the length of the document can be explained by the fact that we view the Constitution as an instrument for social change. By changing some institutions, we achieve desired social changes; we meet the needs of the society as it reaches a higher stage of development along the lines of self-management.

I wish that we could find a better way to pursue that course, to adapt a constitution to new needs. For example, we are aware that the decision-making process is too complicated and too slow on many issues. On all important economic matters an agreement of the republics and autonomous regions is necessary before a decision is taken in the Federal Assembly. In that respect, even what is written in the Constitution has been much extended in practice. It is a widely shared view in Yugoslavia that we should do something to reduce the scope of problems that must be decided on the basis of a consensus among the republics and autonomous regions. It is a difficult problem because the republics and autonomous regions are jealous of their rights and resist any attempt to limit them.

In framing the U.S. Constitution, there was a conflict between federalism and confederalism. During the prolonged discussions in the formation of the Yugoslav Constitution, the main conflict was between those who emphasized self-management—the equal position of self-managing enterprises throughout Yugoslavia and the rights of workers to control social capital and to pool their resources regardless of the boundaries of the republics and autonomous regions— and those who emphasized the rights and sovereignty of federal units and the control of the economy by their governments. It was not, of course, a clear-cut and openly admitted division, but nevertheless it could easily be discerned. One result of this conflict is that among the constitutional amendments of 1971 are those that are intended to strengthen the position of republics and autonomous regions and those that stress the rights of self-managed units. Concrete attempts to reconcile these two tendencies were only partly successful.

In difficult economic crises, which affect Yugoslavia as well as many other countries, the problem of democratic but strong leadership has become more acute. We have paid a high price for the political stability we have achieved. We have precluded the possibility of a struggle for power, for the personal power of one leader. The composition of the presidency of Yugoslavia, for example, is such that ambitious attempts to impose personal rule and to build a personal cult are prevented. But the eight men in the presidency come from eight federal units; they are not elected by the electoral body of the whole of Yugoslavia or by the federal Parliament. They are directly elected by assemblies of the republics and autonomous regions, and their allegiance is primarily to those republics and regions. That strengthens the position of the republics and autonomous regions, but it is not always easy to provide for energetic and enterprising leadership, and that may pose some problem for the future.

We hope that if we fully stabilize the system of self-management, there will be less and less need for state intervention, especially in economic matters. The regulations will be less elaborate, and more problems will be solved on the basis of clear economic roles and with full respect for the rights of workers to manage enterprises and to decide on all problems regarding their organization and the distribution of income. But that stage of stability of the self-management system we have not yet achieved.

The people of all nations in Yugoslavia are aware that Yugoslavia guarantees their national freedom and independence. Only within the structure of the federation could all their rights be ensured. That is for Yugoslavs the main lesson of World War II. The Yugoslav federation was not determined *after* the war; it was determined *during* the war. The main programmatic goal of our fight for national liberation was not socialism but a federal structure for the country; that goal was proclaimed during the war in 1943. The future Yugoslavia we fought for would be a federal state of fully sovereign and equal nations. Yugoslavia was conceived not as a "melting pot" of nations but as a device, a political framework, that guarantees free national development and the equality of Yugoslav nations and nationalities.

MR. STANOVCIC: The problem of values mentioned by Professor Howard is very important. Some values, some aims, always underlie constitutional arrangements, and during the 1950s the whole scale of values was revised or even reversed from the customary scale of values in socialist or communist states. The position of man in society was seen in quite a different way, and the antidogmatism that characterized Yugoslav society in the theoretical works of the 1950s was later expressed in the program of the League of Communists, which rejects any claim to a monopoly over truth. That program says explicitly that neither the party nor the government nor the state has or can have any monopoly over truth, that searching for the truth is a social process in which science must be engaged, and that everyone can search for the truth—religious, philosophical, or ideological—for himself. The program further declares that science is the only judge of itself, that is, that politicians cannot judge whether scientists are right or wrong. This pragmatic approach is in part the answer to how we were able to mix elements from Marxism, from the U.S. Constitution, and from the Weimar Constitution. The program of the League of Communists also says that nothing whatever that has been accomplished can be considered so sacred to us that it cannot be superseded by something believed to be more progressive, freer, or more humane.

The concept of self-management of workers was introduced in 1950. The idea behind it was that state socialism did not provide much to the workers; they were hired by government and were often even less free than in capitalist enterprises because, although one can complain about an individual owner, one must not complain about the government. Self-management was further developed through the addition of other concepts: that those who work should enjoy the results of their work and that a worker has an inalienable right to income and to participate in making decisions concerning the income of an enterprise. It is, of course, inconsistent to give workers the right to participate in making decisions about the income distribution of an enterprise and allow the income taken by the federal government to be invested or distributed somewhere else. We had to accept that the income created in a region cannot be taken from that region to any other by an act of government, except by the will of those who live in the original region. When these regions are inhabited by people of different nationalities, this principle is quite understandable, but it leads to some very bad economic consequences. It is very difficult for the social capital of one region, of one nationality, to be invested in another. That is a problem that we have been facing in Yugoslavia for a number of years.

Another problem that we face concerns the presidency and the movement toward confederation. It is true that the composition of the presidency and its functioning can be used as an argument by those who claim that the Yugoslav system is very close to being a confederation, but the problem is not in the presidency, because a solution can be found relatively easily among eight or nine men. With eight legislative bodies scattered around the country, however, where interests and pressures are felt much more directly, solving problems is much more difficult. The problem in Yugoslavia is in reaching an agreement not among those nine persons in the presidency but among those eight legislative units. It would be difficult for anybody who knows the situation in Yugoslavia to conceive that a single person could be found who could gain the support of all those legislative bodies. Those who serve in the presidency have to exercise power in turn.

In my view, what is wrong with the Yugoslav federal arrangement is not the distribution of powers between the federation and the republics—that is not much different from the distribution of power in the United States. The federal government provides for the national defense, controls foreign policy with the participation of the republics, and regulates what we call the unitary market. But the federal government is left without the proper means to exercise its constitutional powers. Everything must be done by the republics and local communities. The federal government does not have its own courts or its own organs of power throughout the country. It is just twenty persons who meet in Belgrade; for any execution of federal decrees, orders, and so on, it must rely on the power structure of the republics, and that, as we know from the American experience during the Confederation, is impossible. The federal government also lacks any autonomous financial resources; it depends on custom duties, contributions of federal units (which are always finding ways to avoid their obligations, just as in the United States under the Articles of Confederation), and a percentage of a federal turnover tax that is collected by the republics and local communities.

Another feature that is very similar to the American experience is that all human rights are protected within the framework of the republics. The entire judicial process for an individual has to be completed within a republic or an autonomous province. Only a person sentenced to capital punishment has the right to appeal to a federal court. The republics have supreme courts that are not supervised by any federal court.

MR. GOLDWIN: From what you said, may we infer that there are, practically, eight markets in Yugoslavia?

MR. STANOVCIC: You are right, although many in Yugoslavia will not recognize that. Some Yugoslav leaders were talking ten years ago about national economies and the need for a common market as in Western Europe. Later politicians nominally accepted the unitary market and rejected the nonsense of having a common market and eight markets of the republics. But that is what we have, and balances of payment for foreign trade are supposed to be calculated for each republic separately, although that, of course, is probably technically impossible.

6
The Writing of the Constitution of Spain

Francisco Rubio Llorente

The Francoist "Constitutional" System

The political regime of General Francisco Franco, which arose following the Spanish Civil War (1936–1939), never built a system of social and economic stability that would outlive its creator. Franco's military uprising against the government of the Second Republic, which began as a reaction to economic and social disorder and violence in the streets, took place without questioning the legitimacy of the existing constitution. In the first days' proclamations, the confessed aim of the uprising was to defend the regime against weak, corruptible, trifling governors who it claimed were mere puppets for "aliens and alienators," among whom "Soviet agents" figured prominently.

"Bolshevik zealotry" and "Marxism" were said to be the forces that held republican institutions prisoner and had to be destroyed for those institutions to regain their freedom. In the beginning, the government denounced the attempt to "present the conflict as a battle between the workers' parties and the rest of Spanish society"; it soon accepted the idea, however, that subversion was being supported by "Spanish capitalism" in cooperation with "certain religious associations." No one can seriously assert that the Spanish Civil War originated in the differences that pit Catholics against non-Catholics, but the Catholic church's association with conservative social forces often obliged the progressive forces to adopt a sharply anti-Catholic attitude. This attitude offered those who arose against the Second Republic an excellent justification of their rebellion; consequently as soon as the Francoists did consider their rebellion to be an endeavor not to reestablish an effective republican government but to create a new state, they adopted the idea of religion as an inspiration for the new state. This idea had already appeared in a well-known discourse by General Emilio Mola, and it would not disappear completely until the last years of the Franco regime, when the Spanish church began to accommodate the modernization *(aggiornamento)* embraced by Vatican II.

In the twentieth century it is clear that, at least in the West, no political system can base its legitimacy solely on religion. In Franco- ism, religious legitimization is tightly bonded to exacerbated nation- alist sentiment. This bond mythicizes the past and disregards three centuries of history, especially the entire nineteenth century, when, even in the face of deep crisis, Spanish political life was organized on the principle of national sovereignty.

The "national" catholicism that made up the nucleus of Francoist political thought, does not, however, provide an "explanation" of reality; it is not an ideology, but a sentiment, and as such does not provide a plan for the organization of political life. It rests on the existence of an absolute truth—which is not so much a religious dogma as a kind of metaphysical essence. This sentiment, in which nationalism and religion are inextricably woven together, is related to a view of "the Spanish truth" pervasive in the rural areas predom- inant in Spain until recently, that grouped the Moors with the French and both with Protestants and Jews as enemies of Spain and the Church. It rejected liberalism because of its relativism; political parties, as protecting relative truths; and above all, any movements for re- gional autonomy (of Catalonia and the Basque region in particular) whose different characteristics were regarded as an affront to the uniqueness of Spain.

This is not the place for a critique of the basic beliefs of the Francoist regime; its internal contradictions are evident (like all po- litical traditionalism, it is stubbornly obliged to deny entire centuries of history), and it was clearly an anachronistic effort in the fight against modernity. What is noteworthy is the purely negative char- acter of that system on the political level. The new state—and, even earlier, the thought of José Antonio Primo de Rivera—had to look off the Spanish tradition for ideas that could not be construed as spring- ing either from democratic-liberal principles or from Marxist ideology. Fascism, introduced into Spanish political life through the Falange but still not widespread at the beginning of the civil war, was quickly transformed—as much because of extrinsic needs (the help provided by Germany and Italy from the very beginning to Franco's rebellion), as because of intrinsic ones—into an important element for the construction of the state.

From the outset, the program, principles, and structure of the new state worked to transcend individualism. The state was to be organized upon three basic principles. First the subordination of the individual to the interests of the community in which he lived (which in Spain is not a matter of ethnicity but of country—a concept with connotations more traditional and less linked to nineteenth-century liberalism than that of the nation); second, the superation of capitalism and Marxism by means of a corporatelike organization of the economy and of labor; third, the concentration of power in a charismatic leader "responsible only to God and to History." An armed movement enforced the adoption of these notions, a fact that completely distorted the function of the single party, the characterizing trait of other fascist regimes.

In 1936 the Spanish Falange of the JONS was practically the only fascist-style party in existence.[1] General Franco united JONS with the Traditionalist party, another political organization very active in the fight against democracy but of different origin and thought. This new political coalition was defined, in its first statutes, in terms reminiscent of a single party such as the German NSDAP or the Italian Fascists. But, one should not be misled by the definition or the functions that are attributed to it rhetorically. The "movement" created by the Unification Decree of April 1937, not only brought together two very distinct political forces but also brought into the fold all the officers of the army, whether they liked it or not. From that moment on, the legal requirement that certain posts in the state and para-state apparatus be held by FET and JONS militants did not serve as a tool for the domination of the state by the party, but rather as a channel for the bureaucratization of the party.[2] The party's already confused and heterogeneous ideology then became even more diffuse and in fact lost whatever efficacy and political dynamism it once possessed. Thus General Franco's regime developed not as a single-party regime but as a regime without parties.

The corporate organization of the economy, especially of labor relations, inspired Spain's first crude constitutional provisions, using concepts originating in nazism and fascism. With the outbreak of World War II, General Franco dictated a series of "fundamental laws" in which the fascist influence was less explicit. Franco's own political ideology remained hidden behind a screen of propaganda; but he was certainly more sensitive to tradition than to the pseudo-modernity of the German and Italian systems. These fundamental laws, in effect throughout the longest constituent period in Spain's history, formed a kind of absolute monarchy, which was, during Franco's reign, a kingdom without a king. After General Franco's death, an oligarchy of questionable legitimacy, which was supported neither by the people nor by tradition, took charge.

In its last days, the Franco regime attempted to revitalize the political structure by giving a little degree of autonomy to the main currents of opinion inside the National Movement; but the effort ended in enormous failure. Already in the final years of Franco's life, it was apparent that his government was incapable of dealing with the tensions brought about by changes in the economy and the society and no one in Spain seriously believed that the structure he had created could be maintained without major changes after his death. The tensions emerged first, from a continuous process of economic development into which Spain was dragged rather than led by European prosperity, and, second, from the reemergence of Catalonian and Basque aspirations. This was true especially of the Basque separatist movement, which gave rise to a terrorist organization, radical also in its political orientation.[3] Unhappily, this terrorist organization counts among its successes the assassination of the president of the government, Carrero Blanco, the first named by General Franco after nearly forty years of direct personal rule.

The Constituent Decision

After the death of President Carrero Blanco, Arias Navarro assumed the presidency. The standard bearer of the so-called Openness Doctrine, which had neither authenticity nor goals, he was the father of the previous attempts at diversification within the National Movement. It was this same Arias Navarro, confirmed by the king as president of the government after Franco's death, who would preside over the first timid efforts at change. To do so he engaged two dynamic figures, Fraga Iribarne and Areilza, both of whom had been committed to Francoism for many years and who had great energy and will for reform. They, along with the new president of parliament, Fernandez Miranda directed the transition process. Fernandez Miranda was a former teacher and confidant of the king, a subtle, occasionally acerbic, reasonably skeptical man with a notable gift for political maneuvering.

This group of men found themselves in the service of a king who had been given his power by Franco but who had no intention of continuing Francoism; at the same time, they were harassed by an oligarchy that, to a great extent, controlled the state apparatus, wished

FRANCISCO RUBIO LLORENTE

to maintain the status quo, and was confronted with an opposition to the king's regime that grew more active and powerful every day. The group's position was, therefore, extremely difficult. Its only source of support for the transition, even for any slight reforms of the system, laid in the king himself. As heir to a quasi-omnipotent power, the king was, however, vulnerable to attacks by purist, hard line Francoists; they, like the extremists of the French Restoration, appealed to the liberal parliamentarians to increase the power of the institutions they dominated (the kindom's council and the Movement's National Council). The king was also the favorite target of the external (democratic) opposition, which naturally expected him to continue the dictatorship.

In this difficult position, using the emergency procedures devised by Fernandez Miranda, and favored because of the parliament's deeply entrenched weakness in the face of the government, Arias Navarro's cabinet succeeded in getting laws passed that would allow for the convening of meetings and creating of associations to pursue political ends. (This was not a great accomplishment in absolute terms, but was a large departure from the former situation.) The cabinet failed, however, in its attempt to modernize the institutional structure, because it did not pursue substantial enough modifications.

The Fundamental Laws Reform bill, entrusted to a commission composed of members of the government and of the Movement's National Council, aimed at creating a second chamber, elected by popular vote, which would share legislative power with the corporate chamber.[4] Like the corporate chamber, the new chamber would lack effective means of controlling the government, which would continue to be accountable only to the king. Arias Navarro's project, however, did not reach its goal. It was rejected as much by the Francoists, who saw it as an opening that would lead to the destruction of the system, as by the democratic opposition, which interpreted it as an attempt to paralyze or at least hamper radical change, and did not even manage to get the support of the government that launched it.

The king himself resolved the crisis in government at the beginning of July 1976, by employing the old Francoist model and wielding all the power at his disposal. In all probability it was the king who asked for Arias Navarro's resignation and who suggested to the king's council including the name of Adolfo Suarez Gonzalez (former secretary general of the Movement) on the list of three persons from which the new president would be chosen. Paradoxically, the king's use of his authority (that is, suggesting to the body whose job it is to counsel him the proposals or advice that he wants to hear) resulted in a break away from authoritarianism.

As the new president of the government, Suarez Gonzalez—without a doubt the most obscure person of the three names on the list prepared by the kingdom's council and whose selection was looked upon with great distrust both by the regime's most liberal sectors and by all of the opposition—affirmed from the beginning (in a televised speech on July 10, 1976) his intention that Spain be governed only with the consent of the governed. The affirmation was not new, but the feeling behind it was. Far from continuing the projected reform of the fundamental laws of Francoism by adding to the old structure or by preparing a new constitution, the new government undertook, almost immediately, the preparation of a new fundamental law, calling for the convening of a constituent assembly.

The Political Reform Bill. The government presented its Political Reform bill in September 1976.[5] The bill created considerable confusion both among the old Francoist political class and among members of the opposition, primarily because of the ambiguity of its proposals, the goals of which were never clearly articulated. It seems evident now that the government's recourse to ambiguity was its way of routing forces it could have confronted openly only with the help of others. And it could not call on those others (members of the democratic opposition to Francoism) without negating its own legitimacy. The method was effective in bringing about the bloodless transition from dictatorship to democracy—a possibility that Spaniards did not believe until they saw it—but its adequacy in restoring the governors' moral prestige was less obvious.

The ambiguity of the Political Reform bill was a function not only of the way it was presented to the public and of the manner in which the parliament's approval was sought, but also a function of the very nature of the bill. Formally, the Political Reform bill was a new fundamental law (the eighth), which neither repealed nor expressly modified any of the previous laws. It did, however, tear down the extremely complex and unviable structure that housed the laws: it affirmed the principle of popular sovereignty, contradicting the previous system; and it provided for creation of a parliament elected by popular vote.

The bill maintained, in appearance, the existing institutional structure, and it tried to accommodate some of the basic institutions of the old system (the Commission of Legislative Urgency and the kingdom's council, for example). In fact, though, the old structure should disappear with the promulgation of the new act, and a new period begin, during which relations among the high-level state organs were guided by only the common sense and patriotism of a few men.

In addition, the Political Reform bill established a bicameral parliament, a structure hardly adequate for a constituent task and that, in fact, had no such mandate. It regulated the procedure for reforming the constitution but did not emphasize it in the face of ordinary legislative procedures and made no clear reference to the possibility of a new constitution.

The process that led to the enactment of the Political Reform bill was characterized, as we have noted, by that same radical ambiguity maintained by the apparent connivance of almost all the participants. The Movement's national council approved the act, and it was debated and voted upon by Francoist members of parliament as if it actually would deal with the reform of the Francoist fundamental laws, not simply with their destruction. The anti-Francoist parties fought against the act, calling for abstention in the referendum vote (December 15, 1976). As a result, 23 percent of the voters abstained, but the act was approved by 72 percent of the votes cast (the negative vote cast by the Francoist right was only 2 percent).

The Making of the New Constitution

Once the institutional framework was established, it was necessary to make political action possible. This required, first, creating a political party associating those who inside Francoism or out of it had pushed for change. Second, the right, which considered the change excessive, and the left, which considered it insufficient, needed to be incorporated into the legitimate political process.

The move to accomplish the first of these tasks, begun even before the change of government, was led by the Christian Democrats; they created a Popular party, later transformed with the incorporation of other small liberal or social-democratic groups—into the Union of the Democratic Center (UCD). The bond between this organization and the government grew even tighter on election eve (May 1977) when Suarez became its president and undisputed leader. Although the UCD was formally a coalition of parties knotted together as a single party, the public considered it dependent on the government. This identification with the government, especially with the already popular president, enabled the UCD to win two successive elections (in 1977 and 1979) but became an insurmountable obstacle to creating a party with a solid popular base and internal stability. The first National Congress (November 1978) modified the formal structure of the UCD, but its substance remained the same. The aligned parties had fused into a single party, but internal divisions remained.

The second task, incorporating the forces of the opposition into the political process, was not a problem of organization, since they already were organized, but one of political balance—to offer them conditions for public activity that, while acceptable to them, would not provoke resistance among the still powerful Francoist forces. This problem existed only with the parties of the left and the Catalonian and Basque nationalists, whose cooperation was required for the legitimization of the democratic process. The rightist opposition presented no problem. Fraga Iribarne, one of the central figures of the period, had succeeded in incorporating the right into the constitutional work by creating the Popular Alliance, a coalition of many of the less frantic factions of Francoism.

But the leftist opposition was split into two parties, the Socialist (PSOE) and the Communist (PCE), both of which had kept alive the doctrine of "breaking away" (that is, opening a constitutional process under a provisional government in order to eliminate Francoism). Each party had created an apparatus to bring other political forces into its fold: the PCE, the Democratic Junta in Paris in 1974; the PSOE, the Platform of Democratic Convergence in Madrid in 1975. From the beginning the Suarez government attempted to legalize the Socialist party; its activities had been openly tolerated, unlike those of the Communist party. For some time, Suarez, through many legislative reforms approved in the Arias Navarro era, continued these efforts, but they would be fruitless because the Socialists could not accept a system that excluded the Communists. By spring 1977, convinced of the futility of his efforts, Suarez gave up and legalized the PCE, thus incorporating the democratic opposition into the legitimate political process.

Once legalized, the Communist party joined the group of principal players in Spanish political life, which included, in addition to those already mentioned (UCD, AP, PSOE, and PCE), the Christian Democratic Federation (headed by two men who were the most prominent in the sector that did not want to join the UCD), the long standing Basque Nationalist party, and the Democratic Pact for Catalonia, a new and less nationalistic Catalonian group. These were not, of course, the only parties that existed (there are literally hundreds of entries in the party registry), but they were the only ones with a reasonable chance for success in future elections.

The Election of the Constituent Parliament. The step prior to the actual convocation of the Constituent Parliament was the promulgation of an electoral act, derived from the Political Reform Act. The opposition negotiated openly with the government even before the legalization of its parties, and they easily reached agreement on the provisions of the act. Several elements of the system (the province as the electoral district, the proportional representation system for the Congress, and so on) were defined by the Political Reform Act, excluding, therefore, any need for negotiation on them. Also, both sides were interested in establishing a regulation to ensure maximum purity of the elections and, in creating procedures that would favor the large parties and impede vote dispersion. The application of the d'Hondt system for relatively small districts, with distribution of the remaining votes only within the district, ensured the result more effectively than the Sperrklausel of 3 percent, which, however, was also introduced with unanimous approval.

The elections of June 15, 1977, were preceded by a lively campaign and yielded noncontroversial results. In large measure, results coincided with opinion poll predictions. The UCD, the government party, received 35 percent of the votes for Congress (the decisive chamber) giving them 165 seats (47 percent of the total). It was followed by the PSOE (with 29 percent of the vote and 118 seats or 34 percent) and trailed by the Communist party (with 9 percent of the vote and 20 seats); the Basque and Catalonian nationalist groups received 11 and 8 seats respectively. The only surprising results were the poor showing of the Popular Alliance and the total defeat of the Christian Democrats, who failed to win any representation at all.

Conditional Political Decisions. The promulgation of the Political Reform Act was, in fact, the beginning of a constituent process. All the parties had accepted the idea that the incoming parliament would be a constituent parliament. For the parties of the left (who had renounced both the doctrine of breaking away and the formation of a provisional government), a constituent nature was the only thing that made parliament acceptable and legitimate. The Popular Alliance, and to a lesser extent the UCD, believed that the parliament's legality determined its legitimacy but also that the constituent task was the more important one to be pursued. But the existence of the new parliament already had changed the power structure substantially and was itself the source for a new constitution.

Work on the constitution took place on two levels: the explicit level, which led to the writing and formal approval of a constitutional code; and the implicit level, which produced decisions affecting the territorial power structure, the relationships among the highest level state organs, and the system for instituting the fundamental rights of citizens. I will discuss first this group of preparatory decisions and later, the process of writing the text of the constitution.

247

The Powers of the Monarchy. The king acceded to the throne, not as heir to the kingdom of his father, Don Juan of Borbon, but through the fundamental laws dictated by Franco who, in July 1969, invited Parliament to elect Don Juan Carlos de Borbón as "heir to the title of king in the headship of the State." The king's symbolic detachment from this Francoist origin was essential for the safeguard of the legal transition. Other symbolic acts were also necessary to strip him of the powers that Franco's fundamental laws had conferred upon him, powers that were incompatible with a system based on democratic legitimacy.

Several days before the beginning of the election campaign (May 14, 1977) Don Juan of Borbon renounced his right to succession in favor of his son Juan Carlos who then became king *and* legitimate heir to the dynasty that had reigned in Spain until 1931. The new regime thus achieved the character of a restored government, which was very important in order to secure the loyalty of the army and of a large sector on the right. And the king, on the opening day of the new parliament (July 22, 1977), affirmed his "recognition of the sovereignty of the Spanish people" and declared that it was not his province, as constitutional monarch, to propose a concrete program or to offer guidance in carrying out a program, "as this is the duty of the political powers." At that moment the Crown ceased to be an institution endowed with political powers and became a vague moderating power.

This change also necessitated a rearrangement of the relationship between the government and the parliament. If the Crown ceased to be a political power, the government could no longer be considered (as the fundamental laws established) an instrument of the head of state, disregarding parliament. Certain parliamentary debate (especially over the Blanco case of September 14, 1977 and the new Rules of Procedure of the Congress of Deputies of October 17, 1977) already reflected the changed relationship. The rules included a reference to the institutions (censure motion and the question of confidence) that usually ensure government's dependence on the parliament, but the complete regulation of this matter was deferred to a special statute. The new statute was approved on November 14, 1977. Even though it was never used and is frequently overlooked by students of the Spanish constitution, it was a first-class constitutional rule establishing a new interdependent relationship between the government and parliament.

The Parliament and the Parties. Other measures taken were primarily technical ones designed to enable the new institutions to function or were initiatives with no relation to the constitutional process. Two, Cortes's Provisional Rules of Procedure and the Moncloa Agreements, are especially significant because they combined to achieve the same result, that of increasing the emphasis on political parties as practically the only players in the new democracy's political life.[6] The provisional rules issued by the Cortes presidency enabled the parliament to function in its early days. They required the deputies and senators to remain in a parliamentary group, established a close connection between the parliament and the political parties, and entrusted the actual direction of the parliament to the group's board of spokesmen, that is, to the parties' leaders or to their delegates. The Moncloa Agreements were negotiated and signed by the heads of the principal parties and by the president of the government at his residence (thus the name).

Government and parliament also made implicit constituent decisions dealing with fundamental rights, decisions that established conditions for the explicit constituent process. The most important, perhaps, were those that permitted previously prohibited activities. It is worth singling out two such decisions: the act (technically, a decree-law) that permitted the creation and growth of free labor unions; and the Amnesty Act of October 1977.

The new parliament approved the Amnesty Act as the conclusion of a long series of amnesties begun when the king acceded to the throne; they were intended to eliminate, to the extent possible, all the sanctions imposed since the beginning of the civil war in 1936. This act extended amnesty to all those punished for acts of "political intention," invalidating all dictatorial restrictions on political activity. The statute also excluded the pardon of those whose "political intentions" had been antidemocratic.

Among the principal beneficiaries of the Amnesty Act were some of the people condemned for ETA terrorist attempts, whom the act refers to euphemistically as people motivated by the desire to "vindicate the autonomy of peoples of Spain." The government also addressed the issue of territorial autonomy and resolved it largely through agreements adopted on the fringes of the formal constitutional process.

Maintaining the unity of the state was the most difficult political problem Spain has faced in the twentieth century. The slow dismemberment of the old empire, culminating at the end of the nineteenth century in the loss of Cuba, Puerto Rico, and the Philippines, was connected with the uprising of the non-Spanish-speaking population of the peninsula. Those nationalities either wanted to create their own states or demanded, at the very least, a profound transformation of the Spanish state, which they identified with domination by Castile. This splintering nationalism, especially active in Catalonia and in the Basque country, two of Spain's richest and most industrialized regions, met with some support during the second republic, when a constitution opened up the possibility that those regions could, if they wished, govern themselves. After the civil war the government of General Franco had strictly repressed such splintered nationalism. This repression, which was entirely ineffectual against nationalistic sentiments, was very effective in establishing a connection between the idea of democracy and Catalonian and Basque autonomy.

The Suarez government—well aware of the problem and under pressure as much from the Catalonian and Basque nationalist parties as from the parties of the left (Socialist and Communist) that had converted to federalism—made one of its most daring and consequential decisions concerning the future constitution: that of provisionally restoring autonomous rule to Catalonia and to the Basque region and extending autonomous rule to other regions of the country, the vast majority of which had not demonstrated any interest in having it. The strategy behind the move was clear. On the one hand, the strategy was to prevent Catalonian and Basque autonomy from seeming to be a special privilege; on the other hand, the government hoped that the Catalonians and Basques would lower their aspirations, since they could no longer be considered exceptional cases. Between September 1977, and October 1978—that is, the period during which the constitution was worked out—the government, by means of decrees, created the map of Spain, dividing the country into autonomous territorial entities, to be approved by the constituent parliament.

In sum, the authors of the constitution were presented with a series of options to which they simply had to give form: the state would not be unitarian, but compound (federal or quasifederal); the government would be a parliamentary monarchy; parliament would be bicameral; political life would be dominated by the parties; and rights and liberties that were standard in Western democracies would be recognized and guaranteed in Spain as well.

The Leading Players in the Constituent Process. The Political Reform Act made it possible for the newly elected parliament to be a constituent one. The act did not resolve, however, the question of who would draft the constitution and by what means the parliament would accept or amend the draft. This question was important because most of the members of the chambers had little political experience and were strongly bound by party discipline, making it likely that they would make few substantive modifications in the texts submitted to them. The Socialist party proposed that the new constitution be prepared by a commission designated by the parliament and not by the government or in any other way, and no party opposed the suggestion.

This last decision in large part determined the final form of the constitution. A constitution worked on by the parliament alone meant that the text would be prepared not *only* by the majority in parliament but also by the important political forces in the chamber. This was the origin of consensus, that is, of agreement reached through compromise rather than by majority vote. Naturally, this concept of unanimity through consensus was an ideal and did not fully coincide with actual practice. The consensual method made it impossible for texts to be approved only by the right (Popular Alliance) and the center right (UDC), which together made up the mathematical majority. But it also made it impossible for agreements between the center and the left to be imposed on the right (or on a regional minority). It was a method designed to unite legality and power on the one hand, with democracy on the other.

Though compromise and consensus were the guiding forces behind the writing of the 1978 Constitution, these praiseworthy ideals also created problems and were responsible for the constitution's principal defects: technical imperfection and the insufficient solution to the problem of territorial distribution of power.

The actual writing of the text was entrusted to a commission, known as the Ponencia working group, itself a subcommission of the constitutional commission formed of members of the Congress of Deputies. In fact, neither the congress nor the commission made any decisions. Both merely formalized agreements made by the parties, and the chamber determined how many representatives each party would have on the constitutional commission. This process was adequate for a situation in which the parties determined the constitutional process and the "authors" of the constitution became mere spokesmen of the parties.

Not even the number of representatives delegated by each party for the constitutional work was of particular importance, since it was the party itself that was to act. After some complicated negotiations among the parties, they agreed that the subcommission would be composed of seven members, three (Sres. Pérez-Llorca, Herrero, and Cisneros) representing the government party (UCD), one each representing the Socialist (Sr. Peces-Barba), Communist (Sr. Solé Tura), and Popular Alliance (Sr. Fraga Iribarne) parties, and one representing the Catalonian minority. This left the National Basque party without representation; its point of view would be articulated, with that of the Catalonian nationalists, by Roca Junyent, a Catalonian. The formal absence of a Basque party spokesman did not correspond with the real situation, since, in addition to the part it played through Roca Junyent, the National Basque party participated very actively in decision making. Though only apparent, this exclusion contributed to its estrangement throughout the process.

As noted earlier, the function of the Ponencia was more to represent the parties' positions than to make decisions on the form of the constitution. Fraga Iribarne, a man with a strong personality and many years of political experience had, as leader of his own party, a substantial role in determining the party position. His freedom of action was increased by the marginal position, with respect to the constitutional consensus, of his political group, which experienced the greatest divisions (in fact, the only ones) during the final vote on the constitution. The capacity for determining their party's positions was lower among the representatives of the Socialist party and the Union of the Democratic Center. They frequently interrupted negotiations to consult with their respective parties. And they left direct negotiations to the two men to whom the parties had conceded maximum authority: D. Fernando Abril, vice-president of the government, for the UCD; and D. Alfonso Guerra, vice-secretary general of the PSOE. Their authority was exercised, however, only when conflict arose during negotiations at the lower level.

Abril and Guerra had studied engineering, but all of the seven members of the constitutional Ponencia were jurists, and all but Roca Junyent were civil servants. Fraga Iribarne (AP) and Solé Tura (PC) were professors of constitutional law, but José Pedro Perez Llorca (UCD) and Herrero Rodriquez de Minon (UCD) also were considered constitutional experts. Peces-Barba was a professor of legal philosophy, Roca Junyent was a lawyer, and Cisneros Laborda (UCD), in addition to being a civil servant, was a well-known journalist. Only Abril, Cisneros, and Fraga had had any political connection with the Franco regime; the other four Ponencia members had opposed the regime in one way or another. Only Fraga was over fifty; most of the rest were approaching forty. Given all of this, it is very risky to make any statement about the personal contributions of each to the writing of the constitution, which was really the work of the political parties.

Writing the Constitution. The Ponencia wrote the first draft of the constitution between August and December 1977. Although it furnished summaries of its progress after each of its meetings, it did not publish the preliminary drafts. The press lamented and criticized the semisecrecy during this period; it is difficult, though, to imagine how the Ponencia could have worked efficiently on the constitution by means of continous negotiation and reelaboration had the text been subject to day-to-day publicity. At the end of November, however, a magazine with which Peces-Barba had close personal connections published the first forty articles of the constitutional draft, and they were published in identical form by the rest of the press a few days later. Although it is possible to hypothesize about the "leak," it is impossible to determine precisely its origin or the motivation for it. The leak prevented the Ponencia from including any purely technical corrections in the rough draft of the constitution published officially on May 5, 1978.

The rough draft, which all the members of the Ponencia supported, included each party's proposals for modifications of the draft. The most significant proposals were those of the Popular Alliance, the Socialist party, and the Catalonian minority concerning the territorial organization of the state, and those of the Socialist party on the monarchic form of government.

As an official pre-bill *(anteproyecto)* the draft was submitted for study to the party deputies, who had thirty days to formulate their amendments in writing. The amendments were abundant (779 of them, some very extensive, with references to numerous articles of the text) though obviously of little importance since the parties' positions remained reflected in the individual proposals published with the text. The deputies' amendments did offer, however, a new opportunity to negotiate. These new negotiations, lasting from the end of February to April 1978, were perhaps the most fruitful of the entire period.

In the course of this second phase of the subcommission work, an incident took place that is indicative of the tensions that existed between the members of the Ponencia and the parties they represented. Citing a "breakdown of consensus" Peces-Barba (PSOE) resigned from the subcommission. It was a surprising move, not only because of the minimal importance of the passages he objected to (some alterations of the articles concerning religious freedom, the right to education, and workplace lockouts), but also because the members of the Ponencia were free to voice their personal differences with the majority point of view, while the parties were able to maintain their own in the public discussions. Some believed, therefore, that Peces-Barba's withdrawal from the subcommission was due to internal party matters, the changes in the text serving only as a pretext. In any case, the ostentatiousness of the move, which briefly raised the fear of a crisis in the political process of transition, ultimately had little effect. When the time came to approve the new constitutional text, Peces-Barba rejoined the Ponencia and signed along with the rest of the members, although he went on the record as desiring to keep the original text, on the points mentioned.

Public debate of the new and final draft of the constitution began with its publication on April 17, 1978. Spanish parliamentary procedure required four debates (two in the Congress of Deputies and two in the Senate) on the same topics. In addition to showing the low level of Spanish political rhetoric (not surprising after forty years of obligatory silence), an event during the opening discussions revealed the true protagonists in the constituent process and the true meaning of the consensus. In the first days of debate, the commission's work proceeded arduously, and differences were often resolved by votes in which the UCD and the Popular Alliance imposed their solutions on the other parties. At the beginning of the eleventh session, however, the president of the commission announced jubilantly that the "majority" of the political groups had reached an agreement on the first fifty articles of the constitution. But this majority agreement, reached by Abril (UCD) and Guerra (PSOE) the previous night in a Madrid restaurant omitted the views of the Basques and of the Popular Alliance. Agreement between the two major parties was important so as to ensure a successful constituent process, but the agreement also signified a change in the relationship among members at the heart of the governing party. In the commission, the minister of justice, Landelino Lavilla, and the principal spokesman, Miguel Herrero, who were the main representatives of the governing party, both leaned toward positioning with Fraga. After the agreement, the constitutional position of this party (UCD) was mainly shaped by Abril and Pérez Llorca, who both favored the understanding with the Socialist party.

The commission's work began with a general judgment by the different parties on the constitutional draft. The two principal parties argued about the latitude and writing of the work; in the opinion of the UCD the former was excessive and the latter defective. The PSOE disagreed, however, and its representative, Peces-Barba, explained the Socialists' insistence on creating a constitutional code instead of a series of constitutional laws. He argued also that the "breakdown of consensus," had caused him to resign from the Ponencia and that his party's vote in favor of a republican form of government had no purpose other than paradoxically to reinvigorate the monarchy, the questioning of which was necessary to make it acceptable to the people. The Communist representative agreed with Peces-Barba that the lack of regulation of the Senate and the constitutionalizing of lockouts were unacceptable.

Fraga welcomed consensus but warned against reaching it through ambiguity and reasserted his opposition to the use of the term "nationalities" and to the solution arbitrated for the problem of territorial distribution of power. Speaking for the other sides Roca Junyent justified the textual ambiguity and, with some reservations, praised the organization of the autonomous regions. Finally, in the National Basque party's first public intervention in the constituent process, its highest-ranking representative spoke for the party's conception of the state as a free group of sovereign peoples who voluntarily limit their power—a conception, he argued, that "constitutionalism" had destroyed.

Debating the text. The constitutional commission of the Congress of Deputies held its sessions between May 11 and June 20, 1978. Its members agreed on a text that, with the exception of a provision referring to the "historical rights" of the Basque country, was not intended to be modified but only corrected and adjusted. Because of this, the successive steps in the process were much shorter. From a juridical point of view, the focal point of the constitutional process was the debate in the plenary session of the Congress of Deputies, carried out in twenty days (from July 1 to July 21), during which the chamber found sufficient time to debate and approve a law that profoundly transformed the income tax.

In the Senate debate, a large number of amendments (1,133) were proposed, which surely must be ascribed in large measure to the ingenuousness of a number of senators who were still not aware of the almost purely preposterous look that must have been attributed to the public debate by the time the negotiations between the parties had been concluded. The Senate, however, in its work between the end of August and the beginning of October, did manage to improve the writing and organization of the text. The Senate commission approved, by a slim margin, the provision that the Basques had introduced unsuccessfully in the full Congress, but the Senate, in the final session, eliminated it decisively.

The Political Reform Act entrusted the resolution of the differences between the texts approved by the Congress and the Senate to a combined commission made up of the president and four members from each of the chambers. This commission, which included Abril and Guerra, met during October and, thanks to the presence of these two individuals, acted with great speed and freedom to modify the text where the Senate had made no modifications whatsoever and on which no differences had to be reconciled. Once again, though, the commission operated almost purely for the sake of appearance. When a confrontation occurred Abril and Guerra frequently left the meeting, sometimes for many hours, only to return later, still together, with the problem resolved. The commission, whose members had remained inactive during their absence, then happily adopted their solution with no further discussion. Fortunately, there were few confrontations; the decisions already had been made, and the corrections needed were, in general, ones of simple editing. Sometimes, however, simple things also became passionate political problems, as was the choice of the name (Castilian or Spanish) for the official language of the state (article 3 of the constitution). A solution was arbitrated, which Perez-Llorca rightly praised in his final speech, since it was the model for many other solutions arrived at by the same procedure of sacrificing logic and grammar for the sake of politics.

The subject requiring the hardest bargaining in the commission's discussions dealt with a simple transitory arrangement, and, as such, was destined to have a short life. At issue was the wish to ensure that once the Constitution was approved, the government would depend on the confidence of the parliament. The Socialist party insisted on putting a provision guaranteeing the necessity for parliamentary support of the government in written form into the Constitution. The extensive references to the subject by the party's secretary general on the occasion of the final vote on the constitution were indicative of the profound distrust that the Socialists had of the government. They had never come to believe in the democratic sincerity of the ruling party. In fact, this distrust was the origin of some of the peculiarities of the Spanish Constitution.

The final text. The commission submitted the final text to the Congress of Deputies and to the Senate simultaneously on October 31, 1978. It was approved in a referendum (December 6) and was promulgated by the king in a joint session of the Congress and Senate on December 27. In the final vote by parliament, the constitution was overwhelmingly approved. Only the extreme right (five votes in the Congress and three in the Senate) and the extreme left (one vote in the Congress and two in the Senate) voted against it. The Basque deputies and senators abstained; this reserved attitude was reflected in the results of the constitutional referendum as well. In the three Basque provinces, although there were more affirmative than negative votes, there was a much higher proportion of negative votes (and of abstentions) than in the rest of Spain. The negative vote in the entire nation was only 7.8 percent of the total vote, but negative votes outside the Basque provinces meant rejection of the democratic system only.

The principal speakers in the final session (Gonzalez Marquez and Perez-Llorca) emphasized the idea of concordance, of the constitution as a pact, reached through consensus—whose harmful effects (secrecy and ambiguity) were minimized. Only the National Basque party did not join in the chorus of satisfaction; its representatives affirmed, once again, that the opportunity to resolve a secular problem had been lost. Perhaps most disquieting was the fact that at least one of these representatives (Senator Antonio Monreal) asserted that the solution to the problem of territorial autonomy had not been reached precisely because there was no desire to approach the problem with the same ambiguity devoted to the rest of the problems: "ambiguity is the fundamental element of consensus, and the integration of the left and of the Catalonian minority in respect to the Constitution requires the double, triple, or quadruple interpretation of any one of its articles."

Constitutional Models and Influences

Models. The objective shared by most of the authors of the constitution was that of "conformity with Europe," that is, imitation of a model. The intrinsic imprecision of the European constitutional model explains its capacity to motivate all the political forces from the Popular Alliance to the Communist party although the Constitution's concrete solutions cannot be traced to any European model. Europe represented to any one group whatever that group wanted it to, and neither the organization of the parliamentary system, nor the system of rights, nor the provision for the guarantee of either system, nor the territorial organization of power could be explained by reference to a European model. The desire for "Europeanization" (an old theme in Spanish politics), however, eliminated the "third worldist" or simply socialist initiatives from some sectors, oriented the system toward "Europeanism" as a guarantee of perfection, and established an internationalist slant for the whole constitution. This was projected as much in the strength with which the Constitution endorsed international treaties (article 96.1) (superior, in a certain sense, to that of the law), as in the quasiconstitutionalization of the international pacts on human rights, which would serve as criteria for interpreting the precepts to which the constitution was dedicated.

The European constitutions most clearly reflected in the constitution of Spain are those of the Federal Republic of Germany and of Italy, although some of its precepts are inspired by the constitutions of Portugal and Greece, which were written closer to the time of Spain's Constitution. The German influence (from which the notions of constructive motion of censure and the regulations on constitutional jurisdiction came) and the Italian influence (which inspired some general declarations and definitions of rights) were very strong; this is explained in part by their practical solutions to problems faced by the writers of the Spanish Constitution and in part by the well established cultural bonds between the countries. The juridical doctrines of West Germany and Italy are the best known in Spain today, Spain's former dependence on the teachings of French public law having disappeared long ago.

Influences. It is more difficult to pinpoint the interests that influenced the writing of the constitution than it is to identify its models. Obviously, though, international relationships must have exerted some influence on the various parties. And it is possible to detect the desire of certain parties outside the country to influence their Spanish conformers or social groups that in time could influence the constitutional work. Among the press, the Madrid daily *El Pais* was most influential; its editorials were read widely by the political community and took on the task of defining what was truly European and modern, and what was antiquated and Celto-Iberic. Of the rest of the large dailies, only *Ya*, closely tied to the church, was a constant mouthpiece for interests that claimed to be influential in the making of the constitution.

The different interest groups generally acted through parties and expressed their desires directly only when their connections were insufficient or nonexistent. Labor unions, therefore, which were closely tied to the Socialist and Communist parties did not intervene, and the initiatives of management (especially those of the Spanish Confederation of Managerial Organizations) became less frequent as communication with the right and center right parties became easier. The church commented directly (in the Declaration of the Episcopal Conference of November 26, 1977) or through its affiliated organizations (such as the Catholic Federation of Family Parents) concerning its points of view on divorce, abortion, and freedom of education. The church and the parties of the right and center right took similar positions on these issues and, though they accepted the principle of separation of church and state, they succeeded in keeping in the constitution (article 16.3) a specific reference to the Catholic Church with whom a "relationship of cooperation" would be maintained. The parties of the right and center right also introduced into the constitutional text (article 8) a reference to the armed forces. While the organization of the state did not require this, it was a symbolic acknowledgment of the importance and function of the armed forces, and undoubtedly it served to dispel fears—of the army and the public—fears that changes of political regime and bloody assaults on military leaders had promoted and maintained.

It would be impossible to discuss the constitution-writing period without mentioning the fierce terrorist activity of nationalist organizations (the Basque ETA, among others) and of ultra-leftist groups that was occurring at the same time. That this process developed and reached a happy conclusion, in spite of the "politics of assassination," is a fact that should not be forgotten in making a fair evaluation of the constitutional work.

The Text of the Constitution

The text of the constitution is moderately long: 159 articles; four additional dispositions; nine transitory dispositions; a disposition of repeal; and a final item. The language used is both emphatic in some of its proclamations of principle and rhetorical in its enunciation of certain rights. Its defects are due to the method of consensual preparation previously discussed and to the "verbalist" tradition of our politics, emphasized during Francoism; to some extent, especially concerning the rhetorical enunciations, the defects have more concrete origins.

The defects, however, should not obscure the merits of the Spanish Constitution of 1978, the foremost of which is that it both organized and effectively limited the power of the government. A system of constitutional jurisdiction ensuring the maintenance of all the organs of power was arbitrated without precedent in Spanish history. This pact between diverse political forces expressed a new understanding of the relationship between society and the state, in accordance with which the "social and democratic" state would work to remove the obstacles that had impeded the progress toward freedom and equality (article 9.2). One could call this new constitution an adequate realization of the modern constitutional ideal.

The constitution, which attempts with uneven success to maintain a spirit of consensus—requiring approval by strong majorities for certain laws (those called "organic" laws; article 81) and for certain appointments (those of the magistrates of the Constitutional Court and members of the General Council of Judicial Power, among others)—must be considered rigid, even extremely rigid if one considers its bill of rights and the monarchic form. Any reform affecting these matters must be approved by a two-thirds majority in two successive legislatures and afterward by a referendum; reform of the rest of the constitution also requires strong majorities (two-thirds or three-fifths,

259

depending on the item) and a national referendum, but does not require the dissolution of parliament.

Fundamental Rights and Their Guarantee. Title I of the constitution, which contains the bill of rights (chapter II) and the guarantee of those rights (chapter IV), also includes the governing principles for social and economic policy (chapter III), perhaps the area most affected by the empty rhetoric I mentioned earlier. Title I had its origin, in part, in the inclination to consider indispensable certain phraseology in the style of progressive literature, occasionally making the order and placement of adjectives a state matter, and, in part, in the different parties' desire to win over many diverse groups (including youth, women, children, the elderly, environmentalists, and the physically and mentally handicapped) through the verbal satisfaction of their aspirations. (A classic example of this policy of coopting marginal groups is seen in the Socialist party's wish to guarantee constitutionally the "right to the free development of sexuality and emotions." But no one ever explained exactly what that right consisted of.)

The use of the constitutional text as a political instrument undoubtedly distorted title I, but it did not diminish the importance or the essential worth of the document as a whole. The bill of rights is extensive and complete, its formulation generally sufficient, and its guarantees great. The fundamental rights are enforceable by all courts (article 53.1), and the right of freedom (including political participation and the right to education) is protected by a special procedure and by the Constitutional Court (article 53.2), to which every citizen has access through what is called recourse to protection (*recurso de amparo*). The constitution also established a commissioner of parliament as ombudsman for the defense of fundamental rights (article 54), although the effectiveness of this institution in the Spanish juridical system is doubtful, since traditionally this task had been entrusted to the courts of justice and the attorney general.

Title VI of the constitution ensures the independence of the judicial branch. Its government and administration are entrusted exclusively to a general council (article 122), part of which is elected by parliament and the rest by the judges themselves.

The declaration of rights was not particularly controversial. The left accepted, without objection, the constitutional guarantee to private property (article 33) and to free enterprise (article 38). The right and center right did not object to limiting the right to property, "in accordance with its social function," to framing the freedom of enterprise in the "social economy of the market" (article 38), or to the recognition of public initiative and the possibility of setting aside for the public sector "essential goods or services, especially in cases of monopoly" (article 128).

Controversy did occur, however, over the right to education. The right to education, especially insofar as it implies freedom to establish schools traditionally has been one of the most serious points of friction between the right and left or between the conservative sectors, who were closely linked with the church, and the laic forces. The constitution of the second republic couched the right to education in terms unacceptable to the church, whose doctrine until then had been a mandatory subject in the schools; it was upon the church, directly or indirectly, that the majority of the middle-level schools (serving ten-to-seventeen-year-olds) depended. The Franco regime had placed education in the hands of the church, entrusted to it the teaching of morality, and favored it with a policy that channeled state funds into the promotion of private education rather than into the creation of public schools.

The transformation of Spanish society in the forty years of Francoism, the *aggiornamento* of the church, and the new pragmatism of the Socialist party—which, while it maintained in its program some of the old formulas (that of the "single and public school," for example), manifestly did not propose to eliminate private education or even to deprive it of public subsidies—all had transformed the nature of the question but did not remove the old distrust. Negotiation on that point was especially difficult and resulted in another "breakdown of consensus." As a result of those tensions and the difficult negotiations, article 27 of the constitution dealing with education is exceptionally long, containing matters of dubious relevance and leaving uncodified important issues connected with the new form of the state.

The constitution also foresees (in article 55.1) the possibility of temporary suspension of certain rights (such as the inviolability of one's home, freedom of expression, assembly, movement, strikes, lockouts, and others), but only in exceptional situations, and only if authorized by the Congress of Deputies (article 116). A person under criminal investigation (because of presumed connection with terrorist activities, for example) may also lose certain rights, such as the right to privacy in communication and the inviolability of the home (article 55.2).

The Organization of the Central Powers of the State. The monarchy did not encounter resistance other than that from the Socialist party, which was surely telling. The belief that the form of government was decided and could not be changed again without risking the entire constituent process, and the king's assurance that he favored the transformation of Spanish political rule, facilitated the work of the parliament in establishing the powers of the Crown. These powers were only those of the parliamentary chief of state whose function was almost purely symbolic and whose authority depended exclusively on his own personal conditions. Some members of the Ponencia wanted to give the king effective powers—making it easy for him to designate the chief of government, for example—but the parliament did not endorse this move, and the monarch's role was left as a purely symbolic one.

The parliamentary form of government also provided for a bicameral legislature. The bicameral form was vigorously defended by Fraga, for often repeated reasons: the effectiveness of the high chamber as a control over radicalism; and the conservative tendency of the rural vote, which had greater weight in the Senate than in the Congress. In Spanish practice, though, these justifications were not convincing. The rest of the members of the Ponencia (and their respective parties) had trouble justifying the Senate's existence. For some time (until the public debate in the constitutional commission of the Congress), the solution was entrusted to a future organic law, to which the Socialists and Communists were vigorously opposed. Nevertheless, article 69.1 established the Senate as a "chamber of territorial representation." So formed, the representation of the provinces (simple administrative districts) outnumbers the representation of the autonomous regions, whose representation would not reach even a fifth of the total (articles 69.2 to 69.5). The Senate was not given the power to demand the government's political responsibility and in the legislative process had only a veto that could easily be overridden by the Congress of Deputies. The constitution gave the Senate several specific functions regarding the autonomous districts (see, for example, article 155), but they were not sufficient to give the Senate real power. The constitution also included, because of Socialist insistence and in spite of resistance from the right, articles calling for proportional representation in the Chamber of Deputies but not in the Senate. (It is presently a restricted majority system.)

The regulation of the government and of its relations with parliament followed the German model closely. The king would propose the head of government to the Congress of Deputies, which then would approve the proposal after hearing him present his program; the government, to be formed later, would not require parliamentary approval. This predominance of the president over the rest of the government was inspired by the desire to strengthen the executive; in fact, however, it only guaranteed his stability.

Territorial Organization of the State. The problem of territorial distribution of power was the most serious of the many problems the constitution had to resolve. Although the constitution provided for a state made up of autonomous regions, it did not determine precisely how that autonomy would be organized. The idea of autonomy was very different in force and character in those regions where it had always existed than in the rest of the country where, when it existed, it often had a purely emergent or simply reactive character. The constitution had to deal with two separate issues: on the one hand, the right to autonomy had to be reconciled with the problem of constituent power; on the other hand, the practical link between the central powers of the state (in the constitution there was no concrete term to designate the joining of these powers) and the powers of the autonomous communities (the designation applied, after some wavering, to the future territorial divisions endowed with political autonomy) had to be addressed.

On these questions, there were two theses: that of the Catalonian and Basque nationalists who believed their regions should have the right to establish their own political systems with absolute freedom; and that of the rest of the country, which felt there should be one Spanish nation with one constituent community. The Basques and Catalonians did not insist on the independence of their regions but did insist that the constitution allow for the free expression of distinct territorial wills. The rest of the population, even the Socialist party and the Communists, preferred to retain Spain as one undifferentiated whole and to consider the Spanish state the political expression of a single Spanish nation.

The authors of the constitution leaned toward the second of these positions (article 2), and rejected the compromise proposals of the Basque National party on this issue. The eventual wording of the constitution was not absolutely clear, though. The provision declaring "the indissoluble unity of the Spanish nation" also declared the right to autonomy of the "nationalities and regions that form it," thus introducing the word "nationalities" which, besides lacking precise meaning in Spanish, was insufficient for some people (those who saw a multinational Spain) and inadmissible for others (those who believed in one nationality). The ambiguity (so much greater here than in any other place, because the Constitution left unspecified which were the "nationalities" and which were the "regions") also affected the division of power between the central government and the autonomous communities. The constitution did not define autonomous communities or limit their number. In fact, as I have said, it already had been decided that all Spanish territory would be divided into autonomous communities, and to achieve this the parliament was given the power to "create" autonomy in those parts of the country that did not want to exercise it (article 144.c).

The imprecision of Spain's political map and the impossibility of establishing a homogeneous system for the entire state led to the failure of the Socialist party's proposal to resolve the problem with a clear system of division between legislative and executive competences. The political impossibility of postponing the satisfaction of the Catalonian and Basque aspirations also impeded Fraga Iribarne's proposal to leave the definition of autonomous governments to a later organic law.

The final solution distinguished two levels of autonomy, and called for a formal state law to define the statutes of each autonomous region. In many cases, this law would result from the pact between the state and the region, and in all cases it would require the consent of the region for its modification. Some lower-level autonomous communities would be able to assume only the powers that the constitution enumerated (article 148); others, the higher-level bodies, would assume all the powers that the constitution did not reserve for the state. The major defects of the system were not the technical insufficiencies of the constitutional provisions or of the statutes of autonomy of the Basque and Catalonian countries, though they were many; those insufficiencies can be eliminated by the Constitutional Court, whose work is in large part dedicated to this task. What was most worthy of criticism was the establishment of procedures as the criterion for distinguishing between the two levels of autonomy, rather than historical and sociological facts such as culture and language differences, both of which could be easily proven. The regions that previously were autonomous (such as Catalonia and the Basque country), or where the autonomous initiative was adopted by quorum (as in Andalusia) were at the highest level (article 151); the new autonomous regions had to begin at the lowest level. (After five years, and through the reform of the statutes, however, they could arrive at the highest level.)

Because autonomy initiatives are voted upon by the parties themselves, the placement of the regions and communities at different levels of autonomy generated serious political tensions—tensions that will probably resurface each time it is decided that a community should move to a higher level. It is likely, moreover, that those communities already at the highest level will begin to demand the "delegation" of state faculties that the constitution (article 150) makes possible. A more orthodox approach to the issue of regional autonomy might have created fewer difficulties; as it is, the constitution has established a permanent constituent process.

Notes

1. Falange Española y de las Juntas de Ofensiva Nacional Sindicalista (FE y de las JONS).

2. The baroque denomination of the unified party was Falange Española Tradicionalista y de las JONS (FET y de las JONS).

3. Euskadi eta Askatarsuna—ETA—literally Basque Country and Liberty.

4. The parliament in the Francoist regime was organized in reflection of the corporatelike structure of economy and labor we mentioned before; there were also representatives of municipalities and the families.

5. In parliamentary systems the draft for a regulation presented by the government to the parliament is called a bill. Only the parliamentary approval transforms it into an Act.

Commentary

José Pedro Pérez-Llorca

Mr. Rubio Llorente begins his study of the constitutional process in Spain by linking it with the immediately preceding events of the Civil War and the Franco regime. For a revealing and analytical consideration of the process, this evidently constitutes a methodologically correct point of departure. It is useful, however, to place the constitutional process within a sociologically broader and historically more remote context. The Spanish constitutional process of 1978 was one attempt—we hope the last—to organize Spanish political life within a modern context; for the vast majority of Spanish people today that means a democratic and Western European context. Consideration of the constitutional process, therefore, should include not just this one successful attempt, as a singular and isolated effort, but also the protagonists in the process and the citizenry in a long historical process whose primary characteristic was repeated failure.

If only to illustrate the nature of the threat with which the writers of the Constitution felt themselves confronted, it seems useful to outline some features of Spanish constitutional history. These features have been perceived, with different emotional and ideological connotations, by the whole of Spanish society. This generalized social consciousness is a basic factor in the constitutional process that must be considered. Yet it points to unanswered questions for historians: At what point, from which moment, and by what means did our constitutional history depart from that of other countries in Europe? How and when did we acquire constitutional idiosyncrasies at odds with other European countries?

The naturally limited process of reform during the Enlightenment was brought to a halt with the trauma that most greatly affected the leaders of that earlier time, the French Revolution. The subsequent Napoleonic invasion brought to Spain an unprecedented upheaval, which dominated most of the nineteenth century. In the middle of that century the first attempts at liberal constitutionalism began.

266

The first Constitution in Spain was granted by Napoleon. However interesting its text may have been, it is generally considered to have been an instrument of occupation and usurpation. Faced with foreign invasion, deprived of the only embodiment of national legitimacy—the monarchy and the national dynasty—a majority of the people tried to respond to the threats of invasion and war and to organize the state and society on a modern, liberal basis. The fruit of this disorganized but enormous effort was the Constitution of 1812, enacted by a freely elected parliament in a city that was at that time the only part of the country not under occupation.

Even with its defects, this Constitution of 1812, advanced in some respects for its time, could have been transformed into a document that would have dominated our political and constitutional future. But it was not to be so. The restored national dynasty, aided by the "European modernity" then ruled by the Holy Alliance, abrogated it twice, the second time in conjunction with an armed French invasion mandated by the Congress of Verona. Thus the possibility of a continuous constitutional guideline crumbled, and the very opposite tradition, marked by discontinuity and violence, began.

The Spanish upheavals of 1808 and 1834 brought about the failure of conciliation as well as a series of great civil wars that gave rise to exclusive, imposed constitutions. The period of "the two Spains" began, the last and most bloody manifestation of which was the Civil War of 1936–1939.

The constitutional process was long and complex and flowed through many channels. Among its effects is that it produced a new phenomenon: constitutional texts ceased to be the outcome of general agreement among existing political or social forces and became the ideological, political, and institutional reflections of one faction of the country, imposed—in most cases by violent means—on another. This was the phase during which the Constitution of 1812, which had an integrational bent, was defended by one of its partisans with the very nonintegrational slogan "swallow it." It was at this time, too, that a lucid writer created an epitaph for the epoch: "Here lies half of Spain; it died from the other half."

It would be out of place here to enter into even a general description of the profound social processes that caused this division in Spain. It would not be out of place, however, to describe another abstract result of our constitutional experience. The various constitutional texts—under which a veritable wealth of instability ensued—increasingly tended to reflect the results of a sometimes bloody conflict and were created to exclude the opposition and to impede its access to power. In the face of this reality, although attempts were

267

made to integrate factions, the defeated forces often chose with-drawal. That is, they tended to situate themselves outside the con-stitutional order, which they considered partial and transitory. The objective of the opposition, therefore, was not to use constitutional channels to reach power but, by staying on the outside, to bring about a constitutional rupture through which they could impose their own constitutional text. Frequently, they did so by means of a *pronuncia-miento* that excluded or provoked the withdrawal of the new oppo-sition, whose aspiration was to bring about the same result in turn and thereby initiate a new cycle.

Although constitutional forces for integration existed, they were always limited. Since the political game was restricted to the partisans of the system in force, certain people were always excluded and held back. These were the factions whose participation through legal chan-nels would have been considered illegitimate and dishonorable by both the excluders and the excluded. With the failure of the last integrational effort, under the Constitution of 1876, this process was exacerbated; being restricted to certain social forces at its beginning, it was then widened and radicalized by the start of the delayed Span-ish industrialization, through which the new working classes began to participate in political life.

The republican Constitution of 1931 instituted integrational ele-ments and efforts, but in some of its fundamental ideological for-mulations it was not wholly different from the tradition of exclusivity and partiality described above. The sociopolitical tensions of the 1930s and the Civil War constituted an unprecedented upheaval for Spanish society, comparable in its effects only to the period of upheaval at the beginning of the nineteenth century (although it was much more costly in human lives and material destruction).

At this point, then, the cycle concluded with elements very sim-ilar to those at its beginning. In the war and the regime that was based on it, the characteristics of dogmatic partiality and exclusion of losers were aggravated to the point of paroxysm after 1939.

When the writers of the 1978 Constitution, each with a different cast of ideological interpretation, were faced with the problem of endowing the country with a political constitution, they found a num-ber of common characteristics of past constitutional experience that they all realized they must avoid. These characteristics were discon-tinuity, instability, violence, and a tendency toward dogmatism and exclusivity. Past constitutional texts were designed not to regulate the competition between different political opinions but to authorize the predominance of one political sector and the proscription or jus-tified withdrawal of the others. This experience brought the writers of the Constitution to an underlying agreement that was part negative and part positive. It was not possible to organize political life on the basis of historical constitutional texts. None of the previous texts had the characteristics of continuity and historical consensus that would have permitted the reestablishment of a consensus of legitimacy and would have guaranteed the acceptance of a new text by the various potential power holders. That greatly distinguished the Spanish situation from that of other countries: Argentina, for example, in spite of tremendous political instability, has a written constitution whose legitimacy no one disputes; the Argentine Constitution of 1853 confronts problems only in its enforcement and its functional modernization. In Spain we had to start from scratch as far as the text was concerned, and it was this first, preliminary agreement that was ever present in the minds of the constitution writers.

The constitution writers were also able to agree on a basic principle without recognition of which one cannot explain the constitutional process. Because the earlier constitutional texts failed to provide for stability and continuity, the new effort was to formulate a constitution that would offer the possibility of such stability and continuity. Moreover, the basic characteristics of the earlier texts being exclusivity and imposition, the writers tried to formulate a text that was not in any way based on the patrimony of one party, that would be as open as possible to the entire spectrum of the country's political forces, and that would not be directed at anyone or even against the past. It would be formulated in the most peaceful and orderly way possible and thus be safe from any charge of violence or partiality in its origin. Since the preceding constitutional process had been characterized by absolutely ideological, dogmatic, and partial constitutional texts, the authors of the new Constitution tried to endow their work to reflect to the greatest extent possible what all the political factions had in common and to avoid polemics. Finally, to escape from the mistakes of the past, the new Constitution would have to reflect a sincere will to permit the free access to power of the different factions and not to exclude any of them.

This basic agreement was foreshadowed by an evolution in Spanish society. Having been one of the legislators concerned, I am witness that they were aware of that social agreement and tried to incorporate it in the constitution. This was possible not only because there was a common historical experience—albeit with different ideological interpretations—but also because the terrible trauma of the Civil War continued to weigh heavily on us as on the whole of Spanish society, and its repetition was to be avoided at all costs.

Spanish society, in its economic, social, demographic, and cultural evolution, provided positive values that allowed the negative and abstract consensus to be molded into a written text. This positive aspect was based on the internalized acceptance by Spanish society—though, at times, through mythical representations—of democratic, Western European values and, more specifically, of the models in force in Europe's Common Market. This acceptance was seen as necessary not only for recovery from the traumas of the past but also for the modernization of the country. As Professor Rubio certainly must recall, this linked the transformation of collective representations during the constitutional period of 1977 with what existed precisely at the beginning of the cycle—what I referred to briefly as the important impulses toward "modernization" and "Europeanization" in Spanish society.

The general awareness of a long historical experience of trauma and failure, the reality of important socioeconomic changes, and the mythical, but still real, acceptance of a model are the three bases without recognition of which a detailed analysis of the constitutional process would be insufficient. The detailed process is correctly described by Professor Rubio Llorente, and I will refer only to the parts of his paper where a complementary analysis might be of interest.

Before June 15, 1977, a situation was created in which the democratic opposition forces, under shelter of precisely that social process mentioned above, were able to provoke a crisis of confidence in the regime and its leaders and to create insecurity in the very structure of the system. They were unable, however, to bring the system down or place it in serious danger. This is important for understanding that the initiative, at its decisive early moments, was always in the hands and under the control of the system itself and its various institutions. The Law for Political Reform, of great importance both as a text and as an example of the self-destruction of a system, perhaps not sufficiently considered, and the sweeping referendum by which it was approved can be understood only by looking equally at the three bases of the constitutional process cited above. It was this law that made the elections of June 15, 1977, politically and legally possible.

Although the meaning that Professor Rubio attributes in his paper to the elections of 1977 is not quite clear to me, I do not believe there is any dispute about whether the elected Parliament was to formulate a constitution. In my judgment, as much for the political forces of the left as for the moderate forces, the preparation of a new constitution was the most important mission of the future Parliament. The content, procedures, pace, and other points of the constitutional process were discussed in the election campaign, and the objective of preparing a constitution received general approval. Once Parliament was assembled, although there were determined, propagandistic efforts to claim authorship, the proposal to create a constitutional commission (which had already been foreseen in the Law for Political Reform) was written, presented, and approved by unanimous agreement of the various parliamentary groups and enacted by a unanimous vote of Parliament.

This is how the commission and its core, the Ponencia, were constituted. Without entering into the details of the negotiations to create the Ponencia, I may say that the temptation to have an exclusively bipartisan composition—that is, from the Union of the Democratic Center (UCD) and the Spanish Socialist Workers' party (PSOE)—was overcome. The Ponencia was opened to other groups, a decision that was not really conscious or planned but that was absolutely correct. The absence of the Basque Nationalist party (PNV), which Professor Rubio points out, was due to the rules governing Parliament at that time; the Catalonian minority and the PNV formed a single parliamentary group for all practical purposes.

The ample representation of the UCD in the Ponencia was due, in the first place, to the necessity of keeping in the very core of the Ponencia—which was responsible for writing the text of the Constitution—the potential for a majority decision, as was possible in the Parliament. (The rules did not at first allow for the possibility of a vote within the Ponencia according to the strength of each group.) Second, the representation of the UCD was due to the need (which I believe was felt by its highest leaders) to direct the UCD on this issue in a collegial manner. During the first session of the Ponencia, on August 22, 1977, many of its members expressed views (each with his own nuance) on the historical constitutional experience, on its palpable results, and on the weight of that experience. That day decisions were made that are relevant here. First, important procedural decisions concerning confidentiality were made. Under self-imposed confidentiality, the progress of the text was not to be made public until a later stage, and the *ponentes* were bound to keep their deliberations secret from the press and from the parliamentary groups. Only the top people of the parties would be thoroughly informed about the progress of the text. This agreement on confidentiality was criticized at the time by the majority of the press, by large sectors of public opinion, and by many parliamentarians; it seems obvious today, however, that without that confidentiality, agreement on the Constitution would have been much more difficult to reach.

Other procedural decisions were no less relevant to the making of the Constitution. One rule held that no party or *ponente* could present a complete constitutional text; the Ponencia itself would formulate the agenda of questions with which the Constitution would deal and would consider the partial documents to be presented by the *ponentes* addressing matters under their responsibility. This decision was important since it determined, from the very beginning, that the resulting text would not be of singular authorship. This proved enormously significant in the ensuing process.

The Ponencia also agreed to work alone, that is, without consulting experts (a debatable decision, although I believe it was basically sound), except for congressional legal advisers who were specifically asked to participate (among them the invaluable Professor Rubio), and without the assistance of other political officers of the Congress, such as the president of the commission. Each *ponente* assumed the role of president of the session and directed the work in rotation.

During the first meeting of the Ponencia and another immediately following it, it was decided that a formulation of a single text would be chosen, which seemed obvious from the results of the general election. Although that implied opting for a constitutional process proportionately longer than a process of considering successive texts— a decision that seemed to carry with it certain risks—experience has clearly demonstrated that it was the right decision. Professor Rubio tends to generalize perceptions about the relations between the *ponentes* and their parties that he probably grasped only indirectly. These relations were different in each case, corresponding to the different natures of the parties and their different responsibilities. It thus seems hazardous to generalize that the two leading parties maneuvered their representatives like pawns. My direct experience leads me to just the opposite conclusion. It was the *ponentes* who, owing to a sense of responsibility, frequently went back to their party—in our case, to the government—to determine their position on issues. We were not given a general text, and only occasionally, at our own request (particularly in certain specialized fields), were we given a draft suggestion. For us, as for the others, there was a process of consultation derived from a sense of responsibility. We represented the majority party whose decisions were incorporated in the text, and that party had the responsibility not only for governing the nation but for carrying out the process of transition and the constitutional process itself.

I believe we must put equal emphasis on the politically important period of September, October, and November 1977. First, the PSOE directed a motion of censure against the Minister of the Interior (which still could have opened the way for a "nonrational" parliamentary system). (This found response in the law that Professor Rubio describes.) During those months, while serious progress was being made by the constitutional Ponencia, two other major agreements were reached: the economic-social agreement of Moncloa and the agreement on the amnesty law. Professor Rubio seems to focus especially on the procedural aspects of these two important political decisions and on the more or less leading, or formal, role played by the Parliament. Without criticizing his position, which is accurate, I believe it is important to note how the political forces initiated the constitutional process and, with evident signs of progress, felt it necessary to complete it with an amnesty law. That law was meant to overcome a previous pattern of violent encounters and to keep the constitutional process safe from socioeconomic tensions by means of a social and economic agreement. The parties thus placed the culmination of the constitutional process ahead of resolving immediate tensions and worries, which would have commanded their principal attention in any other situation. At that time it became clear that the political forces and all of Spanish society wanted to break the cycle that I have described.

I agree for the most part with Professor Rubio's description of the ensuing process. I part company with him, however, over his understanding of the so-called consensus, the origins and mechanics of which were more complex than he describes, and also over his description of the work of the joint committee. The joint committee was used for more than its strictly defined mission of reconciling the work of the Congress and the Senate, but given the complicated and difficult constitutional process in Spain, minimizing the role of the committee would have been a great mistake. I also do not agree with his view of how this committee worked, which was not in accordance with his description of a group of silent parliamentarians waiting for the decision of two absent members. To my recollection, such a situation occurred only once, the absentees were more numerous, and the issue was strictly a practical political problem. But since this happened only once, it should not be given the prominence that Professor Rubio gives it—perhaps as a consequence of his undeniable literary talent.

I agree with Professor Rubio with respect to the fundamental decisions about the Constitution. Naturally, the first decision concerned organizing our political life in a democratic and modern way, by formulating a text to break the seemingly permanent cycle of winners and losers—a text, that is, that would preside over political and civil life in Spain through different men and parties and to prevent the predominance of one political faction to the exclusion of the oth-

273

ers. Professor Rubio describes with particular insight the reasons for the general acceptance of the monarchy, which continues to unite historical and functional legitimacy.

Because of the existence of the monarchy and because of the context of our democratic traditions, the motives for choosing a parliamentary regime (in the technical sense of this term in political science) and for incorporating in it the process of rationalization, which recalls the constitutionalism of the postwar period, seem obvious. This system of rationalized parliamentarism was particularly precise compared with the much more traditional parliamentarism, such as the postwar French and Italian systems. The position of the UCD linked a logical concern for stability of government—that is, a view of *parliamentary* instability as one cause of our past *constitutional* instability—with a better understanding of the German chancellorial system and a greater ideological identification with the Fundamental Law of Bonn. That, together with the electoral system and the decisive influence of television on that system, made clear that beneath the appearance of a rationalized parliamentary system, one can speak somehow of a de facto presidential system in Spain.

It is interesting to note the bold strokes used to frame the power of judicial review of the Constitutional Court. A great failure in the 1931 experience, the creation of the Constitutional Court has become—thanks to a good organic law and the prudent practice of the court itself—one of the most prestigious and effective institutions in our political system.

The court is the one element that, without deviating from its strictly jurisdictional role, is helping to close the obvious gaps and correct the imperfections of Title 8 of the Constitution, which concerns the territorial organization of the state. Without the existence of the court, the application of that title and most of the conflicting statutes of autonomy (concerning Catalonia and the Basque country) would have been difficult, if not impossible. That title of the Constitution addressed a major political problem and brought to light a major technical deficiency. It was problematic because Spanish regional problems have a long history, going back virtually to the beginning of our existence as a modern state. The contemporary cycle, to which I have already referred, exacerbated the problem, which lacked those elements of implicit consensus that contributed to political decisions in other areas. The problem did not permit a solution based on foreign models. The constitutional text reflects some ambiguous agreements in which the consideration of certain Basque and Catalonian points of view carried the most weight. The necessity of their inclusion, in a scheme of general and abstract pursuits, was clear. This explains

274

the technically deficient result and the label "problematic," pinned to this issue. Even with a partial solution, it continues to be the fundamental problem in Spanish political life. It is precisely in this area that the Constitutional Court's action has been more important.

Given the historical experience I have described and the explicit acceptance of things European as model, the *ponentes* from the UCD proposed a formula, both wise and naive, to overcome the most important stumbling block, the ideological content of a Constitution written in 1978. By referring directly to the European human rights conventions and the European social charter, we were attempting to shorten the duration of the Ponencia's work, make an implicit consensus explicit, and incorporate in the constitutional text a democratic, European character. This attempt failed, however, because of unanimous rejection by the other political parties, which led to the consequences Professor Rubio accurately describes. Apart from the trouble caused during the drafting of that dogmatic part of the Constitution, however, there have so far been no particular difficulties in its enforcement. Thanks to the Constitutional Court's close attention, a process of careful maturation has begun, which will enrich what was described as an apocryphal compromise.

Of external influences on the constitutional process, the influence of German doctrine and texts was incomparably greater than that of any other. The reasons have been outlined here and more extensively addressed by Professor Rubio.

The experience of the application of the Constitution since 1978 permits us to formulate an initial positive judgment about the results of that work. The Spanish Constitution truly has ruled political life in Spain; its acceptance continues to be very high; and the operation of its various elements and institutions has been generally successful, with the possible exception of Title 8. Although the great regional issue in Spain remains unresolved, we can affirm that the writers of the Constitution of 1978 found the formulas to break decisively the repetitious cycle that had so often placed in jeopardy the collective navigation of the Spanish ship of state along a free, peaceful, orderly, and democratic course.

Discussion

ROBERT GOLDWIN: The Spanish political situation had very strong, fixed characteristics that no constitution writers could change, but at the same time those constitution writers were bound to no particular existing form. So the possibilities for very great success or partial success or even disaster were there. Spain lacked the towering figure of other national constitutional experiences and also seemed to lack political experience because of the lengthy era of dictatorship. Nonetheless, it is clear that constitution writers had a good deal of political sagacity, a pervasive prudence, and amazing skill in the face of ambiguity.

Mr. Pérez states that the writers of the Constitution had to start from scratch as far as the text was concerned because of the previous character of their constitutional experience. But the more I think about it, the more it seems to me that they did and did not have the opportunity to start from scratch, because there were both a very narrow range of possibilities and also, at the same time, something of an opportunity for a new beginning. I put these conflicting thoughts before you in the form of a question: To what extent did the writers of the new Spanish Constitution have an opportunity to start from scratch? To what extent can any modern constitution writers have such an opportunity?

FRANCISCO RUBIO LLORENTE: It is extremely difficult in a country as old as Spain, with a long constitutional history, to start from scratch. First, we should remember that Spain's first Constitution was adopted in 1812. With such a long history we could never have begun with a clean slate. Second, Spain is part of a distinct cultural world within which are certain accepted ideas at any moment in history. We never begin from scratch.

The terms in which, politically, we approached the problem of the transition from the dictatorship of General Franco to a democratic regime were rather simple. The institutions that existed under the

276

Franco system, including a parliament without real representation, were legally the depository of power. They also included the state machinery, the administration, the armed forces, the police. But all these institutions had retained power only through the person of General Franco and therefore lacked a legitimacy of their own. The Francoist legitimacy did not conform to the accepted ideas or values that legitimize political systems in the Western cultural world. At the time of General Franco's death some people wanted a continuation of the Franco kind of government with adaptations to accommodate the political structure to the modernization of Spanish society, and some people wanted to start from scratch.

The latter group wanted to do away with the institutions of Franco absolutely and give power to a transitional government (the form of which was never quite as clear as it should have been). They even wanted to do away with the monarchy and to institute a constitutional system that would break completely with the previous regime. This was the so-called rupture idea, which was supported especially by the leftist parties, as against the idea of continuing Francoism by adapting it to modern times. Neither of these two ideas prevailed.

A middle way was found that allowed us to unite legal power with politically legitimate power. It allowed us to fashion a new constitution that had nothing to do with the previous one but without eliminating the legally existing government and without naming a provisional government, which would have provoked a terrible crisis in Spain. The new Constitution was drafted while the government continued to function. The courts not only were not opposed to the new constitutional process but assumed the task of helping that process work.

This radical change without rupture also meant acceptance of some of the structures from the past because we were operating on the basis of those structures without even realizing it. The most basic of these structures was the monarchy. When we wrote the new Constitution, no one seriously questioned the logic of continuing to use the monarchical system. First of all, the monarchy is the fundamental element that permits us to speak about a degree of continuity. It is what prevented us from talking about revolution, and this satisfied the conservative forces. Furthermore, the monarch has frequently been the main catalyst for change in Spain. The constitution writers thus found that they could not question maintaining the monarchy. Certainly, some proposals were advanced to substitute a republican for a monarchical form of government, but these were more of a political gesture than a real intention of their proponents.

The writers of the Constitution faced the replacement of a unitary, centralized state by a federal state. A new territorial distribution of power was needed that would accommodate the different territories of the country. This was especially true of those territories with a history of professing autonomy rooted in their national feeling, such as Catalonia and the Basque country. That these territories might have a greater degree of autonomy and self-government was central to the debate about the form of the new distribution of power. This was a question to which the constitution writers had to respond to address the political needs of a large segment of the Spanish people.

The constitution writers also had to decide what powers of self-government the territorial entities would have and how those powers would relate to the central powers of the state. They had to decide whether autonomy should be granted only to those parts of Spain with an old tradition of autonomy, such as Catalonia and the Basque country, or to all the regions. The drafters decided to open up the possibility of self-government to all the Spanish regions. Autonomy was not given equally, as in a federal system where all the states have more or less the same powers and authority, but in a very differentiated way in which some regions have greater autonomy than others. This process of distributing power lengthened the process of making the Constitution. To answer Mr. Goldwin's question, then, the constitution writers operated with freedom, but freedom within a particular cultural world; certain options were possible and others not possible within that context. We did not begin completely from scratch, because we could not ignore our constitutional history.

José Pedro Pérez-Llorca: The most interesting element of our political transition and the history of the Constitution is the distinction between the great political options that the constitution writers considered and the actual constitutional text. The text is very important. Some democratic systems are established on the basis of shared national values; sometimes the text itself turns into a symbol that integrates those values and affirms the democratic system. We find this in the United States, for example, where the text of the Constitution is treated as symbolic of American nationality and the democratic system. There are many ways of recovering democracy after a long period of dictatorship; a previously existing democratic constitutional text might have the historic legitimacy to place it above particular circumstances, thereby preventing the need to start from scratch. An archaic text might need to be adapted and modernized, but the difficult process of drafting a modern democratic constitution for a country that has had a long history would nevertheless be avoided.

There was, of course, a lack of freedom in Spain, a country whose problems, whose characteristics, whose history were familiar to the constitution writers. But they might have depended somewhat on the preexisting constitutional texts, and we must ask why they could not do so. First, Spain's nineteenth- and twentieth-century history was characterized by political instability and therefore constitutional instability. We did not have any legitimized text that could help us in 1978 in drafting a constitution. In this respect we were starting from scratch. We did not use the methods of any existing historical text. We started from what I would call negative conditioning.

Several people on the commission writing the Constitution were convinced that there had been a continual cycle of constitutional change, of imposed constitutions, that gave rise to instability in the country and that we had to break that cycle. The effort was to preclude an imposed constitution that served just one sector of the society. Our desire to be sensitive to the needs of all sectors of society led us to seek a consensus. In seeking a consensus, however, we had to start from scratch because this had not been done before in Spain. Generally, constitutional texts had been the product of revolutionary history or imposed by force. Here we had an opportunity for an absolutely atypical process of change from a political regime of dictatorship through an electoral convocation. We started from scratch because we were not bound either to a revolutionary system or to dictatorship.

Our possibilities were limited theoretically, but there were some positive aspects as well. Obviously we had to endow Spain with an efficient democratic system that would provide stability. If you want a reason for saying that we started from scratch, I may say that we recognized the weight of history, we recognized the weight of our problems, and we recognized the will of the Spanish people to find themselves once again in what Anglo-Saxons call the mainstream of European society.

We have had republican constitutional texts, we have had monarchic constitutional texts, and we have had democratic constitutional texts. It was not possible, *ex novo*, to regulate the Crown in a democratic system in the same way as under the constitutions at the end of the last century. If this Constitution had really exhibited continuity, more than just small parts of the old texts would have been incorporated in it in 1978. We have provisions concerning the institutional relationships of the government, for instance, that might have come from any previous constitution, the last republican one being that of 1931. But they were not used, because it appeared to be necessary to incorporate the system of "rationalized parliamentarianism" of the postwar period with the monarch as the head of state. We could not rely on French or other foreign formulas but had to think of a way to stabilize the office of president of the government, who was the real executive in the country. The best approach we found was the German, which we followed in the role of the chancellor as well as other aspects. Again, we cound not find, and we could not base our work on, historical texts. We had to do something else.

BRUCE E. FEIN: One distinctive phenomenon about the drafting of the Spanish Constitution enabled many of the delegates to reach a successful compromise, and that was the almost universal rejection of the Franco regime as a model to be followed. There seemed to be a common desire to establish a system that was plainly different from what had prevailed under Franco. To be sure, several restraints or conditions were imposed by the history of the time, for instance, the various regional differences, but by and large the Spaniards enjoyed a great degree of freedom in drafting their new Constitution because of the overwhelming consensus around the rejection of the Franco regime.

I would also like to point out a similarity between the way in which the Americans tried to resolve the problem of slavery in drafting the U.S. Constitution and the Spanish constitutional treatment of autonomous regions, specifically, the Basque and Catalonia regions. In the United States the ambiguity of the status of slaves under the Constitution necessarily led to decisive rulings by the judiciary rather than to decisions of the legislative or executive branches. On the whole the judicial treatment of the issue was a disaster, reaching its culmination in the odious *Dred Scott* decision, which clearly contributed to the onset of the American Civil War. Similarly, one of the most divisive issues in Spain results from the ambiguous status of the Basque country and Catalonia. It has given rise to terrorist activity, and, like the slavery issue in the United States before the Civil War, no clearly prescribed legislative solution to the problem can be defined in the Constitution. The judges in Spain, it seems, will have a great degree of authority over how the problem of autonomous regions is ultimately resolved. I would like to pose this question: Because of the ambiguity and in light of the authority of the courts to resolve the problem of autonomous regions, will the Spaniards face an American version of *Dred Scott* in laying out exactly how much power the Basques and Catalonians may exert in defiance of the central government? More generally, is there a danger, when constitution writers seek to cloak very divisive issues in ambiguity, that the ultimate result, within a system of judicial review, is that those issues will be decided without reference to the popular will?

DIOGO FREITAS DO AMARAL: I would like to stress three points. The first is the importance in our time of the peaceful transition from dictatorship to democracy that took place so successfully in Spain. The success in Spain compares favorably with the unsuccessful attempts at peaceful transition in Portugal, which led to a revolution. This reminds me of President John Kennedy's saying that "those who make peaceful revolution impossible will make violent revolution inevitable."

Second, Professor Rubio's paper contains an important element in emphasizing that the Spanish Constitution was deliberated and approved by the political parties within Parliament, rather than by individual members of Parliament as in previous phases of constitutional history. Today, of course, democracy is based on the existence of political parties, and to a certain extent they monopolize power within Parliament. Therefore, the collective decisions of the parties, not the influence of individual members, determines what will be approved.

Third, in three southern European countries—Greece, Spain, and Portugal—we see the great importance of formal contracts or agreements signed outside Parliament between the executive and the political forces, be they parties or persons, ensuring the transition to democracy. In Greece during the Cyprus crisis, the military president called together important persons in political life who signed an agreement that opened the door to the transition to democracy. In Spain the Moncloa pacts were signed between the prime minister and the political parties, and in Portugal two pacts were signed between the military and the political parties. It is necessary to emphasize the importance of contractual elements outside Parliament in making possible the process of evolution toward democracy.

In my view, however, there is at least one important difference between the pacts signed in Greece and Spain and those signed in Portugal. In Greece and Spain the agreements were signed to facilitate the transition to democracy. In Portugal, on the contrary, the Armed Forces Movement signed agreements or pacts with the political parties to try to prevent full democratization. In Portugal the military wanted to retain its supremacy and to impose certain rules that the parties were obliged to include in the constitutional text. The parties in Portugal accepted this agreement because it was the only way they could ensure that free elections would be held. Only after those elections, based on the popular vote, was a strategy adopted to eliminate, in four or five years, the presence of the military in politics. But in all these cases contractual pacts were important to the constitutional process.

MICHAEL DECLERIS: I would like to respond to the important point just made by my colleague from Portugal. The Greek pact that he referred to was not formal; no contract was signed between the military and the civilians. The general who was then acting president convoked a council composed of selected politicians, and a kind of gentlemen's agreement was entered into. Of course, the decision reached between the military and the civilians to hand power to civilian rule was unanimous and was confirmed in the preamble of a subsequent decree whereby Karamanlis was invested with the power to form a coalition government. It was formally stated in that decree that he gained power by the unanimous decision of the military and the political forces to reestablish democracy. This preamble revealed the true character of the earlier, informal pact that initiated the constitutional change.

Another point I would make is that there is a difference in transition between Spain and Greece. In Spain there is a strong element of continuity. In the Greek process there was a clear *dis*continuity between the previous regime and the regime that succeeded it. The previous regime was suddenly declared illegal by the constitutional regime instituted afterward. Perhaps the time factor had something to do with it. In Spain an autocracy lasted for about thirty years; in Greece the military regime lasted only seven.

GUSTAVO PLANCHART MANRIQUE: Messrs. Rubio and Pérez-Llorca have spoken about the constitution writers working within a historical, circumstantial framework that limited their freedom in the sense that the solutions to the problems they confronted were limited. But I believe that more was involved. Mr. Rubio tells us that before the drafting of the Constitution began, the government had already made certain decisions that defined the political formulation later found in the Spanish Constitution. Two matters of special importance in Spain can be identified. One was the view of the king, who held that the new regime would necessarily tend toward a constitutional monarchy in such a way that neither republicanism nor absolute monarchy would be possible. It is quite curious, given the attempt in 1931 at a second republic, which led to civil war in Spain, that when the Spanish Constitution was discussed in 1978, not the least intention was expressed of instituting republicanism except, according to Mr. Rubio's account, for a kind of symbolic "salute to the flag."

According to Mr. Rubio, the government also decided to grant a certain degree of autonomy to Catalonia and the Basque country. Here, again, the government made what appeared to be a political decision: Let us not look to federalism; let us look to regional autonomy, which the republic had already tried in 1931. The possibility of a federal arrangement was thus practically eliminated because of a position taken earlier. The government should have considered the existing consensus regarding regional autonomy since everyone realized that this was the basic political problem that Spain had to resolve. It is very strange that no attempt was made to resolve it in any way during the dictatorship of Franco. It remained suppressed, so that it continued to arise and the same situation existed as in 1936 before the Civil War.

A second comment has to do with what Mr. Fein referred to as the ambiguous treatment of divisive issues in the Constitution. This, in fact, is probably necessary for compromise and consensus. The treatment of certain issues must be ambiguous at times, but the evil of this is that problems are then deferred to the future. In the Venezuelan Constitution, which applies the Spanish solution, the obscurity and ambiguity surrounding an issue are presented to a court that is in charge of interpreting the Constitution. This has been achieved with great success in the United States. The U.S. Supreme Court has a permanent constitutional power and resolves all constitutional problems with greater or lesser certainty. One of these resulted in the *Dred Scott* decision, which contributed to the Civil War, but the Supreme Court has also achieved a legitimacy in the United States that is not possessed, at least in its constitutional aspects, by any other supreme court in the world. In France, the court has such judicial power but only in the administrative field. That is the only other court in the world that commands general respect comparable to that of the Supreme Court of the United States. This is the way to resolve the problem of ambiguity in the Constitution.

The Supreme Court is formally a juridical court, but it has to be a court with great sagacity and intelligence. We see this in the way Chief Justice John Marshall achieved the slow imposition of his interpretation of the American Constitution through his opinions, which were, quite apart from their legal importance, quite admirable in their prudence and political intelligence. These kinds of jurisprudential solutions to constitutional ambiguity are reached only if the court acquires legitimacy in the political system to which it belongs.

NANI A. PALKHIVALA: I will make four brief points. Mr. Rubio mentions the restoration of monarchy. I am reminded of the observation of Plato that human history reveals the following cycle: monarchy, oligarchy, democracy, dictatorship. Then the cycle begins again, from dictatorship back to monarchy. The surprising thing is that the human race invented democracy as a substitute for monarchy. The curious fact is that the majority of monarchies in the world today are constitutional ones, and the majority of republics are dictatorial.

The Spanish Constitution provides that on certain issues, if the Constitution is to be amended, the amendment must be approved not only by two successive legislatures but also by a referendum of the people. That is a very salutary provision. It is a myth, a fallacy, to think that the will of Parliament is the will of the people. A person is elected to Parliament on a number of issues and not necessarily—in fact often not at all—on a given issue being addressed by constitutional amendment. That is why the old Constitution of Belgium provided that if the Parliament wanted to amend the Constitution, first it had to formulate the amendment, then it had to be dissolved, and then an election had to be held on that single issue; whether the amendment was desired by the people. The candidate would say, I am in favor of the amendment or I am against it, and the Parliament would be reconvened. For 140 years the Constitution was amended only five times, because the members of Parliament dared not risk going back to the people.

In Australia the current Constitution took effect about 1900. In eighty-two years, thirty-two amendments were approved by the Australian Parliament. Only five were approved by the people by referendum. In 1973 the prime minister brought up two amendments in Parliament, both of which were approved by an overwhelming majority. But the Australian Constitution, like the Spanish, requires a referendum, and when the referendum was held, every state in Australia rejected both amendments by decisive majorities.

The Spanish Constitution also provides that fundamental rights can be suspended during an emergency, but the suspension requires the legislature's approval. In India we had a similar provision for the declaration of an emergency but without requiring the approval of the Parliament. The executive could declare an emergency, and that was enough. Our experience was most sad. In 1975 an emergency was declared, and overnight a democracy was converted into an authoritarian state. The number of free people in the world was halved overnight. After the emergency ended in 1977, our Parliament amended the Constitution; now no emergency declared by the executive is legally effective unless it is approved by Parliament within sixty days.

The last point I would like to make concerns proportional representation. In the United States people may not appreciate the virtues of proportional representation because there are two parties that speak the same political language. Third world countries have a desperate need for proportional representation, and we do not have it. In India we began with the British system, and we have continued with it. It has been called the system of "first past the post." The result has been that no party in the history of the Indian Republic has ever polled 50 percent or more of the total votes cast. Never. Yet these parties with less than 50 percent of the total votes have a three-fourths majority in Parliament and thus can push through amendments that require such a majority.

Proportional representation is the only answer in the third world, and it would interest my colleagues to know that in England, when proportional representation was the subject of a public poll, the majority of the people said they would prefer it. But proportional representation has not yet been proposed for the simple reason that the parties are elected under the present system and do not want to take the risk of change. No one realizes that at the next election he may be not the beneficiary but the victim of the present system. So I commend the system of proportional representation and hope that more third world countries will follow this example of the Spanish system.

MR. PÉREZ-LLORCA: Professor Fein has raised a key question in all of constitutionalism about the dangers of ambiguity. We are living in Spain amid the consequences of ambiguity, and there are a series of questions about regionalism. There is danger in ambiguity, but the dangers of clarity in certain parts of the constitutional text were so great that they impeded compromise and would have made the drafting of the new Constitution impossible. Although I do not think all parts of the text should be ambiguous, in many cases ambiguity is the best solution to constitutional problems.

The system of proportional representation in Spain has been adjusted so that the districts are not similar. We have thirty-two representatives elected in Madrid and Barcelona, where the system works proportionally, but a multitude of districts vary in their numbers of deputies. The system, then, is a majority system, as a result of a political pact that gave it the character of proportional representation. It has been corrected because of rural factors, a procedure that was very much criticized, particularly by Mr. Rubio.

I would like also to refer to what Mr. Decleris said about political agreements. In Spain during the transition there was no express formal pact, no written pact with the military power or with military men. On the contrary, the agreements that were made were among the political forces. Three agreements were made in the autumn of 1977. The first was among the political parties in the Parliament without intervention by any other sector. The second, a social pact among the political parties, was also made in the Parliament without any intervention. Finally, the amnesty, which is also a kind of pact, was carried out by representatives of the political parties. The government was present, and the government was represented by the minister of defense, but we cannot talk about it as a pact with the military.

MR. RUBIO LLORENTE: Ambassador Palkhivala spoke about the emergency suspension of rights. On this point our Constitution is analogous to most constitutions in Europe, which provide for certain emergency circumstances. The constitutional guarantees can be suspended by the government only when it is necessary and only after obtaining the Parliament's approval. We have a bizarre example in our contemporary history. During our Civil War, from 1936 to 1939, when the Spanish people were killing each other in the fields of Spain and a million people died, constitutional guarantees and freedoms were not suspended in the territory dominated by the government of the Republic until three years after the war began, because the anarchists considered that it would be absolutely intolerable to suspend freedoms although Spain was divided in the trenches.

In response to the comments of Gustave Planchart about the relation between the constitution-writing process and political decisions, quite clearly any constitution-writing exercise faces two problems. One is the building of the nation, and the other is the building of the state. Together they can be solved either through reflection and deliberation or through force and power. Our Constitution employed neither. We chose a third way, time. As an old Spanish proverb has it, you give time to time. In writing our Constitution, the problem of territorial distribution of power was an enormous one. Although we might have had the support of a majority of the nation, we could not even construct a general theory that could solve this problem, because of the many positions on this subject. We therefore opted for a solution by which the territorial structure of power finds itself with time. That is the reason why federalism was not chosen.

Certainly, the autonomous communities in Spain have infinitely greater powers than those held by most of the member states of the federations that now exist in the world in all fields—financial, public order, education, social security. But to opt for federalism would have meant opting for a particular solution, and we were not sure whether this was the solution that everyone wanted, even if it was the solution that responded to the interests of some of the Spanish regions. We allowed for the time to find a solution without imposing it by force and without reaching it through deliberation. This explains why we did not choose federalism and why we opted for ambiguity. I wholly agree with Mr. Pérez Llorca that clarity often has the same disadvantages as ambiguity. An old Spanish proverb says, If we cannot make good laws, let us at least make obscure laws.

Of course, our Constitution contains principles conveyed in the meanings of words that form mandates for the legislature. In these simple mandates we talk about rights, for instance, and we say everyone has a right to health, to a home, and the like. The simple use of the word "right" in this context creates a notable ambiguity. In my opinion, ambiguity should have been avoided in these fields, but not in others.

I agree with Mr. Fein, who made a very acute observation on this point, that there is a danger in allowing the Constitutional Court to decide about an ambiguous issue in the Constitution. This court has on its shoulders the burden of construing the powers of the state and the powers of the autonomous regions. Our system, therefore, is now the responsibility of a Constitutional Court, and the construction of the state is an enormous responsibility. If we manage to avoid a decision such as *Dred Scott* it will be because we have a Constitutional Court with enough authority that its decisions will be accepted by all the litigants, including the Basques and the Catalans. Only time will tell if the court has been accepted.

Recently, the court invalidated a law by which the Parliament claimed that it was supplementing the Constitution and established the limits of both the central and the regional powers. The Constitutional Court struck down that law as unconstitutional. It claimed for itself the function of determining the exact limits of the central and regional powers. This implies enormous responsibility for the court, and the most important part of its work centers on these problems. We hope that we will not produce a solution that will lead to a civil war, but that is just a hope.

7
The Writing of the
1971 Egyptian Constitution

Ibrahim Saleh

Although the constitution in any country is the supreme law and the law of laws, democracy—that is, the rule of the people by the people for the people—will not necessarily be achieved just because there is a written constitution. Hence, I believe that an in-depth study of the provisions of a constitution for guarantees on behalf of the governed is not sufficient since such provisions—as has been pointed out by Professor Maurice Duverger—though they may be phrased neatly in the most elegant style, may in reality amount to no more than empty words. Any reader, after perusing some constitutions, might gasp, "My goodness, there is a world of difference between the text and the practice!" We remember distinctly, for instance, Joseph Stalin's statement in presenting the 1936 Constitution, "Although it preserves the dictatorship of the proletariat, yet this constitution is the only one in the world that is democratic." I agree with Professor Jean-Jacques Chevallier that the rulers in all political regimes—whether deep-rooted democracies or dictatorships—are a small minority in number and in power compared with the governed.

The true criteria for evaluating the political life in any system are provided by answers to the following questions. Who exercises the power: Is the power exercised by the masses, or is it in the hands of a small minority? From whom does the power originate: Is it the offspring of the people's will through free and direct elections; do the governors rule on their behalf, or is their rule the outcome of the usurping of governmental power by the military or a single party? In whose interest is the power exercised: That is, does a selected group— a family, a social class, a supreme committee, or a certain party— obtain the lion's share of the national product? Is the national product distributed on a fair basis? I believe that any attempt to understand the provisions of any constitution is futile, as is any in-depth study, if it is focused primarily on the text rather than on objective criteria for identifying the political elements in a given society and the extent of protection and guarantees provided for them in the society's constitution. Such political elements include

- *Political parties.* One must evaluate the freedom in forming them; the extent of restrictions on their activities; their role in expressing the various interests of social classes; the scope of opportunity for them to assume power; and their right to oppose and restrict those in power. It is not enough for a government to allow for a multiplicity of parties. Most important are the parties' programs. Is the philosophy of the system based on a dialogue representing diverse opinions, or is one opinion thrust upon the parties, a monologue to be parroted by all? Do parties have the right to establish newspapers to express their respective philosophies?

- *Information media and the press in particular.* An in-depth, objective study must consider the extent of freedom to establish and run newspapers; the freedom exercised by newspapers, or the restrictions imposed on them, regarding the formation and expression of public opinion; the right of each citizen to write what he wishes to express his beliefs or opinions, whether they be in conformity with or in opposition to those of the government.

- *Public opinion.* A basic element in every political system is enlightened public opinion, which avails itself of correct and objective information concerning national domestic and foreign policies. Restrictions imposed on citizens' ability to gather information simply crush the will of a people and obstruct the emergence of a powerful public opinion that would ultimately be effective in mapping out a nation's policies.

- *Pressure groups.* Pressure groups formed in academic circles, labor unions, and feminist organizations are among the elements conducive to social equilibrium in political societies. Restrictions on establishing such groups, interference in their affairs, or surveillance of their activities would inevitably deprive the political social system of an effective tool.

- *The army.* Study of the role of the army in any political system is of even greater importance than the study of constitutional texts. The army is one of the political forces in all systems, yet its status as such has critical ramifications. Is the army a shadow force, or does it have a monopoly on politics? If the latter, any constitutional provisions concerning it would be utterly useless, regardless of how elegantly they are phrased and how much is said about their sanctity. There is ample proof of this. It suffices to glance quickly at regimes under the control of army generals in Africa, Asia, and Latin America.

289

Study of constitutional texts alone is not enough to achieve full understanding of a constitutional system as it is applied in any political society. A constitution legalizes basic economic, political, and social principles and designates constitutional powers as components of a political equilibrium. The rest of the political system is defined by other laws not covered by the constitution.

Understanding nomination and election systems and their constitutionality is also important. Pertinent questions include: Do all citizens have the right to be nominated to membership in Parliament, or are there restrictions? The same applies to voting rights: Are there categories of citizens deprived of their right to vote? What guarantees are provided to safeguard elections? Who supervises elections? At the same time, internal regulations of Parliament also need to be scrutinized, as should parliamentary controls on government exercised by members and rules governing parliamentary procedure. Finally, how are laws determined to be constitutional, how are they organized, and how effective are the means to ensure that their constitutionality is not arbitrarily revoked?

In telling the story of the writing of a constitution a certain amount of imagination, an ingredient of narrative fiction, might creep in. Hence, the approach might be subjective rather than objective. To avert such a pitfall, I have adhered to bare facts, from which I have drawn my conclusions—a method of writing known as witnessing to history—noting that truth and intellectual honesty are the hallmark of such testimony.

Egyptian Constitutionalism before the Proclamation of the 1971 Constitution

The 1971 Egyptian Constitution was promulgated on September 11, 1971, by the president. There is a long story to this Constitution; its text is the outcome of successive events over nineteen years beginning with the assumption of power by the army in 1952. This period witnessed tremendous hardships and oppression under which the Egyptian people bitterly suffered. Therefore, it would be useful to review the socioeconomic and political developments prior to the drafting of the 1971 Constitution. My aim is not to present the political thought of the pre-1971 Constitution era; however, most of the basic principles incorporated in the 1971 Constitution were not devised by the Constitution Writing Committee but were handed down as a constitutional heritage contained in the Constitution of 1956, endorsed by means of popular referendums, or contained in the provisional constitution of 1964.

Some provisions were responses to the situation existing at the time, for instance, those provisions concerning the president of the Republic and his qualifications for nomination to the presidency that were almost required by those in higher echelons. Article 120 of the 1956 Constitution provided that the president-elect shall be Egyptian, of Egyptian parents and grandparents, enjoying civilian and political rights; that his age shall not be less than thirty-five years; and that he shall not be related to the royal family of Egypt. The age prerequisite of thirty-five years was stipulated because President Gamal Abdal-Nasser was then still in his thirties. In the 1971 Constitution, however, article 75 on this point provides that "the president of the Republic shall be an Egyptian, born to Egyptian parents and enjoying civil and political rights. His age must not be less than forty years." The prerequisite stipulating "Egyptian grandparents" is nonexistent because it did not apply to President Mohammed Anwar al-Sadat. Thus the Constitution Writing Committee had to accept these and other provisions, such as those concerning the republican system, the method of electing the president by means of a referendum, the forbidding of multiple presidential candidates, the adoption of the one-chamber parliamentary system, the forbidding of political parties, the establishment of a one-party regime, the requirement that at least 50 percent of the members of all elected councils be from among the laborers and peasants, and the eligibility of civil servants and public sector employees to run for elections while retaining their original jobs and their right to promotion even though they were not working at those jobs.

Other legal precepts have been carried over from one era to the next, as in the area of agricultural land ownership. The first and most important of the laws that went into effect in the wake of King Farouk's abdication was promulgated on September 9, 1952, limiting agricultural land ownership to 200 feddans (1 hectare = 2.5 feddans). In 1958 and 1961, other laws, providing a maximum limit on land ownership per family (husband, wife, and children) of 100 feddans, were issued. One law, issued in 1963, forbade foreigners to own land or to transfer their land ownership to the state in return for compensation. Another law, in 1976, forbade ownership of real estate by foreigners, with the exception of one housing unit, subject to the approval of the Council of Ministers. The 1971 Constitution, therefore, provided in article 37: "The law shall fix the maximum limit of land ownership with a view to protecting the farmer and the agricultural laborer from exploitation, and asserting the authority of the alliance of the people's working forces in villages." This is a repetition of the provision found in article 12 of the 1956 Constitution, which also

291

stated: "Non-Egyptians shall not be allowed to own agricultural land with the exception of cases indicated by law." This was also provided in the 1964 Provisional Constitution, article 17.

Such principles were the outcome of events taking place in Egypt during that earlier era. The researcher might wonder about the role of the Committee for Writing the 1971 Constitution in light of its concern with legalizing or repeating in the 1971 Constitution established premises. Actually the committee played a different historical role. The 1971 Constitution represents a transition from the revolutionary legislative stage to the constitutional legislative stage, an undoubtedly quite critical transition in the political system and in the guarantees provided for the governed. Therefore, this chapter will first deal with the political and economic circumstances leading to the drafting of the 1956 Constitution. The era of that Constitution goes from 1952 to 1961. Then the discussion will turn to the 1964 Provisional Constitution and the period from 1961 to 1971. It was during this latter period that the 1971 Constitution was drafted.

The 1956 Constitution

Although the Constitution Writing Committee actually started its work in June 1971 and issued the 1971 Constitution on September 11, 1971, the basic principles incorporated in that Constitution were deeply rooted in earlier times. The committee was neither a constituent nor a national organization, oblivious of earlier principles and ideologies, assigned to draft the Constitution from nothing.

After the death of Nasser on September 28, 1970, Sadat assumed the presidency on October 16, 1970. Sadat's accession was not the result of a revolution or a coup d'etat. It was rather an extension of the preceding era despite several changes and ideological modifications. Hence, the Constitution Writing Committee had to abide by certain principles that are actually part of constitutional tradition; they are known as irrevocable, basic principles.

Events Leading to the 1956 Constitution. The pre-1971 constitutional events began on December 10, 1952, the date the 1923 Constitution, which was then in effect in Egypt, was abolished. The abolition of that constitution was the outcome of events in Egypt when, after midnight on July 23, 1952, units of the Egyptian army, in accordance with a plan drawn up by the Officers Command Committee under the name of "Free Officers" seized the main centers of the army command, including those in Cairo and Alexandria. They also took over several important state utilities, such as the main broadcasting station in Cairo. At 7:00 a.m. that day, the Army Movement Command Committee issued a statement to the people, read by Sadat, who was then a lieutenant:

> Egypt has undergone a critical time in her recent history. It has been a period of gross corruption and governmental instability, and these factors have had a great influence on the army. People who received bribes contributed toward our defeat in the Palestine war. Traitors plotted against the army after the Palestine war, but now we have purged ourselves; and our affairs within the army have been placed in the hands of men in whose ability, character, and patriotism we have faith. The whole of Egypt will welcome this news. No harm will be done to former military personnel who have been arrested. The entire army is working for the interest of Egypt within the Constitution, and without any designs of its own. I appeal to all Egyptians not to resort to acts of sabotage or violence. Any such action will be met with unparalleled firmness, and offenders will be punished immediately for treason. The army will undertake responsibility for law and order in cooperation with the police. I want to assure foreigners of the safety of their lives and property, for which the army considers itself responsible. God is the Grantor of success.

Undoubtedly, the statement was met with deep satisfaction and a sense of relief by the Egyptian people, regardless of their ideologies, in view of the political, social, and economic collapse that had beset the country. (This collapse was made evident by the defective arms case, during the first war staged by Egypt against Israel in 1948, in which several of King Farouk's courtiers were implicated.) What really helped the army movement was the prevailing democratic climate; the emergence of the press as a political force, stirring and whipping up the bottled emotions of the masses, especially the poor and middle classes to which most of the Egyptian intelligentsia belonged; the escalating effect of two ideological extremist parties, the Moslem Brotherhood and the Egyptian Communist party; and the people's utter trust and faith in the patriotism of the young army officers. Regrettably, many thinkers adopted in their writings at the time the theme of the "just despot" who is able to bring about desired reforms. This theme proved to be totally wrong.

I do hope third world nations will benefit from this Egyptian experience and its serious negative repercussions on political life in Egypt, from which we still suffer. Only God knows when these vestiges will disappear. We now can point to two important factors that expedited the seizure of power by the army, namely, the abrogation of the Anglo-Egyptian Friendship Treaty in October 1951 and the ensuing events, including the Cairo fire on January 26, 1952, as well as King Farouk's abominable conduct and notoriety. Eminent Egyptian historian, Abd al-Rahman al-Rafei, was driven to exasperation when he produced his book, entitled *Farouk Paves the Way for the Revolution*. Also among the important factors in this respect were the investigations of September 1952 in which I took part. They proved that a coded cable was sent from the Egyptian ambassador in London to the chief of the Royal Cabinet, to the following effect: "Last night I was sitting with Mr. Bevin. He said to me that these last fatal accidents which happened now in Egypt are due to officers attached to high quarters. Tell King Farouk this is a weapon with two edges." Investigations proved that King Farouk had formed an outfit known as "The Iron Guards for the Dissolution of Certain Politicians."

Therefore, following the broadcast of Anwar Sadat's statement on July 23, 1952, King Farouk assigned the late Aly Maher Pasha the task of forming the cabinet. He also dismissed his notorious courtiers. In the meantime, the army was heading to Alexandria, the summer quarters of the king and the cabinet. On the morning of July 26, General Mohammed Naguib, assigned by the Free Officers as their chief, issued the following ultimatum to King Farouk:

> In view of the general chaos sweeping all of the nation's public utilities as a result of your misguided policy tampering with the Constitution, and degrading the will of the people to the point where each citizen feels insecure regarding his life, property, and dignity; and in view of Egypt's stigmatized reputation among nations because of your persistence in such conduct—granting traitors and corrupt elements protection, security, and immense wealth at the expense of the hungry poor people (This was evidenced clearly in the Palestine war, the ensuing scandals involving defective arms, and the subsequent trials in which you openly interfered, thus twisting facts, shaking trust in justice, and helping traitors to flourish unrestrained, becoming richer and richer, corrupt and more corrupt . . . why not? Aren't people fashioned after their kings?), therefore, the army, the representative of the people's power, has delegated me to request Your Majesty abdicate the throne to your Crown Prince, Ahmad Fouad, providing that this take effect not later than Saturday, July 26, 1952, at 12 noon and that you depart before 6:00 p.m. the same day. The army holds you responsible for all consequences resulting from your refusal to acquiesce in the people's will.

Farouk abdicated the throne to his Crown Prince Ahmad Fouad and departed in the evening of that day from the land of Egypt forever.

Since the 1923 Constitution, promulgated in January 1924, had been in effect in Egypt during Farouk's reign, the commander general of the armed forces deemed that that constitution had to be abolished—on December 10, 1952, according to his proclamation—and that the government should begin to form a committee to draft a new constitution to be endorsed by the people. The new constitution would avoid the pitfalls of the old one and thus realize for the nation a clean and sound parliamentary rule.

On January 13, 1953, therefore, a decree was issued for the formation of a Constitution Writing Committee to draft a new constitution "in conformity with the objectives of the revolution." The committee was formed of fifty members representing various ideological trends, educational levels, parties, and social categories. Aly Maher was elected as the committee chairman. The committee was divided into subcommittees, including a five-person subcommittee to inquire into the form of rule—either a monarchy or a republic. The subcommittee unanimously decreed that the monarchy be abolished and that a republican system be established. In its report, the subcommittee pointed out the deficiencies of the monarchy and the benefits to be accrued from a republic.

On January 17, 1953, the commander general of the armed forces, who served temporarily as chief of the Revolutionary Command Council, issued a proclamation containing a decree to abolish political parties and expropriate all their funds, all in the people's interest. Political parties were said to have jeopardized the objectives of the 1919 revolution and to have tried to undo the 1952 revolution so the nation would backslide to the previous state of affairs. (This first change actually represented a constitutional rule which was applied until 1979 when it was abolished by a constitutional amendment.) The proclamation also limited the transitional period to three years ending on January 16, 1956, pending the writing of a new constitution defining the regime of the country.

On February 10, 1953, the Revolutionary Command Council issued the first constitutional proclamation, a provisional constitution in extremely condensed form. It consisted of eleven articles defining rules for organizing powers during the transitional period. It adhered to general phraseology and avoided details. The idea behind it was to keep away from such phraseology that would hinder the progressive march of the revolution. The text of that constitution reflected the desire of the authors of the revolution to avoid restricting themselves to detailed precepts, definitive rules, or certain systems. All in all, the text was so general that it did not even define the form of government.

Among the ensuing major political decrees was the Revolutionary Command Council's decree of June 18, 1953, proclaiming the republican regime and the downfall of Mohammed Ali's rule, which had governed Egypt since 1805. The decree stated that the history of Mohammed Ali's dynasty in Egypt consisted of a series of treasons committed against the people.

> The first treacherous act was manifest in Ismail's profligacy and the subsequent debts that infested the nation, marring its reputation and causing its bankruptcy. This created a pretext by which imperialist powers infiltrated into the land of this secure valley. Tawfik, who, in his attempt to retain the throne after his succession, climaxed the treacherous drama by encouraging the onset of occupation armies in order to protect himself. In seeking the help of the enemy against the people, he paved the way for the imperialists and the throne to join hands in a mutually profitable deal. Either party upheld the other in a bid to promote its selfish interests to the detriment of the people. The throne served as a facade behind which the imperialists operated to squeeze and demoralize the people and undermine their freedom.
>
> Farouk outranked his predecessors of that dynasty. His incredible wealth, promiscuity, tyranny, and ungodliness mapped out neatly his horrible fate. It is high time for the nation to liberate itself of all vestiges of slavery imposed on it due to such conditions. We, therefore, today, declare in the name of the people:
>
> First—abolition of the monarchy; the elimination of the rule of the Mohammed Ali dynasty and the abolition of titles held by its members;
>
> Second—proclaim the Republic. The president, chief of General Staff, Mohammed Naguib, leader of the revolution, shall assume the presidency and, in the meantime, shall retain his present authority under the provisional constitution;
>
> Third—this regime shall remain in force throughout the transitional period. The people shall have the last say concerning the kind of republic to be established, and the selection of the president upon the endorsement of the new constitution.

Hence, the republican regime was proclaimed on that date and was decreed by the Revolutionary Command Council, becoming one of the bases for the system of government in Egypt sustained by the

1956 Constitution, the 1964 Provisional Constitution, and also by the 1971 Constitution, the subject of this paper.

These were the changes in the framework of the system of government brought about by measures adopted by the Revolutionary Command Council. The monarchy was abolished, and the republican system was proclaimed. All of the political parties were disbanded and their funds confiscated. The only exception was the Moslem Brotherhood Society, which was a political power with tremendous weight. Its one million members and supporters formed various chapters throughout the country. They boasted of an armed military wing, help from which was sought by the army, and from which one of the cabinet ministers was appointed. In the meantime, civilian and military courts were formed to try members of the old parties as well as key political figures. Criminal charges incurring capital punishment were leveled against many of them. In September 1954, a Moslem Brotherhood youth opened fire on President Nasser in Alexandria. Investigations uncovered a plot to stage a coup d'etat. Six people were sentenced to death, and the executions were carried out. A decree was issued for the liquidation of the Moslem Brotherhood Society. Thousands of its members received long-term sentences, including hard labor for life. The Revolutionary Command Council proclaimed six principles to which it would adhere, including the establishment of a sound political life and the eradication of feudalism and of stooges of imperialism. The radical socioeconomic and political changes, which took place later, were actually derived from these six principles, the underlying philosophy of which leaned toward socialism. Many of the ruthless measures taken against citizens were perpetrated in the application of these principles. The culmination of developments concerning the application of the six principles led to the iron-fist control of the Intelligence Service and the General Investigations Agency and to widespread panic among citizens, all under the pretext of protecting the objectives of the revolution. Such was the climate of political life in Egypt until the death of President Nasser on September 28, 1970.

Principles of the 1956 Constitution. Many of the underlying principles of this era assumed a degree of constitutional continuity with the past, particularly in regard to the tightening of control over presidential affairs, the prerogative of the president, the role of the legislative power, and the equilibrium or disequilibrium among various political powers.

As stated above, a committee was formed for drawing up the draft constitution. The resulting draft conformed to the objectives of the revolution and was referred to the prime minister on January 17,

1955. This draft constitution adopted a parliamentary republican system. It was submitted to President Nasser who noted, however, that "it did not realize the objectives of the revolution in bringing about a radical change in the system of government, the eradication of imperialism and its stooges, and that its general framework was not different from that of the 1923 constitution." President Nasser broadly outlined the philosophy upon which the constitution was to be based, and it was proclaimed on January 16, 1956, at the end of the three-year transitional period. The draft constitution provided that "a referendum on [it] shall be held on Saturday, June 23, 1956" (article 193) and that "it shall go into effect as of the date of its endorsement by the people" (article 196). In other words, the constitution would go into effect only after a referendum was held and the draft was approved by the people. Holding such a referendum was in fact a precedent that crystallized into a constitutional rule contained in both the Provisional Constitution of 1964 and the 1971 Constitution.

This 1956 Constitution was in effect only a few months for reasons to be discussed later. Among its main features, however, was the adoption of the republican system, the one-chamber parliamentary system, and aspects combining the parliamentary and the presidential systems. The most important innovation was the adoption of the one-party system, which was derived from the Portuguese system during the Salazar era. This replaced the former, multiparty system. Article 192 of the constitution provided that "citizens shall form a National Union to work for the realization of the objectives for which the revolution was staged and to exert efforts for the establishment of a sound sociopolitical system in the nation. The National Union shall undertake nominations for membership in the National Assembly." The one-party political system became a basic constitutional rule, which the 1971 Constitution, in its fifth article, followed. Also among the prevailing rules was one providing that the president serve as chairman of the single party, which was later called the Arab Socialist Union. Another important feature was the introduction of the method by which the president would be elected and regulated; article 121 provided that the National Assembly would nominate the president, and that this nomination would be followed by a referendum. The candidate then would become president of the Republic upon receiving an absolute majority of the electorate votes.

Two laws promulgated in 1956 related to the regulation of political rights and the prerequisites for membership in the National Assembly. They were laws 73 and 246, respectively. Among the most important precepts of law 73 was that it reduced the voting age to eighteen years; it decreed for the first time women's right to vote; and it secured the right of the military to exercise political rights. Law 246 provided, in its sixth, seventh, and eighth articles, that nominations to the National Assembly would be submitted to the single party, the National Union, which would prepare slates of *unopposed* candidates in each constituency. Its verdict in this respect would be final and uncontested by any means.

Egypt under the 1956 Constitution. The 1956 Constitution, the key provisions of which have been presented, was, as mentioned above, in effect only a short while. On July 26, 1956, President Nasser declared the nationalization of the Suez Canal, which was followed by the Suez war. This war started with Israel's aggression on October 29, 1956, followed by the Anglo-French invasion on the eve of October 31. Because of the fortitude of the valiant Egyptian people, the relentless Egyptian army, President Dwight Eisenhower's historical stand vis-á-vis that invasion, and Premier Nikolai A. Bulganin's ultimatum early in November, the aggression ended with the withdrawal of armies on December 24, 1956. Hence the National Assembly elections were not held until June 1957. Shortly after the convocation of the assembly, steps were taken toward a union between Egypt and Syria, which had already reached a stage presaging the establishment of a United Arab Republic. Both the Syrian House of Representatives and the Egyptian National Assembly agreed on February 5, 1958, to establish the Unity. On that date was issued a constitutional proclamation consisting of seventeen articles of general principles for a system of government during the transitional period. The last article stipulated that a referendum was to be held on the Unity and for the election of the president of the United Arab Republic on February 21, 1958. The referendum resulted in the election of Nasser as president. President Nasser then issued, on March 5, 1958, a provisional constitution consisting of seventy-three articles defining the system of government in the new republic. This provisional constitution was in turn abolished with the collapse of the union between Egypt and Syria on September 27, 1961, as a result of a military coup staged by the Syrian army officers.

In this context, I would like to highlight the events which led to the dissolution of the union between Egypt and Syria. That era witnessed radical legislation that extensively altered the existing constitutional framework and institutions. Because such legislation was regarded as a coercive constitutional legacy, the Committee for Writing the 1971 Constitution had no choice but to legalize it and incorporate it into the new Constitution and to include controls over the type of legislation under which the Egyptian people had previously suffered. In this respect, the events of the 1960s completely undermined the morale of the Egyptian people. It is no exaggeration to contend that they crushed the national and the constitutional conscience.

Perhaps the most serious legislation issued during the first year of the period under the 1956 Constitution was law 156 (1960) organizing the press, by virtue of which the ownership of newspapers was transferred to the National Union (later called the Arab Socialist Union), the only party allowed. Article 6 of the law provided that "the National Union shall form special organizations to run its own newspapers. A board of directors shall be appointed for each organization to assume responsibility for running its newspapers." To resolve the dispute that arose over the legal nature of such organizations, law 151 (1964) provided that these organizations be considered public and that the responsibilities of managers and personnel be the same as those stipulated in the penal code regarding export-import operations.

The nationalization of the press and the transference of its ownership to the one legal political organization actually legislated the status quo. Freedom of the press already suffered from censorship by a censor appointed to each press organization and by the public censor. Furthermore, the general atmosphere was not conducive to the emergence of any free opinion or independent thought. As a result of the nationalization of the press, journalists became no more than functionaries liable to be transferred to any other press organization or to simply any other organization. Such deplorable developments may be evaluated against the glorious history of the Egyptian press, a history of great writers and eminent thinkers who have enriched Egyptian thought since the Orabi revolution of 1882, during the 1919 revolution, and throughout the first half of the twentieth century.

In addition, a new agrarian reform law was issued on July 23, 1961, decreasing the maximum limit of land ownership to 100 feddans per family. This law was followed by other socialist laws leading to the nationalization of all private activities; companies, banks, and other institutions were to be treated as public domain (owned by the people) and the public sector, which exercised control over all aspects of economic activities, was established. The first vice-president, Marshal Amer, whose conduct was among the reasons for the collapse of the Egyptian-Syrian Unity and who was solely responsible for the defeat of the Egyptian army in the six-day war of June 1967, was quoted as saying that during his visit to the Soviet Union, following the promulgation of the socialist laws, Khrushchev said to him: "You have gone much too far, and we are concerned about the extent you have reached in nationalization."

The 1964 Provisional Constitution

The 1960s witnessed a host of economic, social, and political changes. As of 1961, Egypt had undergone radical changes with the promulgation of the socialist laws on July 23, 1961, which were carried into effect in both Egypt and Syria. The secession of Syria from the union with Egypt took place on September 27, 1961, however, and on that day armed forces from Fatna Camp seized the radio station, besieged the general command building, and broadcast statements announcing the secession of Syria from the United Arab Republic.

Events Leading to the 1964 Provisional Constitution. After the secession, a phase of indescribable oppression, coercion, insecurity, and panic swept Egypt. President Nasser declared, in his October 16, 1961, speech to the people of the United Arab Republic that he had decided to review all political conditions since 1952 and bring about the necessary changes that would destroy the causes leading to the secession. He concluded that the so-called reactionaries were responsible and consequently should be counteracted and destroyed. Since his initial steps were unsound, the resulting measures were devastating. In a nutshell, he deduced that the reactionaries were ready to align themselves with imperialism to regain their privileged exploitative positions. He contended that the secession conspiracy would not have succeeded had it not been for the inefficiency of the people's organization. The new organization, therefore, should confine its membership to workers, fellahins, the intelligentsia, professionals, landowners whose ownership was not based on exploitation, and men in the armed forces. In addition, labor unions, peasants' cooperative unions, universities, and professional organizations, as well as feminist organizations, should all become centers that radiated creative ideology to regenerate the revolutionary work.

President Nasser, however, failed to comprehend fully the causes for the secession, which were due, in fact, to the oppressive conditions that he himself had imposed on Egypt and wished to carry out in Syria: the July 1961 socialist laws and a rule based on tyranny, deprivation, and lack of human dignity. Questions that remain unanswered are, Did the leaders of this system of government really believe in the socialist philosophy or was its application aimed at doing away with the landowning class, depriving the class of its economic power and consequently of its political influence, only to win the favor of the poor class? Most important, was President Nasser really the man at the helm at that time, or was he manipulated by Field Marshal Amer and his entourage? Other questions are related to that: Did

President Nasser want change, and could he bring it about? The answers to those questions were provided in the wake of the humiliating defeat of Egypt in the six-day war in June 1967. The solutions Nasser had resorted to are summarized as follows:

On November 8, 1961, President Nasser issued republican decree 1879 (1961) calling for formation of the Preparatory Committee for the People's Forces National Congress. No sooner had the committee discharged its mission than a presidential decree was issued in the form of law 34 (1962) concerning the political isolation characterizing categories of people to be deprived of their political rights. This law, called the political isolation law, was used by the regime as a dangerous political instrument against the citizens. It not only deprived citizens of their political rights but also served as a means of political isolation. Regrettably, it was carried out throughout the years of President Nasser's rule, and even President Sadat resorted to it in 1978 to get rid of several members of old parties. By virtue of this law, the people deprived of exercising their political rights for ten years were placed under administrative precautionary measures in accordance with the Revolutionary Command Council decree of June 22, 1956: those who were subjected to any of the measures referred to in clauses 6 and 7 of article 3 of law 533 (1954) concerning martial laws or in clauses 1 and 4 of article 3 of law 162 (1958) referred to during the interval between January 23, 1956, and the date of promulgation of this law; and those whose landownership was limited in accordance with law 178 (1952) and law 127 (1961). Any citizen could be considered politically isolated once a decree was issued for his arrest or detention even for a few hours.

The People's Forces National Congress convened on May 21, 1962. It endorsed a ten-point draft charter presented by President Nasser that was to serve as a guide for national work. President Nasser then issued a constitutional declaration on September 27, 1962, consisting of twenty articles concerning the formation of the so-called collective leadership. A Presidential Council was formed to serve the supreme authority for state power and to map out and implement its policy. President Nasser also decreed the formation of an Executive Council to serve as the executive authority for the state power. The charter was considered a constitution; some even regarded it as superseding the 1956 Constitution. Its text contained socialist terminology and even included full passages translated from the 1847 *Communist Manifesto*.

Syria's secession from the Unity on September 27, 1961, initiated a phase of oppression, violence, and destruction in Egypt, touched off by President Nasser's speech on October 16, 1961. Nasser had been made to believe by the security and intelligence machinery that the prerevolutionary statesmen were conniving to strike at the regime, capitalizing on its vulnerability. Information media subsequently launched a campaign against the so-called enemies of the people. The government confiscated assets and properties of rich families, who were subjected to strict surveillance, arrest, and imprisonment. Such measures were applied even to relatives and friends of these detainees. The situation in Egypt was aggravated even more by censorship of the mail, of telephone calls, and of private and public meetings. The Yemen war in September 1962 was used as a pretext for escalating these exceptional measures.

The constitutional declaration issued by President Nasser on March 23, 1964—really a provisional constitution—was carried into effect on March 25, 1964; and it remained in force until the drafting of the permanent Constitution in 1971. The declaration stipulated that the National Assembly formed earlier should draft the permanent Constitution, which then would be voted upon in a popular referendum.

Principles of the 1964 Provisional Constitution. It is relevant at this point to highlight some principles introduced in the Provisional Constitution of 1964 that relate to the Constitution of 1971.

1. The first article defined the United Arab Republic as a "socialist state established by the working people's forces alliance." This provision, a result of the inevitability of the socialist solution as defined by the charter, underscored the socialist philosophy influencing the laws of July 1961. These laws were actually among the main causes for the Syrian secession from the Unity. In contrast, the first article of the 1971 Constitution provides that the "Arab Republic of Egypt" is a "democratic socialist state." This phraseology reveals the constitution writer's approach. The word "Egypt," which had disappeared as a result of the use of "United Arab Republic," was retrieved. It was an expression of the Egyptian people's sentiment for and desire to use the word "Egypt" in their constitution. Also of significance is the use in 1971 of "democratic socialist state," compared with the text of the first article of the 1964 Provisional Constitution.

2. The provision in article 2 of the 1964 Constitution for sovereignty of the *people* can be compared with its 1956 constitutional counterpart, which stated that sovereignty be of the *state*. Such textual discrepancy is intentional and stresses the principle of the people's sovereignty adopted by most contemporary constitutional systems. This provision appeared in article 3 of the 1971 Constitution, with only a few changes.

3. Article 9 of the 1964 Constitution provided that the economic basis of the state be socialist and that no form of exploitation be allowed, thus guaranteeing a socialist society buttressed by sufficiency and justice. Article 23 of the 1971 Constitution states:

> The national economy shall be organized in accordance with a comprehensive development plan that ensures raising the national income, fairly distributing it, raising the standard of living, solving the problem of unemployment, increasing work opportunities, connecting wages with production, and fixing minimum and maximum limits for wages guaranteeing smaller disparities in income.

About this point, the 1964 and 1971 constitutions agree on the following principles:

• The 1964 Constitution provided for control by the people over the means of production and direction of the surplus in accordance with the development plan laid down by the state with a view to increasing wealth and raising the standard of living. This parallels article 24 of the 1971 Constitution.

• There are three kinds of ownership: state ownership (ownership by the people); cooperative ownership (ownership by all participants in cooperative societies); and private, nonprofit ownership. The 1964 Constitution recognized and protected private ownership, but only subject to the supervision and control of the people. The 1964 Constitution also provided that the people *be in control of* all means of production but did not provide that the people *own* all means of production. Control meant mere supervision, guidance, and subjection to the general development plan. This provision paralleled article 29 of the 1971 Constitution.

• The 1964 Constitution stipulated that private ownership not be expropriated except for the general welfare and only in exchange for fair compensation in accordance with the law. Private ownership, according to the 1964 Constitution, is not an absolute right, however. It is restricted as a social function regulated by law. The 1971 Constitution refers to that principle in articles 32 and 34; however, to avoid earlier sequestration measures, the writers of the 1971 Constitution implied, in article 34, that private property should not be sequestered except in cases defined by law and in accordance with a judicial decision. This provision ensures protection of wealth.

• The 1964 Constitution encouraged the state to work with cooperative ownerships and look after cooperative institutions in their various forms. This principle is provided by article 27 of the 1971 Constitution.

- In the 1964 Constitution, the state guaranteed social security services, providing help for Egyptians in cases of old age, sickness, disability, or unemployment. This provision appears in article 17 of the 1971 Constitution.
- The 1964 Constitution ensured that work is a right of all able citizens. Work is not a mere negative freedom but a right of citizens guaranteed by the state. The state, according to the 1964 Constitution, also was to provide work opportunity for all Egyptians. This principle appears in article 13 of the 1971 Constitution, which also adds: "No work shall be imposed on citizens except by virtue of law, for the performance of a public service, and in return for a fair remuneration."

4. Concerning the method of selecting the president of the Republic, the 1964 Constitution provided for a referendum, not for elections. It divided the nomination process into two stages, however: the proposal stage and the voting stage. It also stipulated that the proposal for nomination be made by at least one-third of the National Assembly members and that to be nominated a candidate must receive the majority of two-thirds of the National Assembly vote. The 1964 Constitution was no more satisfied with an absolute majority of National Assembly members for nomination than was the 1956 Constitution. Like the 1964 Constitution, the 1971 Constitution (article 76) requires that the candidate receive the majority of two-thirds of assembly members' votes. Then the candidate is referred to a popular referendum. The candidate is considered the president of the Republic if he receives the absolute majority of votes in the referendum. If the candidate fails to secure such a majority, the assembly proposes the nomination of another candidate, and the same procedure is followed.

In this connection, I wrote an article in the newspaper *Alakhbar* on December 30, 1975, calling for an amendment to the Constitution to allow more than one presidential candidate to run for an election. I wrote that lawmakers in the West contend that a referendum is more or less like a horse race in which a single horse runs, and that in the case of the "yes or no" plebescite, it is unthinkable that all the electorate would vote "no" or that the office would remain vacant. President Sadat rejected this idea at the People's Assembly, asserting that he was the head of the Egyptian family.

5. The 1964 Constitution introduced the office of the first vice-president in article 107; but upon the death of President Nasser on September 28, 1970, there was no first vice-president. President Sadat had served as the vice-president since December 20, 1969, and it was decided that he be considered the sole vice-president; he was nominated, therefore, by the National Assembly. The 1971 Constitution

eliminated the idea of a single vice-president and stated this point explicitly in article 139: "The president of the Republic may appoint one or more vice-presidents, define their jurisdiction, and relieve them of their posts. The rules relating to the calling to account of the president of the Republic shall be applicable to the vice-presidents."

The 1971 Constitution, however, worked out a new solution, in the event of the disability or death of the president. Article 84 states:

> In case of the vacancy of the president's office or the permanent disability of the president of the Republic, the speaker of the People's Assembly shall temporarily assume the presidency. In case the People's Assembly is dissolved at such a time, the president of the Supreme Constitutional Court shall take over the presidency on condition that neither one shall nominate himself for the presidency. The People's Assembly shall then proclaim the vacancy of the office of the president.

In the weekly *Alshaab*, organ of the opposition Socialist Labor Party (September 1981), I called for the inclusion in the Constitution of one or more articles of basic law to regulate the process of choosing the vice-president. I proposed that the People's Assembly and the Shoura Council rather than the president nominate the vice-president. I also called for procedures concerning vice-presidential jurisdiction and the method of the vice-president's appointment and removal.

6. The 1964 Provisional Constitution introduced the Council of Ministers system and adopted the bilateral executive power concept. That constitution did not regulate the executive power in the same fashion as in a parliamentary system, however; it did not regard the president as a mere figurehead. Rather it vested in him actual power to exercise real prerogatives. He would positively participate in governmental affairs as stipulated in article 113 of the 1964 Constitution and in article 138 of the 1971 Constitution: "The president of the Republic, in conjunction with the cabinet, shall lay down the general policy of the state and shall supervise its implementation in the manner prescribed in the Constitution."

The difference between the texts of the two constitutions is that, whereas article 113 of the 1964 Constitution stipulated that the president lay down the general policy of the state in conjunction with the government and supervise its implementation, article 138 of the 1971 Constitution uses the phrase "in conjunction with the Council of Ministers" and says that "they shall supervise its implementation."

7. Although the 1964 Constitution, a provisional constitution, had introduced the principle of joint responsibility of ministers and had distinguished between the president and the prime minister, the

1971 Constitution regressed by not adopting the principle of the ministerial joint responsibility. It sanctions withdrawal of confidence from a deputy prime minister or a minister, but it does not sanction the withdrawal of confidence from the entire government. It did introduce the possibility of interpellating the prime minister, but the procedure has been made very complex (see articles 126–128 of the 1971 Constitution, appendix A).

Moreover, this possibility is merely a rhetorical matter because neither the People's Assembly nor the National Assembly has ever used this constitutional right against any member of the cabinet or a prime minister.

8. The 1971 Constitution inherited from the 1964 Constitution the legacy whereby numerous prerogatives are conferred upon the president of the Republic. Although the cabinet is responsible before the People's Assembly and may be subjected to all means of parliamentary control, such as serving notice, interrogation, and requests for debates, giving this political system some parliamentary characteristics, yet in view of the president's prerogatives, the prevailing characteristic is presidential (articles 73, 74, 139, 141, and 152 of the 1971 Constitution, appendix B). The 1971 Constitution also provides the president with administrative prerogatives, as stipulated in articles 137 and 146 (appendix C); legislative prerogatives, in articles 108 and 144–147 (appendix D); political and emergency prerogatives, in articles 143, 148, and 151 (appendix E); and judicial prerogatives, in article 149: "The president of the Republic shall have the right of granting amnesty or commuting a sentence, but a general amnesty can only be granted by virtue of a law." In this vein, the president also heads the Supreme Council for Judicial Organization by virtue of law 82 (1969), promulgated simultaneously with the judicial reform laws.

9. Under the 1923 Constitution, which was abolished by a decree of the Revolutionary Command Council on December 10, 1952, Egypt had a two-chamber legislative parliament: a House of Representatives and a Senate. Perusing the minutes of the two chambers, one cannot help but be filled with a sense of dignity and pride; the enriching parliamentary debates followed admirable parliamentary traditions.

The 1971 Constitution, however, has followed in the footsteps of the 1964 Provisional Constitution and the 1956 Constitution, adopting the one-chamber parliamentary system consisting of 350 members, at least half of whom are workers and fellahins. Article 82 of the 1971 Constitution provides that the president may appoint ten members.

Such were the features of the 1964 Provisional Constitution compared with those of the 1971 Constitution.

Egypt under the 1964 Provisional Constitution. In 1965, intelligence services claimed to have uncovered a conspiracy engineered by the Moslem Brotherhood, the activities of which had been banned since 1954. This claim resulted in a sweeping wave of terrorism and a crackdown on thousands of Moslem Brotherhood members, some of whom were prosecuted and given death penalties, while others received life imprisonment with hard labor. About the same time, in a Kamshish village in Lower Egypt, following the murder of a Marxist advocate, there was a crackdown on the family accused of the murder. The slogan "Wipe out Feudalist and Reactionary Pockets" was hoisted, and a "committee for the liquidation of feudalism and reactionary elements" was formed in May 1966, chaired by Field Marshal Amer, first vice-president and commander in chief of the armed forces. Thereafter Egypt was subjected to various ruthless measures including detention, travel restrictions, and property confiscation.

It is noteworthy that the 1964 Constitution was provisional, awaiting the writing of a permanent constitution. A Preparatory Committee was formed to draft a permanent constitution; and on June 2, 1966, it started studying the provisional constitution to discern its shortcomings. It began reviewing the National Charter to dig out principles not legalized in the provisional constitution, researching and preparing comparative studies concerning basic principles underlying various constitutions in the world, and compiling reference works needed for writing up the draft constitution. On February 11, 1967, the committee started listening to representatives of various social strata until a blueprint of the draft constitution was drawn up. The project, however, was interrupted by the June 5, 1967, aggression; and the National Assembly was unable at that time to endorse the draft constitution and refer it to the people for a public referendum.

The humiliating defeat of Egypt in 1967 was the natural outcome of prevailing political conditions based on empty slogans and of the crackdown on personal freedoms. In the wake of the defeat, President Nasser reshuffled the armed forces to rid them of corrupt elements that maintained an upper hand. Key figures held responsible for the defeat were brought to trial. Underlying the causes for the defeat was the sense of "not belonging to Egypt." President Nasser then attempted to reform internal conditions after popular demonstrations had swept the country. He issued the March 30, 1968, declaration containing political principles for preserving freedoms and steps for initiating socioeconomic reform. The March declaration may be considered an important constitutional document, although the ensuing period witnessed the most flagrant violations of judicial power. On September 1, 1969, several laws, known as the judicial reform laws, were issued, resulting in the isolation of hundreds of members of the judiciary, the dissolution of the Judges' Club, and the disbanding of its board of directors. This era ended with the death of President Nasser on September 28, 1970.

Perhaps the best description of the situation at that time was given by President Sadat in his book, *In Search of Identity*:

> When the people felt a little uneasy about one thing or another, their uneasiness was regarded as counterrevolutionary; their private property was put under state custodianship and mass arrests were made. This was how human dignity was shattered in practice.
>
> I have had the opportunity to observe that the gravest injustice done to the Egyptian people was the "cultivation of fear," that is, rather than trying to build up the inner man we did all we could to make him feel frightened. Fear is, I believe, a most effective tool in destroying the soul of an individual—and the soul of a people. The livelihoods of all the people were in the hands of the ruler; it was up to him to give or deny, although in the latter case a man wouldn't be merely denied a livelihood—he would be arrested and thrown into a detention center, while the members of his family would lose their jobs and be subjected to persecution.
>
> People thus turned into dummies. They became puppets in the hands of rulers, who did what they liked with them. Travel abroad was forbidden. No one could say anything that appeared to contradict the official line of thinking (the penalty being arrest and loss of livelihood). People's passivity increased daily until one day no man felt he could be secure unless he had completely kept to himself, cut himself off entirely, both from public events and from the very stream of life around him, as though he wanted to see nothing, hear nothing, and say nothing.
>
> It is this that makes me say that just as the July 23 Revolution was colossal in its achievements, so it was equally colossal in its mistakes. In time, however, the achievements fizzled out. They either vanished altogether or turned into cold reality, deprived of all glory. The revolution was reduced to a huge, dark and terrible pit, inspiring fear and hatred but allowing no escape.
>
> It would be a mistake, all this notwithstanding, to think that the spirit of the Egyptian people could ever be stifled. It is a great spirit, capable of enduring all hardships, and is

never subdued by adversity. Our people have withstood the worst types of oppression, both domestic and foreign, and emerged unharmed. It was the great fortitude and self-confidence of the people that enabled them to endure the pain; the bleeding, they knew, would stop and the wounds would heal.

Such is the real spirit of the Egyptian people, in whom I have always had total confidence. I hope I shall be able to remove the present obstacles on their road to progress and so enable them to be in complete control of their destiny. They will then, I am sure, work miracles.[1]

The 1971 Constitution of the Arab Republic of Egypt

The Constitution proclaimed on September 11, 1971, which was the first permanent Constitution of Egypt since 1952, is significant for defining the system of government on the basis of a constitution, thereby ending Egypt's revolutionary phase. It has been supplemented by several complementary laws, aptly called *Lois Organiques* (organic laws) in French constitutional law (because they underlie guarantees safeguarding the life and freedom of citizens), and it underwent basic changes in 1980.

Sadat's Role in Writing the 1971 Constitution. Sadat assumed the presidency on October 16, 1970, succeeding President Nasser after the latter's death on September 28, 1970. President Sadat was nominated by the National Assembly, and a referendum was held on the nomination according to the 1964 provisional constitution. He received the percentage of votes required.

When Sadat assumed the presidency, a power struggle erupted between him and the so-called Nasserites. The struggle climaxed on May 13, 1971, when all the Nasserites resigned from the government. A conspiracy to topple President Sadat, known as the May Conspiracy by Centers of Power, was later discovered. The conspirators were brought to trial, and the Revolutionary Court passed sentence on them.

On May 20, 1971, President Sadat appealed to National Assembly members to draw up a permanent constitution without delay. In his statement, President Sadat outlined the following basic principles:

• The Constitution should express the true Egyptian way of life and tradition. It should stress Egypt's affiliation to the Arab homeland.

• It should protect, reinforce, and expand socialist gains, including ensuring that at least 50 percent of members in the People's Assembly and elected people's councils at various levels would be fellahins and workers, as prescribed by the charter.

• The state should be subject to the power of the law just as individuals are.

• Sovereignty should be for the people only, and every power should be derived from the people and represented in elected councils.

• Sovereignty of law should be established. The people should have the right to administer justice through the jury system in a manner that would ensure the democracy of the judiciary.

• The government should be administered through well-defined institutions with specific jurisdictions.

• Power should be associated with responsibility to render accountability feasible.

• The people should elect the president of the Republic, his will being derived from the people's will and protected and guided by the popular front.

• The three forms of ownership should be underscored: public sector, cooperative, and private. Provision should be made to protect and guarantee each one of them.

• Each citizen should be entitled to have his pension ensured, in case of disability, through the expansion of social security.

• The labor unionist movement should be encouraged to develop further.

• Various unions and organizations should be entrusted with drawing up a code of ethics to regulate their activities and to stress ethical values in the new society.

• Parliament should be called the People's Assembly, not the National Assembly.

Procedures for Drafting the 1971 Constitution. The National Assembly convened on May 24, 1971. The speaker related to the members the president's order to draft a permanent Constitution. He announced that a fifty-member Preparatory Committee drawn from the assembly would be formed for that purpose. Nonmembers would be entitled to attend meetings or submit memorandums containing their views. The Preparatory Committee would seek the assistance of scholars, law experts, religious leaders, and others. The draft Constitution would be submitted to the assembly for debate before July 23, 1971. The speaker resolved that the entire assembly be considered as the Committee for Writing the Constitution and that the Preparatory Committee would consist of those willing to participate in its activities.

311

He called for nominations to the Preparatory Committee stating that it would be formed during the following session.

The National Assembly convened the following day. The speaker announced the formation of the Preparatory Committee consisting of those willing to take part. He called on the assembly to increase the committee membership to eighty. Members included university professors, judicial experts, and religious leaders. No specific rule governed the choice of such experts, except that they should be authorities in their respective fields. Several of these experts were chosen by the speaker of the National Assembly, the minister of Justice, and the chairman of the State Council.

Three main committees were formed, each of which was to study one part of the Constitution and make appropriate proposals. A fourth main committee was to receive suggestions from citizens. The tasks of the various main committees were as follows:

- Committee I—to study the basic components of society, freedom, and ethical values
- Committee II—to study the system of government
- Committee III—to study local government and basic laws
- Committee IV—to receive suggestions, that is, collect suggestions from the people, classify them, and submit them to the above-mentioned committees

The full Preparatory Committee held a meeting on May 29 under the chairmanship of the assembly speaker. It consisted of the members of the National Assembly and members selected by the committee from among experts and specialists.

The speaker of the National Assembly, who served as chairman of the committee, stated that "foremost among the guidelines to which the Committee on Writing the Constitution should adhere are the National Action Charter; the March 30, 1968, declaration; the 1964 Provisional Constitution; and the works of the former Preparatory Committee on Writing the 1966 Draft Constitution." In this respect, the Committee for Writing the Constitution was not free to choose constitutional principles, particularly the thirteen principles outlined by President Sadat in his statement before the assembly.

The four main committees convened, selected their office staff, and formed subcommittees as shown in table 1.

Each subcommittee held several meetings and prepared reports on principles recommended for the Constitution. Subcommittee representatives met with members of the main committees to discuss the results of their research on principles. The Committee for Receiving Suggestions received 103,000 suggestions of which 89,500 were on

TABLE 1
COMMITTEE STRUCTURE

Main Committee	Affiliate Subcommittee
Committee on the Basic Components of Society	• Subcommittee on Social Components • Subcommittee on Moral Components • Subcommittee on Political Components • Subcommittee on Economic Components • Subcommittee on Public Freedoms
Committee on the System of Government	• Subcommittee on the Socialist Union • Subcommittee on the Nature of Governmental System • Subcommittee on the People's Assembly, People's Control, and People's Councils • Subcommittee on the Head of State, Vice Presidents, and Ministers • Subcommittee on the Specialized Scientific Councils • Subcommittee on the State Control Institutions • Subcommittee on the Masses' Organization • Subcommittee on the Judiciary
Committee on Local Administration and Basic Laws	• Subcommittee on Litigation Rights • Subcommittee on Socialist Union and Elections and Membership Law • Subcommittee on the Press and Information Media • Subcommittee on Basic Laws
Committee for Receiving Suggestions	• Subcommittee on Stimulating Masses • Subcommittee on Studying Suggestions Concerning the Basic Components of Society • Subcommittee on Studying Suggestions Concerning the System of Government • Subcommittee on Studying Suggestions Concerning Local Administration

the basic components of society; 9,000 suggestions were on the system of government; and 4,500 suggestions were on local administration. Furthermore, the Preparatory Committee gave its members leave to visit various provinces to hold meetings with citizens and hear their views regarding the Constitution. Members of the Committee for Receiving Suggestions submitted reports to the other committees concerned. Information media also encouraged the people to voice their views.

When the main committees ended their meetings, a Committee for Drafting Principles was formed, and it was chaired by the chairman of the Preparatory Committee. Now the principles upon which the Constitution was to be based were to be defined.

On July 14, 1971, the Preparatory Committee met to discuss the principles, and several constitutional amendments were introduced. The Preparatory Committee decided to submit them to the National Assembly before referring them to the General National Congress of the Arab Socialist Union.

The National Assembly convened on July 23, 1971, and eighty basic principles for the Permanent Constitution of the Arab Republic of Egypt were endorsed, although some were rather controversial (these shall be discussed below). The assembly speaker announced that supplementary laws would be issued with the Constitution. The draft of the Constitution was submitted to the Arab Socialist Union Congress, which in turn endorsed the principles and assigned a central committee to phrase them in specific articles. The central committee selected from among its members an ad hoc committee to draft the Constitution in accordance with the general principles approved by the National Assembly. After revising the articles of the Constitution, the ad hoc committee submitted the entire draft to the central committee on September 8. The latter endorsed it after introducing some amendments to its provisions. The draft Constitution was then referred to a general referendum on September 11, 1971. The establishment of a permanent Constitution for the Arab Republic of Egypt was endorsed, and the president issued the Constitution in accordance with article 193. The president also ordered that the documents concerning its promulgation and proclamation be on file at the People's Assembly.

Context of the Writing of the 1971 Constitution. Several interesting questions arise concerning the Preparatory Committee and the eighty principles they defined to be incorporated into the Constitution. How and why were these principles laid down, and what was the controversy surrounding some of them? Were they all incorporated into the Constitution, or were some of them discarded? Perhaps the major question is, why did the Preparatory Committee choose to draw up a permanent Constitution in the first place? Was it merely because Egypt had to have a Constitution, or were there other valid reasons? Also, what were the prevailing ideas that the Egyptian public opinion wished to see documented in the Constitution? Objectivity and impartiality are required in answering such questions, which involve Egyptian public opinion.

Before the 1971 Constitution the panic-stricken Egyptian citizen lived under oppression and tyranny. The six-day war of June 1967 brought disappointment and bitter feelings of failure and frustration to the average Egyptian, particularly regarding the high hopes pinned on the leadership of President Nasser, the national hero. Following Nasser's death on September 28, 1970, the whispers about atrocities being perpetrated became loud talk. Field Marshal Amer's suicide in 1967 touched off a court case involving a plot by army officers to topple President Nasser and seize power. The case revealed the way Egypt was being ruled and the role of the intelligence apparatus and military prisons in committing abominable crimes against the dignity of man. In 1971 a conflict between President Sadat and the Nasserites, or centers of power, erupted. I cannot reveal secrets of this conflict, however, since I was personally involved as one of the investigators.

The Egyptian press, in the meantime, carried lengthy stories about, and photos of, various aspects of torture of many Egyptian people. Hundreds of republican decrees were issued with orders such as the following: "To be fired from his job," "to be arrested," "sequestration of his property and that of his family." The Sequestration Department paid a meager salary to victims and their families, though barely enough to cover their needs. The department also was reported to have misused sequestrated funds and to have mismanaged real estate. To cite an example of the prevailing chaos, President Nasser was quoted as admitting in his May 1966 speech that, although he succeeded in running the Suez Canal, he failed to manage Kasr al-Aini Hospital (a major medical university hospital in Egypt). Commenting on this speech, the chairman of Medical Syndicate said that if he were given the facilities for the operation of the Suez Canal, Kasr al-Aini Hospital would have fared better than the canal. That same day the chairman was placed under sequestration with his friends who had applauded him.

Several means of torture existed. Intelligence services recruited young people to spy on and frame members of their own families, and thus the seeds of dissension were sown among the rank and file. No one was to be trusted. There were fake trials in military courts; people were deprived of their legal rights.

Egyptian public opinion at that time followed three trends. First, the religious trend came from the general belief that the humiliating military defeat and the deteriorating conditions in Egypt resulted from a widespread drift from religion. The solution was to go back to religion for building character. Egyptian public opinion endorsed vehemently such a view since religion was and remains the basic factor in the formation of Egyptian character. Both Christianity and Islam have been primarily instrumental in the crystallization of the Egyptian identity. The Egyptians are firm believers in God and in the messages of prophets. Even today they believe that the only means of escape from the stress and strain of modern life is an upward glance to heaven—taking refuge in God. This trend became forceful in the 1970s and early 1980s and reached its high point the day President Sadat was assassinated.

The second trend attributed causes of defeat to socialist ideology and, as the simple Egyptian layman would say, "turning to the left when we should have turned right."

A third, rational, liberal trend, manifested in the provision of guarantees to liberate citizens from fear and anxiety, also existed. To limit dictatorial authority, this view held, Egypt should establish a political system in which state authorities would be organized with lines of demarcation defining their functions, an independent judiciary would serve as a safety valve in disputes between rulers and ruled, and the principle of sovereignty of the law would be established. On June 15, 1971, I was privileged to meet President Sadat, and I said to him: "Egypt's defeat in the 1967 war was not due to Egypt's weakness and Israel's strength; rather, it was due to the loss of a sense of belonging to Egypt. The revolution has crushed the morale of the Egyptians. Mr. President, if it be your wish to lead us to victory you should liberate the people from fear. The six-million-member Socialist Union is no good; we want ideological citizens who believe in Egypt and in defending it. The only way to achieve that is through freedom."

A large segment of the intelligentsia in Egypt believed, even during the British occupation, that the basic issue in Egypt was reform from within. The internal building of Egypt in various fields—economic, social, political, and cultural—was, according to this view, the sound path for its renaissance. President Nasser, as well as President Sadat, to a certain degree, had been fascinated with the glitter of leadership on the international scene. The former fought all his battles outside Egypt—dreaming of the Arab Empire and its leadership—but the end was quite disappointing both domestically and internationally. President Sadat was internationally acclaimed for his courage and statesmanship, but he was oblivious to domestic problems that should have been nipped in the bud. His provocative attitude toward the sentiments of Egyptian youth spelled out his end.

It was natural that the liberal trend should permeate all the others. The call for a return to the old Egyptian family and traditional human relations was echoed on the widest scale.

As mentioned above, the fourth main committee of the Preparatory Committee for Writing the Constitution was in charge of receiving suggestions from the people. It was reported that 86.6 percent of the suggestions centered on the basic constituents of society—an indicator of the Egyptian people's extreme interest in moral, religious, and social issues—in general, on the Egyptian dignity. That report is substantiated by the fact that forty-six of the eighty principles adopted by the Preparatory Committee for Drawing up the Constitution dealt with religious, moral, social, and economic issues, the sovereignty of the law, guarantees for individual freedom, and the independence of the judiciary. The fourth point in the Proclamation of the Constitution emphasized that the main objective of the Constitution was to liberate the Egyptian citizen from fear and to buttress the guarantees for his freedom and natural rights. This point is now the cornerstone of the Egyptian Constitution.

History always will be witness to President Sadat's initiatives in laying the groundwork for the preservation of the Egyptian's dignity. No matter what is said about the major pitfall that heralded his assassination on October 6, 1981, the Constitution and its complementary laws will remain his immortal achievement.

Discussion in the People's Assembly about the Eighty Principles. The National Assembly, in its July 22, 1971, session, discussed the eighty principles prepared by the subcommittees of the Preparatory Committee. All but one of those principles were incorporated into the Constitution; the exception was the principle calling for establishment of a Socioeconomic Council. Of the eighty principles, the most controversial was number 55, which parallels article 89 of the Constitution, stipulating: "Employees of the state and the public sector may nominate themselves for membership in the People's Assembly with the exception of cases determined by law. The member of the People's Assembly shall devote himself entirely to his duties, while his former work or post shall be preserved for him as determined by law."

The 1964 Provisional Constitution exempted public sector employees from the rule banning the holding of both membership in the People's Assembly and their former jobs; the proposed text for article 89 of the Constitution sanctioned the holding of both. That article evoked the criticism of several members who contended that the assembly would consequently turn into a group of employees who are members, and, at the same time, be incapable of exercising its constitutional right of controlling the ministers who are also their own bosses. The text was thus amended to stipulate that membership is full-time and that holding assembly membership without relinquishing a former job is not allowed.

Among other controversial principles was number 56, providing that the electors are entitled to withdraw confidence from a member of the assembly according to conditions and procedures determined by law. The representative defended this principle, saying: "Any representative should be subject to giving account to the electorate, expounding his services for the homeland. Where the people feel that there are members who have fallen short of the standards, they are entitled to voice a protest or withdraw their confidence from the representative." Some members of the assembly opposed this provision, saying that it would lead to instability of parliamentary life, since each member had to compete against twenty candidates in his constituency during elections; only two of the twenty are elected. Those who have suffered defeat would ceaselessly provoke the winners, rightfully or otherwise. Some members raised the question, How will the representative give account, every month or every year? If the principle were carried out, the freedom of representatives would be in the hands of the electors, whereas representatives are the *people's* representatives. Discussion ended at that point, and the principle of allowing the electors to withdraw confidence from their representatives was turned down and not incorporated into the Constitution.

This ends my presentation of the most important views that were voiced during the discussion in the assembly about the basic principles of the Constitution. It will be noted that the discussions of the Committee on Local Administration and the Basic Laws have been omitted. I have devoted a separate study to those laws and have expounded the circumstances that induced the promulgation of them.

Complementary Laws of the Constitution

Constitutionalism is always concerned with general principles and basic rules; details are addressed by laws stemming from constitutional provisions. The provisions of any constitution—concerning, for example, protection of private property and litigation rights—invariably end with the phrase "in accordance with the law." Therefore, one should bear in mind, if the principles incorporated in the constitution are not protected from abuse by executive power, preventing the executive from tampering with the constitution, constitutional provisions would be mere ink on paper or, as Professor Duverger says, "just decor or a camouflage not worth the ink with which they are written or the paper consumed in writing them." For example, both the 1956 Constitution and the 1964 Provisional Constitution provided protection of private property and personal freedom; nevertheless, administrative custodianship was imposed on people's assets, and rights of citizens were trampled by arrests, administrative detention, indefinite confinement, and arbitrary dismissal from work.

The complementary laws of the Egyptian Constitution, mentioned in the National Assembly speaker's speech requesting the formation of a Committee for Writing the Constitution, were actually conceived in compliance with President Sadat's request. (At this point, I note that the late Gamal al-Oteify had exerted tremendous effort—for which Egyptians owe him gratitude—in preparing and defending those complementary laws at the People's Assembly.) The thirteen laws are contained in two volumes. The first, of 656 pages, consists of seven laws; and the second volume, of 951 pages, consists of six laws. Each volume contains a report by the People's Assembly Legislative Committee and an explanatory memorandum.

The two volumes, the product of monumental legislative effort, consist of provisions safeguarding citizens' rights from constitutional flaws that earlier infringed on their freedom and providing guarantees for such freedom at present and in the future. Therefore, I appeal to my colleagues living under various political regimes, aspiring to enhance democracy in their respective countries, to learn from this scientific legislative endeavor.

Perhaps the most important complementary law—number 37 (1972)—concerns protection of personal freedom. It stipulates that assault on the private life of citizens is a crime; that torture and other violations of personal rights are crimes without limits as to when they can be prosecuted; that detention for indefinite periods is abolished; that telephone wiretapping is forbidden; and that authority to declare a state of emergency is restricted. This law was drawn up in accordance with article 57 of the Constitution: "Any assault on individual freedom or on the inviolability of the private life of citizens or any other public rights and liberties guaranteed by the Constitution and the law shall be considered a crime, the criminal and civil lawsuits for which can be brought at any time. The state shall grant fair compensation to the victim of such an assault." (Many citizens who were tortured in Egyptian prisons have filed lawsuits in courts and demanded compensation for physical and moral harm they sustained. They have been generously compensated.)

The executive, before the 1971 Constitution, resorted to laws prohibiting citizens from appealing to the judiciary to contest measures taken against them. Those were the so-called litigation prohibitions, by virtue of which any measures taken by the executive were considered as acts of sovereignty and, therefore, could never be referred to the judiciary. Although article 68 of the 1971 Constitution stipulates that citizens have the right to appeal their cases to appropriate judges, the provision was ineffective because of the prohibitions.

Law 11 (1973), consisting of two articles, has eliminated all litigation prohibitions; it has abolished prohibitions in agrarian reform laws, other agricultural legislation, taxation laws, judicial fees laws, laws concerning the organization of universities, work and social security laws, laws concerning civil servants, and an aid to war victims law.

By virtue of law 23 (1972), on the exercise of political rights, and law 38 (1972), the people's assembly law, political isolation cases—that is, cases in which complete deprivation of political rights applied to detainees and those whose assets were placed under custodianship in the past—were abolished.

Law 37 (1972), guaranteeing citizens' freedom by amending existing laws, was promulgated to change the penal code and the criminal procedures law. Foremost, it refers to the penal code, which now reads: "Every individual holding a public office and every qualified individual ordered to administer punishment to a person sentenced, who personally administered punishment more severe than that prescribed by the law, or who administered punishment that was never sentenced, shall be imprisoned." Other changes in the criminal procedures law, concerning arrest and the searching of individuals and homes, were also made by virtue of this law.

Other laws complementary to the Constitution concern safeguards for the national unity and public funds; the independence of universities; the judicial authorities; the legal departments in public agencies, which like judicial agencies have become independent; the participation of workers on boards of directors; the general budget of the state; the general policy of the state; and the local government laws.

The 1980 Constitutional Amendments

Constitutions are either rigid or flexible depending on the method by which they are amended. A constitution that requires complex measures for its amendment may be categorized as rigid. A constitution that can be amended as simply as any ordinary legislation may be described as flexible.

According to article 184, the Egyptian Constitution can be categorized as rigid; its measures for amendment are complex and of long duration. Amendment of the 1971 Constitution began on July 16, 1979, and ended on May 22, 1980. I shall discuss these amendments, first dealing with procedural aspects and then with the nature and scope of the amendments themselves.

Procedures for Constitutional Amendments. The story of the 1980 Constitutional amendments is interlocked with the Egyptian-Israeli Peace Treaty and its appendixes and the complementary agreement on complete autonomy in the West Bank and Gaza, signed in Washington on March 26, 1979. These two documents were submitted to the People's Assembly in accordance with the Constitution and were ratified during a long session that ended late April 10, 1979. The next day, President Sadat addressed the people, stating that he had issued a republican decree (number 157, 1979), inviting the electorate to vote in a referendum on nine subjects, including a request to dissolve the People's Assembly (see republican decree number 157, 1979, appendix G).

The referendum was held on April 20, 1979. The minister of the interior issued two decrees announcing the results of the referendum. The first decree dealt with the results of the referendum on the peace treaty (and its appendixes) and the agreement on Palestinian autonomy. The second dealt with the electorate's approval to dissolve the People's Assembly.

The next day, Parliament issued republican decree number 178 (1979), concerning the dissolution of the People's Assembly and calling on the electorate to elect members of the new assembly on June 7, 1979. In cases that necessitated reelection, such a procedure would take place on June 14. The decree fixed a date—June 23—for convening the new assembly. Following the elections, republican decree number 271 (1979), concerning the appointment of ten members to the assembly by virtue of the presidential prerogatives stipulated in the Constitution, was issued.

On July 16, 1979, more than one-third of the People's Assembly members submitted to the assembly speaker three requests for amending the Constitution. The first was a proposal to amend articles 1, 4, and 5 of the Constitution and to add to the Constitution the necessary articles to form the Shoura Assembly and to define its powers. Among other changes proposed was the addition of articles for organizing the press as a popular power.

The People's Assembly decided, in its July 18, 1979, session, to form an ad hoc committee, chaired by the speaker and consisting of seventeen assembly members—including two representing opposition parties and one independent—to consider the conditions requiring amendment of the Constitution. The committee was to submit its report to the assembly during the July 19, 1979, session.

Upon submission of the committee report and after deliberation, the assembly announced the following decisions:

- to approve the committee's report and the principle of amending the number of articles in the Constitution and the introduction of others as phrased in the report
- to debate and discuss the articles that the assembly agreed to amend. The ad hoc committee was to examine all suggestions and views and report them to the assembly.
- to require the ad hoc committee to submit a report on the suggestions and views it received

A technical subcommittee of the Parliamentary Committee was formed, and I served as a member. Chaired by the speaker, the subcommittee prepared comparative studies of all constitutional amendments and, subsequently, wrote up the required texts. During President Sadat's meeting with all information media personnel, in August 1979, a decision was made to form a committee for drawing up legislation for the press and the press syndicate. The twenty-two-member committee consisted of nineteen journalists and three law experts, including myself, and was chaired by the minister of information and culture and presidential affairs, Mr. Mansour Hassan. After holding meetings for six months, the committee drew up proposed constitutional provisions concerning the press.

The Parliamentary Committee held two meetings, on April 26 and April 27, 1980, to study suggestions and views submitted to it.

In the committee's report, suggestions fell into three categories. First, from a constitutional viewpoint, the major part lacked constitutional form, were incompatible with the house regulations and, hence, were unacceptable as requests for amending the Constitution. They were irrelevant to the articles that the assembly on July 19, 1979, agreed to amend and also irrelevant to the new provisions concerning the Shoura Council and the press that the assembly agreed to introduce. The second category consisted of basic amendments related to the changes previously approved by the assembly and therefore were open to discussion. The third category concerned topical or textual amendments to articles that the assembly had previously agreed to amend. The second and third categories therefore were to be considered by the committee.

The problem facing the ad hoc committee for amending or introducing the new articles to the Constitution was how to amalgamate such provisions in the Constitution, that is, whether to insert them in the existing text or to devote a separate part to them. Suggested solutions were as follows:

• The new provisions concerning the Shoura Council and the press authority were to be inserted into the text of the parts and chapters of the Constitution dealing with the system of government.

• The new provisions concerning the Shoura Council and the press authority were to appear in two separate parts at the end of the Constitution.

• The new provisions would appear in two successive parts before that concerning general and transitional provisions. The numbering of part IV and of its articles would be changed so that the latter would appear at the end of the Constitution in line with standard procedures.

The committee adopted the second approach and decided to place the new provisions under a separate part with two chapters, namely, part VII under the title "New Provisions." Chapter I would contain articles concerning the Shoura Assembly; chapter II, articles concerning the press authority.

The committee also approved proposed articles concerning the authority of the press that would appear in part VII, chapter II, under the title "The Press Authority."

The report was submitted to the People's Assembly in its session of April 30, 1980, and was approved by the majority as defined in the last paragraph of article 189 of the Constitution. The amendments were referred to the Egyptian people in a plebiscite held May 22, 1980, and the amendments were approved by 99.9 percent of the electorate.

President Sadat and the 1980 Amendments. The People's Assembly, which ratified the Peace Treaty on April 10, 1979, was to be dissolved following a referendum proposed by the president on April 11. In his speech at the inaugural session on June 23, 1979, President Sadat said, "With this new assembly, you are entering a decisive transitional state in the stream of our democratic life coming after the people of Egypt imposed their free will and openly denounced malicious political scandalmongers, fanatics, the bloodthirsty and the politically corrupt; and after the people rejected the peace opposers and those devoting their energy to serve twisted objectives alien to the land of Egypt. Subsequently, the vigilant people buried those elements once and for all."

Those words expressed his extreme exasperation toward the attitude of about thirteen assembly members representing the opposition. They objected to certain Peace Treaty conditions, which they claimed were not in national or Arab interests. Most conspicuous was that twelve of the opposers were defeated in the June elections. Some opposition factions accused the ministry of interior of interfering to prevent their success and claimed that the elections had been rigged.

Nevertheless, President Sadat called in that address for constitutional amendments to lay down the framework for the socialist-democratic philosophy in a bid to achieve political and social freedom for the individual; to defend social peace and national unity; to reinforce socialist-democratic principles; to bring about justice in the distribution of burdens—that the levying of taxes be the sound application of social justice between the haves- and the have-nots; to draw up a declaration of the Egyptian individual's rights, which should be an integral part of the Constitution; to consider the press as the fourth power, ensuring its freedom and affirming its independence in discharging its mission; to discard the one-party system by establishing a multiparty regime; and to establish responsible opposition to maintain moral principles. Actually, amendment of the Constitution was based on these principles, with the exception of the declaration of the Egyptian individual's rights. The ad hoc committee established in July 1979 to consider reasons for amending the Constitution was of the opinion that the present provisions of the Constitution did not require drawing up a new document on individual rights.

Ironically, the 1980 amendments spelled the end for President Sadat. They were followed by a series of laws, the so-called notorious laws, that touched off a serious rift between President Sadat and the opposition and eventually led to his assassination on October 6, 1981, by young religious extremists.

The Egyptian Constitution before the 1980 amendments consisted of 193 articles. Following amendment, it consisted of 211 articles: 19 articles plus part VII were added. The most important amendments concern articles 2 and 5.

Amendments to Article 2. Article 2 stipulated, before amendment, that "Islam is the religion of the state. Arabic is an official language, and the principles of Islamic jurisprudence are a principal source of legislation." Assembly members called for an amendment so the article would read as follows: "Islam is the religion of the state. Arabic is its official language, and the principal source of legislation is Islamic jurisprudence."

The first sentence says that Islam is the religion of the state. It means that both the people and the government adhere to the statutes of Islamic jurisprudence, otherwise the text would be meaningless. That is, if the Islamic jurisprudence statutes were not carried into effect, the official religion of the state could not be Islam.

The text at the end of article 2 says that Islamic jurisprudence is a principal source of legislation, implying that it is but one source among others rather than the only source. Thus other, imported sources would be allowed to infiltrate in contradiction to the statutes of Islamic jurisprudence. The problem would be that the phrase "Islam is the religion of the state" would be a mere formality. Islam is not just a noun but, rather, an applied practice and conduct. If the phraseology were not rectified in this respect, the day would come when this word would be lost. Therefore, since the text of the last paragraph of article 2 deviated from the aspirations of the people and from the Constitution writers' purpose, the amendment was recommended in response to the requests of the masses and in a bid to gratify God and conscience. Upholding the text of the Constitution stipulating that Islam is the religion of the state was also recommended.

Article 2 now reads: "Islam is the religion of the state. The Arabic language is its official language, and the principal source of legislation is Islamic jurisprudence (Shari'a)."

Several other suggestions stressed the importance of depending on Islamic jurisprudence in drawing up legislation; others endorsed the application of the Shari'a, maintaining that there is "no coercion in religion," no discrimination among Egyptians because of differences in religion, and that non-Moslems submit to the precepts of their own faiths. The committee reviewed all these suggestions concerning article 1 and, after a thorough study, resolved that the text of the amended article serves the purpose for which it was intended.

The committee noted in this respect that article 40 of the Constitution candidly stipulates that "all citizens are equal before the law. They have equal public rights and duties without discrimination due to sex, ethnic origin, language, religion, or creed." Article 46 of the Constitution also provides that "the state shall guarantee the freedom of belief and the freedom of practicing religious rites." In addition, the committee noted, any provision of the Constitution should be interpreted within the context of the rest of the provisions, and that this should apply to Article 2 as well. It should be recognized that Islamic jurisprudence rules that non-Moslems are subject in their personal affairs to the rulings of their own creeds. This view was upheld by Islamic lawmakers from time immemorial, in accordance with the Holy Book and practice sanctioned by tradition (Sunna).

After having studied the various suggestions, the committee reached the following conclusions with reference to article 2:

- There is not a shadow of doubt that the right to hold public office and jobs, and the freedom of creed and practice of religious rites, are among the general rights Egyptians enjoy under the Constitution and in accordance with the provisions of the law without any discrimination due to sex, origin, language, religion, or creed.

- Any deviation that occurs through interpreting any constitutional provision in a manner contrary to the principle of equality, freedom of creed and practice of religious rites by Egyptian non-Moslems constitutes a direct constitutional contravention, particularly against the rulings of article 2 and against the duty of Egyptians to preserve national unity as mandated in article 60. It would also contradict the principles endorsed by the people in the referendum of April 19, 1979, concerning the Peace Treaty and the building of the nation.

In the People's Assembly session of April 30, 1980, the minister of justice and advocate of the proposal for amendment of article 2 emphatically stressed the rights of Christian brethren. A Christian representative also spoke eloquently about national unity, stating, "Religion for God and the Homeland for all."

The committee recognized Islam's respect for other religions and its guarantee of others' rights in accordance with their own religious laws. This recognition was mainly addressed to the Christian brethren and was in response to the reservations expressed by some of the latter, including Pope Shenouda, the Spiritual Leader of the Coptic Orthodox Church, concerning amendment of this article and in response to their demand to add to the text a paragraph candidly stipulating that the rights of followers of other creeds shall be preserved.

Amendments to Article 5. Since January 17, 1953, when political parties were abolished, Egypt had known only the one-party system provided for by the constitutions of 1956, 1964, and 1971. Article 5 of the 1971 Constitution provided that "the Arab Socialist Union is the political organization that represents, through its institutions based on the principle of democracy, the alliance of the forces of working people: the fellahin workers, soldiers, the intelligentsia, and representatives of national capitalism. The Arab Socialist Union shall serve as an instrument of this alliance in reinforcing the values of democracy and socialism, in following up national action in all aspects, and motivating this national action toward its prescribed objectives."

The request of the People's Assembly members for amending this article contended:

> The constitutional provision of article 5, that ASU [Arab Socialist Union] is the political organization representing, through its structure, the alliance of the working people's forces, has become invalid since the adoption of the multiparty system regulated by virtue of law 40 (1977) and its subsequent amendments. The adoption of the multiparty system and the freedom for its formation was one of the principles that were referred to the people in the recent referendum, through which the People's Assembly elections took place on June 7 and 14, 1979, and during which the people chose their representatives in accordance with the various party programs.
>
> Therefore, article 5 does not conform anymore to the present political reality based on the multiparty system and should be substituted by a new provision for a political system based on multiparties.

In its report concerning this article, the ad hoc committee said: "The assembly has endorsed the following amendment to article 5: 'The political regime in ARE [Arab Republic of Egypt] is based upon the multiparty system within the framework of the basic principles and components of Egyptian society stipulated by the Constitution. Political parties shall be organized under the law.' After studying the various suggestions concerning this article, the committee noted that some suggestions were already contained in other provisions of the Constitution and that others, dealing with irrelevant textual details, would lead to a total loss of the general phraseology of the Constitution. In this view, the committee approved the amendment of article 5 of the Constitution.

During the April 30 session, one of the assembly members asked why the ascription of 50 percent of the votes to workers and fellahin

327

was not incorporated into the amendment. The speaker said, in commenting on this point, that the percentage ascribed to the workers and fellahin was voted on by the people several times and is now considered as part of the general state system.

The Shoura Assembly. As we noted above, among the three requests submitted by the People's Assembly members was one concerning the creation of the Shoura Assembly. The committee received several suggestions concerning the formation of the Shoura Assembly and expressing the following trends:

• One series of suggestions was to adopt the two-chamber system. Advocates of such an approach contended that the basic prerogatives of parliaments were both legislating and supervising the government. The proposed provisions for the organization of the Shoura Assembly endorsed by the assembly do not mention such prerogatives. Therefore, the suggestion was made that the Shoura Assembly be granted legislative and supervisory powers parallel to those granted to the People's Assembly. This approach was fundamentally opposed to the principle endorsed by the assembly.

In addition, the aim of establishing the Shoura Assembly, approved by the people in the April 19, 1979, plebiscite, was to set up an Egyptian Family Council to express the views of all categories of the populace on public and national issues and to avoid any duplication of legislative and supervisory prerogatives assigned solely to the People's Assembly.

• A second trend, manifested in some amendments that do not affect the basic principles contained in the proposed provisions for the organization of the Shoura Assembly, defines the jurisdiction of the assembly, its method of functioning, and the procedures related to calling it to session and dissolving it.

Having studied the articles endorsed by the assembly in this report, the committee decided to introduce the following changes:

1. Article 1 of the provisions for organizing the Shoura Council consists of a paragraph leaving the law to define the assembly's other prerogatives and the means adopted to preserve the principles of the July 23, 1952, and May 15, 1971, revolutions, providing that the assembly study and propose what it deems necessary to preserve them. Though the Constitution alone should define the jurisdictions of the new Shoura Assembly, articles 1 and 2 of the draft amendment would

have actually defined its jurisidiction, so the committee decided to omit the second paragraph of article 1.

2. The committee preferred to amend the text of the draft to make clear that the Shoura Assembly would be precluded from sharing in the legislative and supervisory jurisdictions of the People's Assembly.

3. Article 12 of the amendment provided that the basis for revoking membership in the People's Assembly be applied to members of the Shoura Assembly. The text noted that among the reasons for revoking membership was the loss of the member's status as worker or farmer upon which basis he had been elected. Therefore, the requirement of 50 percent membership of workers and fellahin, approved by the people in the April 19, 1979, plebiscite, would be included in the law for organizing the Shoura Assembly. The committee, to avoid ambiguity in this respect, preferred to provide clearly in article 3 of the draft amendment that at least half the elected Shoura Assembly members be from among the workers and fellahin.

4. Article 9 of the draft amendment provided that the president of the Republic be entitled to make a statement on the general policy of the state, or any other statements, during a joint meeting of both the People's Assembly and the Shoura Assembly. The original article did not define who would chair the joint meeting; so, to avoid any confusion on that score, since the People's Assembly is the lawful authority to exercise legislative and supervisory powers, the committee stipulated that the speaker of the People's Assembly shall chair the joint meeting.

5. The committee considered that article 2 of the draft amendment should contain a statement clearly indicating that the application of articles in the Constitution not be incompatible with those provisions concerning the Shoura Assembly. This is to ensure a sound basis of interpretation.

The Press as a Popular Authority. Among the amendments of the Constitution that the People's Assembly requested was the introduction of articles stipulating that the press be the fourth authority on which the regime is based. The preamble of the request read as follows:

> Taking into consideration that political life is based on the existence of several parties, and in order to enhance democracy, it is deemed necessary to revise the status of the press and to codify in the Constitution the Egyptian people's opinion, voiced in the April 19, 1979, plebiscite, that the press

become an authority so as to safeguard its freedom and affirm its independence.

The provision introduced into the Constitution concerning the press as a popular authority should be confined to the establishment of bases and principles organizing that authority and its relations with other authorities. Detailed rulings should be governed by a law guaranteeing the organization of press affairs thus achieving legislative flexibility and avoiding the complexity of constitutional amendment procedures.

Provisions in the Constitution concerning the press as a popular authority aim at codifying the following principles:

Article 206: The press is a popular, independent authority exercising its vocation in the manner stipulated in the Constitution and the law.

Article 207: The press shall exercise its vocation freely and independently in the service of society through all means of expression. It shall thus interpret the trend of public opinion, while contributing to its formation and orientation within the framework of the basic components of society—the safeguard of liberties, rights, public duties and respect for the sanctity of the private lives of citizens—as stipulated in the Constitution and defined by law.

Article 208: The freedom of the press is guaranteed, and press censorship is forbidden. It is also forbidden to threaten, confiscate, or cancel a newspaper through administrative measures, as stipulated in the Constitution and defined by law.

Article 209: The freedom of legal persons, whether public or private, or political parties to publish or own newspapers is safeguarded in accordance with the law. The financing and ownership of newspapers and the funds belonging to them come under the supervision of the people, as stipulated in the Constitution and defined by law.

Article 210: Journalists have the right to obtain news and information according to the regulations set by law. Their activities are not subject to any authority other than the law.

Article 211: A Supreme Press Council shall deal with matters concerning the press. The law shall define its formation, competences, and relationship with the state authorities. The Supreme Press Council shall exercise its competences with a view to consolidating the freedom of the press and its independence, to upholding the basic foundations of society, and to guaranteeing the soundness of national unity and social peace as stipulated in the Constitution and defined by law.

I hope I have succeeded in presenting the controversial issues and the subsequent solution worked out by the constitution writers. I am confident that constitutional life in Egypt, which started with the 1866 Constitution during the reign of Khedive Ismail, will continue and that the democratic current will spread toward the enhancement of sound democratic principles.

Note

1. Anwar Sadat, *In Search of Identity: An Autobiography* (New York: Harper and Row, 1978), pp. 209–210.

Commentary

Mohamad Taha Al-Shaeir

When one discusses the Egyptian Constitution, it is appropriate to examine the fundamental elements that determine the way it was drawn up. First, every society has its own political system by which it defines its government, organizes the relations between ruler and ruled, and thereby achieves harmony between power and freedom. This political system evolves with the society. Second, every society, regardless of its level of civilization, has its own ideology that stems from historical, international, economic, social, religious, and philosophical influences. The political system governing a particular society is inspired by the ideology on which the state is based. Various systems of government develop differently according to their respective socioeconomic factors as well as their environmental circumstances. A political system suitable for one country may not be at all suitable for another. It might not even be suitable for the former if existing conditions were to change.

Whoever is entrusted with the task of drawing up a constitution or with amending such a constitution will ultimately face several basic issues or problems. Considerable study may lead to many solutions for each problem, but only one may be chosen as following the spirit of the constitution under consideration and taking into account the existing circumstances.

The constitution now governing the Arab Republic of Egypt is the 1971 Constitution. On September 8, 1971, the central committee of the Arab Socialist Union ratified the draft Constitution. On September 11, the Constitution was approved by popular referendum, and the establishment of an Egyptian constitution was announced. The president of the Republic issued the Constitution and ordered that the proclamation and promulgation documents be deposited with the People's Assembly.

On July 16, 1979, more than one-third of the People's Assembly members filed requests to amend several constitutional provisions, namely, articles 1, 2, 4, 5, and 77, concerning the state regime, the principles of Islamic jurisprudence (Shari'a) as a basic source for legislation, the economic basis of the state, the Arab Socialist Union, and the presidential term. They also advocated the addition of a few articles on the organization of the Shoura Assembly and on the press as an independent popular authority.

The People's Assembly decided on July 18, 1979, to form an ad hoc committee to study these amendments and report on them. The assembly studied the report and approved it on July 19, 1979. Although in July 1979 the assembly approved these amendments in principle, it debated the articles to be amended during its July 30, 1980, session and finally endorsed them. They were then approved by the people in a popular referendum and put into effect. In the wake of these constitutional amendments, the Shoura Assembly law, the political party system amendment law, and the press law were issued in July 1980.

As one looks at the circumstances affecting the 1971 Constitution, the attitudes of its authors, and the ideology underlying its provisions, it is helpful to recall the constitutional status in Egypt before the 1971 Constitution.

Constitutional Status before the 1971 Constitution

The constitutional system in Egypt began in the truest sense with the establishment of the 1923 Constitution. The different system of government that existed before then may have been the prelude for the 1923 constitutional system. In this sense, we may consider the rule of the Mohammed Ali dynasty as the starting point in the study of constitutional systems before the 1923 Constitution. There is a close link between those systems and that of the 1923 Constitution on the one hand and the present system on the other.

The Egyptian revolution was staged on July 23, 1952, and the king was ousted on July 26 of the same year. In a statement on the morning of July 23, 1952, the commander in chief of the armed forces said: "I assure the Egyptian people that the whole army today is now working to promote the interest of the homeland under the constitution, void of any vested interest." With the success of the revolution, the existing constitution was abolished, and on December 10, 1952, the Revolutionary Command Council issued a statement to that effect. It also set up, for the meantime, a committee to draft a new constitution for endorsement by the people. On January 13, 1953, a decree was issued for the formation of a fifty-person committee to draft a new constitution. The situation compelled the revolution's leaders to proclaim a transitional period starting January 15, 1953. The transition was limited to a three-year period, during which a provisional constitution was to go into effect. The commander of the revolution proclaimed on January 18, 1953, the abolition of the monarchy and the establishment of the republic in Egypt. The constitutional declaration issued on February 10, 1953, proclaimed a brief constitution but did not elaborate on the organizational framework of any power or related matters. The revolution's leaders wished not to be restricted by detailed rulings in rebuilding and reorganizing the nation politically and socially.

No sooner had the three-year period expired than the president announced the articles of the new constitution drawn up by the Technical Bureau of the Presidency. The draft constitution was submitted to the people in a referendum on June 23, 1956. The 1956 Constitution is thus considered the first nonprovisional (permanent) constitution after the beginning of the revolution.

The 1956 Constitution was short-lived; it was actually enforced for no more than twenty months. The union between Egypt and Syria was proclaimed on February 21, 1958, and the constitution became legally inconsequential on the date the Unity was established. On March 5, 1958, the president of the Republic proclaimed a provisional constitution for the United Arab Republic to regulate the work of the government in the new republic during the transition period, pending completion and ratification of the permanent constitution.

That provisional constitution lasted, however, only a short while also. The Unity, abolished on September 27, 1961, resulted in the abolition of the provisional constitution. On September 27, 1962, a constitutional proclamation regarding the amendment of the 1958 constitutional provisions was issued.

The provisional constitution of the United Arab Republic was issued on March 13, 1964, to go into effect as of March 25, 1964, until the National Assembly completed its assigned task of writing up the draft of the permanent constitution. The draft constitution was then submitted to the people in a referendum. Through the people's free will such a constitution is vested with the power to become the source of all powers. The government drew up that provisional constitution, which was promulgated by the president of the Republic through a proclamation.

The provisional constitution is not drawn up in the same manner as the permanent constitution, that is, by convention or a constitutional referendum. Rather, the provisional constitution is drawn up by the ruling power alone. Because of temporary and exceptional circumstances, therefore, the 1964 Provisional Constitution was promulgated by presidential decree. The elimination of such circumstances would ultimately lead to the abolition of the provisional constitution.

The 1956 Constitution was the only permanent constitution during the period prior to the promulgation of the 1971 Constitution, the second permanent constitution in the revolution's era. Although the 1956 Constitution was in effect for a short while, it was never meant to be provisional.

Actions before the Writing of the 1971 Constitution

According to the Provisional Constitution of 1964, a Preparatory Committee was formed to write the draft of the permanent constitution. It started work on June 2, 1966, by studying the 1964 constitution to detect any flaws. It revised the national charter drawn up in 1962 to extract from it the principles codified in the provisional constitution, prepared research and comparative studies on the basic principles contained in various constitutions throughout the world, and compiled relevant reference materials to facilitate the task of writing up the blueprint of the draft constitution. On February 11, 1967, the committee started to listen to the views of various social groups. Those open sessions were held until the end of May 1967 when the committee completed the blueprint of the draft constitution. The conditions during the aggression of June 5, 1967, however, prevented the achievement of this vitally important work. Consequently, the National Assembly was unable to ratify the draft constitution, and it was never sent to the people by referendum.

On May 2, 1968, a popular referendum was held on the March 30 declaration that stipulated that a permanent constitution should be written, to be voted upon by popular referendum following the elimination of all traces of the aggression. This was followed immediately by elections of members to the newly formed National Assembly as well as by presidential elections.

The March 30, 1968, declaration, though endorsed by the people, could not be considered a constitutional document. It amounted to no more than a work program offered by the ruling authority to dilute the people's dissatisfaction with the political situation at that time. In other words, the declaration was but a political commitment on the part of the government, containing principles and rulings to be observed in its future policy. In that respect it was more or less similar to a statement by the government submitted to Parliament. Any deviation from it would not constitute a constitutional contravention, though the government was not absolved of its political responsibility.

335

The Methodology by which the 1971 Constitution Was Drafted

After he assumed the presidency, Anwar Sadat called on the Egyptian National Assembly (May 20, 1971) to draw up the basic principles for the Constitution of the Arab Republic of Egypt. Thereafter the assembly formed a Preparatory Committee composed of several members who sought the advice of religious leaders, the judiciary, scholars, public opinion experts, and university professors. The committee also considered the opinions and suggestions voiced by the populace. It finally worked out a draft of eighty principles upon which the Constitution was to be based. The draft was submitted to the National Assembly and was endorsed during the July 22, 1971, session.

When the General National Congress of the Arab Socialist Union held its first meeting after the reelection of its members on July 23, 1971, the draft Constitution was submitted and approved. Furthermore the Congress entrusted the central committee of the Arab Socialist Union with the task of putting those principles into the form of specific articles. The central committee selected an ad hoc committee from among its members to write up the Constitution according to the general principles approved by the General National Congress. When the ad hoc committee completed the revision and phrasing of the constitutional articles, it submitted the final draft to the central committee on September 8. The latter ratified it after having introduced amendments to several of its provisions. These amendments included articles 41, 87, 118, and 156, pertaining to the private freedoms of individuals, the membership of the People's Assembly, the final account of the state, and the powers of the Council of Ministers.

The central committee had endorsed the draft Constitution before submitting it to a popular referendum. The matter was never submitted to the General National Congress, considered the supreme authority within the Arab Socialist Union at that time. Rather, the committee was satisfied that the congress had earlier endorsed the principles of the Constitution and had assigned the committee responsibility to cast those principles into specific articles.

The draft Constitution contained this provision in article 193: "The Constitution shall be in force as from the date of announcing the approval of the people in this respect in the referendum." Following the approval of the draft Constitution by the central committee on September 8, 1971, the draft was submitted to a popular referendum on September 11. After approval of a permanent constitution was announced, the president issued the Constitution and ordered that both the proclamation and the promulgation documents be deposited with the People's Assembly.

The 1971 Constitution clearly was issued by popular referendum, after which its draft was drawn up by the people's representatives, whether members of the People's Assembly or the Arab Socialist Union. In other words, the people drew up the constitutional document, either through their representatives during the writing stages or through their own approval and ratification.

Reasons for Expediting the Writing of the 1971 Constitution

According to the declaration of March 30, 1968, the permanent Egyptian Constitution was expected to be promulgated after the nation succeeded in eliminating the vestiges of the aggression. Egypt's experiences following the death of President Gamal A. Nasser on September 28, 1970, however, instigated corrective measures, including a hastened effort to write a permanent constitution that would preserve national unity and the sovereignty of the law and enhance the Egyptian citizens' belief in socialism and democracy.

The writing of the Constitution was expedited by the establishment of the Federation of Arab Republics (embracing Egypt, Syria, and Libya), the basic provisions of which were drawn up in Bengazi on April 17, 1971. The republics of the federation were committed, according to the provisions of that constitution, to make their respective constitutions conform to the federal constitution for which a referendum was scheduled to be held on September 1, 1971.

The writing was accelerated by the desire to turn from revolutionary legitimacy to constitutional legitimacy and to provide justification and self-expression for the new system. The revolution of July 23, 1952, had, since its beginning, espoused six principles, namely, eradication of imperialism and its stooges, elimination of feudalism, extermination of monopoly and of capital's control over the ruling authorities, establishment of a strong national army, establishment of social justice, and establishment of a sound democratic life.

Although the revolution focused its efforts during the pre-May-1971 phase on achieving the first five goals, those goals were reached at the expense of the freedom and security of the Egyptian citizen. The objective was, therefore, to institute safeguards that would guarantee the Egyptian citizen enjoyment of rights and freedoms through the sixth principle of the revolution, namely, the establishment of a sound democratic life.

President Sadat had put this fact on record in his October paper when he said: "Although the revolution had achieved much in the realm of social freedom, we, in all honesty, have to admit that political freedom was not achieved in a manner satisfactory to the people.

337

Restrictions and procedures were so numerous that the social transformation procedures deviated from their original humane goal and were exploited to serve personal rancor or the interests of certain groups."

That was the reason he had supported, since becoming president, the principles of the sovereignty of law and the abolition of detention camps and of sequestration. When President Sadat assumed control of the government in 1970, the Egyptian people had already been shattered by the 1967 defeat, by worsening economic conditions, and by their diminishing leadership in the Arab world. It was necessary to strengthen the people's identification with their political leadership.

Establishing democracy and constitutional legitimacy would legitimize the regime and accurately express the true sentiments and aspirations of the populace. To affirm and codify the principles in a new constitution was the only means to assure the people of the sincere intentions of the political leadership. President Sadat, therefore, took his initial steps toward the establishment of democracy by issuing the 1971 Constitution. In his statement before the National Assembly on May 20, 1971, he called for the speedy establishment of a permanent constitution and gave thirteen principles on which that constitution should be based. It was clearly evident, after a close look at these principles, that they had stemmed from the overpowering desire to put into effect the sixth principle of the revolution, namely, establishment of democracy. Those principles also affirmed the socialist gains that constituted a legacy fixed indelibly in the mind of the Egyptian citizen during the preconstitution era. Relinquishing that legacy was not easy.

Since the fundamental objective of the constitution was the achievement of democracy, the 1971 Constitution incorporated that objective and, for the first time in the history of Egyptian constitutions, contained a special part on the sovereignty of law. The following were stipulations: the sovereignty of law is the basis of the state regime; the state is subject to the law; the right to litigation is an inalienable right for all; the judicature shall be prohibited from exercising control over any act of administrative decision; and any person arrested or detained shall be informed forthwith of the reasons for his arrest or his detention and shall have the right to communicate with whomever he sees fit, to inform them of what has taken place, and to ask for help. (He must also be notified, as soon as possible, of the charges directed against him, and he may lodge a complaint to the courts against any measure taken to restrict his personal freedom.) The Constitution also stipulated for the first time that any assault on individual freedom or on the privacy of citizens or any other public rights and liberties guaranteed by the Constitution and the law shall be considered a crime. The state shall grant a fair compensation to the victim of such an assault.

The Individual Freedom Committee had to grapple with two basic lines of thought; the first was that the Constitution provide, in detail, for the freedoms and rights of citizens; the second was that guarantees be laid down for the exercise of such rights. In both, the objective was to heighten awareness of safeguards for freedoms in a manner that would discourage all means used in the past to encroach upon those freedoms.

Political Components Underlying the 1971 Constitution

In analyzing the articles of the Constitution, before the Constitution's amendment in 1980, we can distinguish the following political elements that permeated that Constitution:

• The rights and freedoms of the individual were affirmed and their protection guaranteed. The Constitution's third part provided for public freedom, rights, and duties. It was primarily concerned with regulating such rights and freedoms. All public rights and freedoms are subject to the basic principle of equality, whether the freedom of an individual, the freedom of opinion, or the freedom to hold meetings. To safeguard these freedoms, one of the main objectives of the Constitution was to affirm the sovereignty of the law and ensure guarantees for individuals—bearing in mind that the sovereignty of law not only is required for the freedom of the individual but also is the only basis for the legitimacy of power.

• The Arab Socialist Union system was adopted. At the beginning of the July 1952 revolution, public opinion was ready to accept the decision taken on January 16, 1953, to dissolve political parties. People were aware that parties had dismally failed to achieve national aspirations and to realize social justice. Interparty conflict also had disfigured the images of some political leaders, giving the public the impression that those leaders represented corruption, bribery, and nepotism. Democracy was never put into effect because the minority parties monopolized the government most of the time. Likewise, when the majority party exercised the upper hand the few times it had access to power, it stifled the minority's dissenting views.

It was therefore expected that when the transition period had expired and the 1956 Constitution had been promulgated, political parties would be banned. Nevertheless, the 1956 Constitution created the National Union to serve as the only political party and to become part of the Egyptian constitutional system. Egypt then lived under a totalitarian regime, later evident in the Arab Socialist Union. The pretext given for the totalitarian regime was that parties led to dissension that in turn threatened the newly born independence of the state. Also the development problems faced by the country required a pooling of efforts not achievable under a multiparty system.

The revolution's adherence to the totalitarian regime and the one-party system became a fait accompli. It was impossible at the beginning of Sadat's presidency to renounce that system. Therefore the 1971 Constitution upheld that legacy and provided in article 5 that the Arab Socialist Union was the political party representing the alliance of working people. This provision was affirmed by law 34 (1972), regarding national unity, that prohibited the establishment of political organizations outside the framework of the Arab Socialist Union.

• The republican system became the foundation of the regime. On June 18, 1953, the republic in Egypt was officially proclaimed following the decision by the committee formed in 1953 to draw up a new draft constitution that the monarchy was no longer suitable for Egypt and that the republican system with its advantages was a constitutional and a national exigency. The people were to be considered not only the source of power; they should be also the source of reference. The revolution's constitutions also affirmed the republican system. The 1971 Constitution laid down guarantees for the protection of that system and blocked any venue for the return of the monarchy. Severe penalties against disloyalty were also provided.

• A semiparliamentary democracy, or parliamentary system with some democratic features, was adopted. The Constitution incorporated the popular referendum, and thus the people would actually participate directly in the exercise of power. This provision was effected under the overpowering pressure of public opinion for the electorate to play an effective role in directing the government.

• Some features of the presidential system were incorporated into the semiparliamentary system. The Constitution applied the most important characteristics of the parliamentary system: it physically separated the office of the president of state from that of the prime minister. It adopted a system that had a council of ministers, the most important element of the parliamentary system, and also a separation of powers with cooperation. It made the ministers accountable to the People's Assembly, though it laid down a special rule governing the responsibility of the prime minister and granting members of the People's Assembly the right to question members of the executive department to hold an investigation and the right to offer public debate on issues. The government, however, had the right to interfere in parliamentary work by inviting the assembly to convene a meeting and to dismiss the ordinary parliamentary meeting. The government was also granted the right to dissolve the People's Assembly.

Although the Constitution had adopted the fundamentals of the parliamentary system, it did not totally disregard features of the presidential system. It had granted the president of the Republic many powers that he could exercise directly, without going through his ministers, as stipulated by the parliamentary system rules. The presidential system was also evident in the way the cabinet was organized. Article 127 granted the president of the Republic a large role in determining the responsibilities of the prime minister.

Amendments to the Constitution

These amendments are closely linked to the experience of Egypt after the Egyptian-Israeli Peace Treaty signed in Washington on March 26, 1979. They are linked also to the emergence of the multiparty ideology that had supplanted the one-party system (the totalitarian regime) represented by the Arab Socialist Union in 1976. The referendum approved by the people on April 19, 1979, contained certain fundamentals for the reorganization of the state.

On July 16, 1979, more than one-third of the People's Assembly members submitted three requests calling for amendment of the Constitution. On July 18, 1979, the assembly formed an ad hoc committee to look into the principle of the introduction of amendments and conditions stipulated in article 189 of the Constitution. The committee submitted its report on July 19, 1979, and the assembly decided to approve the amendment of several constitutional articles and the introduction of new ones in conformity with the text of the committee's report. It also decided to open a public debate on the articles to be amended. The committee was entrusted with the task of accumulating and studying the various suggestions made during the debate and giving a report in that respect.

The committee received several suggestions and viewpoints on the amendment of the Constitution and compiled a study on April 26–27, 1980. The People's Assembly discussed the amendments and ratified them on April 30, 1980. They were approved by the people in a referendum on May 22, 1980, and were in turn issued by the president and put into effect as of the date of the referendum results.

We mentioned earlier that these amendments included articles 1, 2, 4, 5, and 77, stipulating that the state is socialist-democratic, that the principles of Islamic jurisprudence are the main source of legislation, that the economic system is socialist-democratic, that the political system is based on the multiplicity of parties, and that the presidential term may be renewed any number of times.

The amendments added the Shoura Assembly and the press as a popular authority. A dispute about the formation of the Shoura Assembly and its powers erupted. Some held the view that the Shoura Assembly should be considered as a second legislative assembly alongside the People's Assembly and should be granted legislative jurisdiction; others contended that it should serve as a mere consultative assembly. The constitutional amendment chose the latter. A similar case applied to the press. Some considered it as an authority equal to the three known authorities; others believed that the provisions for the press were intended merely to realize the latter's independence and liberate it from any domination that would affect its loyalty and keep it from serving the people and looking after their objectives, principles, and values. The amendment, in its final form, stipulated that "the press is an independent popular authority."

The provision about the multiplicity of parties was a fundamental issue that mirrored the prevailing conditions prior to the amendment of the Constitution. Because of the misdeeds of the one-party system of the Arab Socialist Union, the consensus was that adopting the multiparty system would bring together citizens with a common belief in a certain ideology, cultivate popular leadership, spare the nation from the threats of class conflicts, and permit a peaceful change of governments. The paper on the development of the Arab Socialist Union submitted in August 1974 provided the appropriate opportunity to bring into the open the idea of multiple parties. Discussions ensued, and platforms emerged. In July 1975 the General National Congress of the Arab Socialist Union decided to endorse the idea of platforms on the condition that they be determined not through administrative decree but through actual practice and debate. Their natural development should not be restricted, and their course should be determined by practice. The Congress called for conditions under which diverse approaches would flourish and develop into permanent platforms. In March 1977 the Committee for the Future of Political Action was formed. It reported on the emergence of several platforms within the Arab Socialist Union, including the Democratic Socialist platform, the Socialist platform, and the Unionist Progressive platform. In the true sense of the word, those platforms did not represent parties. None of them boasted a specific ideology or a definite political philosophy or even advocated different views.

As a result the three platforms would be transformed into political parties that could develop the political will of the people and cement democratic principles. Law 40 (1977) was enacted for the organization of political parties. The first article stipulated that Egyptians have the right to form and join political parties.

In affirming the role of political parties and attempting to resolve a dispute (it was contended that Article 5 of the Constitution of 1971 for the organization of the Arab Socialist Union provided for the possibility of multiple parties), the constitutional amendment provided that the multiparty system would be the basis of democratic practice. This was followed by law 144 (1980) that amended the rulings of law 40.

The future of democracy and political parties in Egypt is irrevocably contingent on ethical practices, the opposition's curtailing force, and the balance between the opposition and the majority. A clear definition of the duties of both sides is indeed most essential.

Discussion

ROBERT GOLDWIN: The Constitution of Egypt contains so many unusual and striking features that I suggest we narrow our focus and
begin with one central point. This Constitution is unique among the
ones we are discussing because of its provisions having to do with
religion. It is the only one of those we will discuss that provides for
an established religion or an official religion. I suggest that we focus
on that characteristic of the Constitution since this will be our only
chance to explore the consequences of a constitution that explicitly
establishes an official religion. Dr. Saleh's paper provides the text of
the provision as recently amended: that Islam is the religion of the
state, Arabic is the official language, and Islamic jurisprudence is "*the*
principal source of legislation." "Before amendment, the provision
was that the principles of Islamic jurisprudence" are *a* principal source
of legislation." I therefore pose this question: What effect does such
a provision have on a constitution, not just on the document but on
the life of the people, on the political system, and on the character
of the nation?

IBRAHIM ALY SALEH: This question necessitates and emphasizes several other questions. In what direction is Egypt headed? Is it acceptable in modern times to allow for the mutual involvement of religion
and politics? How can this be acceptable in Egypt if all other constitutions separate religion and government? We now teach our students
that this provision must be in accordance with the wishes and opinions of the people governed. It is accepted that it must satisfy the
thoughts and wishes of the nation. One of the important characteristics of Egypt is that our religion is at the core of Egyptian nationality
and personality. Religion has built the Egyptian personality—both
Christianity and Islam.

DANIEL ELAZAR: The Egyptian Constitution of 1971, like most of the
other constitutions we have discussed, is a constitution marking the

end of the postwar generation. We should view it like the other constitutions of the 1970s as a statement of principles and patterns that emerged out of the crucible of experience of the post–World War II generation. In Egypt this was of particular significance because it was a generation of revolution against its own older regime. That is one of the reasons why the Constitution is so rich in the kinds of details that we may not see in other constitutions.

I would like to speak about how the Egyptian Constitution fits into a general pattern of what would conventionally be called the Middle East but may more appropriately be called the eastern Mediterranean and western Asia. The states there were constituted out of the old Ottoman Empire but were built around peoples whose ancient roots are such that the youngest of them as a people is essentially 1,000 years old. For thousands of years these peoples have persisted while boundaries and regimes and polities have come and gone, in contrast to the United States, in which the nation and its polity came into existence within the same generation, or Europe, where territorial states tried to create national states out of often diverse populations. Constitution making in Egypt was therefore somewhat different from constitution making in either the United States or Europe. The Egyptian Constitution reflects that difference, as do virtually all the other constitutions in the region.

Yesterday we discussed the Greek Constitution, in which the religious question is addressed by reference to the Greek Orthodox church as the prevailing religion. We may consider the Turkish situation, in which a radical effort was made to separate religion and the state fully, an effort that was substantially readjusted to reflect the realities of culture in the region where the two are so closely intertwined. And I will say a word or two about the Israeli example, which falls very much into the same category.

One of the ironies of the Middle East is that even peoples that think of themselves as far apart are part of the same regional family and function in the same general constitutional tradition. The pregnant terms describing Egypt as an Islamic state with Arabic as the official language and the principles of Islamic jurisprudence lead us in a direction worth pursuing with regard to every Middle Eastern constitution, each in its own way. This model could be described as the modern adaptation of a traditional constitution; indeed, that is what generally characterizes the constitutions of those states. They all rest on traditional constitutions in the really old-fashioned sense of the term. Whether it is Shari'a or Halakhah (Jewish law), the notion is that a fundamental constitutional law is inherited that must somehow be adapted to the needs and exigencies not only of a modern

345

state but of modern republicanism. Certain dilemmas arise in that adaptation.

In this region both Islam and Judaism are religions that are not churches; they are religions of law and institutions that are not confined to what in the West is considered the religious realm. That, of course, is why their traditional constitutions remain important and require adaptation to modernity despite the dilemmas involved in doing so. For example, under the older regimes minorities were granted certain autonomy as ethno-religious communities and their institutions were empowered to carry out certain functions. Modern states, however, all of them, deny that kind of autonomy to ethno-religious communities, and a dilemma is posed by the persistence of the minority communities. An effort is made to guarantee their autonomy in some spheres (personal status is the one that has usually survived in the region), but they are not granted the same autonomy in the civil spheres, where modern states have superseded their authority.

Israel, for example, has no established religion. Israel's Constitution consists of the Declaration of Independence and eight basic laws adopted by special majority. The original Knesset was elected as a constituent assembly but, in view of certain political realities, decided not to write a complete constitution but to assemble one piecemeal through the adoption of basic laws as consensus was reached subject by subject. Again, that was a response to the fact that they had to grapple with a strong constitutional tradition. The Israeli Declaration of Independence provides that Israel shall have no established religion, but the term "prevailing religion" would certainly apply to the Israeli situation. What Israel has done is to officially recognize individual religious communities and to provide them with government support. It is easy to become a recognized religious community with appropriate legal and institutional support. Of course, the Jewish majority (over 82 percent of the population) has somewhat special legal and institutional support.

Traditional Jewish jurisprudence includes civil as well as religious laws. In 1982, the Knesset determined to anchor the law of the state to Jewish sources rather than continue to rely on English common law. A formula had to be found that would do so in such a way as to satisfy both old nineteenth-century secularists and traditionalists. The result was to shift the basis of Israel's law from English precedents to the "principles of freedom, justice, equity, and peace of the heritage of Israel." Jewish case law goes back 2,500 years. Much of it has now been computerized, and one can use key words to find case decisions on a range of civil as well as religious issues. Thus there is a strong basis for the change. The formula was designed to satisfy everyone and offend no one. It is the same kind of problem we find in Egypt.

I would summarize by saying that the reason for the traditionalism of the region is partly the existence of peoples who have had their own laws and institutions since ancient times. But it is more than that. It is not simply making do with reality; it also reflects the serious questioning in many quarters—and Professor Saleh alludes to this in his paper about the religious revival in the late 1960s and subsequently in Egypt—as to whether the Western liberal way is the correct way to deal with the problems of human nature or whether even a modern state needs to have a religious basis for civic virtue, which must be considered somehow in the constitution.

CONSTANTINE TSATSOS: I have a question about the provision stating that Islam is the religion of the Egyptian state, that Arabic is its official language, and that the principle of Islamic jurisprudence is the principal source of legislation. This article reminds me of Article 28 of the Greek Constitution, in which the generally acknowledged rules of international law are applied and are therefore an integral part of domestic Greek law and prevail over any contrary provision in the law. That is, we created a corpus of laws that does not derive directly from the constituent power of the state; rather, the Constitution refers to international law. The question in Egypt is whether Islamic law prevails over other internal laws of Egypt. In Greece we employ international law, and we know what it says. If there is a Greek law opposed to international law, the Greek law has no precedence. Is this true in Egypt?

My second point concerns the term "prevailing religion." The Greek state is a secular state; it is not a religious state in any sense. The word "prevailing" in the Greek Constitution means only that the majority of the people, 97 percent, are Orthodox and that the church has some minor economic privileges. Article 13 provides that all known religions shall be free, that religious rites shall be performed unhindered, and that freedom of religious conscience is inviolable. The enjoyment of individual and civil rights does not depend on persons' religious beliefs. That is, we have a secular state, not a religious one.

MR. GOLDWIN: President Tsatsos, in your account of the writing of the Greek Constitution, you say that there is no way to understand the present Greek constitutional experience without starting with this characteristic of the Greek people: that religion is an essential part of the Greek character and has kept the Greeks a nation even when they were not a free state. I pose the question to you, and your response

347

will be a question to Mr. Saleh: Why does the Greek Constitution not establish an official religion and provide that all law should derive from the principles of the Greek Orthodox church?

PRESIDENT TSATSOS: When we drafted the Constitution, many members of the committee said that the provision of a prevailing religion made no sense from a juridical point of view. It was included as part of the continuing, long story of the Ottoman Empire, during which the church, having certain privileges, was able to maintain the national consciousness and to get certain freedoms accepted by the empire. It had nothing to do with the Greek Constitution. You must accept that every religion in Greece is completely free and equal. If you ask, What will prevail, Greek legislation or the gospel? my answer is that the gospel is not law for Greece. It is a religious belief; it has nothing to do with the law. The question is for the Egyptians: Is the Koran a part of legislation, yes or no? Does it prevail or not?

A. E. DICK HOWARD: I would like to sharpen the question of religion and the state by drawing a comparison between Egyptian and American practice. The First Amendment to the U.S. Constitution includes a religious freedom provision of two parts. One part forbids an establishment of religion, and the other protects the free exercise of religion. In the current state of American affairs, the free exercise principle is far more generally agreed and acted upon than the no establishment part. Most of the current controversies over church and state or religious matters invoke the establishment clause rather than the free exercise clause. I have in mind such quarrels as those over prayer in public schools and tuition tax credits for parents of children in church-related schools. This continues to be a very contentious area among American citizens because there is a lingering, indeed growing, notion among some people that some religious atmosphere, some generalized support of religion, is essential to maintaining ethics, civic virtue, perhaps patriotism throughout the country. This remains a battlefield in this country. The Egyptian and the American constitutions are similar to the extent that both prohibit coercion in religious practices, which is to say that both have a free exercise principle.

Practice obviously diverges in the two countries on the question of an establishment of religion. The question I raise therefore—and I hope it is not a parochial question—is whether it is logically possible to have a genuine noncoercion principle without something like a nonestablishment principle, however that may be applied in practice. I am not suggesting at all that a constitution can be viable if it departs

348

from the realities of a particular country. One of the realities of Egypt
is Islam, and the Egyptian Constitution must respond to that reality.
What does puzzle me a bit is whether the Egyptian Constitution can
have it both ways. Can it protect the citizen against coercion and at
the same time establish a religion that reaches secular law?

MICHAEL DECLERIS: From a comparative viewpoint, one can identify
many possible relationships between church and state, ranging from
a clear separation of religion and the state to a situation in which the
religious sphere prevails over the political system. In between, however, are a great variety of relationships. It is in this context that the
provisions addressing church and state in the Greek Constitution
should be understood.

First, those provisions have symbolic value for the reasons that
President Tsatsos has explained, but there is a great difference between having a prevailing religion and having a religious state. Under
the Egyptian Constitution a law may be unconstitutional if it is opposed to a principle of Islamic law, but in Greece the opposite would
be true. The provision in the Egyptian Constitution does not seem
strange to me, however, because even a secular state sets limits on
the power of the lawmaker. I am thinking about Germany, which is
a secular state. German law explicitly states that everyone's rights
have limits set by the prevailing moral law. In Greece we adopted
that rule of German law. By establishing the preponderance of Islamic
law, the Egyptians simply opted for a religious moral system.

LESLIE WOLF-PHILIPS: It is very difficult for me to decide whether
Islamic states fall into what I would call a family of constitutions. I
can think of Commonwealth constitutions, military constitutions,
Francophonic constitutions, and socialist constitutions. There are clearly
defined families of constitutions, and I have difficulty fitting the Islamic countries into such a family. I will describe what I see as the
problems; in doing so, I return to the questions posed by the chairman.

First, some countries that have large Islamic populations—for
example, Bangladesh and Turkey—have no Islamic provisions in their
constitutions. The Turkish Constitution says that Turkey is a secular
state. Albania, the Soviet Union, and China have large Moslem populations but, as far as I am aware, also do not have Islamic provisions
and, in fact, fall into the socialist family.

Second, if Islam provides a complete ideology, does it indicate
and, if not, should it not indicate, clear guidelines for distinctive
institutions? Is it not true that most constitutions of Islamic countries

have but one article on religion, similar to article 2 of the Egyptian Constitution? Pakistan and Iran have extensive sections concerned with Islam, but they are exceptions. Is it not true that although one might put Islamic states into one Islamic family, they are really quite conventional presidential or parliamentary systems? The two questions are, Can Islam be said to provide a complete ideology if it does not indicate distinctive Islamic political and social institutions? and, If Islam does present a complete ideology, why do secular states such as Turkey not accept that Islam should entail distinctive political and social institutions?

TERENCE MARSHALL: I want briefly to turn to the experience of the American Constitution and then come back to the question of Egypt. The problem of despotic rule, of course, is not alien to popular governments. It is possible to have popular governments and despotism at the same time. If so, how is it possible to prevent despotism in the name of the people, just as we may raise the question, how is it possible to prevent despotism in the name of feudal authority? *Federalist* No. 37 states the general purposes of the American founding in the construction of the constitutional design. Those purposes are to establish political stability and energetic or competent government and at the same time to establish conditions of political liberty under the conditions of popular government. These conditions are said to be somehow in conflict with each other, and the art of constitutional statecraft would be to resolve the conflicts in the best way possible.

One means to resolve such a conflict would be to create constitutionally economic conditions that could prevent despotic power exercised by any class, whether popular or feudal or other. The solution we find in the United States is the creation of a political economy by fragmenting interests and preventing class politics. We see this in the early policies of James Madison and Alexander Hamilton and in the early decisions of the U.S. Supreme Court concerning commerce questions. The point to be made about the fragmenting of interests in relation to the question of constitutional rights is that this would require a policy allowing equality of opportunity in the economy. But it might also require a policy of opposition to equality of results, which would bear on the issue of social rights versus civil rights.

The reason for encouraging equality of opportunity combined with decentralized and divided political power is that such equality encourages the formation of interest groups concerned with limited and specific objectives as opposed to mass political movements and the dangers they would pose. If, then, it were necessary to encourage equality of opportunity, it would also be necessary to oppose equality

350

of results, because a policy of equality of results obviously offers no incentive for the formation of interest groups. In the American context this suggests that constitutional statecraft requires maintaining the conditions of equality of opportunity but opposing equality of results. Obviously, there are problems in this. The conditions of equality of opportunity require some sort of starting line that allows people to advance themselves. Nonetheless, the distinction may be a reasonable one. This would be one means of preventing unequivocal domination by any power while preserving the independence of each of several powers and thus one constitutional means of preventing despotic government.

The problem in this kind of regime would be how to create coherent politics in such a context, and this would lead to the relationship between executive and legislative powers. In Egypt the problem concerns presidential power versus parliamentary power. The distinction between presidential and parliamentary governments does not apply to American government, of course. It is neither of the two, and when we examine the relationship between the two powers, we see how the aim of preventing despotic power would require a particular design in the separation of powers. It would require excluding simultaneous membership in two branches of government while allowing some intermixing of functions between the two to prevent one branch from monopolizing a domain of authority. It is useful to note that fragmenting economic interests prevents broad mass movements and the divisions in a community that such movements promote. This might provide a basis for a broad national consensus on the highest ends of the society, a consensus that might allow for some degree of coherent politics.

Egypt has a different problem in attempting to establish civil rights on the basis of socialism on the one hand and of religious provisions in the Constitution on the other. It would be interesting to know whether the protection of those civil rights depends on the chance factor of who is in power or whether there are structural conditions for preserving them. It would also be interesting to know whether the religious stipulation is a substitute for change in Egyptian politics and whether that stipulation is a sufficient means of overcoming it.

MR. SALEH: In response to Dr. Marshall I would say that in every political system there are several political forces—political parties, the press, public opinion, pressure groups, the army. If the people are trying to modernize, to establish a system of institutional government, it is important to keep in mind that political forces will defend any system.

I would say to President Tsatsos that when we amended our Constitution, the change did not at all mean that we were changing from a secular to a religious state. That must be understood. Only the second provision stipulates that Islamic jurisprudence is to be the principal source of legislation. What part of Islamic jurisprudence is to be taken as that principal source of legislation—the Koran, the Sunna, the saints and prophets? According to Islamic rules, there are different sources. If you do not find the rule you are looking for, it does not exist; you have to accept what is acceptable generally in the world. It is very difficult to translate into English what we mean by accepting the rules that are not included in Islamic jurisprudence. When we speak about Islam, we should not think of a fanatic system, because Islam is a well-known religion. When we speak about it, we must guard against these old and incorrect ideas.

If any international rule contradicts an internal provison of the Constitution, we cannot deny the international law. That is a rule we need not stipulate in our Constitution. Different systems and different leaders recognize international laws; French professors always say that General de Gaulle detests international institutions. No one can deny the obligation to obey laws that are obligatory for all members of the international community. I assure you that in Egypt this is considered an indisputable rule without being stipulated in our Constitution.

Finally, I would like to comment on the laws that regulate the situation of Christians. The Constitution provides that the rules of their religion must be applied, and Article 40 states that all citizens are equal before the law. They have equal public rights and duties, for instance, without discrimination on account of sex. Article 46 stipulates that the state shall guarantee freedom of belief and freedom to practice religious rites. In 1981 President Sadat organized a committee of leading religious people, including Christians, but within a month the Council of State decided that the decree by which he organized that committee was unconstitutional. It was therefore obligatory for the government and the president to put an end to that action. I myself believe that the system of checks and balances is a great guarantee of freedom and of the constitutionality of law, and in Egypt the Supreme Court now plays a very important role. In protecting civil and social rights, then, the judicial organ is a very important instrument.

8
The Making of the Venezuelan Constitution

Gustavo Planchart Manrique

The Venezuelan Constitution that has been in effect since January 23, 1961, is the twenty-fifth constitution of Venezuela. The first constitution, written at the dawn of Venezuela's independence in 1811, represented hardly more than a political desire of the Venezuelan people. Only seven or eight of the constitutions have been effective. Only four constitutions—those of 1830, 1864, 1881, and 1961—have lasted ten years or more. Six constitutions—those of 1811, 1830, 1858, 1864, 1947, and 1961—embodied either important constitutional conceptions or significant departures from what had gone before. All the others merely varied existing constitutions, either to accommodate the whims of the tyrant, *caudillo*, or dictator of the moment or to meet fleeting political expediencies.

This long constitutional experience influenced the writing of the present constitution. Some constitutional formulas and expressions have become traditions. No Venezuelan constitution since the first has been written without being influenced by its predecessors.

In addition, Venezuelan constitutions have always reflected foreign constitutions: the U.S. and the French, whose influences have been continuous; the Spanish Constitution of 1812; the Italian, on the writing of Venezuela's 1961 Constitution; and various Latin American constitutions which have greatly fostered the Venezuelan constitutional process.

Politics and the Constitution in Twentieth-Century Venezuela

The Dictators. The first thirty-five years of this century were characterized by the domination of two of the cruelest dictators in Venezuelan history: Cipriano Castro, from 1899 to 1908; and Juan Vicente Gomez, from 1908 until his death in 1935. Both were from the Andes in the southwest of Venezuela, they integrated that region into the rest of the nation. One might say their regimes represented an Andean conquest of Venezuela. Because they were more brutal, they "liquidated" the other regional *caudillos*. Such leaders had been present in Venezuela since—and perhaps as a result of—the (federal) civil war that bled and impoverished Venezuela between 1858 and 1863. Their victories over the regional *caudillos* ended almost fifty years of nearly constant civil wars—small and large—that oppressed Venezuela from 1858 to 1903. Gomez also created some state structures that have served as a basis for subsequent institutions, in particular those dealing with the organization of public finance and the role of the military.

The Lopez Contreras Period. When Gomez died he was provisionally succeeded by his minister of war and the navy, General Eleazar Lopez Contreras, who was elected president of the republic in 1936 for a seven-year period. He was expected to continue the dictatorial practices of his predecessor, but he did not: from the beginning, he sought a peaceful transition from the previous tyranny toward a democratic regime and a climate of tolerance, which would permit the evolution of democracy. We could characterize this as a "controlled" or, to borrow a term from the French professor Georges Burdeau, "governed" democracy, which allowed Congress, also in 1936, to promulgate a new constitution. That constitution did not break the tradition of earlier ones, as it retained previous constitutions' provisions for electing the president, senators, and deputies, provisions depriving illiterate members of the population of voting rights, restricting free expression of thought, and prohibiting Communist and anarchist propaganda.

The 1936 Constitution included for the first time, however, the equivalent of a declaration of rights, providing for social rights and work laws to "improve the condition of the laborer or worker." And most important, the new laws were put into practice. In 1937, the first labor law, which recognized the formation of unions, was enacted. At the same time the constitution reduced the presidential term from seven to five years. The reduction in the length of the term, in a strict legal sense, did not apply to President Lopez Contreras. To serve as an example, however, he accepted voluntarily a two-year reduction of his own term in office. The importance of this act was primarily psychological: he sought to demonstrate to the people the government's willingness to uphold the law and to support a rule of law (estado de derecho), or at least a willingness to evolve toward or to create such a rule.

In 1937, however, Lopez Contreras felt politically obliged to expel from the country a group of about seventy persons. The majority were young people under thirty-five who were accused of being Communists. Among them were two future presidents of the republic and others who would later become ministers, senators, and deputies; in fact, virtually all of them were to play a leading role in Venezuelan national politics. By 1939 the government had begun to allow their return, and by 1940 all of those expelled in 1937 had returned, forming, with different degrees of difficulty, various political groups. The government tolerated these groups, permitting them freedom of expression and thought and, in particular, criticism of the government. Until that time in twentieth-century Venezuela these freedoms had been unthinkable.

What was important in the Lopez Contreras period was not so much the changes made in the constitution, but the behavior of the government. The government's support of the new constitutional provisions for personal and political liberty was the biggest factor in the improvement of Venezuelan life and the political environment.

The Government of Isaias Medina. The Lopez Contreras period ended in 1941. Under the restricted and indirect electoral system mandated by the 1936 Constitution, the Congress elected to the presidency General Isaias Medina, who until then had been President Lopez's minister of war and the navy. The government of General Medina was characterized by an accelerated evolution toward democracy, further broadening the climate of liberty in Venezuela. Political opposition parties were formed and newspapers were founded, or those that already existed were utilized more widely to wage political campaigns—sometimes virulent ones—against the government. The climate was one of respect for human rights; the government took no political prisoners and persecuted no one for his political ideas. Union organizations multiplied: the majority of them were founded by the principal opposition party, Accion Democratica (AD or Democratic Action), which was made up of many of those who had been expelled by Lopez Contreras. The Communist party functioned (although not under the name) and even aligned itself with the government party organization for the municipal elections of 1944. This alignment led to the election of a congress that was entrusted with electing the president of the republic for the 1946–1951 period.

The Medina government instituted compulsory social security, enacted the first income tax law, reformed the Hydrocarbon Law, and

355

raised taxes on those foreign enterprises that mined Venezuelan petroleum. Also, the Medina presidency upheld the Venezuelan constitution of the time and made it a reality, especially insofar as it dealt with human rights. In short, Medina worked to solve rather than to create problems.

In 1944 and 1945 the Medina government itself promoted several small constitutional reforms, in order to reconcile the constitution with reality. It eliminated the ban on espousing Communist or anarchist doctrine, permitting the legalization of the Communist party. In addition, to reform the electoral system, the government established direct election of the Chamber of Deputies and allowed women to vote in municipal elections. It also enacted a technical reform, the so-called nationalization of justice, through which the states, as members of the Venezuelan federation, lost their power to designate the judges in their jurisdictions. That power was passed to the central authority or, as it was called in the constitution, the federal authority. Finally, in recognition of the economic and financial difficulties created by the Second World War the government authorized the president of the republic, with the approval of Congress, to exercise extraordinary power in matters concerning Venezuela's economic welfare. These reforms began what is known as the constitutional period in Venezuela, which would not end until fundamental reform of the constitution took place.

Government reforms in the electoral system provoked public debate, led by the opposition, concerning the direct vote for the election of president of the republic, the right of women to vote in all elections, and the prohibition of voting rights for illiterates, who at that time composed a majority of the population and even now form some 20 percent of it.

The reform nationalizing the judicial system raised the problem of the meaning of Venezuelan federal organization. Venezuela had long considered itself to be a federal state, but with the nationalization of judicial power, the last vestiges of federalism were lost. Thus, whoever proposed calling elections for a special constituent assembly must have understood that such a reform, dealing with such a fundamental aspect of the constitution, would require the approval of the original constituent authority, not just Congress and the legislative assemblies of the federal states.

These reforms of the constitution were promulgated on May 5, 1945. Scarcely five months later, on October 18, 1945, the government of General Medina, just six months short of the end of its term, was overthrown by an uprising of young officers of the Venezuelan army with the help of the principal opposition party, the AD. We have no reason to enter into a discussion here of the causes of that event or of the controversy over the political advancement or regression that it signified for Venezuela. The revolution of October 18 did not begin solely to make a structural change in the constitution, although such an aspiration existed and was important, at least to the civilians who participated in the coup.

The Rise of the Accion Democratica. The government resulting from the October coup was a junta with seven members, five civilian and two military. Rómulo Betancourt, a civilian and founder and leader of the AD party, presided. He had been the principal force in the opposition to the Lopez Contreras government as well, and many of his opposition party's principal members had been apprentice leaders in the opposition against Gomez and had endured both jail and exile. All the other civilian members of the junta were equally prominent members of the AD, except one who was an independent. This junta constituted a *de facto* government, assuming both executive and legislative powers.

In March 1946, the junta promulgated a statute for the election by direct vote of a National Constituent Assembly. This statute acknowledged universal suffrage for all Venezuelans: men and women, the illiterate, and all those eighteen years of age or older. It applied the voting system of proportional representation by party, utilizing the d'Hondt method.* Such a statute in and of itself constituted a true reform of constitutional principles (what Carl Schmit has called fundamental political decisions), which have remained part of Venezuela's constitutional order. At the same time the junta promulgated a provisional decree of guarantees acknowledging fundamental rights as embodied in the Constitution of 1936 and, with only slight variations, in the reform of 1945. This was to create a propitious climate for future constitutional decision making.

In the elections of October 1946 the AD party received 79.8 percent of the vote. Among the other three parties, Copei took 13 percent, and the URD (Union Republicana Democratica) and Communist parties about 4 percent each. Copei and the URD had been founded only a few months earlier, in contrast to the Communist party, which was,

---

*The method of proportional representation prescribed by the election law is a variation of the "highest average" formula invented by Victor d'Hondt, a Belgian university professor, in the nineteenth century. For additional information see Henry Wells, "The Conduct of Venezuelan Elections: Rules and Practice," in Howard R. Penniman, ed., *Venezuela at the Polls: The National Elections of 1978* (Washington, D.C.: American Enterprise Institute, 1980), pp. 30–55.

in some ways, the oldest of the parties participating in the process, even though it had not always used that name.

The National Constituent Assembly was installed on December 17, 1946, and immediately embarked upon its work, establishing itself not only as a constituent body (that is, a body entrusted with the formulation and approval of the constitution) but also as a legislative body. Six months after its installation, on July 5, 1947, the assembly approved and promulgated a new constitution. The period that began with the electoral statute of 1946 and that formally ended with the approval and promulgation of the Constitution of 1947 was the period of greatest intensity and evolution in twentieth-century Venezuelan constitutional history. This period gave birth to a new life for Venezuelan political parties and their struggle for power, and ideas about constitutional decisions were debated with a vigor and passion only fully understandable at the time. At that time, too, the government made fundamental political decisions about the structure of the constitution and not just about its technical details.

The government not only opened sessions of the National Constituent Assembly to the public, which is normal, but broadcast the sessions on the radio; and though this was before the days of the transistor radio, those broadcasts reached at least the principal cities, if not the countryside. The constitutional debates were disseminated to the most important cities and towns, with constant coverage by the print media, including journalistic debate about all the issues then under discussion.

The Constitution of 1947

The Constitution of 1947 can be distinguished from previous constitutions by its declaration of rights; besides affirming traditional individual rights which, in one form or another, had been affirmed in all foregoing Venezuelan constitutions, it also spelled out social rights, augmented the role of the state in the assurance of those rights, and introduced, for the first time in a Venezuelan constitution, the petition of *habeas corpus*. While this constitution recognized economic rights (property, free enterprise, business), at the same time it made them relative; one might say that it began the trend toward a welfare state, acknowledging an interventionist role for the government in the economy.

The 1947 Constitution also called for election reform, institutionalizing provisions contained in the electoral statute, which had served for the election of the National Constituent Assembly. The new constitution provided for universal, direct, and secret vote in all elections, without distinctions of sex or race or social status, or of educational background; it also called for a system of proportional vote counting for legislative bodies and a single term for the president of the republic. Likewise, following the custom in Venezuela, the presidential system was reaffirmed, and, as the constitution was modeled on the Latin American system, it was infused with some institutions from the parliamentary system, such as ministerial counterbalancing and a cabinet or council of ministers presided over by the president. The constitution required that the council of ministers approve all presidential acts—thereby accentuating presidential-parliamentary liberalism—and provided for the censure and removal of a minister with a two-thirds vote of the Chamber of Deputies. It instituted separation of powers among the legislative, executive, and judicial branches, as did the earlier constitutions, but clarified it by expressing that the branches must collaborate for the realization of the ends of the state. The constitution adopted the federal form but, in reality, this was just for appearances; the constitution was one of centralism, retaining only remnants of federalism.

The government approved the constitution, and decreed a new electoral statute based on the previous statute. On December 14, 1947, the president of the republic, the National Congress, the legislative assembly of the member states, and the municipal councils were elected. Once again, the candidates from Democratic Action won with just over 70 percent of the vote; Copei increased its share of the vote to over 20 percent; and URD garnered about 4 percent, just ahead of the Communist party. The new government was installed on April 19, 1948, and on November 24 of that same year it was overthrown in a bloodless military coup.

The new military government first imprisoned and later exiled principal members of the previous government; others fled the country; some sought asylum in embassies and later left for the exterior; some went directly into clandestine political activity; and others returned to organize the opposition to the ruling military regime. The coup prohibited the Democratic Action and Communist parties from functioning but allowed the other parties to do so. In 1952 the government called for new elections for a National Constituent Assembly under the principles of direct secret universal suffrage and proportional representation.

The government falsified the results of that election, however, giving itself a majority vote. URD, which had really won the election, and Copei both protested. URD did not accept the election results, and its leaders were expelled from the country. Copei opposed the election but considered it better to continue as a legal opposition force. Nevertheless, it abstained from joining the constituent assembly.

The Constitution of 1953

In 1953 a new constitution abandoned the model of 1947—except in its references to the electoral procedure—and returned to the 1936 model. The two constitutions differed particularly in their treatment of individual rights: the earlier government respected the constitution's declaration of rights and attempted to carry it out, whereas the military dictatorship that emerged from the coup in November 1948, saw the value of the constitution only in its external manifestation, that is, that a constitution gave the government an apparent respectability. The government's new constitution, though, with its transitory ordinances, placed restrictions on human rights, stripping all effectiveness from the declaration of rights contained in its text, especially regarding freedom of expression and guarantees against unwarranted imprisonment and arrest.

On January 23, 1958, the dictatorship fell in a military uprising supported by practically all sectors of the population—parties (clandestine and not), professions, merchants, the church, and the general population—with street demonstrations lasting three days. A *de facto* provisional government emerged, made up of three military persons and two civilians. The constitutional law of the government kept the Constitution of 1953 in force. And in May the junta promulgated a new electoral statute that retained the principles of all electoral laws since 1946 and called for elections of the president of the republic, the National Congress, legislative assemblies, and municipal councils. Peculiarly, however, the junta did not call for the election of a new National Constituent Assembly, as was traditional practice in Venezuela after a revolution. Rather, it called for election of the public powers, the governmental organs, provided for in the Constitution of 1953. Thus, it was the constitution promulgated by the overthrown dictatorship that was to reign in Venezuela until it was reformed by the enactment of still another constitution. That reform followed effectively the procedure established for constitutional reform, which was inspired by the procedure established for reforming the U.S. Constitution.

We must ask why, on January 23, 1958, as the dictatorship was overthrown, the government retained its constitution, instead of returning to the 1947 Constitution the dictatorship had abolished and supplanted. We also must ask why the new government called only for the organization of the public powers provided in the Constitution of 1953 and not for the creation of a Constituent Assembly.

Neither of these questions can be answered with certainty because the actors have not given any explanations. Thus we are able only to make reasonable conjectures. The members of the junta knew that the Constitution of 1947 had been debated bitterly; they knew that, in a certain sense, it reflected the opinion and the political will of only one party, Democratic Action. But Copei and URD, though still minority parties, over the years had grown in importance. Also the armed forces, important in the overthrow of the dictatorship, had been almost solely responsible for the 1948 overthrow of the government that had emerged from the Constitution of 1947. The members of the junta probably preferred to avoid, therefore, the problems and the controversy surrounding the Constitution of 1947, focusing instead on promoting national unity. Thus, they prudently retained the Constitution of 1953, despite its volatile origin.

The members of the junta could also have chosen to return to the Constitution of 1945, but that (in addition to being considered by Democratic Action as a personal attack) would also have been seen as a return to the system of restricted elections. This would have been a step backward, unacceptable to the immense majority of the country, if not the entire population.

The junta chose instead to retain the Constitution of 1953, which gave extensive powers to the executive. In a period of revolutionary transition and sociopolitical instability, this was an advantage, as demonstrated between 1959 and 1960. During that period the democratically elected government, in order to stay in power and to stand up to its many violent enemies, both of the left and of the right, found it necessary to use the extensive powers conferred on it by the 1953 Constitution. This advantage, however, seems like a rationalization or justification after the fact, since the decision was made in a very short period of time, scarcely hours under very turbulent circumstances. The people in the streets were in a state of joyous exultation; the barracks of the military police were stormed to set the prisoners free amidst the uncertainty of not knowing if part of the army would join them or resist.

All of this causes one to wonder whether the decision to maintain the 1953 Constitution was the result of intuition or rashness rather than rational thought. It could even have been the decision of the secretary of the junta, without the other members having been consulted.

The decision not to call for elections of a constituent assembly is simply explained. The junta and the political parties were interested in returning to an elected government and in doing away with the provisional government. If the junta had called elections for a constituent assembly, it would have first had to hold such elections and, then to wait while the assembly debated and approved a new constitution. Such a process could have taken two or three years and would have submitted the country to two successive elections, with their attendant costs and politicization of the national life. The junta preferred to call elections to elect the public powers who, in turn, shortly ended the functions of the junta and took on the problem of constitutional reform through the ordinary process established by the 1953 constitution.

Writing the Constitution of 1961

During the electoral campaign of 1958 a political agreement was reached that, in my opinion, was to have fundamental importance concerning the process of writing the Constitution of 1961. The three principal parties, AD, Copei, and URD, signed a pact in which they agreed that no matter who won the election the government formed would be a coalition of the three. This guaranteed the government an absolute majority in the Congress as well as vast political support that would permit it to confront political vicissitudes. AD again won the election, with nearly 50 percent of the vote; URD won approximately 33 percent and Copei 15 percent.

Bicameral Commission on Constitutional Reform. The National Congress was installed in January 1959, and the new government took office. On January 28, a few days after both the Senate and the Chamber of Deputies were installed, each chamber agreed to create a commission with the "mission of studying and drafting a new constitutional proposal." These elected commissions assembled on February 2 of that year and agreed to meet jointly as a commission, the Bicameral Commission on Constitutional Reform. The commission was composed of twenty-two members (eight from AD, four from Copei, four from URD, three from the Communist party, and three independents) and was presided over by Dr. Raul Leoni (AD), president of the Congress and of the Senate, and Dr. Rafael Caldera (Copei), president of the Chamber of Deputies. Each was later elected president of the republic for the periods 1964–1969 and 1969–1974, respectively. One of the independent members of the commission was Dr. Arturo Uslar Pietri, elected on the URD ballot, who had been a minister and chief political adviser in the regime of General Isaias Medina.

In this way, the Bicameral Commission on Constitutional Reform represented the gamut of national political opinion except for those who had supported the earlier dictatorial regime. The commission was dominated by persons between the ages of forty-five and sixty, with only three members between thirty and forty. The election of the commission was not controversial: its creation was proposed in each chamber on the same day (in the Senate by a member of AD and in the Chamber of Deputies by one from Copei, both of whom were elected members of the commission). Likewise, all of the members were elected by common accord on the same day, demonstrating the unity that, however brief, then existed in Venezuelan politics.

The cabinet was formed from the tripartite coalition of AD, URD, and Copei and was presided over by the president of the republic, Romulo Betancourt, who also had directed the government between the coup in October 1945 until April 1948. The absolute majority that the governing coalition enjoyed gave it security: it held nearly all the seats in Congress, permitting it to be generous to the Communist party, the only other party represented, and to the independents elected on the plank of each party. During the nearly two-year life of the commission some members were replaced, some temporarily, others unexpectedly; but they always were replaced by others who were from the same party or shared their political views.

The commission heard the opinions of specialists on certain specific points: regarding citizenship, two eminent professors of international law; regarding judicial organization and independence, members of the Supreme Court of Justice and professors of procedural law; on questions of city organization and administration in general, professors of administrative law; and regarding drafting the constitution, a philologist, a writer, and a professor. Also, the members responsible for each area consulted often with the executive. This spirit of unity, security, and compromise among the three principal parties continued throughout the creation, approval, and sanctioning of the Constitution of 1961.

From the first work session of the commission, each party expressed its opinions about the issues it considered most urgent: whether the Constitution of 1953 should be modified or replaced, since it was the constitution of the dictatorship; whether the Constitution of 1947 should serve as the blueprint from which the commission would work; and whether, as a method of work, the parties would raise the points on which they felt modification of the constitution should be introduced.

During the session on February 26, 1959, the third formal meeting of the commission and its second working session, an event took place that illustrates the political thought of the moment. The Communist party proposed that within thirty days the commission introduce the "necessary adaptations of technical or formal character to the 1947 Constitution, which achieve total consensus among all the political factions represented in the parliament, and the express abolition of the Constitution of 1953," and that this be the proposal presented to Congress. But the Communist party at the same time reserved its right to express openly in Congress, when such a proposal was to be debated by it, all of its views on the substantive reforms that should be made in order to preserve a public image of political harmony within the coalition.

Dr. Leoni, president of the commission (he was also president of the Congress, a prominent member of AD, party chief of the governmental coalition, and later, president of the republic), had stated that the propositions of the Communist party might provoke a philosophical discussion in Congress, the very thing that should be avoided. He argued that, in a public debate, the members of Congress could make a show of the same volatility, intransigence, and verbal violence that was demonstrated in 1947, reopening the wounds that the discussions in 1947 had produced in the parties. Dr. Leoni's intention was to keep the debate within the commission, where flexibility and the possibility for changes in position were greater than in public debates, and leave to Congress the discussion on technical details and the forms of drafting the constitution.

To a large extent, Dr. Leoni's wishes were carried out. The fundamental discussion of changes in the constitution took place within the commission, and the public congressional debate was primarily a debate about form and style. The consensus that the Constitution of 1947 should serve as a model for the new constitution revealed that, after twelve years of hot and impassioned discussion, the public still supported the political goal that served as the foundation of the 1947 Constitution: establishing a democratic state, with tendencies toward a welfare state. The members sought technical improvement, to polish the roughness in the 1947 Constitution. There also was some interest among the members in an eventual evolution of the welfare state to a so-called social state of law, a system derived from postwar German political thought.

Party Concerns. The Commission discussed first the issues of concern to each party.

URD. The first party to present its list of concerns was URD, in the session of March 3, 1959. The party chose four general areas of concern, and identified issues within those areas that they considered to be of particular importance. The URD's general areas of concern were: the rights and duties of citizens; the national economy; municipal power; legislative power and its relation to executive power.

Issues raised in the category of citizen's rights were: equality of participation in the military service; widening the guarantees of privacy in communication by telephone and telegraph; defining and widening guarantees of social security; establishing the principle that national education should be reconciled with the demands of the economic development of the country through the regionalization and diversification of instruction; imposing on the government the duty of founding technical schools and handicraft centers in all the cities and towns of the country. Issues raised by the URD regarding the national economy suggested giving wide guarantees to foreign investment in those areas not effectively developed by Venezuelans and developing a heavy or basic industry to be controlled by Venezuelans. Regarding municipal organization the URD suggested recognizing the autonomy of each municipality, setting aside a percentage of the budget of the state to be distributed among the municipalities, and augmenting the taxation power of the municipalities. Issues in the fourth group, concerning legislative and executive power, suggested: that regulations affecting the relations between executive and legislative offices be made more flexible; that a distinction be made between the functions of the Senate and those of the Chamber of Deputies; that "functional senators" (senators not elected by the member states of the federation but by groups that carry out functions in the country) form part of the Senate; that the commissions of the chambers of Congress receive constitutional recognition as organs of the legislative power, with power to investigate and summon ministers; and that the system of ministerial reports, serving no real purpose, be eliminated.

Copei. Copei presented its issues for discussion in the session of March 5, 1959. It proposed: the adoption of the *juicio de amparo*, considered to be more extensive than *habeas corpus*; the introduction of a right to housing; a prohibition on establishing hindrances on Venezuelans reentering the country; and the recognition of political parties as more than a simple derivation of the freedom of association. With regard to judicial power, Copei raised the issue of establishing a means for guaranteeing its independence. Concerning legislative power, it proposed that reelection of the president of the republic be prohibited and that ministers be allowed to delegate constitutional or legal functions to subordinate officials. Regarding constitutional reform, it suggested adopting a more rigid system, in particular one that would distinguish between constitutional reform and constitutional amendments.

Communist party. The Communist party made its presentation on March 10, 1959. Its proposals regarding citizens' rights included: increasing penalties for crimes of embezzlement and for abolition of the Constitution during a coup; enforcing the rights of individual members of political, social, economic, and cultural groups; that the right of association and the right to unionize be established separately, as distinctive rights; that foreign investment be limited in those areas that could be exploited by the state, and that the state be obligated to establish a heavy industry; that any suspension of guarantees be delegated to the legislative power upon proposition by the president of the republic with his council of ministers. In municipal matters, it supported municipal autonomy. Regarding legislative power, it proposed a unicameral system and greater participation by the legislature in the direction, orientation, and practice of international politics (for example, submission to the legislature of designations of chiefs of the diplomatic missions for its approval). Regarding federal organization, it suggested that the people of each federated state elect a governor by direct, secret, and universal vote. Last, it proposed establishing the office of vice-president of the republic, a position not provided for in the Constitution of Venezuela since 1922.

In the following session, some independents proposed eliminating the legislative assemblies of the federated states. This would, however, have been equivalent to erasing what little federalism remained, and still remains, in the Venezuelan Constitution. Another proposal, which would have eliminated the word "federation" from the text of the constitution, immediately produced a discussion of federalism that lasted through the following session. The century-old arguments heard throughout Venezuela's history—whether evils derive from federalism or from centralism, and whether federalism signifies a tendency toward dispersion and disintegration—were repeated. Dr. Gonzalo Barrios, an important member of AD who was to become a candidate for the presidency of the republic (he is now president of the AD party and has been one of the most sagacious politicians of Venezuela in the last forty years), expressed something easily comprehensible to Venezuelans: that in Venezuela the word "federal" has an egalitarian and anti-oligarchical meaning, and that it is in that sense that "federation" should be understood. The problem is that, from 1859 to 1863, what was called a federal organization in Venezuela imposed a long and bloody war on its people. Although the federal organization was always more an appearance than a reality, federalism came to be identified both with the high price in blood that was paid for it and with the great social mobility that has been interpreted as the triumph of social egalitarianism in Venezuela.

Thus, in one form or another, Venezuela has become attached to the word federation and to the vestiges of federal organization. For example, in 1953 Congress changed the name of the Venezuelan state from the United States of Venezuela to the Republic of Venezuela. When the effort to eliminate the country's characterization as "federal" was made, however, the only heated debate of that Congress resulted, and the word federation was left indefinitely in the constitution. In 1961 the commission again debated, only in different words, the relative merits of federalism.

If we analyze the parties' initial proposals, leading up to the promulgation of the 1961 Constitution, we see that the revisions to the 1947 Constitution they suggested were primarily technical: the changes improved the constitution's provisions for problem-solving, without transforming or modifying its structure or altering the fundamental political principles that had formed it.

Problems and their Solutions. The parties found solutions to problems through rational debate; and most of the long debates were resolved by almost unanimous consensus. They debated the form of the constitution most often; when debating something on which no consensus could be reached, a subcommission of the commission recommended a compromise. (Dr. Jose Guillermo Andueza, a young professor of constitutional law and a member of the Copei party, was nearly always a member of these subcommissions.) Compromises usually were not difficult to reach because, in many cases, the parties' points were not incompatible and often differed only in nuance.

The commission debated the issue of human rights, for example, at great length, but concerned itself more with the form than with the content of the constitutional position. Copei's initial proposition— that the *juicio de amparo* (similar to a writ of *habeas corpus*) be adopted because it is broader than *habeas corpus*—was welcomed, but the commission established *habeas corpus* as a transitory provision of the constitution for immediate application while the provisions of *amparo* were drafted. It is noteworthy that a *ley de amparo* has not yet been enacted and that *habeas corpus* continues to apply; but other laws (for example, the Law of Administrative Procedures, the Organic Law of the Supreme Court of Justice, and the Tax Code) have introduced principles of *amparo*. The commission also welcomed the proposition of URD regarding equality of participation in the military services, perhaps because it was implicit in all the previous constitutions. The Constitution of 1961 reaffirms this equality.

The commission adopted a procedure dividing the several chapters of the constitution among its members, assigning to each of them reports that would result in proposals for discussion. (It is noteworthy that the members of the Communist party were assigned no reports and were not involved in the other reports.) The members then debated the constitutional topics, but in technical form, because they had already agreed upon the principles they would support. Let us look, nevertheless, at some problems to which the commission gave special consideration and at the solutions they found.

Venezuela and federalism. In light of the previous discussion about federalism in Venezuela, it may seem strange that the drafting commission gave much attention to the topic of federalism. The commission's discussion, however, did not center upon whether or not a Venezuelan federal regime should be established because the apparent consensus was that federalism in Venezuela was not convenient at that time or in the foreseeable future. The idea was not abandoned but was held out as a distant goal toward which to strive. It was Gonzalo Barrios who, intervening again, maintained that the federal form was an ideal toward which the Venezuelan state should move. The important thing was first to reconcile the centralist reality with an aspiration toward a federalist state. The commission found two formulas that seemed wise, making a concrete decision in favor of centralism but leaving to the ordinary legislator the power of promoting greater federalism. It authorized Congress to provide in the future for: 1) the direct election of governors of the federated states rather than by presidential appointment and 2) state authority on matters which, according to the constitution, are in the national scope or are under central power.

Nevertheless, the commission established safeguards that make it very difficult for these alternatives to occur. One of these safeguards is that it is necessary that the two chambers of Congress, senators and deputies, meet in a joint session, enter into discussion of the proposal, and pass the proposal with a two-thirds majority. It is not clear whether something like this can occur within the near or even foreseeable future, since the political structure is so highly centralized. No party that believes it can win the election for the executive power really supports the direct election of governors, just as Congress presumably would not trim its own authority in favor of the legislative assemblies of the states. The method by which the constitution declares the federal system the form of the Venezuelan state reveals the psychological division of Venezuela over this problem. In addition to the fact that the system, in theoretical purity, is not federal, there is the fact that Venezuelans refuse to abandon the historical significance of federalism in their country. The constitution declares the Republic of Venezuela to be "a Federal State in the terms consecrated by this Constitution," which is to recognize that it is a federal state in the planning stage, or in a very *sui generis* form. It must be noted that the 1961 Constitution is the first to use the wording just cited; previous and less candid constitutions called Venezuela a federal state, without clarification or qualification.

Municipal organization. The municipal organization of Venezuela was also the subject of long discussions and is addressed in one of the most innovative chapters of the Constitution of 1961. In order to understand why it is so innovative it is necessary also to understand a peculiarity of the historic-political evolution of Venezuela. It is not known what symbiosis of psychology, politics, and culture caused Venezuela to see, in municipal autonomy, a corollary of federalism. People who are familiar with federalist governments know that federalism and local autonomy do not necessarily go hand in hand and that some highly centralized states, such as England or France, have possessed or possess strong local governments. In Venezuela the traditional solution had been to leave the problem of municipal jurisdiction to the law. The Constitution of 1947, however, recognized the principle of municipal autonomy in its text, thus protecting it from the whim of ordinary legislation. The constitution of 1961 does the same, but whereas that of 1947 established a uniform system of municipal organization, the 1961 Constitution proposed a law to create diverse municipal regimes for each type of class or municipality, mindful of "the conditions of population, economic development, and other factors of importance." It is sad to say that the Organic Law of the Municipal Regime, which was drafted six years ago (sixteen years after the drafting of the constitution), took very limited advantage of this opening in the constitution.

The constitution, in effecting the division of jurisdiction among the national power, the states, and the municipalities, really makes a distinction only between the national power and the municipal power. The areas are scarce in which the states have jurisdiction, and the majority of them are subject to principles dictated by the national power, especially regarding taxation. In this area, the federated states are practically powerless. (Dr. Allan Brewer Carias has attempted to establish some power of taxation for the states. He also inspired the preparation of, and helped to draft the constitutions of the states of

369

Yaracuy and Zulia, which tend to serve as models for the other constitutions of the federated states of Venezuela.) In contrast, the power of taxation of the municipalities is considerable. The municipalities, at times, are wealthy due to their own taxes, whereas the states live only on the percentage (15 percent) of the national budget that is awarded to them through the constitution. Part of this "constitutionally situated" allocation, however, must be divided among the municipalities of each state.

The Senate. Another of the innovations of the constitution was the augmentation of the functions of the Senate. The Communist party, according to its theoretical tradition, had proposed a unicameral legislature, but the member states defeated the Communist proposal almost without discussion, retaining the bicameral system. In Venezuela constitutional tradition gave the Senate and the Chamber of Deputies almost equal authority, and URD saw from the beginning that, in order to continue bicameralism, it would be necessary to distinguish the Senate from the Chamber of Deputies, either through the form of election of each or by designating their specific authorities or both.

Concerning the elections of each body, the URD proposed that half of the Senate be elected through representation of interest groups: unions, employers' federations, universities, etc. This proposition was rejected quickly, which is strange, because Copei, which is the Democratic or Christian Social party, always has demonstrated, through doctrinaire principle, a form of corporatism. The commission's rejection of the URD proposal was due, in part, to the fact that it was probably unacceptable to AD (which was the predominant member of the coalition) and, in part, to the practical difficulties of carrying it out. The decision may equally have been due to the fact that an election of that form would constitute a weakening of the federal principle, taking from the Senate its character as the chamber representing the component states of the federation. There remained, nevertheless, a vestige of this proposition in the constitution of 1961, which stated that former constitutional presidents of Venezuela after 1936 were, *ex officio*, lifetime senators.

At the time of this decision, the only former constitutional president still living was General Eleazar Lopez Contreras, whom the AD government had exiled in 1945 after the October revolution; he had been subject to a trial by a special tribunal and condemned, unjustly, for pursuing personal enrichment to the detriment of the state. The adoption of this measure allowing Lopez Contreras's return therefore signalled AD's desire for national reconciliation.

In addition, the provision concerning the Senate permitted all future presidents, as their terms ended, to become lifetime senators. The specific functions of the senators were augmented in two areas: exterior relations, where they were given the power to authorize the appointment of the chiefs of permanent diplomatic missions; and the discussion of laws authorizing treaties and international conventions, were to be started in the Senate. Also, the Senate must authorize other appointments, such as the General Procurator of the Republic, and must approve any attempt to prosecute the president of the republic.

Separation of powers. The new constitution maintained the principle of separation of powers but, in accordance with the Constitution of 1947, it clarified the meaning of this principle by expressly stating that "each one of the branches of the Public Power has its own functions; but the organs which exercise power will collaborate among themselves for the realization of the ends of the state." We can interpret this as an inclination toward a flexible interpretation of powers or, going even further, toward a system of collaboration of powers with interdepartmental controls and functions. It has turned out to be more than was foreseen in the constitutional text.

This clarification of separation of powers brought with it greater congressional controls over the executive power. In Latin America, due generally to the period of *caudillos*, there always has been the belief that intergovernmental controls must be created to limit the power of the president of the republic. Many Latin American constitutions, among them Venezuela's, have adopted two institutions typical of the parliamentary system of government: the ministerial countersignature, by which the acts of the president of the republic, except for a very few, are required to be signed also by one or more ministers who have jurisdiction in the particular subject area; and a Council of Ministers (presided over by the president), with authority to rule on many of the acts of the president, such as regulating, promulgating, and vetoing laws, declaring the suspension of rights, and reestablishing rights.

Another institution of the parliamentary system, preserved by the drafting commission of the 1961 Constitution, recognizes the power of the Chamber of Deputies to censure a minister and to call for his removal if approved by two-thirds of the congressmen in the session. The chamber has, in fact, voted for the censure of several ministers in Venezuela, but never by the majority necessary to remove him.

The constitution also augmented the powers of investigation by the chambers and their permanent commissions, which had been reserved to bicameral commissions on an ad hoc basis. In addition, the ministers were given the right to speak in the chambers, as well as the duty to be interrogated by either chamber, through its commissions. Again, the discussions of the drafting commission centered more on form than on substance in the majority of cases.

Evident in all of the aforementioned proposals were the diminished power of the president of the republic and the increased control of Congress over his actions. The commission reinforced those changes in its drafting of the new constitution and later incorporated into it the president's right to veto legislation. Until 1947 the veto system was inspired by its counterpart in the United States, in which the president's veto of a law could be overridden only if Congress ratified the original text by a majority of two-thirds or more. The Constitution of 1947 changed the law to require only a simple majority. The commission of 1959 long debated the point, considering propositions ranging from the elimination of the veto for certain laws to a referendum in the case of a veto not accepted by Congress. Finally, the members reached a compromise between the position of the Constitution of 1947 and the traditional procedure: If the presidential veto is rejected by two-thirds of the members in a joint session of Congress, the rejection of the veto is final and the president must promulgate the law without further delay; if the veto is rejected by a majority of less than two-thirds, the president has the right to return the bill to Congress for new deliberation. If the veto is rejected a second time the president is obligated to promulgate the law, but if his argument is based on the unconstitutionality of the bill, he has the right to refer it to the Supreme Court of Justice which would rule on its constitutionality. The Supreme Court must make a decision within ten days and, if it does not the president must promulgate the law, regardless of what the Supreme Court may later decide.

All of these rules and controls clearly support the commission's decision to limit the constitutional powers of the executive in favor of the legislature. Nevertheless, they left extensive powers to the executive and in some areas even increased them; for example, the executive, with prior legislative authorization, may exercise extraordinary powers in economic and financial matters. A similar provision had appeared in the Constitution of 1945 and was incorporated into the Constitution of 1947 as well. The 1961 Constitution, however, simplified the wording but in so doing established the possibility of a broader interpretation of executive power than that in the 1947 Constitution.

Reelection of the president. A topic of extreme importance in relation to the president was whether he should be eligible for reelection and, if so, if he should be eligible to serve successive terms in office. The commission determined that a president could run for reelection but only after being out of office for at least two terms.

The armed forces. With respect to the mission and organization of the armed forces, the commission resolved, practically without debate, to eliminate an entire chapter of eleven articles that had been dedicated to the subject. The Constitution of 1961 included only four articles concerning the military within a more general chapter and reinstituted provisions of previous constitutions: the principle that the president is the *ex officio* commander in chief of the armed forces, and that the armed forces constitute an apolitical and obedient institution, organized to ensure the national defense. It added that another of their missions is to "insure the stability of the democratic institutions" as a reminder of the role the armed forces played in the overthrow of the dictatorship in 1958.

Relations between the Catholic Church and the state in Venezuela had been ruled by the principle of Ecclesiastical Patronage since 1834, when Venezuela declared itself inheritor of the same privileges and rights that the Spanish crown enjoyed in relation to the church: appointment of archbishops and bishops in the Venezuelan diocese, and the right to send representatives to the Venezuelan bishop synods. The Venezuelan Constitution of 1961 adopted the words of the 1947 Constitution on these points, recognizing at the same time the freedom of religious faith and of worship, and declaring the prohibition of all discrimination due to religious belief. The state nevertheless reserved to itself the right to inspect places of worship.

The judiciary system. One of the most debated topics in the constitution concerned judicial power, though not in regard to its functions, because in Venezuela, for many decades, the appeal based on unconstitutionality had been recognized as much by way of action as by way of exception. Venezuela was perhaps the pioneer in the appeal based on unconstitutionality through action; whereas in Europe it did not come into fashion until after World War I, in Venezuela it began at the end of the nineteenth century, although not fully developed that early. The fundamental problem of the commission was how to guarantee the independence of judicial power. For this it consulted the members of the Venezuelan Supreme Court of Justice and professors, and studied diverse existing systems in various countries. It was a subject that was not treated as a political point; all the members were in agreement on the principle of the independence of judicial power. In Venezuela, the U.S. system of appointing judges for life has never been favored. Venezuelan judges have traditionally served for the constitutional period, subject to the approval of the supreme court and its recommendations to the executive.

In order to achieve independence of the supreme court, the commission first established that the court's members be elected by the National Congress for nine years, and that the terms of one-third of them be renewed for three years. It was believed that in this way politics would not control the court; during each constitutional period, at least one-third of the court would be elected, and in no period would more than two-thirds be voted out of office. Thus was ensured the continuity and equilibrium of its composition.

At the same time, the requirement of stability among the judges was proclaimed as another principle. Imitating France and Italy, and following that which already had been done in the Constitution of 1947, the commission recognized that a Council of the Judicature should be created. Its composition and functions would be left for a later law, but it was established that the purpose of the council was to ensure the independence of the judicial power and to guarantee the benefits of judicial tenure for the judges. Yet, it did not wish to enter into the details of the organization, leaving that to ordinary legislation.

In judicial matters the commission recognized the equal constitutional stature of the litigious-administrative jurisdiction, and also provided for recourse against illegal administrative acts and for reparation to persons damaged by administrative activity. But even more important, it recognized the rights of citizens to reestablish the "personal, legal situation distorted by the administrative activity," proposing guarantees for individuals whose rights had been injured by the activity of the administration.

Human rights. An important evolution in the guarantee of human rights in the Constitution of 1961 was the transformation of the functions of the General Public Prosecutor of the Republic. In the earlier constitutions the public prosecutor's primary function was to exercise public retribution against those who had committed crimes. In contrast, the Constitution of 1961 makes the general public prosecutor a type of ombudsman, placing him in charge of "ensuring respect for the rights and guarantees of the Constitution" and "ensuring the swiftness and smoothness of the administration of justice." Congress appoints the general public prosecutor, and he serves for five years. In the past few years it seems that these new functions of the general public prosecutor have acquired greater force, making his function as ombudsman more effective.

The economic rights of citizens. The commission paid great attention, as does the constitution, to property and economic rights, realizing their social function. The commission protected those economic rights by prohibiting confiscations of personal property and by establishing the guarantee that no one may have his land expropriated except for reasons of public utility or social interest, and then only with a prior judicial decision and payment of just indemnification. In none of these decisions, however, was the commission the innovator; the idea of limitations and restrictions through law has always appeared in the Venezuelan Constitution, although less directly. The 1961 Constitution simply clarified and strengthened the economic rights of the Venezuelan citizen.

In the area of freedom of industry and commerce the commission reaffirmed laws limiting these freedoms based upon social interest. Specifically, it expressed that "the economic system of the Republic will be founded upon principles of social justice that assure to all an existence worthy and beneficial to the community." With this in mind, the constitution established the principle that the state, although it protects private initiative, has the power "to plan, rationalize, and foster production, and to regulate the circulation, distribution, and consumption of wealth, in order to promote the economic development of the country." The state recognized for itself the role of supervisor and director of national economic progress and established in the constitution the principle of "state capitalism," where "the state will be able to reserve for itself determined industries, operations, or services of public interest, and will tend toward the creation and development of a basic heavy industry to be under its control."

All of these economic provisions received the support of the commission members. And in fact many of the provisions were already being carried out: during the dictatorship, the state had begun construction on the country's first large iron and steel plant and had denied foreign industry the right to construct petrochemical plants to make fertilizers. Of note, too, are the provisions of the 1961 Constitution facilitating nationalization of the petroleum industry and the iron mining industry.

The Constitution of 1961 contains few changes concerning citizens' rights and guarantees. Until 1947 the executive held the power to suspend rights and guarantees without control or intervention by the legislature. The Constitution of 1947 established the system under which the power to suspend rights and guarantees remained with the executive; but the decree stated that, although the suspension would be effective immediately, it was to be sent to the Congress for consideration, where it could be rejected, and in which case it would be without effect. The Constitution of 1961 retained the earlier system with only slight differences.

Of course, the suspension of guarantees can take place only if the peace of the republic is threatened or under grave circumstances affecting the social and economic life of the country. In this vein, the commission introduced in the constitution a provision allowing the executive to declare a state of emergency in case of interior or exterior conflict or when it is believed that one or the other will occur. This decree takes effect immediately as well, though the Congress still had the authority to reject it. A state of emergency might not cause the immediate suspension of rights and guarantees, but once declared, it can serve as the basis for such a suspension. This institution of an emergency procedure is, in a certain way, curious; it arises from the desire to avoid the use of the word war, since war is banished, by international law, in the charter of the United Nations.

The Constitution of 1947 already had made mention of the state of emergency as the authority of Congress, but the 1961 Constitution modified the system and put it under the authority of the executive, with legislative approval required. It can be said that the state of emergency is a euphemism for a state of war or what some countries call a state of alert.

It is interesting to observe that due to an old Venezuelan constitutional tradition the guarantee that prohibits the death penalty can never be suspended; nor can a prison sentence last for more than thirty years (in previous constitutions it was ten and twenty years). The same holds true for the prohibition of the application of torture and other unusual penalties.

Amending the constitution. The drafting commission created two distinct systems for amending the constitution. Since 1864, the system for modifying the constitution was based on that of the United States, requiring congressional approval and ratification by two-thirds of the legislative assemblies of the states; but in Venezuela each modification required the publication of an adapted text. This is why Venezuela can be said to have had twenty-five constitutions, when in reality, there have been nearer to eight. The commission devised a two-step system for amending the constitution: for significant modifications, either in importance or in size, the system requires approval of the Congress, followed by submission to a referendum. The utilization of this system gives origin to a new constitution, and its procedure is equivalent to what had been followed until 1961 for any modification, that is, approval by the Congress followed by ratification by two-thirds of the legislative assemblies of the states. But the innovation is that the text of the constitution is not rewritten; rather, the constitution is published with the amendments following the article to be amended, making reference to the number of amendments that have been made. (The Constitution of 1961 already has officially undergone two amendments, although, in my opinion, it is five, since the second amendment consists of parts that modify several articles of the constitution. Under the old system these amendments would have signified two new constitutions.)

I have left nearly until last a discussion of the preamble to the constitution. In Venezuela the traditional preamble was an invocation to God to protect the country. This custom was broken with the Constitution of 1947, which contained, along with the invocation, a preliminary declaration concentrating on the great characteristics of the philosophical-political foundations of the constitution. The 1961 Constitution retained this preamble, but simplified the wording and put greater emphasis on the ends that the state is proposing: "to protect and ennoble work; to protect human dignity, promote the general welfare and social security; to achieve equitable participation by all in the enjoyment of wealth, according to the principles of social justice, and to foment the development of the economy to the service of man; to maintain social and legal equality, without discrimination based on race, sex, creed, or social condition." With respect to international law, it recognized self-determination for all peoples and repudiated "war, conquest, and economic predominance as an instrument of international politics." This preamble reflects rather well the ideological content of the constitution.

Approval of the Constitution

Given the composition of the commission and its consensus, it was not surprising that the Congress approved the new constitution without much deliberation. It proposed some modifications, none of which changed the essence of the commission's proposal. The legislative assemblies all ratified the proposal once it was approved by Congress, without further discussions or clarifications.

Conclusion

The conclusion can be drawn that the formation of the Constitution of 1961 was not a traumatic process; in a certain way it was smooth, compared with the circumstances necessitating its creation. The country had just been through a cruel ten-year dictatorship, the result of dissent within the country in the years 1945–1948, and of the exacerbated fighting among the political parties in those years. The jailings, exiles, tortures, and deaths during the years of the dictatorship forced the politicians of the left and the center to understand the necessity for a united front and for greater flexibility and tolerance of each other. Thus, the discussion of the Constitution of 1961 was an internal discussion within the commission; it was a commission that reflected all the existing political tendencies and a coalition government that, in turn, reflected the opinions of the immense majority of the population. And although the Constitution of 1947 was attacked harshly in the commission's discussions, the passing of the years had created a certain consensus on the political idea which it embodied, making the adoption of the present constitution much less controversial.

Commentary

Allan R. Brewer-Carias

There is no doubt that the origin of the 1961 Venezuelan Constitution can be found in the democratic revolution of January 23, 1958, and the consequent establishment of certain rules encompassing the general political system and the activities of political parties. After 1958 the political parties took control of the political system in Venezuela. These were the same parties that favored democracy in the three-year period 1945–1948, but they now had a different attitude. The extreme interparty discord typical of the political process in the 1940s was now minimal. Without doubt the discord had caused the overthrow of President Rómulo Gallegos in 1948 by the same military officers who, three years earlier, had brought Rómulo Betancourt into the presidency. After the overthrow of Gallegos, the ten-year period of dictatorship (1948–1958) began. Betancourt himself said, when referring to the new regime beginning in 1958, that "inter-party discord was kept to a minimum, and in this way the new leaders revealed that they had learned the hard lesson the previous despotism taught all Venezuelans."[1]

Unmistakably, these new leaders had learned not only the hard lesson of despotism embodied in the dictatorship of General Marcos Pérez Jiménez but also an even better one: interparty discord taken to the extreme, as it was during 1945–1948, in no way allowed for an operative political system, since the rules of the game were not clear and permitted no real political participation. Therefore, in addition to the experience of dictatorship, what moved the new political leaders to install a new regime was the failure of the political system established in the mid-1940s, precisely because of this kind of extreme interparty discord, which kept the country from achieving political stability.

According to Juan Carlos Rey, "the main feature of the political party system of the 1940s was that the relations of the parties were not based on mutual respect, but on absolute enmity, each hoping to destroy the other."[2] This confirms the statement of Betancourt in 1958: "Venezuelan political parties, previously forced by tyranny to operate clandestinely, now agreed on concerted and joint actions in order to clear the path toward democratic order in Venezuela."[3]

The democratic revolution of 1958 had its roots in party coalition. Hence Ramón J. Velázquez, referring to a meeting held in New York City early in January 1958 that was attended by the chief political leaders of the country, remarked, "They [the political leaders] reviewed the political situation, analyzed the mistakes and the successes of the past, and finally accepted that the future belonged to them as long as they were able to understand that political power is the product of alliances and agreements between the different sectors which make up a country."[4]

The political pact that oriented the democratic process beginning in 1958 sought to eliminate the hegemony of any single party to the exclusion of others in the political process and to establish a system of competitive parties based on mutual respect and, above all, committed to the maintenance of the democratic regime. The formal expression of this political agreement was the Pact of Punto Fijo, signed on October 31, 1958, by the leaders of the three major democratic political parties in the country.[5] The 1961 Constitution can be said to be the direct consequence of this pact both in the organization of the state and in the operation of its political system.

The Pact of Punto Fijo concluded that, for the sake of unity and cooperation, "the responsibility of channeling public opinion towards the consolidation of democratic principles" would fall on the three most important political parties. It was an agreement of toleration whereby all three major parties pledged to respect the outcome of the forthcoming elections, which would ensure a democratic government because of the participation of the various political sectors. I here outline the three general principles that inspired the pact and the political commitments that were made.

First, the parties agreed to establish guidelines for their coexistence based on mutual respect, understanding, and cooperation. This agreement aimed at lowering the tensions between them and drawing together sectarian and partisan opposition, notwithstanding the autonomous organization of each party and their particular ideological characteristics. The guidelines for coexistence were to strengthen the implied unitary front and sought to extend the political truce, encourage objectivity in political debates, and eradicate interparty violence.

Second, this attempt at cooperation between the political forces had an immediate goal; to develop jointly the electoral process to be conducted in December 1958, so that the public powers elected in that process would adhere to the principles of democracy. Therefore, it was by coalition that democracy would be established once and for all.

Third, the pact promised an equitable representation of all sectors of society in the executive and legislative bodies. This promise was based on the hope that stability in the republic would be gained through a popular system of government. Hence the pact actually surpassed the original agreement of mutual respect and cooperation, since its objective would be participation of all sectors interested in establishing a new government. Indeed, this was achieved, not only through the structure of Betancourt's "coalition" administration in 1959, where each ministry included members of each of the three main political parties, but also through the establishment of the principle of proportional representation for minorities. Thus "equitableness" in the legislative bodies would be achieved through representation of all the sectors of society interested in the stability of the republic.

The pact, of course, was an agreement "of all the sectors of society interested in the stability of the republic." It omitted all sectors *not* interested in such stability, such as those representing Pérez-Jiménism, military conspiracy, and the Venezuelan Communist party, which had proved its lack of interest in republican stability through its five years of subversion.

No one who reads this document with care can fail to be startled by the fact that the political parties had actually learned a bitter lesson: extreme interparty discord, based on destroying one's opponent and on the hegemony of one party over the rest, had led to the destruction of the democratic system during the 1940s, which inevitably ended in dictatorship. The Pact of Punto Fijo formally expressed the will to prevent such a situation from happening ever again. It is certainly unusual to find a political pact of this sort proposed as the basis of a political system. This inspired Rey to call it "one of the most outstanding examples to be found in any political system for formalizing and institutionalizing the 'common rules of the game,' and simultaneously demonstrating the brilliant thinking of the elites of the Venezuelan political parties."[6] Consequently, it was through this pact that Venezuela's system of political parties was established on the basis of cooperation in the face of conflict to defend the system against its enemies: the forces of Pérez-Jiménism, on the one hand, and extreme leftists, on the other, both of whom were in conspiracy against the democratic values of the regime.

The Pact of Punto Fijo served as the basis for writing the 1961 Constitution. This assertion follows from the fact that the first task assigned to the senators and deputies elected in December 1958 (two months after the pact was signed) was to write a new constitution. The first anniversary of the 1958 revolution was celebrated on January 23, 1959, and only a few days later, on February 2, the Bicameral Commission for Constitutional Reform was already at work, operating as a bicameral body of the recently elected Congress.

Only twice in the constitutional history of Venezuela has a constitution been created not through a constituent assembly but rather through Congress; these were the 1936 and 1961 constitutions. In 1936, after the death of the dictator General Juan Vicente Gómez, the existing Congress was allowed to revise the constitution. This was possible because once General López Contreras had taken command, although the country went through a period of transition, it did not really break away from the previous political system, even though that system aimed at avoiding the extremes of revolution and despotism. Again in 1958, in spite of the complete rupture of the political process, the decision was not to convene a constituent assembly but to assign to the recently elected Congress the task of drafting and enacting a new constitution.

The Bicameral Commission for Constitutional Reform, therefore, began its sessions on February 2, 1959, and, during the course of its second meeting, on February 23, arrived at three basic agreements to serve as guidelines for drafting the document. First, the commission decided to take the 1947 Constitution as a model for its discussions—hence the similarities between the two constitutions—since that earlier text had been discussed at length by a previous constituent assembly in which all the political parties that signed the Pact of Punto Fijo had taken part. Second, it was agreed that the members of the commission and the political parties would clearly indicate the points they deemed incompatible with the 1947 Constitution. Finally, it was also agreed that points of discrepancy among the political parties would be specified throughout the process of constitutional reform.[7]

At the second session of its discussions, the commission reached a tacit agreement: constitutional reform would be carried out by the commission itself and would not be subject to discussion by the two congressional chambers when sent to them. This agreement was expressed formally in the commission's third session, on February 26, 1959.

The text of Proceeding No. 3 of the commission contains a communication from the Communist party. (Although the Communist party had, in fact, participated in the elections, it was not a party to the Pact of Punto Fijo.) The communication demonstrated the Communists' assent to the use of the 1947 Constitution as the foundation for the new document; they made it quite clear that they would press their views, which they believed should be included in all future discussions of the constitution being written. Senator Raúl Leoni, at that time president of the Senate, said that the communication "had left open the possibility for undertaking a philosophical discussion in the Chamber . . . *which is precisely what we wanted to avoid.*"[8] Avoiding *philosophical* discussions would maintain the existing unifying spirit of the bicameral commission.

Similarly, Rafael Caldera, at that time president of the Chamber of Deputies, proposed that the political parties should raise polemical issues for discussion in the commission but ought not to take stands "since this would lead to ideological divergence."[9] His proposal was intended to prevent the breakdown of debate and the impossibility of reaching agreement due to ideological differences. Therefore, the spirit of the Bicameral Commission for Constitutional Reform was consistent with the idea of unity, mainly because, being a legislative body elected as a result of a pact of unity, the commission was obliged to create a constitution that reflected and responded to that political pact.

This argument for unity is asserted in the Document of Motives, which explains the constitutional draft and through which we are able to follow, step by step, the work carried out by the commission in the drafting of our fundamental law. The document states, for instance:

> the Bicameral Commission has worked with a great spirit of friendly understanding, keeping before it, at all times, the purpose of writing a fundamental text *that does not represent partisan or sectarian points of view*, but on the contrary, presents the basic lines of the Nation's political life, *which may, and will, indeed, contain convergent thoughts and opinions of the vast majority*, and that could well represent the totality of opinion of the Venezuelan people.[10]

This reference in the Document of Motives to the bicameral commission's intention to draft a fundamental text with such features is yet further proof that the 1961 Constitution is the result of a prior political pact to settle on a political party system. The Document of Motives adds:

> This idea has made each and every one of the meetings an occasion to exchange points of view and to channel all efforts towards finding the *formulae of common acceptance*. The discussions have not been kept to the formal limitations of a parliamentary debate; but, beyond that, they can be char-

acterized as sincere and informal conversations, most of the time resulting in *unanimous decisions*.[11]

The Document of Motives, therefore, reveals the persevering interest of the bicameral commission in reaching formulas of consensus, as opposed to partisan or sectoral interests, and formulas consistent with the general lines of the country's political life. The Constitution, then, would not reflect any rigid political-ideological trends. Thus, the Document of Motives explains: "The [constitutional] text allows the common legislator certain flexibility to settle arguments and include modifications consistent with the needs and experiences of the Republic, but without having to resort to constitutional reform."[12]

This point is of the utmost importance, since it shows that the Constitution does not represent a partial point of view and that its provisions can be complemented by the ordinary legislator, who can adjust it to the concrete realities arising from the new experiences of republican life, without having to modify the whole text. Of course, the "flexibility" referred to in the Document of Motives does not mean that the 1961 Constitution is not rigid. The Constitution does specify special methods for amendment and general reform. But it contains no ideological rigidity concerning the possibilities for its development and adaptation through the political process.

This characterization of the 1961 Constitution, the result of the Pact of Punto Fijo, finds support in the opinions of all the men involved in its writing. I quote only three: Dr. Raúl Leoni, president of the bicameral commission; Dr. Rafael Caldera, vice-president of the commission; and Professor José Guillermo Andueza, secretary of the commission.

Leoni, president of Congress when the Constitution was enacted, in his speech before the chambers upon the celebration of the tenth anniversary of the Constitution, on January 23, 1971, said that, after January 23, 1958,

> the chaos existing in the government was eliminated and, logically, this led to the recovery of the sovereignty claimed for the creation of a new Fundamental Law. As the result of a *tacit pact* made by all the political forces, dictatorship was vanquished. A climate of harmony reigns in the Congress as reflected in the writing of the Constitution. And this environment of *compromise and conciliation* surpasses the purpose of the Drafting Commission. Hence, the result has been a reconciliation of ideologies, so often contradictory, aimed at a higher objective, which is the enforcement of a constitution as the instrument for a complete return to legality and

repeal of the impure constitutional rule that should have been abolished. . . .

The 1961 Constitution allows the evolution of Venezuelan society, without the counterpart of the painful sacrifice of freedom. More than a programmatic constitution, which we, its authors, were trying to avoid, it is a *flexible* Constitution, not in the terms provided by orthodox constitutionalists, but in the wider sense taught by semantics.[13]

Plainly, it was Leoni's belief that the Constitution was written in the spirit of unity, compromise, and conciliation that reigned on January 23, 1958, and that it is a *flexible* text, not rigid, thus permitting its future democratic development.

In his recent dissertation for the Congress on Latin American Thinking (sponsored during the celebration of the bicentennial of the liberator, Simon Bolivar, in June 1983), Caldera, former president of the republic, said:

Still fresh were the experiences of the era . . . between 1936 and 1945. . . . The failures, the disappointments, the perils, were undoubtedly a warning. And all this is reflected in a Constitution that contains a mixture of idealism and realism; it is ideal, clear and marked with inspiration; it is straightforward and holds a summary of the difficult experiences and failures suffered in the past.

He had expressed this same thought long before, at the time when the Constitution was enacted. In his speech given at the promulgation of the Constitution, on January 23, 1961, Caldera said:

We wanted a Constitution for all the people and by all the people: a Constitution *by all and for all Venezuelans*. In order to accomplish this, we had to encourage the spirit of *National Unity*, which characterized the Movement of January 23rd. Both in the Commission and in its debates, the spirit of optimism was maintained at all times—and various interventions therein gave testimony to this. The tolerable discrepancies were almost always overcome with a Venezuelan spirit, and those that logically persisted were not able to obscure the ample field of convergence.[14]

Years later, on the celebration of the fifteenth anniversary of the Constitution, Caldera summed up his argument in one phrase: "The basic assumption of the Constitution, lies in *Consensus*, in its general acceptance."[15]

In response to Caldera's remarks, Andueza said, "The spirit of the 23rd of January had, truthfully speaking, its best expression in the Fundamental Charter."[16] Andueza also emphasized the "spirit of January 23rd" as one of the environmental factors of strongest influence on some of the political decisions taken in writing the 1961 Constitution.[17]

In any case, a simple reading of the Pact of Punto Fijo and a quick glance at the political process that followed are enough to confirm that the 1961 Constitution is definitely a direct consequence of that pact. The Constitution was drafted according to the principles of unity and harmony expressed in the pact, with an eye to avoiding interparty discord, searching for conciliation between the parties, and establishing a flexible text, not committed to any specific ideology, that could form the basis for the republic in compliance with this spirit of unity within a democratic regime.

A general consideration of the 1961 Constitution, within the particular focus of the preceding political events, carries the conviction that the "spirit of January 23rd" had a direct effect upon the Constitution, particularly in four ways: the establishment of a democratic system; the enforcement of the democratic system; the reaction against dictatorial rule and abusive power; and the lack of restrictions on the economic and social framework.

The 1961 Constitution is a political pact, and, as such, it must have its own economic and social grounds. It will rule society politically, and every society has its own economic and social structure. The Constitution determines a political superstructure of democratic character, in which the institutions and their enforcement enshrine the reaction against absolute power.

Therefore, the political system in Venezuela has been built upon the experience of absolute power suffered in the past and the subsequent claim for democracy, which gave rise to specific political institutions. Hence it is the result of a compromise to establish a formal—but not rigid—regime to govern the economic and social system, and it is here that the compromise between the various political forces is evident.

Notes

1. Rómulo Betancourt, *La revolución democrática en Venezuela* (Documentos de gobierno presidido por Rómulo Betancourt 1959–1964) [The democratic revolution in Venezuela] [Documents of the Romulo Betancourt government 1959–1964], Imprenta Nacional (Caracas: 1968), vol. 1, p. 9.

2. Juan Carlos Rey, "El sistema de partidos venezolanos," in *Problemas socio-políticos de América Latina*, ["The Venezuelan party system"] in [Socio-

political problems of Latin America], Editorial Jurídica Venezolana (Caracas: 1980), p. 313.

3. Betancourt, *La revolución democrática*, p. 7.

4. Ramón J. Velázquez, "Aspectos de la evolución política de Venezuela en el último medio siglo," in Ramón J. Velázquez et al., *Venezuela moderna, Medio siglo de historia, 1926–1976* ["Aspects of the political evolution of Venezuela in the last half century"] in Ramon J. Velázquez et al. [Modern Venezuela: Half century of history 1926–1976], Fundación Eugenio Mendoza, Editorial Ariel (Caracas: 1979), p. 219.

5. Presidencia de la República, *Documentos que hicieron historia* (Siglo y medio de vida republicana 1810–1961) [Documents that make history] [A century and a half of Republican life, 1810–1961], Ediciones Conmemorativas del Sesquisentenario de la Independencia (Caracas: 1962), vol. 2, pp. 443–449.

6. Rey, "El sistema," p. 315.

7. *La Constitución de 1961 y la evolución constitucional de Venezuela* (Actas de la Comisión redactora del Proyecto) [The 1961 Constitution and the constitutional evolution of Venezuela] [Proceedings of the writing commission of the project], Ediciones del Congreso de la República (Caracas: 1971), vol. 1, p. 5.

8. Ibid., pp. 6–7.

9. Ibid., p. 8.

10. *Revista de la Facultad de Derecho*, Universidad Central de Venezuela (Caracas: 1961), no. 21, pp. 205ff.

11. Ibid., p. 205.

12. Ibid.

13. Raúl Leoni, *X aniversario de la Constitución de 1961* [Tenth Anniversary of the 1961 Constitution], Ediciones del Congreso de la República (Caracas: 1971), p. 11.

14. *Anuario de la Facultad de Derecho*, Universidad de los Andes, Mérida, no. 7, p. 7.

15. Rafael Caldera, *A los quince años de la Constitución venezolana* [On the Fifteenth Anniversary of the Constitution], Ediciones del Congreso de la República (Caracas: 1976), p. 11.

16. José Guillermo Andueza, "Rafael Caldera, constitucionalista," in *Estudios sobre la Constitución, Libro homenaje a Rafael Caldera* ["Rafael Caldera: Constitutionalist"] in [*Studies on the Constitution: An Homage to Rafael Caldera*], Universidad Central de Venezuela) (Caracas: 1979), vol. I, pp. xxvi–xxvii.

17. "Introducción a las actas," in *La Constitución de 1961 y la evolución constitucional de Venezuela*, vol. 1, p. xxiv.

Discussion

ROBERT GOLDWIN: One of the things we have not discussed with any attention is the role of the military in constitution making and in constitution breaking. Mr. Planchart's paper refers to a startling event in which a government in Venezuela was elected by a 70 percent majority and six months later was overthrown in a bloodless military coup. A dictatorship was then established, which lasted for ten years. That is a matter that is relevant to talking about constitutions, and it is not unique to Venezuela or to Latin America. What to do about the military is obviously an important constitutional consideration, in a broad sense, going beyond the constitutional text; it is a consideration in attempting to understand how a nation is constituted.

It is clear that the role of the military is not always harmful, that in many cases the military plays an essential, beneficial constitutional role. Examples of that are in Mr. Planchart's paper and in the experiences of many nations. I propose that we try to concentrate on this question, on the role of the military. What can and should be done about the role of the military in constitution making?

GUSTAVO PLANCHART MANRIQUE: To understand the *coup d'état* of November 24, 1948, which overthrew the regime of President Rómulo Gallegos, who had been elected by a vast majority a few months previously, we must understand the political climate in Venezuela beginning in 1935 on the death of General Juan Vicente Gómez. First, however, I should say that when I mention names of generals in this period, we should remember that they were not real generals. General Gómez and General Castro, who were the two presidents of Venezuela between 1899 and 1935, became generals only in the civil war; they were generals who crowned themselves; they *called* themselves generals. General Castro, for instance, was simply called Senator Castro between 1890 and 1899. General Gómez was a peasant who did not belong to the landholding oligarchy; he had become rich in the Andes region growing coffee. General Gómez proceeded to institutionalize the army. Until that time military people in Venezuela were basically civilians who suddenly took a machete or a gun and started to make a revolution. General Gómez dominated Venezuela for twenty-seven years with such power that he did away with all the other leaders. All the other rural leaders disappeared in skirmishes or were sent into exile.

When Gómez died, the Congress elected as his successor General Eleazar López Contreras, who had been with Gómez the whole time. Everyone imagined that he would continue Gómez's policies, but he was a person who tolerated other people's opinions. He was a liberal thinker who thought it necessary to lead Venezuela toward democracy. The Constitution that had been in effect was modified in 1936, and López Contreras's first gesture was to reduce his term in office from seven to five years.

The elected successor to López Contreras was General Isaías Medina Angarita, a military man trained in the military academy. General Medina was the first professional military man to govern Venezuela. He went much further in the liberalization of the regime. The Communist party operated (though under another name), and we saw the founding of the most important party of the country, the Democratic Action party.

One of the things that Medina did not do was to concern himself a great deal with the army, which was already an army of professionals. In October 1945 Democratic Action, along with younger members of the military, the captains of the army, initiated a *coup d'état* in which at least 150 people lost their lives and established a revolutionary junta headed by Rómulo Betancourt and other members of Democratic Action and the military. This government, which at the beginning found little opposition, began to encounter enormous opposition from other forces created in the country. Two new parties were created, the Social Christian party (COPEI) and the Democratic Republican Union (URD). The climate during these years was one of permanent agitation and unrest in the streets.

With the Constitution of 1947 the government allowed great freedom in the diffusion of radio programs; there were loudspeakers in the streets around the Congress, which led to tremendous unrest, and universal suffrage was introduced. Democratic Action won a tremendous victory in the National Assembly elections, but it proved to be completely intransigent and imposed what might be called a "party constitution," reflecting the thought of the Democratic Action party.

All of this takes us to the election of Gallegos, who had been a professor of philosophy and Venezuela's leading novelist. His books contributed something fundamental to the life of the country, but his government was not efficient. The economy fell into a state of depression, and the government appeared not to know how to rescue it. During the entire government of Gallegos there was enormous civil unrest. University strikes occurred with the intention of creating the necessary climate for the overthrow of the Democratic Action government, which took place on November 24, 1948, without resistance. The next day everything looked as if nothing had happened in the entire country.

From this brief historical survey, I would offer this comment on the role of the military in Venezuela. The military do not produce *coups d'état* in a vacuum. They become involved only when political and civil forces spur them to initiate a *coup d'état*. This is evident also in the overthrow of the dictatorship in 1958. The dictatorship had produced some modernization and progress in a material sense—for example, highways and houses built—but did not resolve any political problems. Instead of having elections in 1958, we had a plebiscite on support for the current government. This produced an opposition. For the first time the three principal opposition leaders signed an agreement of party unity to overthrow the government. The military initiated the movement to overthrow the government, but it failed, and the people both in and outside the parties began a continuous opposition to the regime, which, in twenty-three days, with a new military uprising, produced the bloodless fall of the government.

ALLAN BREWER-CARIAS: The democratic process has been a contemporary phenomenon in Venezuela. Although we have the least democratic tradition, we nevertheless have the longest continuous democratic period in Latin America. Our Constitution is therefore particularly important. Venezuela was the first country in Latin America to have a constitution after the liberation in 1811. It has the longest enduring constitution aside from Mexico's.

Venezuela is a country of paradoxes, as can be seen from the role of the military, but the military did not participate in the contemporary framing of constitutions in Venezuela, especially not that of 1961, which is currently in force. In 1947 the president was elected with over 60 percent of the votes but was overthrown a few months later. In 1958, as Dr. Planchart has pointed out, occurred the downfall of the military regime and the political experience of the hegemony of one party over another. At that time we managed to achieve a system of political parties different from the system that had previously existed. That is, the period of extreme right-wing power linked to the military came to an end. In 1958 a pact signed by the three major political parties established the basis for a democratic political system. Free elections took place for the first time in December 1958, and the Congress was elected by universal suffrage. A constitution was written reflecting this political pact to establish a new political system.

There is a regrettable tendency to identify Latin America with military regimes, but this is not the case in Venezuela. Constitutions and constitutional experiences in Latin America are very diverse, and the experience of Venezuela is distinguished from that of other Latin American countries in that the military played no role whatsoever in the Constitution of 1961. That does not mean that it has played no part in the political process since the War of Independence of 1811. In fact, generals led the movement for independence in Latin America against Spain, and there were bloody internal civil wars and wars between different leaders after that. But that the Constitution of 1961 was in no way influenced by the military is the great paradox of Venezuelan experience.

What, then, were the major influences on the framing of the Constitution? The only way I can explain them is institutionally, that is, with reference to the motives for the establishment of certain institutions. The reaction against dictatorship and absolute power pointed to a presidential system with democratic and free political parties and a system of checks and balances that would help avoid an abuse of power. We wanted to establish a political system having political parties with control over the system through participation and representing the true wishes of the people. In sum, we wished to prevent the abuse of absolute power connected with the military and to establish a system based on democratic pluralism. That is what we have had for the past twenty-five years, during which there has been no military interference. This is one reason for the democratic stability in Venezuela today.

MARK W. CANNON: I would like to comment on Robert Goldwin's question about the role of the military in constitutional experiences. Obviously, the military has not intervened in Venezuelan politics, and it did not play a role in the formation of the written Constitution. But I understood the question to refer to a broader kind of role in the informal constitutional system as against a role in either creating or responding to the written Constitution.

I believe that societies have an absolute, inherent fear of anarchy, which may be subconscious in most countries, and a desire to have some group or institution exercise ultimate decision making to ensure that basic, broad decisions are made peacefully instead of violently.

In more primitive societies decisions may be made by chieftains or village elders or theocratic groups. In many Asian societies consensus, tradition, and social mores determine rules of behavior, and people tend not to be too individualistic but to harmonize with the larger group. Until relatively recent historical times, we created kings who had ruling power. Some people in the United States even feel that we have moved to a government by judges.

There are probably Latin American countries, such as Peru, where there is a cyclical effort to achieve cohesion within the society. First, a democracy is created; then the democracy tends to run amok because of excessive selfishness, or demand, or lack of education and responsibility, or skyrocketing inflation, and the government commits itself to do things that are beyond its capability. Then there is a demand for more discipline, to which the military often responds. It is not primarily one man trying to get control of the country and become its new dictator. Sometimes, after discipline has been restored, the cycle begins again. Obviously, some dictatorships are very long, but some are temporary.

We can only speculate about why constitutional democracy worked in Venezuela, but these are at least some of the things that come to my mind. First, the fires of adversity had produced a remarkable group of leaders in Venezuela, and I think real major political and social change in a country requires people of extraordinary courage, talent, judgment, and wisdom. Very often these turn out to be older people who have lived a long time and have seen many things, like General Charles de Gaulle in France or Konrad Adenauer in Germany. At other times they may be younger people, as in Venezuela, who have had many experiences for their years. Most of the people that I knew in Venezuela who held government positions had risked their lives working in the underground, and that had built in them a depth of commitment that was very powerful.

Second, when these leaders were exiled, three of the future presidents of Venezuela went to Costa Rica and were schooled in a middle-class, democratic system. That helped inform them about what it was that they were to do, particularly since they had been Communist party organizers. This dimension is also important. These leaders were very realistic. They did not have the illusions of many academicians. They knew the enemy, they knew what they were dealing with, and they were very realistic in how they proceeded to establish constitutional democracy in Venezuela.

Third, there was a critical mass of people. Many of them had known each other from their college days, and many were graduates of the class of 1928 at the Central University in Caracas. These people had known one another and, even though some were members of antagonistic political parties, they understood one another.

Fourth, there was a substantial consensus for change. The excesses of the Pérez Jiménez dictatorship were on everyone's mind—the injuries done to people who were trying to work for democracy. This consensus for change among an elite group is often an important factor.

The fifth factor was the power of dispersion. Mr. Brewer Carias mentioned that Venezuelans were afraid to let the president have too much power. In Venezuela, however, the dispersion of power took the form of militant parties, each watching the others and fighting intensely for electoral votes.

A sixth factor was gaining control over the military and incorporating a military ideology. Venezuela differed from other countries in that the role of the military was to defend the constitutional democracy and very careful control was placed over the military leaders.

Seventh, Venezuela did have revenues. It is much easier for an existing government to succeed when it has money. In Venezuela the oil revenues were coming in, and the uses to which they were put were very visible: land reform, education, housing, roads, buildings. Even though these did not address the mass poverty of the country, there was hope because of a sense that things were changing.

Finally, the electoral system was very important. Each party felt that it had a chance of winning the presidency because of the winner-take-all election.

MR. GOLDWIN: Looking at the list of factors Mr. Cannon has just presented, one could think of countries where there has been adversity that produced leaders, exiles who have gone to free regimes, substantial consensus for change among the elite, and so on down the list, but where nothing comparable has happened. When I mentioned this to Mr. Brewer just now, he said it is essential that the military be in accord with the desire to change, to move away from a dictator to democratic government. All these other factors may be important, but apparently the essential ingredient if that movement is to take place is the role of the military. So I renew my question about the constitutional and unconstitutional roles of the military.

JORGE CARPIZO: The military in most countries constitutes a pressure group. This is one of the most important subjects of political sociology. In countries in which the military is institutionalized and there are important social, economic, and political problems, we cannot know exactly how long that institutionalization will last. In Latin America, for example, we considered Uruguay and Chile two of the democracies that worked best, and they had two very institutionalized armies. When social circumstances became more and more serious, their armies became deinstitutionalized. Even though the army in a country is institutional, therefore, a series of measures may be taken by the government because the military has put pressure on it. If we do not look at constitutional law and history with a view to political sociology, we cannot understand constitutional institutions at all.

I would like to make two brief comments about Venezuela. First, through its Constitution of 1961 Venezuela established a presidential system but one with very strong parliamentary aspects. It did so because experience with a presidential system of the classical mold did not work and it wanted to control the executive through means found in parliamentary systems. The system in France, which is also a mixture of parliamentary and presidential systems, was established for the same reason, the experience of past politics. This brings me to the following conclusion. The very important thing is that institutions should be adjusted in light of the experiences of a country, given its history and politics. This is the great merit of the framers of constitutions and one of the reasons why the Constitutions of France of 1958 and of Venezuela of 1961 have worked. They did not adopt classical forms but were framed in accordance with experience.

Second, the Venezuelan Constitution stipulates that the country is a federal state, but if you read the Constitution, you find that it is almost a unitary state. Why? The constitution writers could not have excluded the possibility of federalism because federalism in Venezuela is a very strong ideological element. The people identify federalism with freedom; so the constitution writers did very well to use the terminology of federalism even though it has practically nothing to do with reality. We can see that there is political decentralization in Venezuela, but what is even better is that the door was left open to the legislators to change the system in accordance with reality. The merit of constitution making in Venezuela was that no established constitutional model was followed but classical institutions were adjusted in accordance with the needs of Venezuela to create its own institutions.

MICHAEL DECLERIS: Allow me to offer one point concerning the role of the military which I believe is not properly understood by people who have long lived in a system of stable constitutional democracy. Those people tend to forget their pasts. Those military leaders in developing countries who are both authoritative and effective are not much different from the kings who shaped the Western states in the years after the Renaissance. Those kings were crowned military men. The building of the state does not start with the building of parliaments. It requires a permanent administrative structure, it requires communication, and these are the things that the successful military provides in some developing countries today. They are exactly the same things that the kings provided in the sixteenth century or earlier. The case of Ataturk in Turkey is characteristic in this respect.

Another point is that some countries have experienced unstable environments and war and, despite good intentions in domestic policies, have had to have strong military structures, which have influenced their constitutional development. When a constitutional process is evaluated, the mistake is made of focusing on the national environment and ignoring the influence of the international environment on the domestic process. In this sense constitutional development in England was different from constitutional development in France. England was not involved in the great wars on the Continent that influenced the constitutional development of France, Germany, and other countries.

JEAN FOYER: We have raised the problem of the constitutional role of the army. I believe that if we were to carry out a comparative survey, we would see that almost all constitutions reject such a role. That is, the army has no political role to play, and the majority of the texts would be found to say that the president, or the head of state, is also head of the armed forces. The problem is that theory and practice do not always coincide, and we are never assured of anything. This question is as old as the world, and Voltaire wrote that the first man who was king was a happy soldier.

If we go back to the Roman emperor, we find that he was both created and also overthrown by the Praetorian Guard, and within the past quarter-century in France, when I was minister of justice, there was military subversion. It can happen anywhere. We can see that things vary according to the different traditions in various countries and to the different psychologies of people; there are great differences among countries in the structure, sociology, and politics of the army. Without a political consensus, a military intervention will not last long. The varying conditions in which military interventions take place and aims that they strive toward produce different results.

Sometimes armies intervene because there has been a lapse in power; the temptation is too strong, and it is only a natural reaction. When we spoke about the Greek Constitution, we discussed the way in which military interventions come to an end. Sometimes they disappear because they are no longer supported by the population or because of a popular revolution against them. Sometimes the military feels that it had greatness thrust upon it and is in fact embarrassed by power; it does not know what to do with it and is quite glad finally to set down the burden and move away from political power and the problems associated with it.

DIOGO FREITAS DO AMARAL: The military intervenes in politics for many reasons. The two most frequent are, of course, reaction against anarchy and reestablishment of democracy, but there are others. I would like to stress two. One is the intention of imposing a social revolution. That is not the same as reacting against anarchy. Even if the established government is very stable and peaceful and perhaps authoritarian, the military may still intervene to impose a social revolution of, in their view, historical progress. This was true of the revolution in Portugal in 1974. The military imposed a socialist goal for the new Portuguese order.

The military may also intervene in politics to put an end to a war they do not want to fight anymore. This has happened when the armed forces think that a war no longer is or never was in accordance with national interests. Of course, the question is whether this would or would not be a legitimate intervention. I think it would not, but it is a real motive in some cases.

My second point is that we had in Portugal for eight years a written constitution that gave the armed forces a formal political role. The Constitution of 1976 provided for the existence of a Council of Revolution, composed of twenty representatives of the military captains who led the revolutionary process in 1974. That Council of Revolution had very important constitutional functions. First, it had the legislative and executive powers in military matters, including the approval of military international conventions. Second, it served as a constitutional court and therefore had a veto over laws approved by Parliament. This was of course a very special system, which fortunately ended with the revision of the Constitution in 1982. In that revision direction of the armed forces was given to the government, and control over the constitutionality of laws was given to a constitutional court. We now have a pure, classical democratic regime in Portugal, but for eight years we had an exceptional system.

9
The Making of the Nigerian Constitution

F. R. A. Williams

Introduction

Independent Nigeria. On October 1, 1960, Nigeria became an independent nation after having been a British dependency. On that date all legislative and executive powers formerly exercised by the British government in Nigeria came to an end, but Nigeria continued to have links with Britain. To start with, the newly acquired status of Nigeria was enacted by the British Parliament. The Nigeria Independence Act of 1960, enacted on July 29, 1960, stated: "On the first day of October, nineteen hundred and sixty . . . the Colony and the Protectorate as respectively defined by the Nigeria (Constitution) Orders in Council, 1954 to 1960, shall together constitute part of Her Majesty's dominions under the name of Nigeria."[1]

The Nigeria (Constitution) Order in Council, 1960, enacting the constitution that would become effective October 1, 1960, was a statutory instrument made by the British queen on the advice of Her Majesty's Privy Council.[2] Nigeria's political leaders had agreed to the provisions so enacted at a conference in London. The order in council provided for amendment of the constitution of the federation by the Parliament of the federation. The constitutions of the three regions composing the Nigerian federation at that time were embodied as separate schedules to the order in council. The power to amend the constitution of a region was vested in the regional Parliament. The constitution embodied in the order in council of 1960 remained in force until September 30, 1963.

Constitutional Role of the Queen of England in Nigeria. To appreciate the changes that came into force October 1, 1963, and that paved

397

the way for the 1979 Constitution, it is necessary to understand the constitutional role of the queen of England. As in the older British dominions, the queen had a significant place in the 1963 Constitution. In legal theory she appointed the governor general of Nigeria on the advice of the prime minister, who consulted the premier of each region before tendering that advice. The governor of each region was similarly appointed by the queen on the advice of the premier of the region, who consulted the prime minister of the federation before tendering his advice. The governor general and each of the regional governors were, under the constitution, the representatives of Her Majesty in Nigeria, and they exercised powers conferred by the constitution on Her Majesty as her representatives. As a matter of constitutional law, the queen was part of the federal and regional legislatures, and the executive powers of the federation and of each region were vested in her.

The Constitution of the First Republic. On October 1, 1963, the Parliament of the federation, with the concurrence of the parliaments of each of the regions composing the federation, amended the order in council and enacted the constitution of the federation, which, *inter alia*, provided that Nigeria "shall be a Republic by the name of the Federal Republic of Nigeria."[3] The office of governor general of Nigeria was restyled president of the Federal Republic of Nigeria and was to be filled not through appointment by the queen but in accordance with the provisions of the Nigerian Constitution. The functions of the queen were conferred on the president as head of the federation and on the regional governors as heads of the regions. There continued to be a prime minister for the federation, who appointed ministers and who (with those ministers) was responsible to the federal Parliament in accordance with the British parliamentary system. Similarly, in each region, there continued to be a premier who appointed ministers responsible (along with the premier) to the regional Parliament. The president and the regional governors were thus ceremonial heads of state wielding no executive powers of any significance.

On January 15, 1966, a military *coup d'état* in Nigeria ended the operation of the Constitution of the First Republic. From January 1966 to September 30, 1979, Nigeria was ruled by a military government with autocratic powers. No useful purpose would be served by giving an account of the military system of government. It is enough to say that after ten years of military rule, it became clear that the popular will was to return to a democratic system of government. The stage was set for the making of a new constitution for Nigeria.

The Political Background

Throughout the period of military government, Nigerians, knowing that the military intervention was temporary, gave thought to the kind of constitution they would like to have at the end of the military regime. Nearly everyone who thought about the matter was convinced that the overriding need was for a constitution that would ensure governmental stability and promote national unity. Before it was possible to organize a nationwide discussion of the political problems involved, a civil war (1968–1970) occurred when one of the regions, Eastern Nigeria, attempted to secede from the federation. On the eve of the civil war, General Gowon, then head of the military government, making good use of his arbitrary powers, resolved some of the most difficult of Nigeria's constitutional problems by creating twelve states.[4] It was left to his successor, General Murtala Mohammed, to complete the job by increasing the number of states to nineteen.[5]

Although all Nigeria's leaders agreed that no constitution could be successful under a system comprising only four regions or states, it would have been virtually impossible within a short time for a body of elected Nigerian representatives—or, indeed, any group of leaders—to agree on the number of states to be created. Nothing short of the arbitrary action of the federal military government could, in my view, have resolved the problem of the creation of states. The military leaders of Nigeria clearly recognized the significance of eliminating the problem from the issues the Constitution Drafting Committee had to resolve. In the words of General Mohammed to the inaugural meeting of the drafting committee:

> The fear of the predominance of one region over another has, for instance, been removed to a large extent by the simple Constitutional Act of creating more States. Your aim, therefore, must be to devise a Constitution which will help to solve other problems that may arise in the future.

That the problem of the creation of states had been solved by the military regime considerably facilitated the discussion and agreement leading to the enactment of the 1979 Constitution. Those who participated in the discussion did not feel compelled to deal with the question whether there should be more states in Nigeria. They were content to discuss only the machinery and criteria for the creation of new states.

The Process of Making the 1979 Constitution

The Constitution Drafting Committee. In September 1975 the head of the federal military government, General Mohammed, appointed the Constitution Drafting Committee and assigned to it the responsibility for producing a draft constitution for Nigeria. The members of the committee (of which I was appointed chairman) were carefully chosen to include distinguished leaders from the various states of Nigeria; leading academics from the universities in relevant disciplines, such as law, political science, economics, and history; and persons who had experience in the operation of the constitution of the First Republic. Approximately fifty persons were appointed. The committee commenced work in October 1975, and its report, which included a draft of the new constitution, was delivered to General Olusegun Obasanjo, then head of the federal military government, in October 1976. The report was published, and there was nationwide discussion of the proposals at public meetings, in the universities, and in the mass media.

The Constituent Assembly. By a decree that came into force June 1, 1977, the federal military government made provision for a Constituent Assembly with full powers to deliberate upon the draft constitution drawn up by the Constitution Drafting Committee.[6] The Constituent Assembly comprised more than 200 members from all over the country. It began its work in 1977 and concluded in 1978.

The Role of the Federal Military Government. The members of the federal military government did not regard the adoption of the Constitution by the Constituent Assembly as giving it the force of law. They not only brought it into force by a decree of their own making but also made some amendments to its text.[7]

The Constitution Drafting Committee

Composition of the Committee. The basis of appointment to the committee by the military government was explained by the head of the government, General Mohammed, in his opening address to the first meeting of the committee:

> Members of this Committee were selected, first, on the basis of two per state, to obtain the widest geographical coverage possible and, secondly, from our learned men in disciplines considered to have direct relevance to constitution-making, namely—history, law, economics and other social sciences,

400

especially political science. Eminent Nigerians with some experience in constitution-making were brought in to complete the spectrum. It is not possible within such a small group to include all shades of opinion and all interests. Nor is this necessary. It is enough to ensure that all the broad areas of interest and expertise are brought into the Committee, and I am satisfied that members of this Committee gathered here today represent a cross-section of opinion in this country that can be trusted to do a good job.[8]

The draft constitution produced by the committee was substantially approved by a largely elected Constituent Assembly, thus giving credibility to the claim that the committee sufficiently represented opinion in Nigeria at the time.

Method of Operation Adopted by the Constitution Drafting Committee. The first two days or so of the meetings of the fifty-member committee were spent generally debating the basic causes of instability in Nigeria during the civilian regime and possible constitutional remedies. Memorandums were invited through the mass media, and those wishing to make written suggestions to the committee were given until March 31, 1976, to do so. In the meantime and in the light of the matters that emerged during the general debate of October 1975 and a debate a month later on the address of the head of state to the inaugural meeting of the committee, it was decided to set up subcommittees on a number of issues:

- national objectives and public accountability
- the executive and the legislature
- judicial systems
- the economy, finance, and division of powers
- citizenship, citizenship rights, fundamental rights, political parties, and electoral laws
- public service, including the armed forces and the police
- legal drafting

As chairman of the Constitution Drafting Committee, I was not a member of any of the subcommittees except the Subcommittee on Legal Drafting, which was set up on a different basis from the rest. As far as practicable, members were assigned to subcommittees to which their expertise or political experience would be most relevant and useful. Most members served on only one subcommittee. The only exceptions to this rule were the members of the legal profession, all of whom served, in addition, on the Subcommittee on Legal Drafting. This assignment did not create any problems since the work of that subcommittee could start only after all the other subcommittees had completed their reports. The Steering Committee, which guided the organization of the work of the Constitution Drafting Committee, was made up of the chairmen of the subcommittees; it met from time to time under my chairmanship.

Decision Making in the Constitution Drafting Committee and in the Subcommittees. In guiding debates or discussions about the various matters that came up for decision, whether before the plenary session of the Constitution Drafting Committee or before a subcommittee, the chairman or person presiding had a very important role to play. He had to listen carefully so as to identify the points of agreement and the points of disagreement. He or some other participant could succeed in putting forward a compromise that could lead to a consensus on some or all of the points of disagreement. If the chairman judged that there was little or no hope of a consensus, he was required to end the debate on the issue, formulate a question embodying the issue, and take a poll to determine the wishes of the majority of those at the meeting. (On one topic, however, a different method was adopted.[9] With the unanimous consent of those at the meeting, I did not attempt to ascertain the wishes of the majority on provisions to ensure that the government reflect Nigerian diversity. The decision of the committee was postponed to the end of the discussions, when the legal subcommittee produced a draft for further debate.)

In its final report the Constitution Drafting Committee described the result of the method it adopted for making decisions on controversial issues:

> Each controversial issue was debated and determined by majority decision. For this reason, the fact is that there is no member of the Committee who agrees to every one of the proposals embodied in the text. The proposals are the decisions of the Committee only in the sense that they represent unanimous or majority decisions as the case may be on any particular issue. In some instances the majority was very slight and in other instances it was overwhelming.[10]

When introducing the draft constitution to the Constituent Assembly, I emphasized the same point in the context of the collective responsibility of all the members of the drafting committee for the draft. I then said the following:

> One simple truth about the Draft Constitution which some people have insisted on ignoring is that it is the work of all the members of the Constitution Drafting Committee. No

single individual can claim to be responsible for the draft, nor can anyone who actively participated in the debates that led to the formulation of the ideas embodied in the draft constitution disclaim responsibility or co-authorship of the document. There were differences among us. Those differences were debated and resolved by the democratic process which is the very same process by which we intend to resolve any differences we may have in this Assembly.

Some of the important topics on which decisions were arrived at unanimously were these:

• fundamental objectives and directive principles of state policy (but not the question whether courts of law should be authorized to enforce them)
• fundamental rights (but not the specific question of freedom of the press or the question whether the rights guaranteed should extend to economic and social rights (for example, the right to education, the right to work, and the right to a minimum living wage)
• citizenship
• division of legislative powers between the federation and the states

The following were among the important topics on which decisions had to be made by ascertaining the wishes of the majority:

• the question whether courts of law should enforce the provisions for fundamental objectives and directive principles of state policy
• freedom of the press
• whether economic and social rights should be enforceable in courts of law and so should be treated in the same way as fundamental rights
• provisions to ensure national loyalty and national unity
• control of the economy
• creation of new states within the federation

These examples relate to matters that would have had to be resolved whether the committee decided to adopt the system of a cabinet government, which is a part of and collectively responsible to the legislature (as in Great Britain, Australia, and Canada), or to adopt the executive presidential system modeled on the U.S. Constitution. The decision of the Constitution Drafting Committee to adopt the U.S. model was arrived at after a very lively and lengthy debate. Indeed, it is probably true to say that this issue was one of the two that occupied the largest proportion of time spent in debate. The other issue concerned provisions to ensure national loyalty and national unity. Both issues had to be determined in the end by ascertaining the wishes of the majority.

The Constituent Assembly

Composition of the Constituent Assembly. The Nigerian military government, by a decree issued in 1977, set up the Constituent Assembly.[11] The decree conferred on the assembly "full powers to deliberate upon the draft Constitution of the Federal Republic of Nigeria drawn up by the Constitution Drafting Committee appointed by the Federal Military Government." The assembly consisted of the following:

- a chairman and a deputy chairman, both appointed by the military government
- 203 members elected by local government councils, which were themselves democratically elected
- 20 members nominated by the military government
- the chairman of the Constitution Drafting Committee and the chairmen of its subcommittees

The 203 seats were allocated among the nineteen states of the federation in proportion to population. The number of seats varied from seven (for Niger State) to sixteen (for Kano State). The decree provided that the proceedings of the assembly "be in accordance with the Standing Orders of the House of Representatives as in force on January 12, 1966," with necessary modifications. It was thus implied that the draft constitution should be treated as a bill to be passed through the assembly as if that assembly were the House of Representatives. This was, in fact, what happened.

Powers of the Constituent Assembly. At a very early stage in the proceedings of the Constituent Assembly, members were uncertain about their exact role. Was it to enact a constitution, or was it no more than to make a recommendation to the military government on the subject? General Obasanjo, head of the federal military government, had said in his inaugural address to the assembly on October 6, 1977, that it was to make recommendations for a constitution to the Supreme Military Council, which would thereafter promulgate a decree on the subject. I referred to this issue in my address to the assembly on November 1, 1977.

> A constitution can have an extra-legal origin. What is meant by this is that in its origin the constitutional law of a state

can be enacted by an authority which does not claim to derive its power to enact a constitution from the existing legal order. This happens either following a revolution or with the acquiescence or the permission of a revolutionary regime. A constitution enacted by a revolutionary government will have as much validity as one enacted by a constituent assembly set up by decree enacted by such a revolutionary government.

The Federal Military Government can, if it so chooses, enact a constitution for use upon its handing power back to an elected civilian government. But it has, to its credit, chosen to set up a Constituent Assembly the overwhelming majority of whom are the elected representatives of the people of this country. However, if it is accepted that the will of the people is the supreme law, can a law emanating from the representatives of the people be modified by any other person or authority? I answer in the negative. But this is not the same thing as saying that the government which sets up this assembly cannot, by decree, supersede or purport to supersede or modify the constitution as enacted by this assembly. In my opinion, however, it would not be prudent for them to do so. Nor do I think that the will of the people should be treated as recommendation. It is and it should be treated as law. But the Federal Military Government has a vital role to play in the business of constitution making.

What is to happen if we quarrel among ourselves and fail to reach decisions? What if we proceed at such an inordinately slow pace that we upset the political program of the government thereby creating a situation of uncertainty and instability? In my opinion, if, but only if, such a situation were to occur, then the nation can rightly blame us and look to the Federal Military Government to give them a constitution. The Government would not then be over-riding the will of the people. They would be taking steps to avoid its frustration and ensure its fulfillment. The nation has given this Assembly the mandate to produce a constitution. If we fail, then the Federal Military Government has a duty to do whatever appears to them to be expedient in the national interest.

Many members of the assembly contributed to the debate, and every speaker expressed concern at the possibility that the Constitution enacted by the Constituent Assembly might be altered or substantially modified by the military government. In the end, leading members of the assembly approached the representatives of the federal military government and obtained the verbal assurance that its intention was not to alter the Constitution as approved by the Constituent Assembly.

Decision Making in the Constituent Assembly. Controversial issues before the Constituent Assembly were decided in accordance with the provisions of the standing orders of the House of Representatives, which were binding on that assembly. At the end of debate on an issue, the chairman of the assembly formulated a question raising the issue in controversy. Those in favor and those against indicated their wishes by together saying "aye" or "nay." The chairman then used his best judgment to determine the views of the majority on the issue, and unless there was a demand for a division, the chairman's decision was accepted without further ceremony as the decision of the assembly. When a division was demanded, the members left the chamber to enter one of two separate apartments to sign their names: one apartment for those favoring an affirmative answer to the question, the other for those favoring a negative answer.

Constituent Assembly Debate on the Principles of the Draft Constitution. In accordance with the rules of procedure of the House of Representatives, I presented the bill for a constitution of the Federal Republic of Nigeria to the Constituent Assembly, and it was read for the first time on November 2, 1977. This was a purely formal proceeding. It was followed by a second reading, which involved a debate on the principles of the bill. The following statement contains my reasons for adopting an executive presidential system, based on the American model, in preference to the system of a cabinet with collective responsibility to the legislature, which is the system Nigeria had used before the date of its independence:

> The Constitution Drafting Committee was convinced that the system of Executive Presidency directly elected by the people is to be preferred to the other system of appointing as the head of government the leader of the political party which commands a majority following in the Legislature. The arguments which convinced us on this issue have been clearly set out in the introduction to the Draft Constitution. It is, therefore, unnecessary for me to repeat that now.
>
> It is sufficient for me to emphasize, in the context of the basic ideas which inspired the Draft Constitution, that the majority of the Constitution Drafting Committee were convinced that they saw a clear choice between allowing the people themselves directly to choose the Head of State and Government and accepting the choice made for them by the

political party that happens to win the majority of seats in the House of Representatives. They chose the former alternative.

It was obvious in the course of the debate that the choice between the two systems was crucial. If the decisions of the Constitution Drafting Committee had been rejected, much of the structure of the executive branch of the government as contained in the draft constitution would have fallen apart. The recommendation of the drafting committee was accepted, and the changes made in the draft constitution by the Constituent Assembly were minor. In other words, the bill was approved in substance, with amendments on details here and there.

Clause-by-Clause Consideration of the Draft. The second reading of the draft constitution was concluded on December 16, 1977, when the draft was, in effect, approved in principle. The assembly then broke off for the Christmas recess. It resumed on January 9, 1978, and resolved itself into a committee of the whole house to consider the draft clause by clause. Approximately 90 percent of the clauses were approved as drafted without any textual alteration. A number of alterations were made in the provisions relating to fundamental rights, the election of the president of the federation, the election of the state governors, and the judicial system. At the end of the consideration of the draft clause by clause, the bill was read for a third time and passed.

The Role of the Military Government

Drafting of Amendments by the Constituent Assembly. I prepared the first draft of the Constitution in my capacity as chairman of the Subcommittee on Legal Drafting. In doing so, I used the subcommittee reports as approved by the plenary session of the Constitution Drafting Committee as my drafting instructions. This draft was then submitted for discussion to the subcommittee, which critically examined it and made important corrections and amendments before submitting it for ratification to the plenary session of the Constitution Drafting Committee. I advised the military government that it would be necessary to have a drafting team available throughout the meetings of the Constituent Assembly to assist the members in drafting amendments or putting forward proposed amendments. My advice was accepted, and a drafting team, headed by a judge of the High Court of Lagos State with many years of drafting experience, was appointed for the purpose.

Further Amendments Made by the Military Government. Despite its oral assurance to the members of the Constituent Assembly, the military government did make some alterations in the Constitution as approved by the assembly. In fairness it must be admitted that one or two of the alterations were made in the public interest. The rest, no doubt, were made because the military government felt that it could not trust the members of the assembly to approve them. The opinion is widely held among Nigeria's political leaders that these alterations, however well motivated, should have been made only with the approval of the Constituent Assembly, which could easily have been summoned for that purpose. In a recent decision of the Supreme Court of Nigeria, a Supreme Court justice who was chairman of the Constituent Assembly said:

> It is the duty of this court to bear constantly in mind the fact that the present Constitution has been proclaimed the Supreme Law of the Land . . . that it was made, enacted and given by the People of the Federal Republic of Nigeria to themselves in Constituency assembled—for which reason and because it is autochthonous, it, of necessity, claims superiority to and over and above any other Constitution ever devised for this country—*the unwarranted inter-meddlesomeness of the military authority concerning some of its provisions* notwithstanding [emphasis added].[12]

The portion of the quotation in italics demonstrates that the learned justice of the Supreme Court, who was aware of the oral assurance of the military government, did not take kindly to what he termed its "unwarranted inter-meddlesomeness" with the Constitution as approved by the assembly over which he had presided.

Fundamental Objectives and Directive Principles of State Policy

Throughout the proceedings of the Constitution Drafting Committee and the Constituent Assembly, members of both bodies were conscious of the need to have Nigeria's national goals constitutionally defined and to impose constitutionally binding obligations on governments at all levels to direct their policies toward the achievement of those national goals. Hence the drafting committee set up a Subcommittee on National Objectives and Public Accountability and included the following among its terms of reference:

- to consider and make recommendations on the desirability of embodying national objectives and directive principles in the Nigerian Constitution
  - to suggest what such principles and objectives should be
  - to consider and make recommendations regarding constitutional arrangements to ensure conformity with such principles and objectives, including the procedure to amend this part of the Constitution

We were aware that the older democracies do not have constitutional provisions defining national objectives, nor do their constitutions specify guidelines for the direction of government policies. Our experience in self-government in a world of competing ideologies has taught us, however, that a new and developing nation cannot afford to leave its political, economic, and social objectives undefined. To do so is to leave the doors wide open for national discord when our overriding need and concern is to unite Nigerian society, which comprises diverse ethnic groups, into one nation bound together by a resolve to achieve common political, economic, and social objectives.

The plenary session of the Constitution Drafting Committee accepted in substance the recommendation of the subcommittee. All the articles contained in the chapter of the Constitution dealing with fundamental objectives and directive principles of state policy were very largely based on the subcommittee's report. The plenary session decided, however, after a vigorous debate lasting several days, to reject the recommendation contained in the concluding part of the report, which read:

> It cannot be disputed that the ideology that is most relevant to our society today and one that is accepted by most Nigerians is that of socialism operating within the framework of a participatory democracy and the ideals of Liberty, Equality and Justice. It is the only effective answer to the conditions of under-development, inequality and exploitation that exist in the country. The long-term objectives of socialism in Nigeria should be to place in the hands of the State and people the ownership and control of the means of production and distribution.

Instead of the foregoing, the Constitution Drafting Committee decided that the economic objectives of the nation should be defined thus:

> The State shall, within the context of the ideals and objectives provided for in this Constitution, control and operate the major sectors of the economy while individual and group

rights to operate the means of production, distribution and exchange shall be protected by law.

It was decided to leave it to the National Assembly to define the scope of economic activities that constitute the "major sectors of the economy." In the absence or in default of a decision of the National Assembly on the matter, the economic activities that were being operated exclusively by the federal government on September 30, 1979, "shall be deemed to be the major sectors of the economy."

The Mass Media

The Nigerian Constitution that had been in effect before the military *coup d'état* of 1966 had contained provisions for fundamental rights. These provisions included one relating to freedom of expression, which is relevant in the context of press freedom. Yet, as Professor B. O. Nwabueze has correctly observed: "Few issues in the Constitution at the time it was drafted provoked so much public controversy as the freedom of the press, and this is appropriate to the importance of the subject. Unfortunately, much of the discussion was confused and unedifying."[13]

The text of the constitutional provision contained in the draft constitution and now embodied in section 36 of the Nigerian Constitution is as follows:

(1) Every person shall be entitled to freedom of expression, including freedom to hold opinions and to receive and impart ideas and information without interference.
(2) Without prejudice to the generality of subsection (1) of this section, every person shall be entitled to own, establish and operate any medium for the dissemination of information, ideas and opinions:
Provided that no person, other than the Government of the Federation or of a State or any other person or body authorized by the President, shall own, establish or operate a television or wireless broadcasting station for any purpose whatsoever.
(3) Nothing in this section shall invalidate any law that is reasonably justifiable in a democratic society—
    (a) for the purpose of preventing the disclosure of information received in confidence, maintaining the authority and independence of courts or regulating telephony, wireless broadcasting, television or the exhibition of cinematographic films; or
    (b) for imposing restrictions upon persons holding office under the Government of the Federation or of a State,

members of the armed forces of the Federation or members of the Nigeria Police Force.

Throughout the debate in the Constitution Drafting Committee, the nationwide debate that followed it, and the debate in the Constituent Assembly, the entire corps of press, radio, and television journalists throughout Nigeria mounted a powerful campaign to the effect that the provisions were defective because they did not specifically guarantee freedom of the press. The critics (who included members of the drafting committee and of the assembly) were not persuaded that the provisions quoted were wide enough to give the Nigerian press all the freedom it could legitimately want. They pointed out that the American Constitution expressly prohibited the making of a law "abridging the freedom of speech, *or of the press*" and that the guarantee of freedom of expression under the Nigerian Constitution without any reference to freedom of the press was not sufficient. The majority of the members of the Constituent Assembly were not impressed by these arguments or by the media campaign, however.

The Religious Factor

Nigeria is a society of many religions, the two largest religious groups being Moslems and Christians. Both these religions were brought into Nigeria from outside the country in comparatively recent times, though before the existence of Nigeria as one country. There are Moslems throughout Nigeria, and they predominate in the northern states; in some of those states there has been a long-established hierarchy of courts administering Islamic law. At the time of the Constitution Drafting Committee and the Constituent Assembly, the highest court administering Islamic law was the state sharia court of appeal.

Freedom to Practice Religious Faith. There was no difficulty whatsoever in obtaining unanimity on the issue of religious freedom. This has always been recognized in Nigeria. Section 35 of the present Constitution reads as follows:

(1) Every person shall be entitled to freedom of thought, conscience and religion, including freedom to change his religion or belief, and freedom (either alone or in community with others, and in public or in private) to manifest and propagate his religion or belief in worship, teaching, practice and observance.
(2) No person attending any place of education shall be required to receive religious instruction or to take part in or attend any religious ceremony or observance if such instruc-

411

tion, ceremony or observance relates to a religion other than his own, or a religion not approved by his parent or guardian. (3) No religious community or denomination shall be prevented from providing religious instruction for pupils of that community or denomination in any place of education maintained wholly by that community or denomination.

In addition, section 39 of the Constitution forbids discrimination against any person by legislative or executive action by reason of his religion.

Religion and the Judicial System. The close connection between religion and law among Moslems posed very serious and delicate problems for those on the Constitution Drafting Committee and for those in the Constituent Assembly. Indeed, so sensitive were the issues that each of the two bodies almost reached a deadlock on the issue. The Subcommittee on the Judicial System had recommended, *inter alia*, that a Federal Sharia Court of Appeal be set up to deal with appeals from each of the sharia courts of appeal in the northern states. The obvious intention was to ensure uniformity in the administration of what was essentially the same system of law. A heated debate took place on the subject before the plenary session of the committee. What the non-Moslem critics strongly objected to was having provisions in the Constitution dealing with sharia when there were no corresponding provisions dealing with customary law. Furthermore, they saw no need to set up a federal court to administer Islamic law. Eventually the recommendation was accepted and embodied in the draft constitution. But the bitter debate continued. Both sides had strong feelings on the matter, and the majority decision in favor of accepting the subcommittee's recommendation in no way put an end to the bitter controversy.

By the time the Constituent Assembly met, its members had made up their minds on the issue. Indeed, some of the members from the non-Moslem areas had been elected on a mandate to oppose setting up a Federal Sharia Court of Appeal. No doubt many of the Moslem members were equally determined that, come what might, the recommendation of the Constitution Drafting Committee must be defended. In campaigning for or against the recommendation, the issues were exaggerated and misrepresented. This fact was reflected in part of my speech in the course of presenting the draft constitution to the Constituent Assembly:

It is no secret that most of us have come to this Assembly with our minds made up on the provisions of the Draft Constitution relating to the Federal Sharia Court of Appeal. My personal view is that a very simple and straight-forward problem has been converted by extremists on all sides into an explosive and seemingly intractable problem.

The debate in the Constituent Assembly was more bitter than it had been during the proceedings of the Constitution Drafting Committee. Fortunately, a deadlock was avoided. The proposal to set up a Federal Sharia Court of Appeal was rejected by a majority of the assembly. Because the main ground for opposition was the argument that Islamic law should not have what was regarded as preferential treatment under the Constitution, the critics successfully insisted on having customary courts of appeal for the states. Like the sharia courts of appeal, customary courts of appeal will exist only in states that want them.

Promotion of National Unity

Ethnic and Cultural Diversity. Nigeria is a country of ethnic and cultural diversity. Though ruled as one country by the British, it had no prior existence as a nation. The name "Nigeria" was given to it by the British, who brought the diverse ethnic groups under one rule. By the time that rule came to an end, Nigeria's political leaders agreed to continue to live together as a political unit under a federal system of government. The period of contact between the various ethnic groups during foreign colonial rule was too short, however, to forge a sense of common destiny and common purpose. The consciousness of belonging to a particular ethnic or linguistic group was, at the end of British rule, still stronger than the consciousness of belonging to one country. Loyalty to the ethnic group was stronger than loyalty to the nation. There can be no doubt, however, that Nigerian leaders have a strong desire to remain one country and to foster a sense of loyalty to the nation among its diverse ethnic groups, notwithstanding the almost irresistible temptation of many of the political leaders to exploit ethnic differences to win votes.

Ethnic hostility led to a civil war, which one side regarded as a war for the preservation of the ethnic group and the other side as a war to preserve national unity. Because of that experience, coupled with the long-term causes of instability that brought about the collapse of the First Republic, those who participated in the Constitution Drafting Committee and the Constituent Assembly lost no opportunity to include provisions in the Constitution to encourage and foster the growth of loyalty to the Nigerian nation among its diverse population. I draw the reader's attention here to some of those constitutional provisions.

Protection of Ethnic Minorities. There are three major ethnic groups in Nigeria, namely, Hausa-Fulani, Yoruba, and Ibo. If the Nigerian Constitution were to ignore this division, it would be possible for these three groups—or, indeed, any two of them with a sprinkling of support from minority groups of their choice—to rule the entire nation through a democratically elected government. In the same way, some of the states comprise one or more major ethnic groups that are sufficiently numerous to form the government of the state irrespective of whether they enjoy the support of ethnic minorities within the state. This situation must be kept in mind to appreciate the object of these constitutional provisions.

Provisions to Ensure Participatory Democracy. The chapter of the Constitution that deals with fundamental objectives and directive principles contains provisions designed to ensure that ethnic minorities are not ignored in the scheme of things. Section 14(2)(c) of the Constitution declares: "The participation of the people in their government shall be ensured in accordance with the provisions of this Constitution." More important, subsections 3 and 4 of the same section state:

> (3) The composition of the Government of the Federation or any of its agencies and the conduct of its affairs shall be carried out in such manner as to reflect the federal character of Nigeria and the need to promote national unity, and also to command national loyalty, thereby ensuring that there shall be no predominance of persons from a few States or from a few ethnic or other sectional groups in that government or in any of its agencies.
> (4) The composition of the Government of a State, a local government council, or any of the agencies of such government or council, and the conduct of the affairs of the government or council or such agencies shall be carried out in such manner as to recognize the diversity of the peoples within its area of authority and the need to promote a sense of belonging and loyalty among all the peoples of the Federation.

Section 15 also contains very important provisions. It is necessary to quote only subsections 3 and 4:

> (3) For the purpose of promoting national integration it shall be the duty of the State to—
>> (a) provide adequate facilities for and encourage free mobility of people, goods and services throughout the Federation;

(b) secure full residence rights for every citizen in all parts of the Federation;

(c) encourage intermarriage among persons from different places of origin, or of different religious, ethnic or linguistic association or ties; and

(d) promote or encourage the formation of associations that cut across ethnic, linguistic, religious or other sectional barriers.

(4) The State shall foster a feeling of belonging and of involvement among the various peoples of the Federation, to the end that loyalty to the nation shall override sectional loyalties.

Election of the President and of the State Governors. The president of the Federal Republic is elected directly by the people of Nigeria. He is not, however, declared elected unless he wins a majority of all the votes and not less than 25 percent of the votes cast in at least two-thirds of the states. In short, in addition to winning the highest number of votes cast, a presidential candidate must have nationwide support. In the same way, a gubernatorial candidate must win at least two-thirds of the local government areas within the state, in addition to winning the highest number of votes statewide. If no candidate is elected president in the first election, a second election is held between the candidate with the highest number of votes in the election and the one with the wider national support—that is, the candidate with at least 25 percent of the votes cast in the largest number of states. The same rule applies, with necessary modifications, to gubernatorial candidates.

Political Parties. To ensure that no ethnic, cultural, or other association allows itself to be used for political purposes, thereby generating political hostility against itself, the Constitution provides that no association other than a political party may canvass for votes for any candidate in any election or contribute to the funds of any political party or to the election expenses of any candidate in an election. The Constitution further provides that only registered political parties may function as such and that only associations conforming to the requirements of the Constitution may so register.

One of those requirements is that the political party must have rules that "ensure that the members of the executive committee or other governing body of the political party reflect the federal character of Nigeria." The term "federal character of Nigeria" is defined by the Constitution as "the distinctive desire of the peoples of Nigeria to

415

promote national unity, foster national loyalty and give every citizen of Nigeria a sense of belonging to the nation as expressed in section 14(3) and (4) of this Constitution." [Sections 14(3) and 14(4) of the Constitution are quoted above.] Finally, the Constitution provides that the executive committee or other governing body of a political party shall be deemed to reflect the federal character of Nigeria only if its members belong to no fewer than two-thirds of all the states composing the federation.

One Constitution

Unlike most federal constitutions, the 1979 Constitution of the Federal Republic of Nigeria comprises in one document the federal Constitution and the constitution of the states. No state in Nigeria has a separate constitution. This feature created no serious difficulty since prior constitutions for the regions, though embodied in different instruments, had always followed the same pattern and, indeed, the same wording.

Separation of Powers

The doctrine of separation of powers is embodied in the Nigerian Constitution. To provide for checks and balances against excesses, however, one branch of the government may be authorized by express provisions to interfere with or share functions with another branch. Thus acts of the National Assembly require the assent of the president, and laws enacted by a state House of Assembly require the assent of the governor. At the same time, some important appointments by a state governor require the approval of the state assembly. The judicial powers of the federation and of the states are vested in courts of law; so judicial review of executive or legislative action is available to any complainant with standing.

As a safeguard against possible legislative erosion of judicial powers, there is express provision in section 4(8) of the Constitution, as follows:

> Save as otherwise provided by this Constitution, the exercise of legislative powers by the National Assembly or by a House of Assembly shall be subject to the jurisdiction of courts of law and of judicial tribunals established by law; and accordingly, the National Assembly or a House of Assembly shall not enact any law that ousts or purports to oust the jurisdiction of a court of law or of a judicial tribunal established by law.

416

The Nigerian Supreme Court has decided that this provision enables it to invalidate a law passed by the National Assembly and assented to by the president of the Federal Republic on the ground that in passing it the assembly failed to observe mandatory *procedural* requirements of the Constitution.[14] Moreover, in examining whether those requirements have been met, the Supreme Court has the power and the jurisdiction to receive evidence of the internal proceedings of the Senate and of the House of Representatives, including the journal, minutes, and other printed proceedings of either house.

Conclusion

The making of the present Constitution of Nigeria is clearly a product of the genuine desire of several peoples who happen to have been brought together as a political unit by forces outside their control. In culture and past history, they have very little in common. In spite of their differences, they have discussed and identified certain ultimate objectives that the overwhelming majority share. They have also agreed that government policies shall be directed toward the achievement of those objectives. The organization of the government is to be firmly based on the principles of democracy, with allowances for the need to take account of cultural and ethnic diversities in Nigerian society. The Nigerian Constitution, in sum, is based on the principles of participatory democracy and federalism.

Notes

1. 8 & 9 Eliz. 2c 55.
2. S.I. 1960, no. 1652.
3. Act 1963, no. 20, "An Act to Make Provision for the Constitution of the Federal Republic of Nigeria."
4. States (Creation and Transitional Provisions) Decree, 1967, no. 14; and States (Creation and Transitional Provisions) (Amendment) Decree, 1967, no. 19.
5. States (Creation and Transitional Provisions) Decree, 1976, no. 12.
6. Constituent Assembly Decree, 1977, no. 50, sec. 1.
7. Constitution of the Federal Republic of Nigeria (Enactment) Decree, 1978, no. 25.
8. Constitution Drafting Committee, *Report*, vol. 1, p. xliii.
9. This was on the question of what is now embodied in sections 14(3) and (4) of the draft constitution. See "Political Parties," below.
10. Constitution Drafting Committee, *Report*, vol. 1, p. iii.

11. See note 6.

12. Nafiu Rabiu v. The State, 1981, 2 NCLR 293, per Sir Udo Udoma, p. 326.

13. B. O. Nwabueze, *Presidential Constitution of Nigeria* (1981), p. 460.

14. Attorney-General of Bendel State v. Attorney-General of the Federation and Ors., 1982, 3 NCLR 1.

Commentary

T. Akinola Aguda

The Era before the 1960 Constitution

For a proper understanding of how and why Nigeria came to choose the type of constitution it now has, it is perhaps necessary to go back a little earlier than 1960. At the inception of colonial rule, the entity now known as Nigeria consisted of well over 100 independent nation-states embracing more than 400 ethnic and linguistic groups. The introduction of colonial administration and Western European concepts of governmental institutions commenced with the annexation of Lagos in 1863 and by the turn of the century was complete. Although foreign rule was ostensibly imposed to put a stop to the slave trade, the mode of the incursion and subsequent events belied this assertion. By 1898 there were three separate British administrations in the country. The first was based in Lagos as a British colony and later extended into the Yoruba (western) hinterland to make economic sense of the control of Lagos. The North was organized and secured through Sir George Goldie of the Royal Niger Company, which monopolized the trade there and in some ports and river areas of the South. Third was the southeastern part of the country, the incursion into which was embarked on by the British Foreign Office to protect British palm oil traders.[1]

In 1906 the tripartite administration was reduced to a dual one, with the amalgamation of the enlarged Colony and Protectorate of Lagos with the Protectorate of Southern Nigeria to form the Colony and Protectorate of Southern Nigeria; the Protectorate of Northern Nigeria continued to exist as a separate administration. The gradual unification of the country was given greater impetus in 1912 when Lord Lugard, in his second term in office, was made governor of both the northern and the southern provinces, and by January 1, 1914, the Colony and Protectorate of Nigeria was inaugurated.[2] Thus was born the Nigerian nation with a unified administration. It should be emphasized, however, that while Nigeria was theoretically administered

419

as a unitary state, in practice the British found the diversity among the peoples over whom they ruled so great that they had to exercise much caution in introducing nationwide measures. To a very great extent, therefore, measures were introduced to suit or reflect the traditional political institutions existing in the different parts of the country before the advent of British rule. It was not surprising that three decades after the amalgamation and unification of the southern and northern provinces, very powerful moves toward decentralization of administration were made.

The Genesis of Federalism. World War II gave great impetus to nationalism among colonial peoples, and soon after that war political parties emerged in Nigeria with leaders from various parts of the country. One point is pertinent here: most of the political leaders, in varying degrees and for various reasons, believed that a unitary form of government must give way to federalism.

In response to calls for decentralization of administration, the governor of Nigeria, Sir John McPherson, promulgated a new constitution for the country in 1946. That constitution divided the country into three regions, each under a lieutenant-governor. Although a direct line of command continued to exist from the governor to the lieutenant-governor of a region, to the resident of a province, and down to the district officer, the arrangement provided the genesis for federalism in Nigeria, which finally commenced in 1951, with inevitable political and legal problems.

The problem that was to be solved at the Constitutional Conference of 1947, which ushered in the 1951 Constitution, was not preeminently whether there should be a federal union but how many units the federal union that was agreed upon should comprise and what amount of power should devolve on the units to be created. For some inexplicable reason, however, it was decided that the existing regions—Eastern, Northern, and Western—should continue to be the units of the federation. By this arrangement many ethnically and culturally divergent peoples were grouped together. Concerning the sharing of powers, the 1951 arrangement followed a traditional pattern. As would be expected, the central government surrendered its sovereignty over specific matters to the regions. Pressure for greater autonomy for the regions continued to mount, however, and, as a result of that pressure, the situation was more or less reversed by the constitution that followed closely in 1954.[3]

That constitution made provision for what were called Houses of Assembly and Houses of Chiefs, but these were not legislative houses properly so called. They acted only in an advisory capacity.

The Basic Peculiarity of the Nigerian Situation. Unlike some other federal states, such as the United States, Canada, and Australia, Nigeria started out under what was more or less a central and single administration. In due course that administration shed some of its powers by way of devolution on smaller units created from the existing unit. It is most vital to remember that this arrangement was an unusual one that sowed the seeds of political and legal problems. As a result of this history, it is not surprising that the states making up the federation of Nigeria now have only such powers as are given to them while the federal government retains much power. This situation is, of course, completely different from that of the United States of America or the Federal Republic of Germany.

The 1960 Constitution

On October 1, 1960, Nigeria became an independent, sovereign nation under a constitution that firmly established federalism. Section 2 of that constitution said that Nigeria should consist of regions and a federal territory.[4] The regions were the Northern, Western, and Eastern, and the federal territory was made up of the former British colony of Lagos. Unfortunately, not much thought was given to the inherent dangers in an arrangement that divided such a huge country into three big territories, one of them as large as the two others together.

Essentially, the political arrangements, both at the federal and at the regional levels, were similar to the British parliamentary system. At the federal level there was a governor-general, who was the queen's representative, and an elected prime minister, who was the leader of the political party that commanded the largest number of seats in Parliament. He chose his ministers from among his colleagues in Parliament, and it was he who presided over the cabinet, which initiated legislation. In like manner, each region had a governor and a premier, who presided over a cabinet, which also initiated legislation.

The 1963 Constitution

Although the agitation for splitting the big regions into smaller units persisted, nothing much was done in this regard until the time of the 1963 Constitution.[5] That constitution made the country a republic. In August 1963 another region was carved out of the Western Region, the smallest of the three existing regions. The Mid-Western Region was created to ease the political tension caused by the peoples of that area, who regarded themselves as oppressed minorities. But the tension continued in other parts of the country.

The 1963 Constitution converted the country into a republic without further splitting it into smaller units. The post of governor-general was replaced by that of president, who was appointed, not elected. Each region had its own constitution, which created the office of governor, who also was appointed, not elected. The constitution of each region was enacted by its legislature.[6]

The Political Problems of Nigerian Federalism to 1966

Four very important points must be noted here. The first is the unequal size of the states. The Northern Region alone was much bigger in land area and also larger in population than the other regions and the federal territory together.[7] Second, the organization of political parties followed the pattern of the regions; each political party had its base, its leader, and the vast majority of its followers in one region. Third, the legislative powers of the federal government were specified, while residual legislative powers were reserved to the regions. In other words, the regions were to a large extent more powerful than the federation. Fourth—and by no stretch of the imagination least important—each region was under the domination of a large ethnic group to which the vast majority of its population belonged.

The Imbalance of the Regions and the Problem of the Majority versus the Minority

That the Northern Region was much bigger than the rest of the country was not a healthy sign for a viable federation. Indeed, it was a large part of the cause of the problems that led to the military's running the government of the country for nearly fourteen years, thirty months of which were spent fighting a bitter civil war.

Because the regions were large, it was inevitable that each consisted of many ethnic groups. Each region was dominated by a large majority ethnic group, against which the minority ethnic groups even together were almost helpless; most of the time, they were in a state of open hostility. Naturally, this hostility led in some areas to confrontation and to riots and bloodshed, which gave rise to agitation for the creation of more states with the hope that such an exercise would correct the existing imbalance, particularly in the sharing of amenities, positions, and services. This problem brought into focus the need for accurate census figures, as well as the need for an acceptable formula for allocating national revenue between the federal government and the states, on the one hand, and among the states, on the other.

422

Creation of States

On the eve of the civil war, in May 1967, the Nigerian federal military government split the country into twelve states. This action was clearly one of the maneuvers that enabled Nigeria to survive the civil war. When a new military government came into power in July 1975, one of its earliest actions was to split the country further into nineteen states.

The nineteen-state structure came into being through an amending decree.[8] The formula for the sharing of power between the states and the federal government continued as before. Because of the peculiar nature of military administration, which operates through a definite chain of command, the chances of conflict were quite minimal.

Section 2 of the 1979 Constitution says that "Nigeria is one indivisible and indissoluble Sovereign State to be known by the name of the Federal Republic of Nigeria" and that the country consists of states and a Federal Capital Territory. Section 3 sets down the names of the nineteen states, but section 8 provides for the creation of additional states. The provision of section 8 for the creation of new states is not only difficult to understand but, no matter how it is interpreted, difficult to apply. The effect is that, although almost all the political parties agree on the necessity to create new states, none has been created. Almost certainly none can be created in the near future unless the section is amended, but it is extremely difficult to amend.

The 1979 Constitution

The Role of the Military. Chief Williams's paper has set down in very great detail the processes followed before the promulgation of the 1979 Constitution, and there is little useful I can add. For two reasons, however, I have not been as enthusiastic as Chief Williams in associating myself with the Preamble to the Constitution, which says, "We the People of the Federal Republic of Nigeria . . . . hereby make, enact and give to ourselves the following Constitution . . . " First, the 203 members of the Constituent Assembly were not popularly elected as supposed. The local government councils, which were in most cases corrupt, served as electoral colleges. It was easy, in the circumstances, to bribe ten or twelve members of each council. The result, of course, was that most of those who found their way into the assembly might not have got there if elections for the particular purpose had been conducted.

Second, and very important, the military government made a

large number of amendments to the Constitution that had been agreed upon by the Constituent Assembly without further reference back to that assembly—a point that Chief Williams made very strongly. Many of those amendments were of great constitutional importance; some were outrageous and incompatible with the other basic provisions and scheme of the Constitution.

The General Scheme of the Constitution. The Constitution divides the powers of the government into three areas—legislative, executive, and judicial—and defines the bodies to which each of these powers is assigned. The legislative powers are vested (by section 4) in the National Assembly (for the federal government) and the Houses of Assembly (for the states). The executive powers of the federation are vested in the president. He may exercise those powers directly or through the vice-president or ministers or other officers in the public service of the federation. In the same way, the executive powers of each state are vested in the governor, who may exercise them directly or through the deputy governor or commissioners or other officers in the public service of the state (section 5). Finally, the judicial powers are vested in the courts (section 6). Apart from the superior courts enumerated in the Constitution, some inferior courts exist, and others can be created to exercise judicial powers within the limits specified in the statutes creating them.

The Separation of Powers. Like the Constitution of the United States, the Nigerian Constitution is premised on the separation, as far as possible, of the powers of the state. The legislature is not permitted to exercise executive or judicial powers; the executive is not permitted to exercise legislative or judicial powers; and the judiciary is not allowed to encroach upon the exercise of powers granted to the other two arms of government. In the exercise of its powers, one branch is not allowed to encroach on the powers allocated to the others. But there is some constitutional overlap. A bill passed by the National Assembly does not generally become law until it is signed by the president. The president has the power to make appointments to certain executive positions, but some of these are subject to an overriding veto by the legislature. Similarly, appointments to certain high judicial positions are made by the president subject to veto by the legislature. All told, there is a clear separation in the actual discharge of duties and functions by each arm of the government.

The Legislature. The federal legislature, referred to under the Constitution as the National Assembly, consists of a House of Representatives and a Senate. The legislature of a state consists only of a House of Assembly.

The National Assembly has the power to make laws for the peace, order, and good government of the federation or any part of it with respect to any matter included on the exclusive list; to make laws with respect to any matter on the concurrent legislative list to the extent prescribed there; and to make laws in respect to any other matter about which it is empowered according to the provisions of the Constitution. I confine myself to the federal legislature.

Section 54(1) of the Constitution says that the power of the National Assembly to make laws is to be exercised by passing bills in both the Senate and the House of Representatives and presenting them to the president for his assent. Subsection 2 of the section makes it clear that a bill may originate in either of the two houses but must be passed by both. Even if a bill is passed by both houses, the president may exercise his constitutional power to withhold his assent to it. Subsection 4 says that when a bill is presented to the president, he shall, within thirty days, signify that he assents or that he withholds his assent. A bill to which he withholds his assent may nevertheless become law if, after the thirty-day period, it is passed by each house by a two-thirds majority. Section 55 makes elaborate provisions in regard to money bills, but I need not go into those here.

Finally, Nigerian judiciary has rightly held that once a bill has been properly passed into law, the judiciary has no right or title to inquire into the motives of the legislature or into the rightness or wrongness of the legislation in the abstract. The judiciary has confined its role to two main areas: first, to examine whether all the procedural rules laid down in the Constitution for enacting a law have been followed; and, second, to examine whether a law passed and assented to is *ultra vires* the Constitution.[9]

The Executive. The executive powers of the federation are vested in the president; he may exercise them directly or through the vice-president and ministers of the government or officers in the public service of the federation. Such powers include the execution and maintenance of the Constitution, all laws made by the National Assembly, and so on (section 5[1]).

The courts cannot dictate to the president or his officials how to carry out the powers granted to them under the Constitution; neither can the legislature dictate to the president how he should execute the laws passed by it save as provided for in the laws themselves. The president need not assign specific duties to the vice-president, and a governor has no obligation to assign duties to a deputy governor.

The Judiciary. The judicial powers of the federation are vested in the judiciary by section 6 of the Constitution. In contrast to the situation in some other countries, the powers of adjudication of the judiciary in Nigeria extend to all matters between persons or between the government or government functionaries, on the one hand, and individuals, on the other. That is one principle in respect of which Nigeria, as a democracy, is justifiably proud.

So that the judiciary may perform its functions fearlessly and impartially, the Constitution attempts to grant it some independence from the other arms of the government. Whereas all members of the legislatures and all the governors and their deputies as well as the president and the vice-president are elected by qualified electorates, no person holding any judicial appointment in Nigeria is elected. If one bears in mind the peculiar circumstances of Nigeria, this provision is quite understandable and, in my view, quite right. It is the scheme of the Constitution to insulate the appointment of judges, and the judges themselves, from party politics.

There are twenty judicial service commissions, one for each state and one for the federation. These bodies make recommendations to the state governors or to the president concerning appointment of all members of the superior courts except the chief justice of Nigeria, who is appointed by the president at his discretion, subject to confirmation by a simple majority of the Senate (section 211 [1]).

The Verbosity of the Constitution. The present Constitution is the most verbose—unnecessarily so—that this country has ever had, if we bear in mind that, unlike the previous constitutions, it is one document. The Constitution Drafting Committee and the Constituent Assembly must have felt that they had a responsibility to plug all the loopholes that might lead to misgovernment or misinterpretation of the Constitution. Good government, however, depends on the human beings running the government, not on the length of the constitution. The U.S. Constitution consists of only about 7,000 words; yet it has lasted for two centuries with comparatively few amendments. The Indonesian Constitution of 1959 is much shorter even than that of the United States, consisting of about 1,000 words in 37 articles. The Japanese Constitution, which consists of 103 articles, is contained in a bare eight pages of print. The most verbose constitutions that readily come to mind are the Indian Constitution, with 395 articles plus fifty-three printed pages of schedules, and, of course, the Nigerian Constitution, consisting of 279 sections contained in ninety-one pages of print plus thirty-seven pages of schedules.

The verbosity of our Constitution leaves room for breach without providing for penalties. Many matters that ought to be left to statutory instruments are provided for in the constitution, without provision for punishment in case of breach. Subsection 3 of section 32, for example, says that "any person who is arrested or detained shall be informed in writing within 24 hours (and in a language that he understands) of the facts and grounds for his arrest or detention." The problem surely is, what is the penalty for the failure of the police to inform, in writing, any person arrested or detained of the facts and the grounds for his arrest or detention? It cannot be argued, I hope, that such a failure eliminates any offense that the person arrested or detained has committed. While subsection 6 of the same section says that any person who is unlawfully arrested or detained is entitled to compensation and public apology, a person who is not told of the reasons for his arrest or detention is not even entitled to compensation or public apology.

Fundamental Rights. Every constitution in Nigeria since the independence constitution of 1960 has contained provisions for the entrenchment of fundamental rights. These provisions were contained in chapter 3 of the 1960 constitution and were repeated in the republican constitution of 1963, also in chapter 3. They are now found in chapter 4 of the 1979 Constitution. The 1960 constitution lasted for only three years and the 1963 constitution for only twenty-eight months. The simple, indisputable fact, therefore, is that the present Constitution has survived longest, if we discount the period of military administration, when there was no stable constitution as we understand it.

In modern times, the sustenance of some well-known fundamental rights has become associated with the rule of law, which now establishes that no country can claim to be ruled under law if it fails to observe a minimum standard of behavior toward its citizens and even toward noncitizens within its borders. Such a minimum standard is enforceable through state machinery, mainly through an independent judiciary. That minimum standard has somehow become associated, at least in practice, with the constitutional entrenchment of these fundamental rights.

I have traveled extensively in African countries and in other countries of the so-called third world, and in spite of the reservations many of us have in regard to some acts of state government agencies and, to a lesser extent, of some federal government agencies, Nigeria can rightly claim to be one of the greatest democracies among those countries. Nigeria has reason to be proud of its achievements in respect to the enforcement of fundamental rights by the courts but has no reason to be complacent.

The rights protected under chapter 4 of the Constitution are the right to life; the right to the dignity of the human person; the right to personal liberty; the right to freedom of thought, conscience, and religion; the right to peaceful assembly and association; the right to freedom of movement; the right to a fair hearing; and the right to freedom of expression and of the press. Chief Williams writes specifically about the mass media in his paper, and I should also say a word or two on freedom of expression and of the press.

Freedom of Expression and of the Press. Section 36 of the Constitution says, "Every person shall be entitled to freedom of expression, including freedom to hold opinions and to receive and impart ideas and information without interference." Many representatives of the Nigerian press have expressed the view that this section does not sufficiently guarantee their independence. In a way they are right; they are uncertain about the extent to which the judiciary, especially the Supreme Court of Nigeria, will provide this bare bone with flesh and blood.

There are a few points I would make. First, let me say what is obvious: apart from the electorate (whose decision in Nigeria may, in a vast majority of cases, be based upon ethnicity and sentiment) only two institutions can control the excesses of politicians, and these are the press (including radio and television) and the judiciary. Unfortunately, the majority of the newspapers are owned by the federal or state governments. Most of those owned by private persons are meant to project the political ideas of their proprietors or of their friends. All radio and television stations are owned, according to the Constitution, by the federal or state governments.

In all these circumstances, most of the newspapers and radio and television stations regard themselves as nothing more than megaphones of their proprietors. The result is that there is not much sympathy for the news media. Indeed, in all my travels in Africa and throughout the world, I have come to realize that Nigeria is one country in which certain sections of the press have carried their freedom to a point bordering on an abuse of that freedom. I do not know of any country in Africa or, indeed, in the third world that would tolerate some of the things that have appeared in the Nigerian press in the past four years without very grave consequences for the writers, the editors, and the proprietors of those newspapers. All this having been said, however, the men of the mass media had, and perhaps still have, reason to be apprehensive of the dangers inherent in the bare provision of the Constitution, so long as the common law offenses of "sedition" and "seditious publications" remain on the statute books.[10]

Limits and Enforcement of Fundamental Rights. Naturally, none of the rights catalogued here is absolute. The Constitution contains a "derogation clause," section 41, which says that nothing in sections 34, 35, 36, 37, or 38 shall invalidate any law that is reasonably justifiable in a democratic society in the interests of defense, public safety, public order, public morality, or public health or for the purpose of protecting the rights and freedom of other persons. This provision is most vital since the path of development of the Constitution will to a large extent depend on how the Supreme Court of Nigeria applies it. Moreover, section 42 of the Constitution states that any person who alleges that any of the provisions of the fundamental rights chapter has been, is being, or is likely to be contravened in relation to him may apply to a high court for redress.

Fundamental Objectives and Directive Principles of State Policy. The present Constitution is the first in the history of this country to deal (in chapter 2) with what it calls fundamental objectives and directive principles of state policy. It should be noted, however, that directive principles of the type now in our Constitution were incorporated in the Indian Constitution as far back as 1951. (Similar provisions are to be found in the Ghana Constitution of 1979, which has been aborted.)

One of the most unfortunate circumstances of Nigeria is the lack of an overriding political or economic ideology. This lack is perhaps the greatest dilemma of our country. Whereas, on the whole, the Constitution is premised on a capitalist ideology, the directive principles that were put into it point toward a socialist democracy. Practically all of those who drafted the Constitution and approved it come from the propertied class with very serious and substantial vested interests. The teeming millions of our illiterate or semiliterate peoples had no hand (except in a most indirect and unimportant way) in the making of the Constitution. Therefore, the main provisions of the Constitution are designed to protect the interests of the propertied class and of their children. The makers of the Constitution added chapter 2, but it gives cold comfort to the millions who live in abject poverty. They remembered to make sure that none of the provisions of that chapter are justiciable. Chief Williams has authoritatively stated how the drafting committee and the Constituent Assembly came to the conclusions reflected in the Constitution. It is sufficiently important for me to say a few more words on this subject.

429

Section 13 of the Constitution says:

It shall be the duty and responsibility of all organs of government, and of all authorities and persons, exercising legislative, executive or judicial powers to conform to, observe and apply the provisions of this Chapter [that is, the Chapter dealing with the Directive Principles] of this Constitution.

Section 6 of the Constitution, however, which gives judicial powers to courts, says that such powers

(c) shall not, except as otherwise provided by this Constitution, extend to any issues or question as to whether any law or any judicial decision is in conformity with the Fundamental Objectives and Directive Principles of State Policy set out in Chapter 2 of this Constitution.

My view is that, in spite of this provision, the Supreme Court can, and indeed should, always bear in mind the directive principles when construing the other provisions of the Constitution and other laws passed by either the federal or the state governments. In particular, the provisions of chapter 2 and of chapter 4, which deal with fundamental rights, must be regarded as supplementary one to the other, with a view to the better governance of our peoples.

At the risk of doing some violence to the main provisions of chapter 2, I think it necessary to refer to some of them. I start with section 14 of the Constitution, which is given the fanciful title, "The Government and the People." It says that "the Federal Republic of Nigeria shall be a State based on the principles of democracy and social justice" and, accordingly, "sovereignty belongs to the people of Nigeria from whom Government through this Constitution derives all its powers and authority." Section 15, entitled "Political Objectives," says that "national integration shall be actively encouraged, while discrimination on the grounds of place of origin, sex, religion, status, ethnic or linguistic association or ties shall be prohibited."

Those things follow that it is the duty of the state to provide or secure. Section 16, entitled "Economic Objectives," enjoins the state to "control the national economy in such a manner as to secure the maximum welfare, freedom and happiness of every citizen on the basis of social justice and equality of status and opportunity" and to "direct its policy towards ensuring (a) the promotion of a planned and balanced economic development; (b) that the material resources of the community are harnessed and distributed as best as possible to serve the common good." Section 17(1) says that "the State social order is founded on ideals of Freedom, Equality, and Justice." Subsection 2 goes on to say that "in furtherance of the social order—

(a) every citizen shall have equality of rights, obligations and opportunities before the law; (b) the sanctity of the human person shall be recognized and human dignity shall be maintained and enhanced; (c) governmental actions shall be humane; (d) exploitation of human or natural resources in any form whatsoever for reasons other than the good of the community shall be prevented; and (e) the independence, impartiality and integrity of courts of law, and easy accessibility thereto shall be secured and maintained." Clearly, if the exploitation of human or natural resources in any form is to be for no reason other than the good of the community, then the present economic arrangement in Nigeria is totally and completely faulty. Yet no one has ever thought of reordering the exploitation processes of our human or natural resources to serve solely the good of the community as a whole.

It is significant that the president of the Federal Court of Appeal has stated, "It seems clear to me that the arbiter for any breach of and the guardian of the Fundamental Objectives and Directive Principles of State Policy . . . is the legislature itself or the electorate. Some even think that they represent a future Utopia, the arrival of which the citizens must hope and pray for."[11]

I am concerned that the directive principles are to be regarded as constituting a mere ideal or Utopia, the arrival of which the citizens can only pray and hope for, but in respect of which they can hope for no assistance whatsoever from the courts. If this is so, I find it difficult to see how the expectations and the hopes of a bright future for teeming millions of our peoples who manage to survive at a near starvation level can be achieved.

Notes

1. For a more detailed account see Sir Allan Burns, *History of Nigeria*, 6th ed.; Lugard, *The Dual Mandate in British Tropical Africa*; and Elias, *Nigeria: The Development of Its Laws and Constitutions*.

2. Proclamation of Amalgamation of the Protectorate of Northern Nigeria and the Colony and Protectorate of Southern Nigeria, 1914.

3. Nigerian (Constitution) Order in Council, 1954, S.I. 1954/1146.

4. Nigerian (Constitution) Order in Council, 1960, L.N. 159 of 1960.

5. Constitution of the Federation of Nigeria, 1963, no. 20 of 1963.

6. For the Northern Region, Law no. 33 of 1963; for the Eastern Region, Law no. 8 of 1963; for the Western Region, Law no. 26 of 1963.

7. It is about 75 percent of the total land area. The population continues to be a matter of debate even today, since no acceptable census has been conducted since 1954. The working figures put it at about 55–60 percent.

8. States (Creation and Transitional Provisions) Decree, 1976, no. 12 of 1976.

9. See Attorney-General of Bendel State v. Attorney-General of the Federation and Ors., 1982, 3 NCLR 1. The rule evolved by the judiciary is that it will presume the constitutionality of a law until the contrary is proved.

10. Those offenses cannot stand the test laid down by Justice Goldberg in New York Times Company v. Sullivan, 376 U.S. 254 (1964).

11. Archbishop Anthony Olubunmi Okogie and Others v. Attorney-General of Lagos State, 1981, 2 NCLR 337, p. 350, in which Chief Williams appeared for the plaintiffs/appellants.

Discussion

ROBERT GOLDWIN: Given the problems described in the papers on Nigeria concerning the task of trying to build a nation out of the population within its territorial boundaries, a population of 200 to 300 ethnic group speaking 400 languages, can any constitutional structure cope with that kind of multiplicity of problems? Is building a nation from such a population primarily a constitutional task? I ask that with more than one thing in mind. There is more to good government than constitution writing; not all the problems come from bad constitutions and not all the solutions from good constitutions. What I am asking is this: Is a good constitutional structure the best way to cope with the problems faced by the constitution makers in Nigeria?

CHIEF FREDERICK ROTIMI ALADE WILLIAMS: I would start by reminding those of you who know about Nigeria, and telling those of you who know less about it, that Nigeria was a geographical unit created by the British during the imperial expansion of the twentieth century. The peoples of Nigeria were never a nation, nor did they live together in one country before the advent of European imperialism. It was British imperialist expansion that brought the country now known as Nigeria into existence and the peoples for the first time under the same government. That situation posed a problem of government after the end of British rule. The most important aspect of the problem was that the various peoples speak different languages and have different cultural backgrounds. In fact, the differences between the major ethnic groups in Nigeria are much greater than the differences between the nations of Europe. If you can visualize the problems in places like Cyprus, you can have *some* idea of the enormous problem of building a nation in Nigeria.

There can be no doubt that the peoples of Nigeria do want to live together as one country. This is what has given impetus to fashioning a form of government that will enable all the peoples who have been brought together by the chance of history to stay together. By 1960 the British had withdrawn their rule, and they left for Nigeria a constitution based on the parliamentary system. In fairness to them, it can be said that even if we Nigerians had been completely free to determine what kind of constitution we wanted, we would have devised very much the kind that the British gave us in 1960. That was the system we were used to. But the experience of trying to operate under that system showed us that it does not provide a sufficient basis for the political stability necessary for social and economic development.

I return to the question of the diversity of peoples and cultures in Nigeria. From the constitutional experiments that preceded the granting of independence to Nigeria, we came to believe that federalism offered the best solution to enabling the various ethnic groups to have some form of self-determination and to develop individually while enabling the new Nigerian state to act on matters of common interest. This system broke down, however, and in 1976 the military government set up a body to devise a new constitution. That body also favored federalism as a basic principle, but it made a very important change; it chose to break from the parliamentary system and to adopt a system based on an executive president. That was seen as necessary for stability. It was also necessary because of our desire to weld the various ethnic groups together by giving all of them an opportunity to participate in the choice of the chief executive.

We also wanted a system that would enable all the peoples of Nigeria to have a say in the making of laws for the country. Hence we established a bicameral federal legislature comprising the Senate and the House of Representatives. Further, we decided to have provisions stipulating the fundamental objectives and directive principles of state policy. We believed that what Nigeria needed most was a constitution that would avoid unnecessary discord. One reason for the stability of older democracies, such as the United States of America, is that the political parties "live in the same world." We thought that by discussing and reaching an agreement on the goals of the Nigerian nation and on the policies that would enable us to move toward those goals, we would devise a constitution that would bring about political parties that live in the same world.

Lately we have revised the Constitution to require that our political parties be national parties, that their governing bodies include people from not less than two-thirds of the states of the country, and that all political parties affirm their acceptance of the fundamental objectives and directive principles enshrined in our Constitution. In this way we hope to use the political parties as instruments to bring the people of Nigeria together.

I would like to speak to the role of the military. The Nigerian

Constitution states that the Federal Republic of Nigeria shall not be governed, nor shall any person or group of persons gain control of the government or any part of it, except in accordance with the provisions of the Constitution. Having this provision in the Constitution is, of course, unlikely to be effective. I remember telling my colleagues in the constituent assembly that this provision is futile; if the president of Nigeria were to wake up one morning and find half a dozen gentlemen with machine guns in their hands telling him he is under arrest, there would be no use in his taking out the Constitution and saying, "Gentlemen, this is unconstitutional; go away." He would not create the desired effect. The military must judge whether the conditions are appropriate for intervention and, above all, must be sure that they will succeed, because if they fail they will face criminal charges and trial for treason. If they succeed, of course, they can put through whatever program they have in mind.

Ultimately the role of the military is to carry out the policies of the civil government and to subject itself to the will of the people as expressed by their legislature and by the representatives of the government. I do not believe in any independent role for the military. When the military intervenes, something has gone wrong; military intervention is a sign of breakdown in the working of the government of any country.

AKINOLA AGUDA: I want to begin by commenting on the military. One thing we should recognize is the love of most Nigerians for democratic government. If we admit that as a basic fact, everything else follows. When General Gowon came to power after military intervention, he promised to return the country to civilian rule. Unfortunately, in the independence celebration broadcasts of October 1, 1974, he told the nation that he was no longer going to keep that promise. In my understanding that was the beginning of his end, because Nigerians innately favor democratic government. Only a few months later he was overthrown in a bloodless military coup based on a return to a democratic form of government.

The process of writing the Constitution lasted until 1978, when a decree of the military administration declared the present Constitution to be in effect. In other words, a military administration that did not appear willing to bring about a change to a democratic form of government was overthrown by another willing and able to do so. Consequently, a democratic form of government took effect on September 1, 1979. That is a matter of considerable importance to the whole world.

I want to address the question of how to bring about democracy given the multiplicity of ethnic groups in Nigeria. The process of electing a president of Nigeria is a little different from the election of a president in most other countries. The Constitution provides that the president must have at least 25 percent of the votes cast and the support of at least two-thirds of the Nigerian states. This peculiarity of the Constitution is designed to ensure that whoever is president is acceptable to a very large number of citizens. Someone who has support only in his own ethnic area, without a broader base, will not be elected president. That is one way by which the Constitution tries to address the issue of diversity. But I agree that good government does not depend entirely on a good constitution. The will of people is perhaps most important in making any constitution work.

AMOS SAWYER: Having heard your opening comments and the statements made on the Nigerian situation, I think we have to 'look at constitution writing in a country like Nigeria, or in my country, Liberia, not as an activity designed simply to arrange the means of sharing power or governing a state, major as that undertaking is. We must also see it as a part of a larger process of nation building or bringing together distinct groups of people who may not share common traditions, whose living together may well have been an accident or a design that has not evolved internally. This throws a larger responsibility on the constitution-writing process than it may ordinarily have. In writing a constitution in such a state, it is important to see whether one is engaged in this process in the larger context of engendering within a population, with all its various active publics and interests, a commitment to guarantee the existence of a body politic. One important ingredient in this is a keen awareness of the historical background of the peoples, the trends in their history, and the kind of arrangements that existed in their societies before the nation-state was born.

Going beyond that, I think one has to look with a political and sociological perspective at the cultural composition of the new polity. In many societies cultural norms and traditions or values may be incompatible with the aspirations and ideals of democracy. One has to survey these tendencies and see not only how they might be accommodated but also whether they can be redirected to conform to a democratic tradition. Democracy implies a culture of its own, and the purpose of constitution writing in modern society is not only to arrange the powers but to promote certain ideals and aspirations. Some of these are best promoted, if at all, in a predisposition toward values that reflect a tendency to cooperation among groups that are different. There must also be a predisposition toward values that promote acceptance of competition, especially in elections, where winners are not set on waging war on losers and losers are not seen predominantly as people who must conspire to undo winners. A whole matrix of cultural values relating to the various ethnic societies influence the process and should be understood very carefully.

Constitution writers in such societies also have the responsibility of beginning to build the kind of structures that will promote the ideals and aspirations of democracy without forgetting the socio-cultural background and the historical background. In Liberia a look at the two important questions of national unity on the one hand and the promotion and protection of liberties and fundamental rights on the other demonstrated the need for a bicameral legislature to accommodate the ethnic diversities of the population and at the same time provide opportunities for counties or larger bodies to take the national situation into account. Just as in the American experience, in which a lower house represents people and the Senate represents states, this kind of balance can both cater to individual needs reflected in the population and make sure that a national perspective is maintained.

Given the African situation, particularly the Liberian situation, where we have seen cultural factors reinforcing certain structures of government, one has to be careful in the balance that one strikes. In Liberia the presidency had overshadowed all other branches of government. This arrangement was reinforced by a chieftain-state-oriented culture. The president becomes a superchief, bringing an imbalance into the system, naturally usurping powers that legislative and judicial systems would otherwise be called upon to perform. This distorts what may well be an ideal democratic process.

In dealing with this kind of situation, there is a need, therefore, to look at possibilities, not of reducing presidential powers but of providing a kind of buffer through which presidential powers are subject to some accountability or at least screened by other institutions in the society. Although in our constitutional draft we maintained a unitary form of government, because of the size of our country we found a need to devise a number of autonomous commissions. For example, a president cannot appoint a judge from anywhere he wants; rather, a judicial service commission presents the president with a list from which he may choose. Again, the mode of civil service appointments in a chieftain-oriented society does not function very well. We need, therefore, to institutionalize in the Constitution the assurance of an effective civil service wherein the criterion of merit will predominate, presidential appointments will be limited, and a degree of bureaucratic professionalism will emerge. Many of these kinds of undertakings must be used in the construction of a constitution against the background I have described.

To turn to the question of the military, the military in Liberia has fears that contribute to its facilitating the process of constitution making. The military facilitates this process for a number of reasons that have been discussed, but also because military rule is not an arrangement that most people, especially in West Africa, are comfortable with, and the military knows this. Whatever its aspirations, it finds itself pressured by some factors inherent in the societies to move to civilian rule even if it is a facade; the motions must be made. Moreover, as in Liberia, the military has its own character and what I call a military culture.

Other factors are important in analyzing the military in the African setting, especially the Liberian setting. Despite all its individual characteristics, the military is often a reflection of the divisions, cleavages, and conditions in a society. It is not necessarily a monolithic structure however well armed and well uniformed. The officer corps is made up of people who are part and parcel of certain groups. Ethnic cleavages and economic differences among the rank and file and people at the top are reflected in the military. All the problems in the society that lead to instability, to a need for social engineering, are also reflected in the military. This may well be why in Liberia we had a military takeover led not by the officer group but by people from the very bottom of the social scale in the military. These soldiers identified themselves with what they saw as the aspirations of the rank and file of the country, but their own need for better opportunities was also reflected. The military must be studied not only as a bloc interacting with other blocs in the power chemistry of the state but also in its sociological makeup.

Of course, the fears of the military often arise from the nature of the change that the military has engineered. If a bloody military coup takes place, especially in a small society like Liberia where there are many very personal relations, there will naturally be fears of recrimination. These have to be taken very seriously into consideration, and one has to look at the quality of the policies that the military institutes and the effects of those policies on various elements of the society. This could well be a source of anxiety for the military regime.

There is also the problem of how to prod the military to undertake an effective political change where the act of writing a constitution is part of a larger process of returning to civilian rule. This immediately means a loss of power by the military. In Liberia we have tried to include transitional provisions to offer some sort of comfort to the military. These would prevent bringing the military regime to trial for acts that it permitted while it was the de facto power of the state. These might be controversial, but something has to be done in this respect to get the military to agree to the process.

Finally, there is the question of legitimacy in the view of the larger society. This is a difficult problem where constitutional rule has not really been democratic in the past, where the constitution has existed in form but the people have not seen their interests or their aspirations reflected in its implementation. The task of breaking the cynicism would then be difficult. At a time when political conscious-ness is rising, the people must be kept constantly informed and in-volved. In Liberia we tried to explain to our people what the suspended constitution provided and then to solicit suggestions for changes. Quite clearly, not all the suggestions will deal with constitutional issues. Many people were more interested in talking about the price of rice, which is a major issue in Liberia, or about fares on the bus, and one must listen to these concerns as well as to questions, for instance, about the role of the vice president.

A very good strategy for constitution writing would be mass public involvement at every stage. A constituent assembly should reflect the opinion of the people, the ideas of the people, to ensure that the document will gain legitimacy when it is promulgated.

LESLIE WOLF-PHILLIPS: I would like to take a British and Common-wealth perspective because that has not yet been done. Although British visions were limited and our attitudes were often overpater-nalistic, I think it is generally true to say that the British took a re-sponsible attitude toward the advancement of colonies to independence. If you think of the way in which Belgium and Portugal left Africa, the comparison is not to our discredit. At the beginning of the 1950s, the British Empire in Africa was probably at its fullest extent. Ten years later hardly a Commonwealth territory in Africa was not either independent or close to independence.

Apart from the vigorous activities of nationalist movements and the habit of the British of making future Commonwealth prime min-isters spend several years in jail, this movement was accelerated by two enlightened and progressive figures in the British Conservative party: Harold Macmillan, with his famous "wind of change" speech—delivered, I believe, in South Africa, which made it all the more notable—and Ian Macleod, the liberal-minded colonial secretary. If the present foreign secretary, Sir Geoffrey Howe, or the previous foreign secretaries, Francis Pym and Lord Carrington, were with us here, they would be nodding vigorously. I suspect, however, that they would be not quite in agreement with what I am now going to say.

When we talk about the Commonwealth, we are talking about a billion people. We are talking about forty-nine countries. That is one-third of all sovereign states. The total population of the United States, the Soviet Union, and the European Economic Community is probably equivalent to about 75 percent of the population of the Commonwealth. If one compares the Latin American family to the Commonwealth, one can see the significant difference in population.

What I now want to address myself to is the concept of the "Westminster model" of parliamentary government. The image of it is sometimes of a rather cozy model of rosy-cheeked country yeomen on their horses many centuries ago, having much more common sense and tolerance than anyone else, riding off to Westminster and establishing a system of parliamentary government. Of course, as most of you know, this is a gross oversimplification. Not only were the original inhabitants of what is now the United Kingdom driven into the corners of that country by invaders, but a succession of foreign princes and monarchs—French, Dutch, and German—presided over a very bloody constitutional development. In the first few centuries of the present millennium the struggle was among territorial warlords, who, by the time of the Tudors, established a unified kingdom. We then decided to argue about religion, which preoccupied us for yet another century and ended in the execution of one king and the expulsion of a second. We then invited a member of a royal family from another country, Prince William of Orange, to take over the throne.

One tends to think of British constitutional history in terms of the Glorious Revolution of 1688–1689, but parliamentary *democracy* was still a long way off. The working-class vote in Britain, the inclusion of the broad mass of people, did not arrive until the 1880s, and we did not get full adult suffrage until fifty years ago. We have had parliamentary government for 700 years but a parliamentary *democracy* for less than 100 years. My reason for emphasizing these matters is that I want to try to discourage the endless flow of praise for the peaceful development of the British system, when in fact it was founded on blood and gore and religious intolerance, and which denied the vote to the broad masses of people until it was forced to concede it.

What is the situation today? What is the *real* Westminster model? I am going to deal with this in an unfamiliar way. In Britain we have an authoritarian head of government. I do not mean Margaret Thatcher specifically; I mean that the British system provides for an authoritarian head of government, who gives advice that cannot be refused to a nominal head of state, who holds that position by virtue of hereditary descent. In times of constitutional crisis, deadlock, or even collapse, all the power that no one else can exercise would flow back to the hereditary monarch. We do not have a one-party state, but we do have one-party governments. I put this question to you, and it is only half rhetorical: When was the last time a minister was forced to resign by action of the House of Commons?

"Sovereignty of the people," using the term in its widest sense, is *not* a principle of the British Constitution. The basic principle of the British system is sovereignty of Parliament, and this principle is upheld even when the will of Parliament is known to be contrary to public opinion. The prime minister has the conventional right to advise dissolution; it is not a cabinet function, and it is certainly no concern of Parliament. The prime minister has the freedom to "hire and fire" members of the cabinet, subject only to practical restraints. The courts have no authority over legislation; they must accept legislation as they find it. The electorate transfers its will to Parliament; Parliament transfers its will to the government; the government transfers its will to the cabinet. The prime minister dominates the cabinet, and the cabinet is bound by collective responsibility, which entails that a member must either agree or resign. He or she must agree openly and in public, not just in the cabinet. The courts have to mind their own business.

I submit that this is the *real* Westminster model. Would any of you recommend it to anyone? One can imagine Caesar's ghost as analogous to the "Westminster model" and the general respect for it and recall Caesar's ghost addressing Mark Antony, "You praise me, but you do not follow me." This Westminster model would obviously not be tolerated in Nigeria or in any other member of the Commonwealth. These nations see the value of a stable system with a clear, directing executive, but they have not kept to the parliamentary system because they lack a basic attribute of the system at Westminster, and that is the existence of dominant and disciplined competing parties. I exempt India from this statement because, of course, India does have a dominant party and a party system roughly comparable to Westminster. The designers of the 1979 Nigerian Constitution, however, explicitly rejected the Westminster model.

The Commonwealth has clearly jettisoned both the ideal Westminster model and the one that really exists at Westminster, and it seems that constitutions, like wine, do not always travel well. Again, India must be considered an exception, as the British wine has traveled there very well. But in Africa there has been a complete move away from the old Westminster model of the governor-general heading a prime ministerial system. All the Commonwealth African countries have gone over to a presidential system, rejecting both the monarchy and the parliamentary system. Zimbabwe is still working under the British-given Constitution and retains a prime minister in a republican situation; but, like India, Zimbabwe has a dominant party, a stable majority, and therefore a working system.

ALBERT P. BLAUSTEIN: While we lawyers, historians, and political scientists are discussing the role of the military in constitution making, I cannot help thinking that in some military academy at this very moment a conference is analyzing the role of lawyers, historians, and political scientists in the constitution-making process. Old soldier friends in England tell me that graduates of British military academies do a far better job of administering new nations than graduates of the London School of Economics. The question before us is the extent to which a constitution is important in the relations among ethnic, racial, religious, cultural, and other groups. Of course, this is constitution business of the highest order, because a constitution is not just a structure of government; it is a manifestation of the dreams, aspirations, needs, and wants of disparate peoples. A constitution should be a contract that is a result of negotiation and compromise resolving and reconciling the differing rights of the people.

To approach this question for a moment as a lawyer, I would say, following Mr. Aguda, that the Nigerian Constitution of 1979 is a great modern constitution. It is great because it has made some sense of the jumble of what human rights are. If you ask the average man on the street what the most important human right is, he will respond that it is the right to walk down the street without being hit on the head. It is this particular human right that the military rulers guarantee—stability. Human rights are not just what we lawyers, historians, political scientists, and journalists formulate as human rights.

The United Nations has enumerated many human rights, and these also have to be taken into consideration. There is even something new called the fourth generation of human rights. This includes the right to development, the right to peace, and the right to a clean environment. We have come very far from the original human rights concepts as set forth in English documents and in the American Bill of Rights, and we have to take this into consideration in future constitution making. How do we do it?

I can remember one night sitting in Liberia, during its constitution-making experience, going over the Organization of African Unity charter of human rights. We wondered whether we had left anything out of the Liberian Constitution. Habeas corpus, freedom of speech, freedom of the press, and freedom of religion are things we lawyers can handle in documents. But if a man comes to us and says, I have the right to learn to read, we are not equipped to give effect to that human right.

Here we can turn to one of the great constitutional provisions of all time, article 45 of the Irish Constitution, written in 1937, which teaches us that we can characterize human rights in a constitution as those that are justiciable—those that are lawyer business—and those, such as the right to literacy, the right to a job, the right to a clean environment, and so forth, that are not. In that constitutional provision they divided rights between human or civil rights, which are justiciable, and rights that are directive principles of state action, guidelines, if you will, to legislative, executive, and administrative policy. These principles give effect to the aspirations of the people. The great Indian Constitution developed this in much detail, but we know from the Indian experience that conflicts can arise in reconciling the list of directive principles and the justiciable human rights. It would be a good idea to state in such a constitution that in any such conflict the interpretation should be in favor of the human rights. In such a way we could constitutionally and legally delineate those rights that are directive, philosophical, and aspirational and those that can be translated into justiciable courtroom business.

J. CLIFFORD WALLACE: There is a great tension between providing unity and efficiency of government on the one hand and providing individual rights on the other. If I had been a constitution maker in Nigeria, my first responsibility would have been to form a government that works, because without that no rights can be secured. Still, if I wanted to bring my people together, especially with such diverse groups, I would think about what rights need to be guaranteed so that all would be willing to join in the government. The more rights are given, however, the less efficient the government may become. If due process is guaranteed for every individual, as it is in Nigeria, the government cannot function without providing due process, and that can hinder its efficiency. If free speech is granted, a minority can become very vocal and interfere with the functioning of the government even though the government is traveling a road that will be of benefit to the country. The protection of these rights may become very antidemocratic. The majority wants the government to proceed, and if such rights become too protective, their enforcement interferes with what the majority wants to accomplish.

I have looked very carefully at the protected rights that Nigeria decided were necessary to bring these diverse groups together. I compliment the Nigerians because I think they have done something of great importance in specifically separating rights that will be enforced from those that are but hopes, or aspirations, or guidelines. Chapter 2 of the Nigerian Constitution stipulates fundamental objectives and directive principles of state policy. That is very nice, but I am not sure what role they play. In his commentary Mr. Aguda says that the makers of the Constitution included chapter 2 to give comfort to the teeming millions who are living in abject poverty. I infer from this that a sop was given to the people so that they could come together. Mr. Aguda may well be somewhat cynical about whether those aspirations or goals or guidelines have any real meaning for the person who is waiting to be educated or otherwise find his way in society.

Chapter 4 certainly enumerates significant and important rights. How will they be enforced? They will be enforced by an independent judiciary, which I think is fundamental for the protection of rights. But another clause says that those rights may not be available if they conflict with the interests of defense, public safety, and so on. I wonder whether, after one is granted freedom of speech and other rights, the courts might one day hold that whatever freedoms one has are in opposition to public morality and therefore one no longer has those freedoms. I wonder what guarantees of these fundamental rights have really been provided under the Constitution. I suppose these rights are secure only as long as they are enforceable by somebody that can act in an antimajoritarian fashion. There will always be a tension between efficient government and the quality of life, and that balance may well have been struck as well as it can be, given the situation in Nigeria.

CHIEF WILLIAMS: Judge Wallace has spoken about the role of the fundamental objectives and directive principles. The rules relating to these are vague for the purpose of getting an agreement on the aims of the society in Nigeria; that they are not enforceable by codes of law does not mean that they are not enforceable at all. In fact, the Nigerian Constitution provides that the National Assembly may pass a law to provide for the enforcement of these rights, even though courts of law are created to enforce rules of law rather than guidelines of policy.

It is true that the National Assembly has not passed any such legislation, but the fundamental objectives and directive principles are also binding on courts of law. They are guidelines for the courts of law. If the legislature were to enact a law repealing an earlier law passed in fulfillment of directive principles (for example, a law providing for free health services to certain classes of people), it would be within the competence of a court of law to decide whether the repeal was constitutional, even though the objectives are not directly enforceable. Although there is no judicial precedent, it would mean that a law passed specifically for the purpose of fulfilling one of the directive principles contained in the Constitution cannot be validly repealed by subsequent legislation. A court of law would be permitted to hold such a repeal unconstitutional.

There are limitations on fundamental civil rights. In the American Constitution these rights are set down in broad terms, and the courts must determine their scope and limits. It is not possible to secure these rights absolutely, and the most common factors that weave the interests of society together must prescribe some limits. Even the right of freedom of expression must be limited by the right of people to protect their reputations. It ought not to be permissible for a citizen, in the exercise of his right of freedom of expression, to discredit unjustly the reputation of one of his fellows.

In the same way, references have been made to the requirements of defense, public safety, and public order. Where there is a need for protection of public order, for example, in exercising freedom of expression or even freedom of movement one cannot act so as to threaten the social means of other communities. If you find people worshiping in a mosque, you cannot exercise your right to hold a political meeting next door in such a manner as to cause a disturbance to those who are lawfully worshiping.

The limitations have been worked out by American judges in the case of the American Bill of Rights. In Nigeria we felt that it would be much better to spell out the limitations in the body of the Constitution itself. That is why we have these qualifications.

10
Conclusion

ROBERT GOLDWIN: In the letter I wrote to the authors many months ago to describe what I hoped the papers and this conference would achieve, I included a list of fundamental issues. You all have a copy of that letter. [The list here referred to is included in the Preface to this volume.] Were some of these items simply superfluous? Are there other issues of real importance that were omitted? Should greater emphasis be given to some things than to others? Most important, are there some overarching questions that were not anticipated but that we now have discovered in our week of discourse? What have we learned?

One thing I learned in the conference that I had not known is the variety of constitution-writing tasks that constitution makers may face. Some such tasks really constitute a nation, as we have heard the American and Nigerian constitution-making experiences described. It is appropriate, in such a constitution-writing exercise, that the people who write the constitution would later be called "founders" or "founding fathers" or "framers," all terms that are used to describe, for instance, the men who wrote the Constitution of the United States.

Other constitution-writing tasks are only modernizing tasks, to bring a constitution up to date, to "catch up with reality." Some are restorative—that is, returning to sounder principles of a past constitution that were lost, abandoned, or distorted. Some are corrective—that is, certain flaws needed adjustment, but no fundamental alteration of the forms of society were necessary. And some are innovative—that is, wholly new devices or principles are added to the structure that already exists. These are some differences that have occurred to me during this conference and that are now part of any thinking I may do about constitution writing. What more should be said, or what corrections should be made as we try to build a statement about constitution writing?

CONSTANTINE D. TSATSOS: First, this gathering to examine the making of some of the new constitutions in the world has proven to be a very useful procedure that should be repeated in the future with respect to other constitutions.

Second, to construct a democratic republic there must be a general consensus such as now exists only in the United States and in some European countries. Wherever this consensus is missing, as it is in most states of Europe for several reasons, the state suffers in some way. It can be a slight, though painful illness, or it can be fatal for a democracy.

Third, although every country has its own constitutional features, one may draw some general assessments. No one can deny that a democracy founded upon the will of a free-voting majority is the best of all possible forms of social and political life, because it ensures political freedom and human dignity; and without political freedom there is no freedom at all.

Fourth, human rights, as expressed in the Treaty of Rome and by the United Nations, are the basic preconditions for democracy, but in those cases where historical conditions lead to the formation of confederate or federal states there arise highly difficult and complicated problems. Communities of different national origin, or communities burdened with different history, want general unity and individual autonomy simultaneously. Between absolute unity and absolute autonomy there are many gradations. This problem, which is so complicated and which leads to so many constitutional varieties, could be a subject for another conference like this one.

One more point remains. There is no state, especially no democratic state, without a common defense and a common foreign policy. The state must have a minimum of governmental functions and powers. This requirement does not concern only confederate or federal states but also every nation that wants to unite with other nations to create a stronger confederation. The ten nations of the European Community, for instance, represent social and political conditions whose variety and diversity are beyond our capacity to analyze. Therefore, one cannot state a specific, concrete method for drafting or changing a constitution for a state as a whole. There is no method for determining the particular political aims of all nations, but we may have found some common evidence of how a constitution must *not* be framed and what general mistakes can be avoided by following the principles of the American Declaration of Independence and the Bill of Rights.

J. CLIFFORD WALLACE: We have talked obliquely but not directly about how people who are in the process of constituting a nation intend to enforce rights. Some constitutions enumerate many rights, but they wink at them rather than enforce them. Those rights are apparently treated only as aspirations or goals. The Nigerian Constitution is one, from what we have heard, which attempts to separate rights from ideals. As a result, it creates rights that can be, and are, enforced.

But stated aspirations may raise false expectations and hopes among the people. Sometimes such aspirations may be adopted as a sop for the governed: at once they placate, yet fuel, expectations, which, in fact, will never be fulfilled.

The Bill of Rights in the U.S. Constitution is not really a bill of rights in the sense that most people think about rights. It is more accurately a bill of preventatives: it speaks negatively, about what the government cannot do to people, and not affirmatively, about what the government must provide for the people. The citizens have a right to do something only in the sense that the government is proscribed from interfering. Thus, the Bill of Rights indirectly keeps the government from interfering with actions of people. By contrast, some constitutions, for example, affirmatively grant a "right to work." Had the drafters of the American Bill of Rights intended to protect the opportunity to work, they probably would have said something like, "Congress shall not prevent a person from working," but they would not have said, "There is a right to work." The problem is that the creation of a right to work entails a concomitant governmental responsibility to create the jobs necessary for everyone to work. Otherwise, the grant of the right, in reality, is meaningless. If rights are to be established as part of a governing document, they should be enforced, or else the document loses its legitimacy. A constitution should not be a political instrument that merely tries to raise people's expectations. That should, and can, be accomplished in a subsequent or contemporaneous declaration. My suggestion is that drafters of constitutions should be careful about the types of rights they include and how they are guaranteed. Rights of individuals are of tremendous importance. As a judge, when I study a document like our Bill of Rights, I ask myself, How do we secure these rights? One way is through decentralizing governmental powers.

In the United States, there is a horizontal separation of powers in the national government—among the executive, legislative, and judicial branches—and there is also a vertical separation of powers in our federal system—between the national government and the fifty state governments. These two separations prevent power from being centralized in one area, one person, or one dominant group. This structure, in turn, makes it less likely that rights will be taken away by government. The Constitution, therefore, creates a social structure that, itself, naturally protects rights in a way not simply derivable from any number of the document's parts looked at *in vacuo*.

There are also ways of protecting rights outside of the constitution itself. Ensuring sufficient competition among various interests, for example, tends to protect all interests. The creation of such a political "market" decreases the likelihood that government will infringe rights. If 94 percent of the citizens of a country belong to one religion, for example, it becomes much more likely that the other 6 percent will be discriminated against on a religious basis. If, however, less than, say, 25 percent of the people belong to any particular religion, discrimination is less likely. Competitive interests are significant and important in protecting rights.

Nevertheless, even given these extraconstitutional factors, I believe that separation of powers is the most fundamental protection. The balance it creates protects rights from governmental usurpation, and the general concept can be adapted to nearly all constitution-making situations. The key to the whole system's success may well lie in an independent judiciary, however. What function can a separate and independent judiciary perform? How can it effectively use its power to review legislative and executive acts?

In a theoretical sense, a separation of powers model ensures equality among the branches of government: creating a structure much like a three-legged stool. In large measure, an executive can check the legislature with a veto or similar power. The legislature can check the executive through the power of the purse. If a judiciary, however, has the ability to check both the legislature and the executive by pronouncing their acts unconstitutional, one must ask, What exists to check the judiciary? Where does the check come from?

If the judiciary is to be separate and independent enough to be insulated from political influence, what prevents it from gaining the power to undo the balance? It must be the self-restraint of the judges. The separation of powers is vital for protecting rights, and the first duty of the judges reading the Constitution is to follow that principle. That means that they must share in the history and spirit of that document and avoid reading it in ways that exalt their own role and thus upset the balance among the three branches by inordinate usurpation of power.

NAJDAN PASIC: When we speak about different types of constitutions, we should point out especially those constitutions that are intended to be tools of social change, because those constitutions are now more numerous than in the past. They include the important element of

449

so-called social and political engineering, trying by constitutional means to achieve certain goals. Such constitutions provide guidance for government action. In this sense, I understand, for example, a constitutional provision that everyone should have the right to work. That obliges government to act to ensure the possibility that everyone can work. This kind of constitution has as its aim not to reflect the state as it is, not just to protect certain valued rights, but to determine the line of future development of the country. In third world countries it is rather common to find such constitutions, as in the cases of Yugoslavia, India, and others.

We also should not overlook the function that constitutions can perform in the process of political socialization. We have discussed here how deeply the principles of the American Constitution are rooted in the consciousness of the American people. The American constitution-making generation passed down to successive generations the process of political socialization with the purpose of continuing their values, points of view, and so on. This is a rather important function of almost every constitution, especially those that include protections of social and economic rights.

MR. GOLDWIN: In the United States, a great majority of the people are not familiar with the text of the Constitution. Their allegiance to the Constitution goes beyond a familiarity with the text. For some, to use a term that Abraham Lincoln used, there is a reverence for the Constitution, something like a "civil religion," without knowing much detail about its content. For others, the saying is, "It isn't in their heads; it's in their bones." I think this shows the extent to which the principles of the Constitution are ingrained in the American people without their being able to say what the words of the document are, even what the opening words are. In fact, they frequently confuse the text of the Declaration of Independence with the text of the Constitution.

MR. PASIC: You are quite right. The veneration for people like Madison, Jefferson, and Washington is the result of having a stable constitution that has lasted for so long. The case in some other countries is similar, and we would like to achieve such veneration for the Constitution of Yugoslavia. That is why we have tried to raise the authority of the Constitution as high as possible. Although Yugoslavs also have a very unclear idea of what is written in their Constitution, they often say, when they threaten someone, "I shall pursue you to the constitutional court," meaning, of course, that that court has supreme authority on all matters.

I have one final point: in discussing separation of powers, more emphasis should be put on those forms of government that provide for a federal structure, because it may be very effective for dividing power on a territorial basis. In Yugoslavia, we do not accept the idea of territorial hierarchy. In Yugoslavia, for example, every republic has its own supreme court; at the federal level, there is a federal court, but it is not above the courts of the republics and autonomous provinces. So, it is not only important to have an independent judiciary and a clear division of authority between the executive and the legislative branches; but it is also important to have a decentralized division of power on a territorial basis achieved through the federal structure.

GERALD STOURZH: I suggest the following topics for future thinking about modern constitutionalism. First, we should consider the relations between the legislative and the executive powers. One can look with interest at the "constructive vote of censure," for example, that Spain has borrowed from West Germany, a device to ensure stability in democratic government. As part of this, we should look at the role of political parties under modern constitutions. We have discussed this with respect to Spain and Venezuela but not in any systematic way.

Second, we should study human rights under constitutions, distinguishing those that are judicially enforceable from those that are not, as well as the various methods of constitutional adjudication. The Constitution of the Federal Republic of Germany includes the fundamental right to a remedy in the law. It says explicitly that a citizen who believes that any of his rights have been violated is entitled to a remedy. If no special remedies have been provided in the legal constitutional framework of the country, the ordinary courts are competent to address the citizen's complaint.

Third, a comparative study of federal systems would be appropriate. I remind my colleagues of the saying of Albert V. Dicey that federalism means legalism, and legalism means limitation of arbitrary power. So I fully agree with Dr. Pasic that federalism is a very important kind of separation of powers.

Fourth, we should study what I call the growth or extension of citizenship. In connection with the American Constitution, for instance, the famous phrase, "We, the people," which Professor Walter Berns referred to in his paper, meant something different in the eighteenth century from what it does now. It means something different now as a result of the Thirteenth, Fourteenth, Fifteenth, Nineteenth, and Twenty-Sixth Amendments to the Constitution. So we should

451

not limit study of the U.S. Constitution, for instance, to how it was understood when it was framed in 1787, but we should include historical discussion about the growth of constitutionalism since then, taking into account the growth of the notion of citizenship, of people as holders of democratic power.

Last, I define liberal-democratic constitutionalism as comprising three main components: one, a system of national representation that has led or is leading to universal, equal suffrage regardless of property, creed, race, or sex; two, a system of separated powers and mutual control over those powers; and three, institutional devices for protecting individual rights on the basis of equality before the law. Discussions of constitutionalism should take heed of all three of these components.

MR. GOLDWIN: More and more in international and national documents, there is a listing of rights, with emphasis on their wording, making them more comprehensive. At the same time the violation of rights has increased all over the world. The condition of human rights in the world is dismal, to put it simply. So I would ask, What really secures the rights of people? We all know that words on paper are insufficient; the question is how much the structure of society and the other features of a constitution contribute to the actual securing of rights, beyond their enumeration.

DANIEL J. ELAZAR: While it is true that modern constitutions emphasize rights as their bases, constitutions are not just matters of rights; they also involve constituting and ordering polities or civil societies. We should consider the broader question and not just the narrower question, in part because it will enable us to make sharper comparisons among constitutions, including constitutions that may not be in the liberal-democratic tradition but that, after all, represent perhaps three-fourths of the constitutions in the world.

The essence of this conference is to demonstrate how constitutional choice is fundamental to republican government and has become fundamental especially to modern republicanism. The role of the citizenry in exercising constitutional choice has become a major means of civic identification and involvement with the polity. In some cases this is clearly demonstrable—for example, in the American states and in Switzerland, where constitutional amendments are deliberated and voted upon by the public. In other cases, public involvement tends to be mere window dressing, with frequent plebiscites attaining very high percentages of "yes" votes. In any case, the exercise of constitutional choice reflects a new dimension in political life that deserves investigation.

I suggest three additions to the list of topics. First is the role of preconstitutional acts or covenants in laying the groundwork for the making of constitutions. Although there has been much discussion of this role especially with regard to Hispanic and Latin American constitutions, almost every liberal-democratic constitution was preceded by some kind of pact or covenant that made constitution making possible. These pacts reveal something about how republics are first formed and, therefore, help us to understand how republics are later ordered through constitutional means.

Second, we have a variety of constitutional models. Again, there has been some tendency to talk about liberal-democratic constitutions along with all others without distinguishing among them. In the discussions here, we have made quite sharp distinctions between the various models of constitutionalism.

Third, as part of our efforts we should try to distinguish between constitutionalizing and real constitutionalizing.

IBRAHIM ALY SALEH: A proverb in Arabic says, "No one can know the suffering of love like someone who has gone through it." Those of us here who come from countries of the third world that have suffered under military rule can talk about that experience. Perhaps those who live under political regimes with democratic guarantees cannot understand such suffering. Those countries that have suffered under military regimes have written constitutions that speak about civil rights; they have constitutions that institute a separation of powers; but what is it that guarantees the continuity of constitutional life in these countries? Is constitutional life permanent or transitory when the military rules the country? Because some jurists and lawyers who have served as counselors to the military have spoken of the doctrine of revolution or the legitimacy of revolution, we have a very difficult task in formulating recommendations so that such jurists and legal experts might develop positions on constitutional issues opposed to those of the military. One of my countrymen once said that when jurists engage in constitutional work, they do not recognize many details that make it very easy for the military to take power. Perhaps we can make an effort to establish the rights of nations and the rights of human beings so that nations will be governed by enduring constitutions.

A. E. DICK HOWARD: Listening to these discussions, I am reminded of Wagnerian opera. It is the sort of exercise in which the material is so rich, the characters so numerous, and the plot so complicated, that if you nod for a moment you are likely to lose your way and never get back on track again. Like listening to a Wagnerian opera, however, being at this conference handsomely repays the effort, and it seems to me there are two fascinating leitmotifs running through this conference. One is the ability that has been demonstrated to talk about constitutions generally and to compare them to find what they have in common. The other motif is the particularity of constitutions, which turns on the circumstances and conditions of individual states.

It is interesting as an analytical exercise to talk about the generality, that is, to ask, for example, What do you mean by a constitution? What are its defining features? What is the process of inclusion and exclusion, by which you decide what goes into the document, and what remains a matter of statute, common, or adjudicatory law? One might simply talk about all constitutions in terms of power relationships, and it seems a constitution cannot be called a constitution unless it deals with power in three fundamental ways. First, a constitution must designate who has power and what kind of power it is. One can designate, for example, the executive, the legislative, and the judicial powers of government. Second, a constitution must designate the substantive limitations that are placed upon power. A bill of rights, for example, can declare the individual rights of the citizen against governmental power. Third, a constitution must designate the procedural restraints or limitations on power; through what processes must power be exercised? Through what procedures does a bill become law?

All constitutions deal with power relationships between branches of government, between government and its constituent parts—such as through a federal system—and between government and the citizen. One might well devote a conference to that kind of analysis.

As people talk about their particular states, about their nations, about their constitutions, and about their systems, various perspectives have emerged, and I suspect those perspectives may be conditioned by one's own discipline, training, or experience. I have noted several of these perspectives. First, the biographical approach has surfaced, in particular during the discussions of the French and the Greek constitutions. That is, what role does the so-called "great man" play in the fashioning of a constitution? Second, there is the economic perspective. In the United States, the historian Charles Beard fashioned a very controversial notion that the work of the framers of the American Constitution is best understood by looking at the framers' economic interests.

The third perspective is revealed in Walter Berns's paper on the writing of the U.S. Constitution: the concern for the force of ideas, that is, an intellectual approach, an ideological or political theory point of view.

A fourth perspective is essentially historical or cultural. The Greek Orthodox Church held Greek society together in the years when Greece was not an independent nation, for example.

A fifth perspective, suggested by Dr. Goldwin, is to look at constitutions by asking, from the political point of view, to what extent is a constitution shaped by the process of constitution making itself?

FRANCOIS LUCHAIRE: It would be very useful to establish a list of questions to put before constitution drafters, but I am more skeptical than most about finding true solutions to constitutional problems. If recommendations are very limited, very brief, or very general, then we provide merely a civics manual for elementary classes; if they are more substantive, then everyone will want to slip in what he finds worthy in his own country's constitution, and this would not be of great use either. I am somewhat skeptical, too, about the possibilities of defining democracy or liberal democracy; taking the definition that has been given here, I have the feeling that France would not be judged a democratic regime. Article 16 of the Declaration of the Rights of Man of 1789, for example, states that when individual rights are not defended by separation of powers, there is no democracy. In the French Constitution of the nineteenth century, there was no mention of this claim. In France and England separation of powers has become a myth in light of the system of majority elections.

Declarations of rights, of course, are very important in constitutions, and in Western Europe, for example, there has been considerable progress in recent years. I would say this is true from the legal point of view, too, because, thanks to the European human rights declaration, any citizen of a European country has the right to attack the laws of his own country when he believes that human rights have been violated. An American citizen cannot do this.

Today, we must include social rights in a constitution. We would be accused of conservatism if we did not. We would be accused of going back to the end of the eighteenth century, so we cannot condemn constitutions that have only a vaguely Socialist tinge to them. To include provisions in constitutions that cannot be amended is, I am afraid, unthinkable. It is even dangerous, because when there is a provision that cannot be revised, the only recourse to change is by force and by *coup d'état*. We cannot believe that something that was true at one historical period of time can remain true into eternity. The men of the French Revolution said no generation can subject future generations to its laws.

Finally, we must be modest; we must continue our analytical work. I agree, of course, that it violates our ethics to be counselors to dictators or military regimes.

DIOGO FREITAS DO AMARAL: I would like to add two items to the list of subjects. One would be to consider the importance of the regional state as distinguished from the federal state or the unitary state. There are more and more examples of regional state systems, mainly in Europe. If we are to include the study of the federal system, we should also include this aspect of regional systems.

The other item is to consider the different systems of government. In recent decades, many countries have attempted to discover intermediate systems that fall between the pure parliamentary model, as represented by Great Britain, and the pure presidential model, as represented by the United States. Many interesting intermediate models have been devised, namely, the French semipresidential model, and we shou!ᵈ give the fullest attention to them.

WILLIAM T. COLEMAN: I have four observations to offer. If we eliminate the few remaining spots in the world where we clearly lack constitutionalism, we must ask whether a constitutional arrangement can exist where it is impossible to have one people. If you take the horrible situation in South Africa, for example, it is hard to conceive that the 17 percent of the people there with the power, the money, and the arms, would ever agree to a constitution under which, the day after it was signed, everything they had would be lost in accordance with the concept of one man, one vote.

In the Israel-Palestine situation, can one think of a constitutional arrangement that would recognize and take into account the basic differences that exist there? In Yugoslavia and other places there certainly have been multi-ethnic groups that have been able to work out a constitutional arrangement, but I do not think those situations are quite as striking as, for example, those in the Middle East and in South Africa. Therefore, I propose that the designation suggested by Dr. Stourzh, "different levels or kinds of citizenship," be expanded to include this very difficult problem.

First as an American and second as a black person, I find a constitutional arrangement based upon race inconceivable. Perhaps those constitution makers who have gotten us through some tough problems, however, ought to see whether there is an intellectual method of resolving this type of problem. Incidentally, this problem would arise in the Soviet Union under a constitutional system, because Russians are now a minority there. It is hard to expect that they would give up the power they now have under another arrangement.

My second observation is that whenever we discuss democratic government, particularly in the United States, we say the ultimate protection is with the least democratic branch of government, the judiciary. Judges do not hold press conferences, they do not have open sessions, and they are appointed for life. It is ironic, perhaps, that we have been very successful in the United States in solving many of our problems by relying upon the least democratic branch. As we try to expand the model of democratic government throughout the world, sooner or later some scholars will have to face up to this issue. I have always been intrigued by the extent to which we Americans accept judicial activism without much difficulty. In the Nixon tapes case, in which the Supreme Court dealt with the question of executive privilege, for example, the real issue was not whether executive privilege is recognized in the American Constitution but rather who should make the final determination of whether it is or not, the president or the Supreme Court? I would urge you to read the opinion and see whether you can say, on a strictly constitutional, rational basis, whether the Court ought to be able to tell the president that he does not have executive privilege. More and more, as nations try to solve all their political problems judicially, these are questions that constitutional lawyers will have to face up to.

Third, I have reservations about whether we have developed a constitutional system that can truly handle tough issues, those issues that would drive people to war among themselves if not resolved. In the United States, we have certainly had four such issues: slavery, segregation, the internment of Japanese-American citizens during World War II, and the Great Depression in the 1930s. We were lucky that we have gotten through each one, but I wonder whether, even with the changes we can make in constitutions, we are still living on a precipice. Have we, as free men and women, developed a method to address very difficult situations?

Fourth and finally, under a constitution that designated social rights, if there were a law that set up welfare or other payments to people, could a subsequent legislature try to change the law without a court declaring the change unconstitutional? And, if the court decided the attempted change was unconstitutional, would it then levy the taxes necessary to make the payments? Because so many of our problems are fiscal, when we press for social rights or economic rights, we must question where we place the responsibility for paying the consequent costs.

FRANCISCO RUBIO LLORENTE: I would like to mention three topics to consider in further work in constitutionalism. First, what do we mean when we speak of constitutions? It is not a question of classifying existing constitutions as liberal-democratic or Socialist or as honest or dishonest constitutions. The French Constitution is without doubt a liberal-democratic one, for example, but the word "constitution" does not have the same meaning in France as in America or in England, and it is necessary to bear this in mind.

Second, Dr. Berns's paper is the only one to make a direct connection between constitutional analysis and political theory. We should include this on our list of topics.

Third, in the future, we should devote attention to the relationship in each case between the government of a country and the people who make the constitution. Theoretically, the constitution of a country is made by the people, but the people, at the time of the writing of the constitution, are being governed, and the constitution is drafted and approved by persons who are chosen in one way or another. So the connection among the people, the persons who draft a constitution, and the government of a country is an important issue.

JOSEPH A. L. COORAY: In Sri Lanka, we have had universal suffrage and free elections for the past fifty years and also a Westminster parliamentary model of government for thirty years. We have changed our government peacefully through free elections no less than six times since the attainment of independence. In 1977, we adopted the Constitution for the Second Republic after an experience of about thirty years of working with the Westminster model. We have been facing problems of development, and for third world democracies such as ours it is a matter of develop or die. If development does not work, the very structure of our democratic system of government is threatened. Therefore, it is vital that our Constitution not hinder but help the task of rapid development. For this purpose, the Parliamentary Select Committee, which drafted the Constitution with me as a constitutional adviser, decided that the Westminster model of parliamentary government should be modified in favor of a presidential-parliamentary system together with a comprehensive guarantee of fundamental human rights. We thought it would not be too difficult to assimilate the advantages of the presidential system and combine them with the good points of the parliamentary system. That way we could pursue development with a strong, stable, and fixed executive, instead of with a prime minister who would be dependent for his continuance in office upon a parliamentary majority. A president can take long-term views of matters, and, during the past six years, we have derived the full benefits of a stable presidential system.

If development ceases, totalitarian forces could seize the opportunity to take over, and that would spell the end of constitutional democracy in the country. There are still people who argue that democratic government will not work in third world countries and that the only way to have efficient government is to have a dictatorship of either the right or the left. So we have a tremendous task, which is not always appreciated in developed countries. We have, therefore, this third alternative to the presidential and parliamentary forms of government. The strict Westminster model is not suitable to the political, social, and cultural conditions of our country. At the same time, we realize the value of the dominant characteristics of the parliamentary system and the value of the legal and political institutions that the British bequeathed to us.

It is very easy to provide for fundamental rights in a constitution, but that is not enough. The will of the people is needed together with the means to make those rights effective in practice. Otherwise, no useful purpose is served. With regard to the means to make fundamental human rights effective, as the experience of the United States shows, there must be an independent judiciary for their adjudication. An independent judiciary is essential for the enforcement of human rights. But how do we provide for judicial independence? Our Constitution has provided for it by making, for example, the judges' salaries permanent and their tenure secure, so that they could carry out their functions without fear or favor. There is also an independent Judicial Services Commission.

As James Madison pointed out in *The Federalist*, however, Montesquieu never intended that legislative, executive, and judicial powers should be watertight, mutually exclusive compartments for the existence of freedom. If you have absolutely exclusive departments of government, the ship of state may remain stationary. We want the ship of state to move, and in a developing society, such as ours, we want it to move very fast in the direction of development, while preserving fundamental human rights. Time is of the essence in successful government. We are hoping that this presidential/parliamentary system will help us to attain our goal of political and social justice.

Writing a constitution is to reply to the question, What role in society will be assigned to the state? There are two possibilities. First, the state can be regarded as a necessary evil. We cannot do without it completely, but we must prevent its being oppressive. This is what we find in Article 16 of the Declaration of the Rights of Man of 1789. We can prevent the state from intruding into certain spheres that are reserved to the individual; this is the traditional liberties concept. The other way of looking at the state is to look upon it as the means to ensure the well-being of the people. This may be ensured by economic and social laws. The state would try to ensure stability and efficiency, which are necessary to make the country dynamic and progressive. In this connection, we can quote Anatole France: "I will forgive the Republic for governing badly because it governs little, but the state must try to govern as efficiently as possible."

There are many constitutions that try to reconcile these two possible roles for the state, protecting traditional rights and liberties, on the one hand, and including economic and social legislation on the other. These economic and social laws do not contradict the traditional liberties concept and can be reconciled with it, but in some cases that is not an easy process. How can one reconcile a Socialist economy with private property and free enterprise, and how can one reconcile territorial decentralization and autonomy with centralized planning? For one thing, we must try to determine which liberties are divisible and which are not. Is political liberty possible without a modicum of economic liberty?

It would be interesting to examine, in the drafting of constitutions, the problem of outside influence. Certain constitutions have been imitated greatly, while others have not. But there are certain fashions that have run through constitution making, and certain constitutions have followed very closely others that have preceded them. We can see how they can be adapted to totally new situations.

MR. GOLDWIN: On the question of whether government is a necessary evil, I have always thought that the Declaration of Independence settled the matter. If governments are established to secure the rights of men, government cannot be inherently evil. One does not have to wait for the German Constitution of 1949 to establish social and economic rights. To the extent that the definition of the function of government—to secure our rights—is accurate, the question of government as a necessary good or as a necessary evil was settled in 1776. The argument that government is inherently evil can arise only where the purpose of government or the state is defined in a different or contrary way.

GUSTAVO PLANCHART MANRIQUE: All constitutions have a historical and political background relative to each particular country. Each country has different problems, so there is no identical constitutional formula for all of them. For a constitution to be successful, it is necessary that there be a consensus about the political and social values of the country, and there must be a degree of tolerance and compromise among the political forces. If these ingredients are present, then a constitution will be successful. That is why it would be a good idea to compare different solutions reached by various countries to problems that may be similar. Along these lines, we can talk about a particular model, but to try to copy exactly the institutions of another country always leads to defective solutions.

Although it seems to be a paradox sometimes in drafting a constitution, the best solution to a problem is to introduce the constitution in an obscure or ambiguous fashion or to leave ambiguous passages in the document. It is also obvious that the party system existing in a country has much to do with the success of a constitution. Political parties in America, compared with political parties in the rest of the world, are characterized by a lack of internal discipline and discipline in voting. The American system has been able to survive very well, and in the Congress of the United States there are coalitions of Republicans and Democrats voting against each other. They divide on the basis of regional interests and according to each issue. This does not happen in the rest of the countries of the world, practically speaking, because parties in other countries vote as if they were single persons. In parliamentary governments there could be one representative for each party, and this representative would control a certain number of votes, because decisions are not made in the parliament; they are made in the parties' headquarters.

ALBERT P. BLAUSTEIN: Regarding classification, categorization, and functions of constitutions, the main focus has been on whether constitutions are constitutive, restorative, or the like. I suggest that a constitution is also a generational restatement. Thomas Jefferson said that a constitution "naturally" expires every nineteen years. We need to record the needs, wants, and aspirations of a people frequently. A constitution is a "flag," an ideological manifesto, an inspirational document joining a nation together. A constitution is also an important educational tool. It is more important in third world nations than in others as a text for teaching government and democracy and for preserving and developing democracy. A constitution is also a public relations document, a legal brief to the world court of opinion. More important, a constitution is a contract. It is the result of national compromise and conciliation.

VOJISLAV STANOVCIC: The process of making a constitution is related

461

to very dynamic changes in the contemporary world. In the twentieth century, we have had social, economic, and technological changes that have no parallel in the past, and constitutions have to provide some room for these changes. New technological devices make control over individuals more effective than ever before. In the past, we have had church-controlled societies, government-controlled societies, and party-controlled societies, but we are now faced with the prospect of computer-controlled societies. Authoritarian tendencies in the present-day world are no less intense than in the sixteenth or eighteenth centuries, and we will have to live with authoritarian governments in the future. There is something here that we have to attribute to human nature. People who lust for power are walking around all over the world, so the primary problem of constitutionalism remains.

The problem, then, is not whether separation of powers alone can cope with authoritarian tendencies. Separation of powers is just one institutional arrangement to help disperse power. Other devices exist, such as federalism. The American Founders quoted both Montesquieu and Rousseau to support the idea that in a large state one can avoid despotism only by means of a federal system. Local autonomy or local self-government, together with separation of powers, is very important. James Madison said in *The Federalist* that there should be some autonomy of social and economic groups. We should add today cultural groups as well, because only such broad pluralism can prevent government from acquiring more power than society should allow it to have.

Genuine federalism really means division of sovereignty. We are still accustomed to the concept of sovereignty as expressed by Jean Bodin and Thomas Hobbes, but American federalism was founded on the idea of divided sovereignty. It is really a contribution of the American Founders to federal theory and practice.

We should also address the problem of human rights. The best restraint on government is the fulfillment of individual rights. It is true that we now have more declarations of rights, more rights enumerated in constitutions, and all these rights are less tenable than when there were fewer enumerated rights. I am against the concept that rights are given to people by government. Human rights are above law, above constitutions. They forbid government to act in certain areas. There are, however, many reasons why we should enumerate human rights in a constitution. Psychologically, people like to know what their rights are, and when they know them, and remember them, they are ready to use them. That is better than if they know only what government is not allowed to do. We have human rights today that, if they are not designated in a constitution, are capable of being regulated arbitrarily by the government.

What the Yugoslav constitution makers had in mind concerning the right to work was not just the right to get a job. In some Socialist countries, under forced labor, the worker is not free to move from one place to another. Work is stated to be a social duty, not a human right. But it should be a person's right to work or not. If he has other means, if he can provide otherwise for life, he has the right not to work. The right to work also means that a government agency is not authorized to question how a man earns his livelihood. He does not have to answer, and that's why the right to work, though it hardly can be applied in the sense of a right to get a job—particularly in Yugoslavia, where there are about 1 million people unemployed— still has important meaning.

MICHAEL DECLERIS: Constitution making today is actually the process of constitutional change, and we should distinguish between the need to address structural deficiencies in a system and the simple precipitating events that usually take place in the environment to prompt constitutional changes. The first kind of constitutional change raises many important questions. First, to what extent is the need for change identified, anticipated, or agreed upon, and, therefore, to what extent does the political system respond through a controlled process? On the contrary, to what extent are the necessary changes ignored and unanticipated, until they trigger a crisis or even a catastrophe? I have concluded that no important change has been brought about through a genuine revisionary process, indicating that usually those entrusted with this process have not paid sufficient attention to, or have not anticipated, the need for constitutional change in their countries.

A second important issue concerns the role, the nature, and the causes of constitutional crises. We need a solid crisis theory and a theory of de facto government; both are closely related to classic constitutional theory. They pertain to ethnic conflict and to military and political processes. A third issue concerns the role of strong personalities in constitutional change. Experience in some countries such as France and Greece suggests that this may be very important. Fourth, to what extent and for how long can a significant part of a constitution remain unchanged?

Finally, what is the role of parliamentary committees, as distinguished from the roles of the government and extraparliamentary groups, in making constitutional changes? These are some of the questions that remain, that have been evoked by the papers and discussions in this conference, and that should be studied by us and others in future conferences.

Released from
Samford University Library